INTEGRATIVE MANUFACTURING

TRANSFORMING THE ORGANIZATION THROUGH PEOPLE, PROCESS, AND TECHNOLOGY

THE BUSINESS ONE IRWIN/APICS LIBRARY OF INTEGRATED RESOURCE MANAGEMENT

Customers and Products

Marketing for the Manufacturer *J. Paul Peter*
Field Service Management: An Integrated Approach to Increasing Customer Satisfaction *Arthur V. Hill*
Effective Product Design and Development: How to Cut Lead Time and Increase Customer Satisfaction *Stephen R. Rosenthal*

Logistics

Integrated Production and Inventory Management: Revitalizing the Manufacturing Enterprise *Thomas E. Vollmann, William L. Berry, and D. Clay Whybark*
Purchasing: Continued Improvement through Integration *Joseph Carter*
Integrated Distribution Management: Competing on Customer Service, Time and Cost *Christopher Gopal and Harold Cypress*

Manufacturing Process

Integrative Facilities Management *John M. Burnham*
Integrated Process Design and Development *Dan L. Shunk*
Integrative Manufacturing: Transforming the Organization through People, Process and Technology *Scott Flaig*

Support Functions

Managing Information: How Information Systems Impact Organizational Strategy *Gordon B. Davis and Thomas R. Hoffman*
Managing Human Resources: Integrating People and Business Strategy *Lloyd Baird*
Managing for Quality: Integrating Quality and Business Strategy *V. Daniel Hunt*
World-Class Accounting and Finance *Carol J. McNair*

INTEGRATIVE MANUFACTURING

TRANSFORMING THE ORGANIZATION THROUGH PEOPLE, PROCESS, AND TECHNOLOGY

L. Scott Flaig

BUSINESS ONE IRWIN
Homewood, Illinois 60430

To my wife, Sandy, and
our children, Shawntel, Steven, and Shad,
whom I love, and whose encouragement and understanding
I will forever cherish

Sponsoring editor: Jeffrey A. Krames
Project editor: Gladys True
Production manager: Ann Cassaday
Designer: Larry J. Cope
Compositor: Publication Services, Inc.
Typeface: 11/13 Times Roman
Printer: Book Press, Inc.

Library of Congress Cataloging–in–Publication Data

Flaig, L. Scott
    Integrative manufacturing : transforming the organization through
people, process, and technology / L. Scott Flaig.
        p.   cm. — (The Business One Irwin/APICS library of integrated
resource management)
    Includes bibliographical references.
    ISBN 1-55623-779-0
    1. Manufactures—Technological innovations.   2. Computer
integrated manufacturing systems.   3. Production management.
I. Title.   II. Series.
HD9720.5..F55   1993   92–28262
658.5—dc20

Printed in the United States of America
1 2 3 4 5 6 7 8 9 0 BP 9 8 7 6 5 4 3 2

PREFACE

Learning is a lifelong journey filled with surprises, confrontations, and reinforcements. I have yet to read an article, meet someone, or experience an event that has not offered a learning opportunity. Throughout this book I have attempted to incorporate both my own experiences and the most leading-edge thinking from many of the best industry and technology leaders in the field of manufacturing.

This book represents a compilation of functional and technical ideas from international experts and conclusions emerging from current research in the field. Furthermore, I have interviewed dozens of business executives who are succeeding in their quest for world-class manufacturing, and I am grateful for their insights.

Because manufacturing is not unique, as some might suggest, I have searched out "best practices" from other industry sectors and management leadership from non-industry settings (e.g., the arts and sciences). I have also given considerable attention to the macrotrends (economic, social, political, and technological) that are significantly transforming the *how*, *where*, and *what* of manufacturing.

In the first chapter I will introduce emerging manufacturing paradigms that are being spawned by these macrotrends, including the pervasiveness of global competitiveness, which has created an interdependency of nations and companies competing yet, ironically, still working together. This is the new world that manufacturing executives must understand in a truly holistic context.

The 1980s have painfully demonstrated that growing $10M, $100M, $1B, and $10B companies can fail in the most basic ways: profitability, customer base, and market share. Size and growth have not been the answer. We have downsized, reorganized, consolidated, and restructured, but with very few successes. We have thrown people, then technology, at problems. We have relocated and co-located, but with little comparative progress. We have merged and acquired, with few successes and many failures.

Finally manufacturers have begun to follow the teachings and recommendations of experts such as Dr. W. Edwards Deming, Ollie Wright, and Michael Porter, all of whom have contributed dramatic innovations to our vocational progress. We have even started to share, hug, value, and empower. Overnight, there has been an onslaught of technical acronyms, many of which were preceded by the term "silver bullet."

A manufacturing executive said to me last summer, "I can't wait to get back to normal." This will not ever be! Our world of manufacturing will never return to the way it was: Load and chase. Volume cures. Make the quarter. Waivers. Safety stocks. MRB rooms. War rooms. Informal systems. Red tags. But wouldn't it be great to get hero badges for saving the day . . . again?

Tough guys ruling in chaos are being replaced by intelligent men and women empowering their organizations with knowledge. No, we will never return to the way it was! Nor do I believe the 1990s will be about accelerating the rate of discovery (even though technology continues to innovate and improve). More likely, the 1990s will simply be about making correct, affordable choices and implementing with excellence. There is already enough firepower in today's technical arsenal that, given a sound company strategy coupled with a passion for implementation, a company can reposition itself into world leadership.

For many years I have felt moved to go beyond the one-hour presentation or the 15-minute article and fully develop my experience and my visions of manufacturing competitiveness into a comprehensive book that would tie it all together. A total of 20 years at Xerox and Digital Equipment Corporation has provided me with a reality check and line management experiences in manufacturing operations, materials management, logistics and purchasing, engineering, and marketing. The extension of these experiences, as I worked directly with such great companies as Motorola, Du Pont, Boeing, and many smaller entrepreneurial and family-owned businesses, has given me a front row seat to observe the manufacturing value-chain enterprise. Opportunities to work with manufacturing clients around the world, with such leaders as Ford Europe, Reebok International, Fujitsu, and Posco Huls, have taken me beyond the technical and methodological side of manufacturing and immersed me into the cultural, regulatory, and international issues of globalization.

I am sure many of you have witnessed several manufacturing long-range plans that aspired to dramatic performance improvements (labeled "world-class manufacturing strategy"), only to be disillusioned by what was later understood to be a wish list of resolutions, soon to be discarded. Since my first industry job at GTE in 1966, I have watched with both amazement and disappointment as nearly every company was targeted and hit hard by foreign competition even as business was growing. This forced a series of tactical responses initially promoted as permanent or turnaround fixes, but nearly always found to be stopgap measures. Very few businesses were bold enough to undergo the massive transformation associated with sustainable industry leadership.

United States manufacturing success was once so complete that underlying practices, such as attitudes, systems, and training, have been fossilized. "Success breeds success" has proven to be untrue! It often undermines the continuing and relentless pursuit for better, more innovative ways of managing the business. Intuition has replaced investigation, and the search for truth has been dismissed in favor of consensus building.

For the past year I have worked on this unique authorship opportunity, but with opportunity has come the responsibility and accountability to produce a solution set, a framework for building a world-class manufacturing capability that is visionary and compelling, yet simple and implementable. An effective framework cannot be conditioned by a "start-from-scratch scenario"; on the contrary, it must recognize the reality that work must go on and one cannot miss a beat or a shipment.

I am convinced that U.S. manufacturing can regain its competitive edge, not by independent, departmental, tactical actions, but through an integrative organizational process that will literally transform the business infrastructure.

The purpose of this book is to provide that knowledge base, to give the reader a contemporary view of the breadth and depth of a manufacturing enterprise and the infinite number of powerful business manufacturing alternatives now available. This book is intended to reinforce a rich and valuing view of integrative manufacturing and how it can transform organizations through people, process, and technology.

L. Scott Flaig

ACKNOWLEDGMENTS

It has been truly inspiring and rewarding to have had the opportunity to work with industry leaders in the development of a crucial new manufacturing paradigm that has been on my mind for nearly a decade. As I began this project, it was evident that many pieces of this highly complex puzzle were missing and that considerable research, dialogue, debate, and hypothesis testing were necessary. As a result, countless conversations and individual contributions took place. I extend my deepest appreciation to those people who made this book possible.

The Ernst & Young Center for Information Technology and Strategy, led by its director, Bud Mathaisel, provided a wealth of intellectual capital, research, and contributions. Bud Mathaisel (Organizational Design) and other center partners, including Dr. Tom Davenport (Innovation Methodology) and Dr. Phil Pyburn (IT Strategy Alignment), provided advanced material that has enhanced the visionary elements of the book. Center professionals Mark LaRow (IT Infrastructure), Alex Nedzel (Implementation Methodologies), and Larry Prusak (Information Management) invested major amounts of time and made significant contributions to the book's technical content. Several center research and support personnel have worked hard as well to ensure that the book's concepts are leading-edge yet supported with authenticity.

I would also like to acknowledge key contributions made from other manufacturing professionals throughout Ernst & Young. This book covers a broad set of complex issues that deal with the best thinking and most contemporary developments. Therefore I looked to Dr. Chris Gopal (Logistics Strategy), Chuck Benson (Best Practices), and Peter Crossley (Manufacturing Systems) to provide functional contributions. Their research and experience was most helpful in preparing sections that handled complicated topics.

I especially want to thank our national office for their insights into industry trends and business issues of the 1990s—Terry Ozan, National Director of Performance Improvement Consulting for Ernst & Young; Steve Yearout, National Director of Quality and Director of the International Quality Study; Steve Burrill, Co-National Director of Manufacturing Industry Services and a recognized thought leader in biopharmaceutical industries; and Kathleen Reichert, National Director of Marketing for Industry Services and Management Consulting. They have all provided guidance, encouragement, and technical contributions.

Bill Krag of Ernst & Young, an expert in factory operations and process-control technologies, worked with me throughout the development of the book. His passion for U.S. manufacturing competitiveness, his lifelong investment in operations research, and his portfolio of client experience made him invaluable to many core messages and manufacturing methodologies. Other Ernst & Young professionals who contributed to the completion of this book include Mike Ostrenga, Peter

Santori, George Raftelis, Eric Hillenbrand, Mary Byrd, Linda Morris, Dave Smith, Dave Howells, Randy Lewis, and Mark Hauser.

A book is not practical without authentic cases from which to develop findings and conclusions. The book has many references to case studies, six of which we fully developed with best-in-class companies with the help of Mary Silva Doctor, who developed the Federal Mogul case, and Suzanne Pitney, who developed the Digital Equipment Corporation case. I would also like to thank Ed Mahler of Du Pont, Dick Krutz of General Dynamics, John Gleason of Walgreens, and Fred Musone of Federal Mogul for their company case studies. Additionally, I want to call very special attention to two friends, colleagues, mentors, and industry professionals who, along with major case study contributions, also provided personal encouragement and years of support. Ray Stark, VP Corporate Materials at Allied Signal and past VP of Materials at Xerox, has provided an outstanding case in supply base management; and Lou Gaviglia, VP, U.S. Operations at Digital Equipment Corporation, has provided a comprehensive case in process innovation.

I believe you will agree with me that the future of U.S. competitiveness will largely depend upon the manner in which we manage people, the degree to which we create cooperative cultures across the world, and the value we place on diversity. Hilary O'Donnell, Intercultural Management Consultant, has been a colleague of mine for 12 years, has directed Human Resource Management Operations in the United States and Europe, and is devoted to the inclusionary process of human assets in corporate strategies. Hilary has contributed sections to the book that will enrich our way of thinking on these most important topics.

Quite appropriately, I would like to recognize the team that has given so much to the successful development of the book. Antonia Bloembergen, Janet Santry, and Alison Ross have individually and collectively invested endless days, weeks, and months toward structuring, testing, researching, editing, and developing case studies and figures in an attempt to produce a high-quality product. Most importantly, I want to acknowledge the enormous commitment that Robin Sadowski has made to the overall coordination and success of this book. Robin has added major contributions through her involvement at each stage of this project. Scott Wallace, consultant at Londahl Wallace Consulting, and Richard Sasanow of Ernst & Young provided professional editing and have been immensely helpful. Furthermore, the technical edit and value added by

Professor Thomas Vollman have brought this book to a professional level far beyond my expectations. Thanks, Tom!

Lastly, I would like to thank my wife, Sandy, for her endearing love and support. She listened, provided encouragement, and accepted the compromises necessary to bring this book to its conclusion.

Many others gave support to those acknowledged. To all of you, thank you for your contributions.

L.S.F.

CONTENTS

INTRODUCTION

The old axiom "nothing succeeds like success" has proven untrue throughout the manufacturing world. In the wake of the great recession of the 1990s, some of the world's most distinguished manufacturing enterprises found that their best thinking was not good enough. Many companies lost money, customers, and market share because of economic, social, technical, and industrial developments that created entirely new expectations and challenges for manufacturers.

These developments are, however, providing the industry with valuable lessons and powerful motivation. After all, satisfying customers and outperforming competitors are classic manufacturing challenges. Many of today's prescriptives (such as computer-integrated manufacturing, shareholder-value-based planning, and market-driven organization structures) produce competitive improvement—but only in conjunction with a well-planned, widely embraced, skillfully executed, and highly integrated strategy. The challenge of creating and sustaining competitive products and services, then, is really one of nurturing, aligning, integrating, and focusing the capacities of the manufacturing enterprise—the *entire* enterprise, not just the factory.

A principal message of *Integrative Manufacturing* is that the manufacturing component of the organization is ideally positioned to exert an integrating influence over the whole enterprise. This is not a novel idea. As Peter Drucker wrote in 1990, "In the new manufacturing business, manufacturing is the integrator that ties everything together."[1]

Conditions have never been better than they are now for building on Drucker's observation. The traditional value-adding components of the manufacturing company are poised to help guide the organization's transformation into a highly competitive enterprise for the 1990s and beyond. Every organization expresses interest in improving and optimizing its success, but few appreciate how complex the transformation will be because of the current manufacturing environment and business drivers.

Key to this new vision is an ongoing commitment to improve the utilization of the company's three basic added-value resources—people,

---

[1]Peter F. Drucker, "The Emerging Theory of Manufacturing," *Harvard Business Review*, May/June 1990, p. 101.

processes, and technologies—through a complex variety of issues, disciplines, practices, and philosophies:

- People must be considered in the context of a wide range of basic corporate issues: organizational design, impacts of partnerships and alliances in a changing organization, and policies and procedures concerning human resource recruitment, retention, education and training, and compensation.
- Technology-oriented issues are equally numerous and complex, including factory automation, computer-integrated manufacturing, corporate computing systems, telecommunications, material sciences, and robotics.
- The processes of the organization call for the consideration of such issues as business architecture, quality programs, group technology, JIT/CFM, and business process innovation.

A successful program of continuous improvement is critical to competing in the 1990s, but the complexity involved in improvement and optimization has discouraged many organizations, prompting "paralysis by analysis." They simply choose not to align, integrate, and focus their programs, compounding existing problems by poor decisions (or no decisions) and accelerating performance decline.

Integrative Manufacturing offers a straightforward framework for organizing and simplifying the complexities of improvement and optimization by structuring the development of manufacturing strategy and organizing the many factors that affect strategy enablement. Because the purpose of this framework is to help align, integrate, and focus the resources of an enterprise, it includes an architecture that positions each element of the manufacturing enterprise and helps to assess the interaction of elements throughout the organization and across the entire value chain. It details a concise taxonomy of considerations that each organization must evaluate to successfully enable its strategies, and it organizes and groups these considerations by primary orientation: people, process, and technology.

One underlying premise of *Integrative Manufacturing* is that the enterprise's strategy and strategy implementation must be compatible with its strengths and weaknesses. Without synchronization of organization and strategy, it will be impossible to successfully align, integrate, and focus the company's people, process, and technology resources—and unless alignment, integration, and focus can be sustained, the organization's performance will not be competitive. To preserve leadership and extend market share today, an organization must do the right things, at the right times, in the right order, with the right people, at the right pace, for the right reasons, across the entire manufacturing enterprise. It is an ambitious goal.

Manufacturers worldwide are rising to meet the challenge; the industry is in a period of competitive transition. The vitality of the manufacturing industry, particularly in the United States, has been of great concern since the late 1970s. "Management in the 1990s," a recent landmark research program at the Massachusetts Institute of Technology, concluded that the challenges of this decade are far from over.[2] Businesses will continue to confront a turbulent environment as competitors increase pressure to produce more quickly, at lower cost, in greater variety, and with improving quality. The study also found that, in the years ahead, competitiveness is likely to result not from one or several key advantages, but from numerous improvements in productivity, innovation, quality, financial management, strategic planning, and human resource management.

As you read this book, you will come to understand how technological advancement, cultural transformation, and methodological development will empower manufacturing companies to form "virtual" enterprises, delivering superior products and services worldwide.[3] The most successful of these enterprises will be humble and creative enough to seek out and emulate product and process excellence, wherever it can be found. Operating procedures in these exceptional virtual organizations will reflect best practices that are gathered from competitors and other industries, then carefully tuned and optimized. Case studies and discussions of benchmarking and other methodologies and technologies help readers identify performance enhancements most appropriate to their organizations and circumstances.

Integrative Manufacturing explores important issues that are changing the manufacturing landscape, such as globalization, quality, and time-based competition. Today, growth and profitability depend on a

---

[2]See Michael S. Scott Morton, ed., *The Corporation of the 1990s*, (New York: Oxford University Press, 1991).

[3]The term virtual will be explained in depth in Chapter 2.

company's vision and its determination to establish global preeminence, because competition is as likely to come from across an ocean as across town. The book discusses how quality has become a given, no matter what other factors are involved, and it explores the vital role that time plays in competitiveness. It also highlights strategic alternatives, advances in methodology, and technological breakthroughs that can help an organization prepare for the economic, social, political, and technical challenges to come.

The book is structured in the following manner:

Chapter 1 sets forth the issues and challenges that the major segments of the manufacturing industry are facing as we move toward the new century.

Chapter 2 explores the "virtual" enterprise and lays the framework for the powerful integrative force of people, process and technology.

Chapter 3 discusses the major human resources issues.

Chapters 4 and 5 deal with management and operational processes.

Chapter 6 explores the major technologies and related issues.

Chapter 7 shows how benchmarking and other improvement methodologies, including business process innovation, are transforming the manufacturing organization.

Chapter 8 presents a view of the factory of the year 2000 and what it will mean to manufacturers.

This book clarifies industry segment issues and shows how to develop flexible, integrated solutions focused not only on shop floor concerns, but also on business problems; it also assists in the selection of appropriate strategies for integrating new technologies and methodologies that leverage intellectual capital and human resources. You will learn how to construct measurable, implementable strategies providing product and service advantages that secure market position with natural barriers to competition.

The challenges in the 1990s and beyond will be significant to manufacturers: higher quality, increased productivity, greater throughput, and faster market response. This industry-wide focus on organizational renewal presents substantial risks and rewards to every manufacturer. The stakes are high; indeed, for many organizations it is a matter of survival. But even companies whose survival is relatively secure are concerned, and with good reason.

As the industry reorganizes and renews itself for optimum performance, manufacturers throughout the world are encountering substantial changes in their markets and in market leadership. *Integrative Manufacturing* is designed to help organizations make the most of their resources so that they can build effectively aligned, integrated, and focused enterprises.

CHAPTER 1
CURRENT STATE OF
MANUFACTURING

INTRODUCTION

A new, dependable, and dynamic framework that leverages people, process, and technology will serve as the manufacturing blueprint for the year 2000. This chapter describes the starting point for exploring this blueprint: the current state of manufacturing throughout the world. Included is a brief discussion of the condition of American, European, and Japanese manufacturing, as well as a detailed description of 10 key issues and concerns that manufacturers everywhere will face in the 1990s.

THE PRESENT STATE OF MANUFACTURING

Since World War II, manufacturers around the world have had to come to grips with a daunting stream of developments that continues to transform the landscape of manufacturing. These often-discussed paradigm shifts and megatrends, many of which are noted in Figure 1–1, are changing life not only for manufacturers, but also for their customers and vendors.

Manufacturing strategies are driven as much by these trends as by customer demand and organizational capability. Companies across the globe are forming strategic alliances to respond to the effects of rapid and extensive change. Alliances and partnerships, both formal and informal, maximize the flexibility and capability of members and minimize overhead, benefiting everyone—when sufficient common interest exists. An international study performed in 1990 determined that the competitive priorities for manufacturers around the world are similar, but not identical.[1] These priorities reflect local economic and manufacturing conditions as well as the effects of global competition.

---

[1] Jay S. Kim, Jeffrey G. Miller, Arnoud De Meyer, Kasra Ferdows, Jinichiro Nakane, and Seiji Kurosu, "Factories of the Future: Executive Summary of the 1990 Manufacturing Futures Survey," Boston University, INSEAD, and Waseda University, 1991, p. 5.

FIGURE 1–1
Changing Manufacturing Landscape

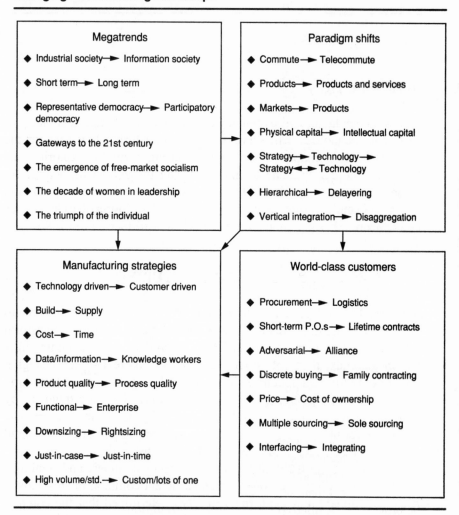

In America, for the first time, manufacturers are under siege and fighting for survival. Many *Fortune* 500 manufacturers are nervous about the 1990s and with good reason. Often, these companies were built on the production successes of the 1950s and 1960s and on mergers and acquisitions in the 1970s and 1980s. They are finding that their manufacturing skills may not be up to the challenges of the 1990s. Manufacturing is much more complex today, particularly in terms of what it takes to be competitive.

The unevenness of the U.S. economy makes broad policy and planning difficult for manufacturers. Indeed, the United States' general economic condition is not expected to ease the burden or to assist manufacturers in their recoveries. If U.S. manufacturers are going to prosper in the 1990s, they must do so on their own without regulatory or outside assistance. Compounding this situation is an overabundance of production and a lack of demand that have resulted in fierce competition.

Technology and improved management methods are exacerbating rather than mitigating overproduction and extreme competition. Downsizing the organization, while often necessary, is not really expected to provide long-term relief. In addition, U.S. manufacturers have historically competed on a single strategy, such as cost. But today, the movement is toward competing on a hybrid of timeliness, value, quality, and flexibility.

The result is that American manufacturers must plan more effectively, execute more effectively, and monitor and measure performance more effectively. With these goals in mind, American manufacturers are emphasizing empowering employees throughout the organization, not just at the highest levels, and are deploying information technology both to increase the efficiency of workers and to more broadly distribute the organization's expertise.

Japanese manufacturers arguably lead the world in delivering manufacturing quality. They pay significant attention to quality function deployment programs and view these programs as a bridge linking customer requirements, product design, and manufacturing. Without neglecting their emphasis on quality, the Japanese have made significant progress in product design methodologies and have improved design systems. Much of this progress stems from aggressive deployment of high-performance computer technology (most notably computer-aided design, or CAD) that shortens design and production cycles.

Major Japanese manufacturers have also emphasized process improvement applied both to new and traditional processes. Such process improvements increase efficiency and better enable enterprises to compete on value and on time. By emphasizing quality and process improvement and by aggressively using information technology, these manufacturers are able to quickly customize products for smaller markets and to handle surges in manufacturing volume more efficiently than American or European manufacturers.

European manufacturers are currently planning for a "borderless Europe." The strategic goal of many manufacturers in Europe is not only to expand distribution, but also to restructure and enhance operations to better serve a larger, more diverse market. Major investments in training on the factory floor and across the organization support this broadening of the European market. European manufacturers are also making major investments in computer technology and process improvement aimed at serving the emerging pan-European demand. Often, these investments are being used to upgrade and leverage the value of existing plants. Because of the soon-to-be-borderless Europe, manufacturers are placing a high priority on timely delivery to customers.

By the end of the 1980s, leading manufacturers everywhere had made a global quest for customers. By the end of the 1990s, manufacturers will have distributed production and business operations more broadly across the globe to better serve their customers and to improve value chain efficiency. Hand in hand with this trend toward globalization comes an increasing likelihood that manufacturers—no matter where they are in the world or what their markets—will face common problems and challenges. In particular, ten common concerns, or business drivers, confront manufacturers of the 1990s: globalization, innovation, time, customer focus, quality, the environment, cost, financing growth, learning and managing change, and regulation and compliance. Each of these drivers is addressed in the following sections.

Globalization

The CEO of Asea Brown Boveri (ABB) provided a viable working definition of a global enterprise when he described ABB as an organization with no geographic center and no national axe to grind, a federation of national companies with a global coordination center. By this definition, globalization means more than international sales. Globalization involves a strategy of profitable indigenous presence—not simply market presence—in selected geographical territories and markets. Globalization requires and implies a local manufacturing, marketing, and support commitment; acculturation of products, services, organizational structure, and procedures to local markets; employment and integration of local staff; and changes in central operations to ensure proper use of non-domestic information and human resources.

Globalization holds a world of change for the manufacturing community. To globalize, manufacturers must reconsider many aspects of production; for example, they must modify vendor selection criteria to accommodate shortcomings in local supply while still taking advantage of geographic and cultural resources. Globalizing also means exploring and learning the value of many different kinds of currency. Manufacturers who globalize need to understand currency futures, cash transfers, minority interests, partnering and alliance formation, licensing, tax transfer systems, and a host of other international financial practices.

Globalization requires investment not only in technology and organizational infrastructure but also in human resources infrastructure. All things considered, becoming global is extremely challenging. Yet, because world-class standards for goods and services are sure to be adopted in most domestic markets, most manufacturers simply don't have a choice of whether or not to pursue a strategy of globalization. For them, competition is already global, so they must evolve their organizations and strategies accordingly.

Innovation

Innovation is the product of being innovative, of consistently exploring new concepts, processes, methodologies, and products. Innovative products are new, refined, redefined, or improved. Innovation in business, marketing, and operations is as critical to manufacturing success as innovation on the factory floor.

If an organization is not facing imminent crisis, the strategy of sticking with a business-as-usual approach and simply trying harder can appear much more attractive than pursuing innovation, which almost always means disruptive change. In fact, it is the organization's increased capacity to change—its capacity for innovation and adaptability rather than its capacity to roll out a specific innovation—that improves the likelihood of long-term success. Successful innovation is usually the result of extraordinary effort. Identifying the attributes of companies that excel at innovation is not simple; but most have effective, flexible, robust information systems and a systematic approach to rewarding innovation. Perhaps of equal importance is an environment and culture that encourages and rewards creativity and innovation.

Innovation relies increasingly upon information technology (IT) to sustain an organization with novel products, services, perspectives, visions, and strategies. Leadership plays an important role in innovation, as does benchmarking. Benchmarking extends the vision of achievable

improvement outside the walls of the manufacturing enterprise and enables an organization to compare its performance to that of other organizations and to identify improvement targets before conceptualizing
how to achieve those improvements. As important as benchmarking has
become in driving innovation, benchmarks today are almost always tactical in orientation and rarely focus on higher-level and more far-reaching
strategic objectives. Combining a strategic set of benchmark-developed
best practices can, however, lead to strategic advantage.

Innovation must be applied to business processes and the processes
of production as enthusiastically as it is now applied to products. In this
instance, innovation is not a redesign or a reengineering of a strategy,
serving only to maintain the status quo. Business process innovation
(BPI) captures the power of information technology to influence, enable,
formulate, design, and implement an entirely new vision and strategy for
the company and its business processes.

Figure 1–2 highlights the increasing opportunities of manufacturers
to innovate. The vertical axis measures increasing capability and performance, and the horizontal axis charts the evolution of major innovation breakthroughs over the period 1950–2000. During this period, the
focus on innovation methods has evolved from labor and departmental effectiveness to process and enterprise effectiveness. Simultaneously,
companies have graduated from short-term tactical activities to long-term
strategic programs.

The innovation breakthroughs shown begin with the application of
automation tools in the factory and, more recently, in the office. Shortly
thereafter, Japan initiated the quality revolution (stemming from the relentless Dr. Deming), which opened up entirely new and far more powerful and pervasive capabilities (including the integrative nature of process
with product).

The traditional and defensive thinking of just-in-case or inventory security was challenged in the late 1970s by the "just-in-time" (JIT) process.
The latest innovation method, "business process innovation," embodies the
emergence of information technology discoveries of the 1970s and 1980s
and has given management the most powerful set of capabilities of the
past decade. This methodology drives across functional lines and extends
through the enterprise, enabling companies once distanced by geography
and time zones to vertically colocate and to manage cooperatively through
the connectivity of their business processes. Each of these breakthrough
methodologies will be developed in depth throughout this book.

FIGURE 1–2
Innovation Chronology

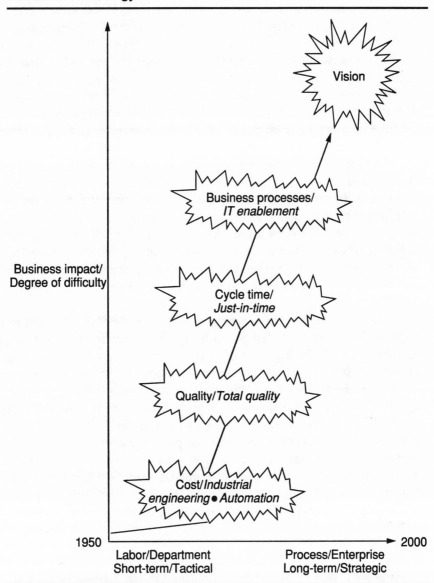

Time

As recently as five years ago, time was rarely considered to be a critical competitive issue. Today, however, time is as critical to competition as price was in the past. "As a strategic weapon, time is the equivalent of money, productivity, quality, and even innovation."[2] One study found that leading companies incorporate two to three times as many technologies in their products and bring their products to twice as many markets in half the time it takes other companies.[3] In order to optimize and compete on time, a company must run parallel, simultaneous operations with no wasted movements or resources.

Manufacturers throughout the world compete on time in at least three ways: manufacturing cycle time, time-to-delivery, and product development time, or time-to-market. In the past, time (in these three senses) was thought of as being the supplier's time; in the future, it will be viewed as the customer's time.[4] Availability and timeliness of delivery has a significant impact on how customers value products and services. In fact, being first to market with a product in demand (i.e., fashion) can negate other competitive issues, such as quality, price, reliability, or function.

Major Japanese manufacturers' emphasis on flexibility has led to a capacity to incorporate changes in design and volume mix faster than the competition. The high rate of employment of computer-aided design (CAD) stations accelerates the design/development process and reduces product development time. Although constant improvement inflates the number of product generations in a given time span, it also challenges other manufacturers to keep up. Japanese manufacturers have had the best rate of improvement in reducing product development duration; however, this rate has not increased as significantly over the past four years as it had in the prior decade. European manufacturers have shown the greatest reduction in manufacturing lead times over this period and are now positioned midway between U.S. and Japanese manufacturers in reducing product development time. United States manufacturers have

---

[2]George Stalk, "Time: The Next Source of Competitive Advantage," *Harvard Business Review*, March/April 1989, p. 41.

[3]T. Michael Nevens, Gregory Summe, and Bro Uttal, "Commercializing Technology: What the Best Companies Do," *Harvard Business Review*, May/June 1990, p. 154.

[4]For further discussion of this idea see Stanley Davis, *Future Perfect* (Reading, Mass.: Addison-Wesley, 1987).

shown the lowest rate of improvement in reducing product development times.[5]

Competing on time has, as its ultimate goal, "instantaneous products."[6] Such products are designed and manufactured in real-time, just-in-time, and provide the foundation for quantum improvements in customer satisfaction.

Customer Focus

Metrics for quantifying product quality and performance are migrating from factors measurable from within the manufacturing enterprise to externally measurable factors based upon the experiences and perceptions of customers. Customers are relying upon suppliers to provide value, not just products and services. Suppliers, in turn, must rely more upon customers to define and quantify value and provide articulate feedback on the supplier's efforts to deliver value. This partnering, or alliance relationship, goes well beyond the traditional lowest-cost paradigm that customers have historically used to select suppliers.

Figure 1–3 depicts the transition of performance criteria from an internal, manufacturing orientation to an external, customer orientation. It

FIGURE 1–3
World-Class Performance: Customer Focus

1980s Criteria	1990s Criteria
Cost/quality performance	→ Value leader
Delivery to commit date	→ Delivery to request date
Availability to promise	→ Promise to be available
Partial ships	→ Completeness
Engineer-to-order	→ Customer configured
Build-to-order	→ Supply-to-order
Contracts/Agreements	→ Relationships/Alliances
Supply/Demand management	→ Demand/Supply management
Environmental compliance	→ Environmental criteria definition

---

[5]Kim et al., 10–11.

[6]Stanley Davis, *Future Perfect* (Reading, Mass.: Addison-Wesley, 1987).

illustrates the transition from the internal behavior of manufacturing companies through the 1980s, driven by the world-class certification, "functional" report card practices, and reward systems, to a new set of behaviors driven by market, customer, and consumer needs. Manufacturers must link their internal performance to customer value, eliminating unnecessary costs while investing in product features and services that enable customers, in turn, to improve their internal performance. The 1990s criteria create the compatibility between manufacturers and customers that builds the bridges for world-class supply chains.

Being attuned to customers is absolutely essential, because customers provide a steady stream of good ideas on improvements and enhancements to products and services. Every organization along the value chain should be considered a customer. If manufacturers are not adding function or service to the value chain, then they are not producing something that the end-customer needs.

According to a recent international study of quality practices, Japanese businesses are more disciplined about translating customer *expectations*, as opposed to requirements, into new products and services than are their Canadian, German, or U.S. counterparts.[7] (See Figure 1–4.) Implications drawn from this study should serve as a wake-up call to U.S. manufacturers: Not only are customers insisting on high-quality products, but, just as importantly, they want the product features and characteristics they need — not just those created by a manufacturer's research and development department. Japanese manufacturers have extended their product development teams to include the customer voice. Ninety percent usually or almost always develop products around customer expectations; in contrast only 69 percent of U.S. manufacturers are similarly oriented. More embarrassing, however, are the 32 percent of U.S. companies who only occasionally or seldom ask the customer for product-need input. This decided lack of interest in customer desires can only stagnate or even further deteriorate the competitive position of the United States.

Quality

Common among all manufacturers is an insistent and increasing emphasis on quality. Once merely a differentiator, quality is now a necessity. But

---

[7]Ernst & Young and American Quality Foundation, "International Quality Study℠ : Top-Line Findings" (Cleveland, Ohio: Ernst & Young, 1991), p.20.

FIGURE 1–4
Frequency with which businesses develop new products/services based on customer expectations

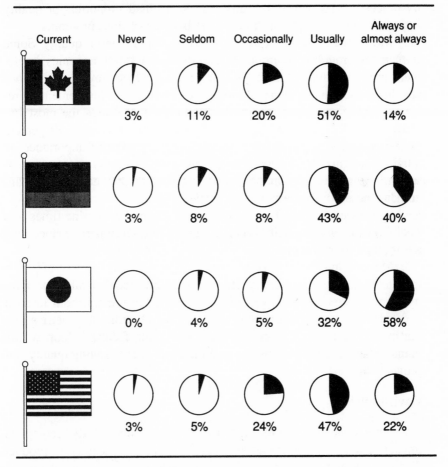

quality is no longer a simple metric of defects. Competition, particularly from Japan, has redefined the concept of quality to mean conforming to both internal and external specifications. Increasingly, delivering quality and meeting customer expectations will be synonymous. Quality consciousness has turned the maxim "If it ain't broke, don't fix it" into "If it ain't broke, improve it."

Quality is a mindset and a discipline for excellence that must pervade the manufacturing process. In the past, improving quality was thought to add to manufacturing costs. Today, we see that good quality discipline results in better products that cost less to manufacture and support. There are a variety of structured approaches to developing quality processes and products—early and determined supporters of quality improvement are beginning to reap the benefits of their programs.

Most organizations express interest in and talk about quality. Some implement programs to improve quality, and a few companies implement programs and measure their progress. But very few organizations are disciplined and dedicated enough to tie quality improvement to rewards. This final step is the most difficult, but it brings the most improvement. A recent study on quality determined that over 50 percent of responding U.S. companies planned to place primary importance on quality performance as a measure affecting senior management compensation.[8] Respondents from the United States led their Canadian, German, and Japanese counterparts on this issue. This leadership could be misleading, however, since U.S. enterprises today are up to nine times less likely to evaluate the business consequences of quality performance than are foreign competitors.

Maximizing the quality advantage is likely to be a very effective long-term strategy, and every effort should be made to raise the ability of an enterprise to deliver quality to all its customers, both internal and external. This effort should include integrating quality metrics into the overall management process and closing the feedback loop within manufacturing organizations by rewarding and compensating quality improvement.

Environment

Consumer concern has been focused for some time on the ecological impact of industrial processes and wastes, and more recently on product disposal. "Whether the issue is hazardous waste, acid rain, the depletion of the ozone layer, the greenhouse effect, or the scarcity of fresh air and water, the root of the concern is the same: the inappropriate use of materials and technologies," wrote Ken Geiser.[9] On many levels and in many ways, manufacturers are responding to environmental challenges. However, manufacturers need to take a more proactive, versus reactive,

---

[8]Ernst & Young, p. 15.

[9]Ken Geiser, "The Greening of Industry," *Technology Review*, August/September 1991, p. 66.

stance in meeting the challenge of environmental concerns. The companies that move in this direction can define the standards by which their competitors will have to be measured and force them to play "catch-up ball."

The environment and human safety have evolved from regulation-driven, niche concerns to issues that every manufacturer must address, particularly in light of globalization. As enterprises broaden their mission statements and their definitions of stakeholders, the impacts of manufacturing processes and products upon communities, as well as upon local and regional environments, take on greater visibility, significance, and risk. Indeed, environment and safety continue to grow as major social concerns around the world.

Effective management of an organization's assets requires integrating environmental considerations into investment and management decisions. Most often, this is not cause for revising financial planning methods, but rather for recognizing the significance of environmental issues and factoring their costs and risks into traditional strategic planning processes. Environmental considerations can affect manufacturing in several ways. Consumer or industrial product sales can be restricted by regulation or by public disapproval. Industrial product sales may decline if a product imposes higher total costs on the customer as a result of environmental restraints on its use or disposal. Changes in environmental regulations may lead to higher manufacturing costs or surges in product demand.

The fundamental requirements for integrating environmental considerations into enterprise planning are threefold: first, monitoring of regulatory developments and project future regulations; second, evaluation of nonregulatory environmental trends to project effects and impacts; and third, analysis of the financial vulnerability of current and planned products and operations to environmental trends and regulations.

Changes in regulations and public sentiment have created a demand for pollution control and other safety and environmental equipment. A number of newcomers to the *Fortune* 500 circle are from the environmental industry. These include Wellman (a plastics and fiber scraps recycler), Zurn Industries (a manufacturer of equipment producing electricity from garbage), and Safety-Kleen (a hazardous wastes recycler). This particular trio of companies is cleaning up by cleaning up.

The impact of environmental considerations extends well beyond the environmental industries. Gerald Glenn, group president for manufacturing at the construction giant Fluor Daniel, predicts that annual spending on pollution control in the United States could reach $100 billion during this decade.[10]

United States environmental regulations are among the most stringent in the world and thus provide U.S. manufacturers with competitive challenges and opportunities. Global U.S. enterprises, by complying with U.S. regulations even when operating in less demanding foreign locales, can promote their organizations as environmentally concerned and "green-thinking." Experience complying with and negotiating environmental regulations provides valuable knowledge and techniques for establishing operations abroad, particularly with the global trend toward tough domestic regulations that provide "protectionist" thresholds to foreign competition.

Cost

For many years, cost has been the predominant point of competition and the primary perspective from which manufacturers reviewed and improved their products and manufacturing processes. Most companies have driven direct costs down to a level that challenges cost accountants to measure accurately. Yet total costs, in particular overhead support, information systems, product introduction, and costs of quality, continue to escalate.

Due to this escalation, the scope of cost improvement efforts has been broadened to include elements of the enterprise not on the shop floor. As a consequence, business processes, in addition to manufacturing processes, have become targets of cost improvement efforts. As organizations move toward becoming "virtual,"[11] alliance-constructed enterprises, there will be increasing need and opportunity for manufacturers to extend cost-improving disciplines beyond the company, into and throughout the value chain (see Figure 1–5). That will be the best way to control total customer cost.

Cost continues to play an important role in customer satisfaction but, like quality, cost is relative. Customers today see value rather than cost as a key measure, largely because purchase price has become less and

---

[10]Joseph Spiers, "A Coming Surge in Capital Spending," *Fortune*, 22 April 1991, p. 116.

[11]The term "virtual" will be explained in depth in Chapter 2.

FIGURE 1-5
Costs Across the Value Chain

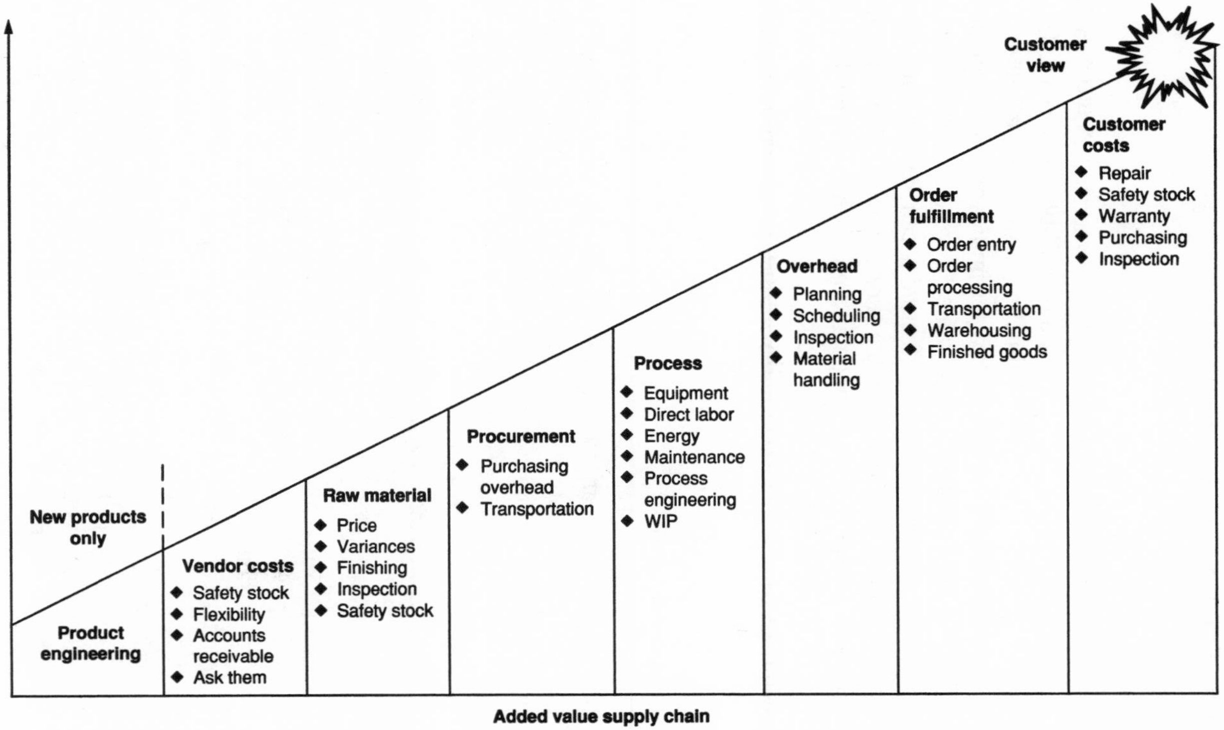

Product engineering	Vendor costs	Raw material	Procurement	Process	Overhead	Order fulfillment	Customer costs
New products only	◆ Safety stock ◆ Flexibility ◆ Accounts receivable ◆ Ask them	◆ Price ◆ Variances ◆ Finishing ◆ Inspection ◆ Safety stock	◆ Purchasing overhead ◆ Transportation	◆ Equipment ◆ Direct labor ◆ Energy ◆ Maintenance ◆ Process engineering ◆ WIP	◆ Planning ◆ Scheduling ◆ Inspection ◆ Material handling	◆ Order entry ◆ Order processing ◆ Transportation ◆ Warehousing ◆ Finished goods	◆ Repair ◆ Safety stock ◆ Warranty ◆ Purchasing ◆ Inspection

Customer view

Added value supply chain

less representative of the total cost of ownership. Value is a function not only of cost, but also of quality, availability, and service. Improvements in cost, quality, service, and timeliness all increase value. Higher costs for products that save time and offer improvements in quality or service still give the customer better value; lowest cost is not always a clear indicator of best value. Manufacturers can be expected to shift focus away from product cost when the services accompanying and supporting products generate more revenue and profit than the products.

Improvements in quality and in manufacturing costs go hand in hand. In fact, a focus on quality almost always reduces the total cost of ownership and often reduces manufacturing costs as well.

Financing Growth

Manufacturers in many industry segments are experiencing unprecedented requirements for cash to fund development and growth. Without access to affordable capital, large companies are unable to grow and small companies are unable to survive. In strong economies, growth is often financed through external sources such as equity offerings, debt, R&D partnerships, or government grants. In weak and troubled economic times, an organization should look to its own operations and balance sheet as the most promising source of funding to finance growth. The most affordable and accessible financing comes from improved corporate performance. Organizations seeking financing in difficult times are well advised to spend more time developing their internal cash machines and less time pursuing external financing strategies.

Even minor quality improvements can pay for themselves many times over and provide recurring internal financing. JIT methodologies and other systems that reduce inventory can be a source of internal cash. Balance sheets may show excess plant and equipment or have accounts receivable three to six months of age. Any of these can be significant one-time sources of capital.

From a financial perspective, strategic alliances offer a means of spreading the manufacturing overhead throughout the value chain. By partnering with suppliers, a manufacturer can closely coordinate investments in production with demand. By partnering with customers, a manufacturer can help cultivate sales by involving customers more in product design and production.

Learning and Managing Change

One of the most significant challenges of the 1990s is the accelerated pace of change in the manufacturing world. "Change is an unnatural act, particularly in successful companies; powerful forces are at work to avoid and defeat it," wrote Michael Porter.[12] Individuals and organizations must do more than simply accommodate change; they must make change work to their advantage. This task would be difficult enough in a more stable manufacturing environment; it is extremely challenging given the competitive and dynamic nature of manufacturing today.

The industrial era of manufacturing has given way to a knowledge era. In the industrial era, capital investment created capital wealth, and the familiar pyramid-structured organization allowed managers to command and exercise control over departments and people beneath them. In the knowledge era, investments in learning are directed toward enhancing individual and organizational competence rather than control. The crystalline or cellular structure of a much flatter organization supports networking and communication. This interconnection, in turn, enables workers to support broadly acknowledged, clearly understood organizational goals.

In order to excel in the knowledge era, organizations must become much better learners. Learning organizations empower employees, placing resources and responsibility directly in the hands of those doing the work. They also provide greater meaning to the work people do and invite a fundamental restructuring of the purpose of a business with respect to its workers and to society.

A variety of definitions of the learning organization have been proposed. A learning organization may be:

- "One which facilitates learning and personal development of all of its employees whilst continually transforming itself."[13]
- "[One which] sets out to maximize the attainment of the individual members' learning goals—through formal structures."[14]

---

[12]Michael Porter, "The Competitive Advantage of Nations," *Harvard Business Review*, March/April 1990, p. 74.

[13]M. Beck, "Learning Organizations and How to Create Them," *Industrial and Commercial Training* 21, no. 3, (1989), pp. 21–28.

[14]A. Huczynski and D. Boddy, "The Learning Organization: An Approach to Management Education and Development," *Studies in Higher Education* 4, no. 2, (1979), p. 213.

- "By definition, an erring organization. The learning organization views policies as hypotheses and programs as experiments. Information is a potential property of data, not their equivalent or something that is automatically derived from that set of data."[15]
- "A community that learns, not only a community of learners, but a self-organizing collective intelligence aware of itself."[16]

The learning organization is distinguished from other organizational types in two ways: the evolution of the organization is intentional, and each worker is central to the organization. Individual learning and development is linked with organizational learning and development in a structured way. Learning organizations maintain a focus on creativity and adaptability. Teams and networking are part of the individual's and the organization's learning and working processes. For the learning organization, creating value is an important personal and corporate goal and is tied to an evolutionary vision of the enterprise and its workers.

Today, for a variety of reasons, the learning organization has come of age. The increased complexity and interdependency of manufacturing requires a systems approach and extensive collaboration throughout the value chain. Competitive pressures with respect to costs, quality, and time are forcing organizations to adopt continuous improvement programs, which in turn require continuous learning and systematic leveraging of what is learned. Value-adding work is shifting from an industrial/task environment to a knowledge/information one. As companies globalize and rise to competitive challenges, they are finding that they must gain maximum benefit from all of their resources, particularly their employees. Likewise, these employees are pushing for greater emphasis on meaningful work and reward and recognition systems.

Coaching (one-on-one mentoring), team learning (training, empowering, and rewarding the collective efforts of teams), and desktop learning (computer access to the information and resources that teams need to do their work) are tactics for nurturing the learning organization. In his recent book, Peter Senge of MIT describes the skills, disciplines, and

---

[15]D. Dery, "Erring and Learning: An Organizational Analysis," *Accounting, Organizations & Society* 7, (1982), p. 218.

[16]G. Por, "What Is A Corporate Learning Expedition?" Paper distributed at the Collaboration of Social Architecture, June 20–21 1991, Cambridge, Mass.

practices that the learning organization needs.[17] These include building a shared vision of the organization's goals and purposes; engaging each employee to develop personally and master the skills needed to support the enterprise vision; specifying, testing and improving the "mental models" of the organization and its processes; developing team learning and team "doing" skills; and integrating and aligning the above four practices by using systems-oriented thinking.

A number of manufacturing enterprises have been hailed as leaders in developing learning organizations: General Electric, Hewlett-Packard, Motorola, Pacific Bell, Honda, Ford, and Analog Devices. Ray Stata, president and chairman of semiconductor manufacturer Analog Devices, noted that "the rate at which individuals and organizations learn may be the only sustainable competitive advantage, especially in knowledge-intense industries."[18]

Regulation and Compliance

Regulatory issues have long been a part of doing business for the aerospace and defense, pharmaceutical, food and beverage, chemical, and healthcare industries. For them, regulatory compliance has been a cost of entry to market, not a competitive differentiator, and this is expected to remain the case.

With the intense pressure on manufacturers to globalize, however, more and more industry sectors will face regulatory and compliance challenges. These challenges will include not only national (and potentially regional) regulation in each market, but also international standards and regulations such as ISO 9000. These regulations and de facto standards are focused on communication, telecommunication, computer networking, workplace health and safety, and environmental issues.

As globalization continues and regulation becomes more prevalent and convoluted, more and more industries will be forced to comply. For the most part, complying with regulations will be a cost of market entry, not a differentiator of products or companies. But manufacturers may find competitive opportunities in how quickly they are able to meet

---

[17]Peter Senge, *The Fifth Discipline* (New York: Doubleday Currency Books, 1990).

[18]Ray Stata, "Organizational Learning—The Key to Management Innovation," *Sloan Management Review* 30, no. 3, p. 74.

regulations and avoid tariff and tax penalties or, if consumer opinion continues to influence purchasing habits, in how consumers view products and services with respect to industrial and environmental regulations.

INDUSTRY PROFILES

The following pages provide overviews of the chemical, automotive, high-tech/electronics, consumer products, aerospace and defense, and biopharmaceutical components of the U.S. manufacturing sector and the pressing industry issues to which each is responding.

The Chemical Industry: Profile and Key Issues

For the chemical industry, there are encouraging developments in new technologies and expanding markets. Yet, intensifying margin pressures and high capital requirements pose continued problems. The chemical industry faces an unprecedented strain on financial and human resources because market and competitive challenges, though not new, are significant.

Quality, Time, and Cost Competition
Management is faced with a growing list of difficult choices and diverse priorities. Although virtually all executives agree that long-term initiatives are essential, short-term results are needed to fund them. In order to compete, chemical companies must improve quality, shorten cycle times, and reduce total costs; the financial and human resources of many companies already seem pushed to the limit. With industry sales growth projected to be below 5 percent, the battle for market share is expected to be fierce. Because the increasing cost and time necessary to develop new products limits the number of strategic options for any one company, companies must focus on the most profitable markets and technologies. Improvements in support methodology and technology are accelerating the development cycle, but only in organizations able to invest resources.

- *Perhaps the most serious industry challenge is an unrelenting pressure on costs.* The industry is largely dependent on petrochemicals, which have a history of significant price fluctuations.

The highly competitive commodity chemicals portion of the industry is also cyclical and is currently at a mature stage of growth.

- *Competitive demands for shorter development times and greater quality have driven increased operating efficiencies.* U.S. producers are beginning to realize the added benefits of JIT techniques (e.g., increased flexibility and responsiveness) and advanced manufacturing techniques. A greater emphasis on quality has been implemented by linking automated process control to quality specifications and methodologies.

Environmental Control

- *The management and investment of resources related to environmental control will be a key issue for chemical companies in the 1990s and beyond.* The chemical industry faces the highest level of government regulations for waste disposal, landfills, and recycling, which have created massive increases in capital expenditures and operating costs that cut into research and development and exploration funds. Chemical companies must also comply with regulations affecting those industries it serves, monitoring equipment and environmental controls and providing environmentally safe packaging and containers.

New Product Development

Even more difficult today is the new product development dilemma. The cost of developing a new chemical product has risen dramatically in the last 10 years, limiting the number of products that can be developed and increasing the dependence on each product being commercially successful.

- *Chemical companies are responding to commodity-cost pressures by shifting to specialty products and high-value-added products, both of which promise higher margins.* Capital has always been scarce, but new factors have made the stakes of the game even higher. New regulations drive up costs, and many new, specialized products appeal only to smaller markets and, therefore, may not justify the product development investment. Yet, without new development, companies are resigned to low-growth, also-ran positions well behind the leaders.

Globalization and Domestic Restructuring

- *Global demand for chemicals is rising, fueled primarily by the growing demand from developing nations.* Recent capitalistic initiatives in Eastern Europe should further increase demand in the 1990s. The weak dollar has made U.S.-produced chemicals particularly attractive abroad. With the reduction of refinery capacity in the early 1980s, there appears to be some room for strong growth in the future, beyond the 2 percent average growth during recent years.

- *Developing countries with vast raw materials are entering the market while domestic chemical suppliers shift from commodity chemicals toward more specialized products.* At the same time, U.S. chemical companies need to expand to new markets, typically offshore, that have sales potential for mature products. But this expansion brings with it margin risks and financial challenges as the value of the dollar fluctuates.

The Automotive Industry: Profile and Key Issues

The U.S. automotive industry encompasses those companies that supply and/or assemble vehicles, manufacture components, or produce raw materials for the worldwide market for passenger cars and light trucks. Although the U.S. auto industry still represents nearly 18 percent of U.S. GNP and almost one U.S. worker in six is connected to the industry, changing customer expectations for quality and performance are necessitating dramatic improvements in the engineering and design process, manufacturing flexibility, quality control, and overall response time.

"The Car Company of the Future," a study of people and change in the automotive industry conducted by Ernst & Young and the University of Michigan, looked at what U.S. car companies need to become tomorrow's leaders, what the operating success factors are for car companies, and what changes are essential for becoming more competitive.[19] The findings of the study were not optimistic—they called for, among other things, the redesign of the fundamental business operating processes in manufacturing, product development, and other areas of

---

[19]Ernst & Young and The University of Michigan, "The Car Company of the Future: A Study of People and Change" (Cleveland, Ohio: Ernst & Young, 1991).

operation to conform to customer expectations and the market's vision of the future.

Globalization and Restructuring

Because the automotive industry operates in a truly global marketplace, the ability to adapt and compete is even more crucial to success.

- *A shifting pattern of investments, alliances, and acquisitions is changing the way automobiles are designed, sourced, assembled, and sold.* For an efficient and cost-effective flow of products, automotive manufacturers must manage supplier networks and worldwide sources of materials.

- *Globalization mandates that companies plan for expansion and be flexible enough to adapt to the nuances of overseas markets.* Manufacturers must be able to design and produce vehicles that meet the needs of consumers in each market. Manufacturing multiple product lines in one plant and on the same equipment will become a necessity.

- *Manufacturing overcapacity in the industry is acute.* The declining market share of Ford, GM, Chrysler, and the growing number of new, foreign-affiliated plants have yielded dozens of excess plants in the United States. A combination of entrenched capacity, the proliferation of more models with lower volumes, and pressures for return on investment encourage companies to strive for the highest utilization of manufacturing facilities.

Time, Quality, and Innovation—Responding to Customer Needs

- *Customers are demanding increasing levels of quality, performance, and service.* Product quality and cost are now the ante to stay in the game. Consumers will consider purchasing only top-quality, low-cost products. Today's differentiators are style and product innovations—how the vehicle makes the consumer feel and the niche needs that the vehicle fills. The challenge for the auto industry is to synthesize information about customer needs, quickly translate it into products, and manufacture the products profitably to top-quality standards. This requires rethinking traditional approaches to product design and manufacturing.

- *Some U.S. car models take up to twice as long as their foreign competitors to get to market, placing them at a distinct disadvantage.*

U.S. car makers must innovate or reengineer their business processes to gain significant improvement in all aspects of their operations—product development, manufacturing, after-sales service, and administration. Concurrent engineering is an example of process innovation, which accelerates the development of products by integrating production planning and process design. Concurrent engineering requires more than technology alone; it requires an engineered approach that addresses the procedural, organizational, cultural, and technological aspects of the operation.

- *The number of suppliers is decreasing, and those that remain play a larger and more collaborative role in designing and supplying finished subassemblies (in contrast to the "make-to-drawing" days of the past).* The trend is for suppliers to interact with one another and form supplier groups. Auto companies around the world are also entering into alliances and joint ventures, to meet the resource demands resulting from investments in plants, accelerated product development, and product proliferation, and to survive the trend toward fewer, but larger, suppliers.

- *Suppliers must be included in the new horizontal organization because they are key partners in achieving time-reduction and quality goals.* These companies may also be grouped into value chain levels. Level zero is the retail distribution network. Level one is the vehicle assemblers. Level two includes companies that manufacture parts, components, and subassemblies ultimately incorporated in vehicles. Level three contains producers of raw materials and basic parts. Suppliers must also form alliances among themselves to meet manufacturers' requirements for fully engineered and produced "black-box" vehicle subsystems.

- *Consumer price and delivery pressures on dealers demand faster and far more cost-effective performance from manufacturers.* A continuous flow of customized product from manufacturer to customer is a must. Streamlining the business processes across the entire value and supply chain will differentiate losers from winners.

Human Resources

- *Management needs to shift toward employee empowerment.* It must encourage input from those with knowledge of what the problems are and how to make improvements. Today's managers need to be skilled in group problem solving, consensus management, and negotiation to support a more inclusive and empowering environment.

Management must also face the challenge of attracting, developing, and retaining qualified people. U.S. automobile companies will not return to profitability through protectionism but rather through an intensive commitment to improve performance throughout their value and supply chain. Level playing fields are essential to a world economy in all industries; but to expect that global regulations will save jobs, produce better cars, and regain U.S. automotive preeminence is short-sighted.

The High Technology/Electronics Industry: Profile and Key Issues

The electronics industry can be segmented into six major categories. They are distinct in their competitive makeup, markets, and operations, but they are highly interdependent and interrelated.

- *Computers and peripherals*: companies manufacturing computer equipment from mainframe computers and supercomputers to minicomputers and personal computers; peripherals include all supporting equipment, such as printers, modems, disk drives, and products providing other snap-in functions.
- *Software*: companies supplying applications, utilities, and operating system software for all categories of computers; also included are computer-aided engineering, design, and manufacturing (CAE/CAD/CAM) suppliers and systems integrators.
- *Voice/data communications*: companies supplying telecommunication and networking products; includes local area networks (LANs) and suppliers of voice/data equipment (providers of long distance/local telecommunications services are not included).
- *Semiconductors and components*: manufacturers of integrated circuits and discrete components.
- *Consumer electronics*: enterprises manufacturing items such as televisions, VCRs, and cellular telephones.
- *Industrial electronics*: manufacturers of test equipment, measurement control devices, and specialized equipment used to design and manufacture semiconductors.

The electronics industry, like many others, is highly stratified, and a small number of the very largest companies comprise the vast majority of total industry revenues. These very large companies, with revenues exceeding $500 million, are responsible for over 85 percent of industry revenues. These transnational corporations are also extremely influential in the industry's pricing, product, and operating standards, and in the introduction and adoption of new technologies. (Transnational is a blend of multinational and global: the world is one market, but products are customized to local preferences.)[20] Their interests and voices are also important in establishing government policy and setting a national agenda for high technology.

Another critical segment in electronics does not have counterparts in most other large U.S. industries: small, start-up, or entrepreneurial companies with significant growth potential. A continuous infusion of new technologies, innovative products, and advanced applications is driven in no small measure by these companies, which are often backed by venture capital. Such enterprises are essential to the health of high tech and are an important source of new ideas for companies of all sizes. Whether these start-up companies grow to be *Fortune* 500 corporations, are acquired by or from alliances with other companies, or fail even as their products succeed, they are the lifeblood of continuous business formation. They play a critical role in keeping the industry vital and sharpening the industry's technology edge.

Technology and Innovation

Although the electronics industry is driven today by global competition, with companies often competing in foreign markets from their earliest stages of development, two of the most important keys to continued success for many large companies are technology and innovation:

- *Attracting and keeping the very best engineers and scientists.* One of the ways that companies are supporting the human side of technology management as they grow is by creating advanced technology teams that extend from their own staff to those of customers and suppliers.

---

[20] For further discussion of the term transnational see Chapter 3 and Christopher A. Bartlett and Sumantra Ghoshal, *Managing Across Borders* (Boston, Mass. Harvard Business School Press, 1989).

- *Managing technology and product development with increasing focus on the customer and on meeting specific needs.* Closer ties with customers and suppliers are having an important impact on how high-tech manufacturers reach decisions on technology and product development programs. The nature of these ties is reflected in the "sell, design, build" model that contrasts with the previous approach of "design, build, sell." This tighter relationship with suppliers and customers, especially in the segments that produce component or linked products, is becoming a competitive priority.

Expenditures on research and development continue at levels exceeding that of any other industry (when measured as a percent of revenue). Many R&D efforts further support companies' efforts to focus product development on areas more responsive to customers' needs and add value to existing, core technologies. "Electronics '91: Framework for the Future," a survey of CEOs in the U.S. electronics industry conducted by Ernst & Young with the editors of *Electronics Business Magazine*, placed the average R&D investment for all electronics companies at 7.7 percent, which is consistent with the previous year's levels.[21] Small companies may spend as much as 20 percent of their revenue on R&D, and software and voice/data communications segments tend to spend above average amounts. Expenditures on applied—versus basic—research are increasing.

Time and Quality: Product Development

- *Reduction of time-to-market is a more important competitive priority than ever before.* Shortening time-to-market is a strategic issue for the long term, a competitive success factor in the short term, and an operational necessity in meeting day-to-day customer needs. Many electronics executives feel that time-based management will be the most important contributor to sustainable success. Competition is driving many companies to find innovative ways to reduce concept-to-customer time. Reducing product design time, increasing speed in identifying markets, and reducing last-minute design changes are early-stage factors that need improvement.

---

[21]Ernst & Young and *Electronic Business*, "Electronics 91: Framework For the Future" (San Francisco, Calif.: Ernst & Young, 1991), p. 14.

- *Competitive pressures are driving U.S. companies to balance innovations with quality and/or speed, for example, reducing time-to-market.* New management approaches enable many development tasks to be accomplished simultaneously. Often called concurrent or simultaneous engineering, the underlying principles of this technique include

  - Integrated teamwork, which brings together various specialists involved in product development.
  - Streamlined communications, which reduce barriers between functions and groups.
  - Simultaneous tasks, which allow specialists to work in parallel rather than in series.

- *Quality is seen by high-technology electronics companies as a necessary investment, a continuing goal, and a customer requirement.* The need for quality is so fundamental to competitive success that it will remain a critical and much-discussed issue indefinitely. Although companies in various segments of the industry respond to the issue of quality from different perspectives, executives throughout the industry are highly sensitive to it.

Electronics executives express concern about the difficulty of measuring quality. Clearly many U.S. companies are devoting significant resources to increase their competitiveness through quality improvement programs (i.e., Malcolm Baldrige award winners Motorola and IBM). But, except for the largest companies, most electronics CEOs believe that they have inadequate measurement tools for assessing quality.

Achieving Customer-Driven Organizations

- *Most executives believe that organizational commitment to the customer is the most effective way to gain customer satisfaction.* Measurement of customer satisfaction is a top priority. Interestingly, many executives see personal contact and direct visits as the best ways to assess customer attitudes and satisfaction. Customer communication and satisfaction can be greatly enhanced by improving the link between customers and employees. Building trust and functional links between design teams and users is becoming an operating essential because of increasingly complex and frequently changing products. This becomes even more important as electronics companies modify products to the various demands of foreign markets.

Strategic Alliances

- *Strategic alliances and a government technology agenda are two additional areas that have received, and continue to receive, substantial attention in the electronics industry.* Over 80 percent of electronics companies have alliances of some type, including marketing agreements, technology licenses, manufacturing agreements, and research partnerships.

The Consumer Products Industry: Profile and Key Issues

The consumer products industry, for purposes of this discussion, is limited to nondurable products that one would typically find in drugstores (except pharmaceuticals) and in grocery, convenience, and mass merchandise stores:

- Foods and beverages, including alcoholic beverages and tobacco products.
- Personal care products.
- Consumer nondurables, including household products, apparel and footwear, sporting goods and toys, small appliances, do-it-yourself hardware and home improvement supplies, and auto care products.

Major demographic changes continue to create new opportunities in consumer products. Many domestic markets are, in general, quite stable and mature, with market shares in major categories showing relatively little change over time. This does not mean, however, that they lack opportunity. In fact, investors recognize food and beverage companies as consistent cash generators that are fairly resistant to recessionary pressures and often target them for acquisition. Globalization of trade channels will also provide significant new markets for many kinds of consumer products. In addition, local and regional demographic trends are likely to fortify market opportunities. In the United States, for example, baby boomers increasingly demand healthful products. Two-income families want more convenient products and have more disposable income with which to pay for them. The result is a huge growth in the number of new products introduced each year.

The basics of marketing consumer products have changed. Gone are the days when advertising on America's three television broadcast networks would make an impression on the vast majority of consumers. Today, marketing to consumers—both domestic and global—is a much more expensive proposition. It is also much more difficult and expensive to create brand preference and loyalty.

Trade Channel Proliferation

It is becoming increasingly difficult for consumer products manufacturers to reach potential customers.

- *During the 1980s, consumer product retailing experienced fundamental changes.* By 1990, channels that did not exist in 1980, such as the warehouse club, accounted for a significant and growing percentage of sales volume. The shifts to mass merchandising and discount and specialty retailing were equally dramatic, with the emphasis on innovative sales and vendor relationship methods.

- *Until 1992, European Community 1992 (EC 92) did not exist.* With EC 92 has come the largest market opportunity in the world. Yet, even with its common financial/regulatory "community," differences remain with respect to product features, imagery, and distribution outlets.

Regardless of the distribution format, a number of consistent buyer needs (or demand themes) have developed. At the most basic level, retailers must always have the right product, at the right place, at the right time, and at the right price. Moreover, retailers in all formats are exploring new ways to meet these needs and make a profit. Although their respective implementation tactics vary, successful retail companies are aggressively finding new and better ways to merchandise, reduce inventory, and eliminate labor. The manufacturer who wants to survive and prosper must help the retailer meet these challenges.

Innovation

- *The trend toward more and more new product introductions continues.* New products are being introduced at an ever-increasing pace. As a result, manufacturers' costs in R&D and inventory have risen.

- *Product proliferation has also led retailers to retaliate against manufacturers as they attempt to control retail costs through slotting allowances.* As retailers introduce and stock more and more new products, they sometimes charge manufacturers slotting allowances to, in effect, rent shelf space for their new products. In this way retailers protect themselves from the heavy costs incurred by repeated product introductions.

- *The development of specialty brands with an upscale image and private label* is in contrast to the trend toward generic products in the late 1970s and early 1980s, when neither the manufacturer nor the retailer had brand loyalty.

Trade Partner Relationships

Though the destinies of the consumer products industry and the retail/wholesale industry are inextricably linked, the industries are separate and distinct. Both face many of the same issues (although often from different and even conflicting perspectives), but each also faces unique issues and challenges.

- *Retailers have introduced other creative charges that allow them to shift their costs to the manufacturers.* The cause of this shift in power is consumer access. It is the retailer that is in direct contact with the consumer and thus serves as a source of detailed information about customers, requirements, and satisfaction levels.

- *Traditional marketing vehicles have been weakened by the increase in the number of options.* There is a diminishing return on larger and larger expenditures in traditional efforts. No longer can manufacturers rely on broadcast advertising to reach the vast majority of consumers—they might miss many of today's niche consumers.

- *More and more, the loyalty that the consumer feels is to the retailer, not the manufacturer.* Purchase decisions are made based on product availability, rather than a preexisting brand preference, and on the services retailers provide.

- *Retailers exert pressure on the manufacturers to regionalize and provide more flexible manufacturing capabilities.* Retailers also gain control over shelf space allocation through point-of-sale (POS) and associated information technology. In addition, POS scanning is providing valuable information for marketing research and logistics, which fosters increased use of tools such as direct product profitability and quick response replenishment.

- *Retailers are increasingly likely to select products from manufacturers that complete orders, deliver on time, and offer responsive pricing and deals.*

- *The primary objectives of these retailers is often to lower inventories and reduce costs.* Technologies that retailers perceive as supporting these objectives were electronic data interchange, product handling systems, direct store delivery, and modular display units. Some retailers have gone so far as to say that these services would be mandatory conditions for doing business with vendors.

Harvard Business Review reported that cost shifting has increased supply-chain costs by as much as 30 percent. Most of these costs were attributed to transportation, manufacturers' warehousing and carrying inventory, unnecessary person-to-person communications, and ineffective promotion and advertising.[22]

Trade partner cooperation is perhaps one of the biggest challenges facing the industry. Manufacturers and retailers must abandon the old adversarial relationships and work together to increase the profitability of the entire supply chain to ensure their own profitability and health. Otherwise, efficient foreign competitors may enter and dominate the market.

Globalization and Restructuring

- *Joint ventures and increased foreign investment have expanded food and beverage globalization.*

Operations Improvement

- *The consumer products industry continues to be market driven.* Producers are increasing the number of new products introduced, as well as associated marketing and advertising expenditures, to increase brand loyalty. However, manufacturers also need to focus on operations and related quality, time, and cost strategies.
- *The consumer products industry has not yet fully embraced the concept of improved operations and remains focused on new product introductions and efforts to build or solidify brand preference.* Most producers have not yet earnestly attempted to adopt operations improvement programs, which have proven effective at generating additional profits through better product quality, shorter cycle times, and increased efficiency.

---

[22]Randy Myer, "Suppliers—Manage Your Customers," *Harvard Business Review*, November/December 1989, pp. 160–168.

Social Issues

Social concerns have affected the consumer products industry in many ways. Among the most pronounced effects:

- *Liability costs have caused manufacturers to rethink their safety concerns.* Old products may be dropped and new products may be delayed or canceled.
- *Environmental concerns have not only affected manufacturing and packaging but have also created an entirely new market, commonly referred to as the market for "green products."* As landfills reach capacity, manufacturers are looking closer at the by-products of the manufacturing processes well as product packaging.
- *The health concerns of consumers are becoming increasingly important.* Food and beverage manufacturers are finding increasing pressure to reduce the additive content of foods. Manufacturers in the alcoholic beverage and tobacco sectors have seen sales declining as vocal opposition groups continue to apply strong pressure.
- *Local pressures increase as more products go global.* As global products become more common, local restrictions take on a greater role. For example, the EC has imposed quality standards on foreign producers. A ban on the use of growth hormones in beef production virtually precludes the import of U.S.-grown beef into the EC.

The Aerospace and Defense Industry: Profile and Key Issues

The aerospace and defense industry, which provides products for both military and civilian aviation, often works in an environment that is regulation-bound and under close government scrutiny. Budget cuts continue to be a fact of life in the military sector, and cyclical demand patterns and financial problems plague many airlines. Low demand and intense competition keep the pressure on manufacturers to stay innovative, cost effective, and responsive to their customers. The two most significant issues for the segment are

- *The shrinking defense budget is squeezing costs.* New procurement and tax rules, as well as fixed-price contracts, are raising costs. Production stretch-outs increase per unit costs as current military programs reach maturity.

- *Industry consolidation forces some suppliers out of business.* More mergers and acquisitions lie ahead, and some suppliers are shifting into commercial markets.

Globalization

- *Global competition has become increasingly fierce.* Domestic companies are seeking foreign partners in design, development, manufacturing, and capital investment in order to access foreign markets. In addition, new aerospace groups, enjoying assistance from their governments, are emerging in both developed and developing nations to compete in domestic and global markets.
- *Defense budgets worldwide have decreased.* But the question "How much is enough?" continues to be debated, with a significant part of the world's resources still allocated to defense.

Quality, Time, and Cost

- *Manufacturing efficiency is a mandate.* Manufacturers must develop strategies and programs to control costs and constantly increase value. This task is complicated by cost accounting and reporting structures that often obscure the true costs of manufacturing.
- *Quality becomes a requirement.* Higher quality is being required by regulation and by demand; quality must pervade every aspect of the business and its culture.
- *Time is an increasingly critical performance metric.* Reducing production time is not enough: time compression from product development through final delivery is essential. Better time utilization can mean improvements in customer and supplier relations, resource utilization, manufacturing capacity, and production flexibility.
- *Research and development costs are increasing.* Fixed-price development contracts, declining tax incentives, and shared research and development are stretching already extended financial resources.

Challenges Ahead

- Increase sensitivity to customer requirements.
- Segment markets and define market share goals.

- Develop systems and manufacturing organizations that are derived from the requirements needed to achieve business objectives.
- Create improvement partnerships with subcontractors, suppliers, and customers.
- Implement plans to meet regulatory compliance mandates and build a communications infrastructure that prevents problems.
- Consolidate resources and eliminate processes that do not add value.
- Create a culture of quality that invites employees and suppliers to participate in the continuous improvement of the manufacturing and business processes.
- Minimize downtime, servicing, and maintenance costs critical to customer success in the commercial marketplace.

The Biopharmaceutical Industry: Overview and Key Issues

Although many analysts once believed that the nascent biotechnology companies would be acquired and overtaken by established pharmaceutical companies, it now looks as though the reverse may be happening. Biotechnology and the companies that specialize in its application are transforming the traditional pharmaceutical business into the biopharmaceutical industry. The relatively young biopharmaceutical industry is already manufacturing and marketing new products with increasing success, including several watershed products released over the past few years. More than 120 new biologics are in clinical trials and over 20 are awaiting regulatory approval.

In its growth during the past 20 years, the industry has overcome many obstacles. As biopharmaceutical companies mature, they will continue to face many challenges—some old, some new. These challenges include attracting capital, choosing which products to develop, receiving regulatory approval, obtaining patents, pricing and selling products, and moving products through manufacturing and marketing processes.

Companies seek to recoup the high costs of R&D, manufacturing, and marketing as they establish prices for new products. For instance, it may cost a company as much as $200 million to bring a new product to market, resulting in a relatively high product price. Unfortunately, the U.S. healthcare system is currently in crisis, with healthcare expenditures accounting for 12 percent of the gross national product. The country's population is aging, and the need for medical care will increase as life spans become longer. Other developed nations have similar circumstances. The question of how to provide medical care for the poor and unemployed today, though unanswered, is being raised and discussed at all levels.

Financing

- *Finding adequate financing continues to be a key concern for biopharmaceutical companies because biotechnology is research-and-development intensive.* Although most businesses finance product development from a sales base, the biotech industry has had to develop products from a capital base in the hopes of generating sales. In addition, as increasing numbers of companies commercialize products, capital will be required to build the necessary manufacturing and marketing infrastructure.
- *The venture capital market, which once provided seed capital for many new companies, has been shrinking and is now more discriminating.* On the other hand, the initial public offering (IPO) and secondary markets were booming for biotech stocks in the early 1990s.
- *Strategic alliances, another important source of capital, are now occurring earlier in a company's development.* Previously, alliances were typically formed between a young biotech company and an older, more traditional company. As the biopharmaceutical industry matures, more biotech companies are forming alliances.

Time and Cost: Product Development

- *Biopharmaceutical companies that are just beginning to develop products often underestimate the time and expense of research and development.* An industry truism is that projects usually take longer and cost more than expected. As product development costs increase, a company may be squeezed by its competition into narrower time frames for recovering costs through product sales. Companies must also strike a budget balance between capital allocations for research and funds devoted to market development.
- *Time shrinkage in getting a product to market has recently become a positive factor for the industry.* Whereas it has traditionally taken from 5 to 10 years (or more) for a new biopharmaceutical to pass clinical trials and receive FDA approval, over the past 2 years the

FDA has begun to implement fast-track approaches for some drugs—primarily in response to advocates for people with AIDS, Alzheimer's disease, and cancer. Parallel-track studies, expanded access, and the concept of compassionate use have allowed patients to obtain therapies before clinical trials are completed.

- *Consumer groups and government agencies are applying pressure to lower the costs of new high-priority, high-priced drugs.*

Regulations

- *Biopharmaceutical companies face broad regulation.* Biopharmaceutical companies can be regulated by local, state, and any number of federal government agencies. Companies seeking to market products internationally must also conform to each country's regulatory requirements. Currently, there is little coordination between regulatory bodies. Even within agencies, the guidelines may be unclear and inconsistent, thereby increasing complexity and creating turmoil for biopharmaceutical companies when they attempt to comply with regulatory standards.

In the United States, government officials are attempting to clarify regulatory requirements. For instance, a recent report of the Advisory Committee on the Food and Drug Administration (FDA) recommended more resources, authority, and autonomy for the agency, consolidation of its facilities, and acceleration of drug approvals.

Cost, Time, and Innovation

- *From a manufacturing and marketing standpoint, a company must decide whether to build an infrastructure for itself, to acquire another company with this resource, or to create a strategic alliance with a company that can provide infrastructure services.*
- *Because capital resources are limited, companies must also decide which of the products in research should be pursued.* In general, enterprises are advised to select products that will sell in important markets that they can dominate or in lucrative market niches. Companies are also urged to target potential products that are easier to manufacture and can generate revenue sooner.
- *Companies also face the technical challenges of product scale-up.* How companies can increase the volume of a substance from

a test tube to a vat without changing reliability and purity is a challenge. Meeting regulatory standards outlined by the FDA and following current Good Manufacturing Practices can be equally difficult.

Patents and Intellectual Property

Intellectual property rights are the foundation of the biopharmaceutical industry—the ability to obtain and defend patents often ultimately determines a company's success. In general, patents are awarded to products that are judged to be new, useful, and nonobvious, that is, not easy to replicate by someone familiar with the art or craft of the field. Although these criteria sound simple, they do not prevent legal confusion among biopharmaceutical companies that may be competing to find solutions to the same "big ticket" diseases, such as AIDS or cancer.

With increasing frequency, biopharmaceutical companies turn to legal systems to determine who holds the rights to certain therapeutic drugs. The competing companies may have independently developed their products along parallel lines at the same time. Fortunately, cross-licensing agreements and strategic alliances can prevent many protracted lawsuits.

The explosive growth in the biopharmaceutical industry has virtually inundated the U.S. Patent and Trademark Office, sometimes resulting in delays of years before a company receives product patent approval.

SUMMARY

Current manufacturing strategies are being driven not only by such traditional forces as customer demand, organizational capabilities, and general changes in the competitive environment, but also by a series of paradigm shifts and megatrends that have changed life for manufacturers as well as for their customers and vendors. The major issues and drivers that manufacturers face today are globalization, innovation, time, customer focus, quality, environment, cost, financing growth, learning and managing change, and regulation and compliance. Every company, if it is to be successful, must seriously consider the ramifications that each of these issues will have on the company environment and deal with them appropriately.

Of course, the many sectors of the manufacturing arena are not necessarily being affected by all of these issues in the same way or to the same degree. Nevertheless, it is clear that even in such diverse industries as consumer products and aerospace and defense, in order to deal most effectively with issues such as globalization, as well as innovation, time-based competition, and so on, people, processes, and technology must combine to create a flexible and responsive manufacturing enterprise.

In the next several chapters, a framework for the virtual enterprise will be explored, including a discussion of the specific roles played by people, processes, and technology in the dynamic global manufacturing environment. In addition, Chapter 2 will introduce a way of choosing the methodology, systems, or human resource policies that are appropriate in light of the drivers and issues facing a given company.

CHAPTER 2
THE VIRTUAL ENTERPRISE AND THE INTEGRATION OF PEOPLE, PROCESS AND TECHNOLOGY

INTRODUCTION

Since the industrial revolution, manufacturers have been pursuing a goal of vertical integration, bringing as much of the value chain inside the organization as possible, largely because of the perceived advantages of and experience with the vertical factory model. The vertical enterprise owns the assets and the capital, directly manages the people, and controls the processes and the inventories involved. Thus, there is no need to negotiate with outside parties.

In the past, the degree to which a company owned, managed, and controlled its production resources was often directly associated with how successful the company was. With growth and throughput as the principal objectives, assured supply and production capacity were the means to success. Ironically, because labor was the major component of production costs, companies practiced cost containment through labor efficiency, paying little attention to systems, technology, and methodology. The value chain was primarily the aggregate of internal factory labor costs.

Such a *vertical* enterprise is no longer the ideal—or, at least, is not the only choice. There are vastly more material alternatives, more specialized advanced electronic and electro-mechanical industrial equipment and tools, more process methodologies, and more nuances within each. Total added value stems more from support functions, knowledge workers, material content, and organizational interfaces at the enterprise level than from labor, skills, and the production process at the factory level. Greater variability in product volumes and customer requirements has created a degree of complexity along the value chain that necessitates unprecedented expertise and investment, and therefore costs, in the massive coordination effort now required in modern factories.

As a result of the various issues and drivers outlined in the previous chapter, manufacturers today face an unprecedented challenge to remain flexible and responsive to customer expectations in the dynamic environment in which they must operate. This chapter introduces the emerging *virtual* enterprise—the aggregation of all the people, functions, and companies that are ultimately responsible for producing a product. In non-manufacturing terms, this entity is analagous to the extended family, including not only the most immediate members, but relatives by marriage, distant cousins, close friends—everyone who plays any role in the day-to-day life of the family unit.

The metaphor of the hospital emergency service also comes to mind. From the initial 911 call, immediate response is made by the paramedic team that performs procedures at the site to stop the bleeding. At the same time, the unit performs diagnostic tests that are fed electronically into a hospital data base, not only for further paramedic support, but also to prepare for total comprehensive service upon arrival. Doctors, nurses, anesthesiologists, specialists, surgery prep staff, support staff, and administration are brought together instantaneously to attend to the patient. Although few of these participants may ever see the patient, or even each other, a common language, a central data base, and a team orientation enable them to function as if they were in the same room.

The virtual enterprise requires maximum performance from its people and depends on the human resources function to empower them with the skills necessary to manage across the organization. Virtual integration has as its goal the linking of disparate entities through information technology so that the overall system is as efficient as if the entities were vertically integrated, or colocated. Achieving virtual integration relies heavily on the formation of strategic alliances, which will be covered in depth at the end of the chapter.

Central to the concept of the virtual enterprise is the term *customer-driven*, which, in the 1990s, must pervade organizational behavior at leading corporations much as *total quality* has been doing since the 1980s. The resulting customer-driven factory will rely on a number of factors for success, including:

- Strategies that address the direction and orientation of the organization, the products and services that the organization will provide to its customers, and the means and methods that it will employ to manufacture and deliver those products and services.

- The integration and alignment of empowered people within knowledge-based organizations that are driven by well-conceived strategies and measurable goals.
- Optimizing processes that can produce a quantum change in operational effectiveness.
- Concurrence of organizational action and the collaborative integration of manufacturing with information systems that will be key to successfully competing on time and customer satisfaction.
- The integration and alignment of manufacturing with other functions, such as engineering and marketing.

Chapter 2 presents a framework that will enable organizations (in particular, but not exclusively, *virtual* organizations) to integrate their people, processes, and technologies, in order to leverage them in creating a manufacturing blueprint for the 1990s. It addresses the business architecture and the conceptual framework that manufacturing companies should use to analyze, develop, and structure their organizational, production, and competitive capabilities. In addition, it focuses on the relationships, interfaces, dependencies, and integration of literally dozens of concepts, systems, principles, methods, and techniques, without which an organization cannot fully take advantage of its core competencies and thereby outperform competitors.

CHOOSING THE APPROPRIATE MODEL: VERTICAL INTEGRATION VERSUS VIRTUAL DISAGGREGATION

The following sections describe the different organizational models, from the traditional vertical to the virtual disaggregated enterprise and their characteristics. In addition, various techniques for achieving virtual integration will be discussed, including logistics and strategic alliances. Other strategic considerations will be explored in depth in Chapters 4 and 5.

The principal choices available involve certain considerations of both benefits and drawbacks for the company. Which of each pair of alternatives allocates present resources to obtain the best future outcome: Should a company bring everything inside, or organize a complex relationship with other companies to accomplish its goals? Should it make physical or intellectual capital investments? Does the market want customization or standardization—and what does that mean for the company? How should it integrate its products and processes? In the end, however, the inspired and dedicated use of people, processes, and technology in pursuit of whichever well-conceived strategy is chosen can result in orders-of-magnitude improvements in an enterprise's performance.

These factors, with technology and methodology at their core, have spawned a new paradigm: *virtual integration*. Through focused factories, supplier and distributor partnerships, and strategic alliances, the virtually integrated company manages and coordinates value chain members, which are decentralized and often autonomous from the core organization. This "virtual" structure results in continuous flow manufacturing, as if these organizational members were physically colocated.

Achieving virtual integration requires a shift in orientation. Organizational processes that were hierarchical become much more peer-to-peer. Ownership gives way to cooperation, collaboration, and communication; direct management and control shift to shared responsibilities and goals. The internal focus and orientation becomes more external. *The driving motivation of the virtual paradigm is to deliver a product that minimizes aggregate cost and maximizes value along the entire value chain.*

Orientation Shift	
Vertical integration	*Virtual integration*
Hierarchal	Peer-to-peer
Ownership	Alliance
Direct management/control	Shared responsibility/goals
Internal orientation	External orientation

In Figure 2–1, two levels of integration are occurring simultaneously: Product flow/added value is shown at the bottom of the figure; information flow initiates from right to left, but certainly is two-way directional as well, at the top of the figure. Customer needs initiate the information added-value chain, whereas product concepts, ideas, and technology initiate the product added-value chain. The integration of information flow with product flow is facilitated by the overlying methods/principles embodied in distribution, manufacturing, and supply.

FIGURE 2–1
Virtual Integration Paradigm: The Integration of the Value Chain

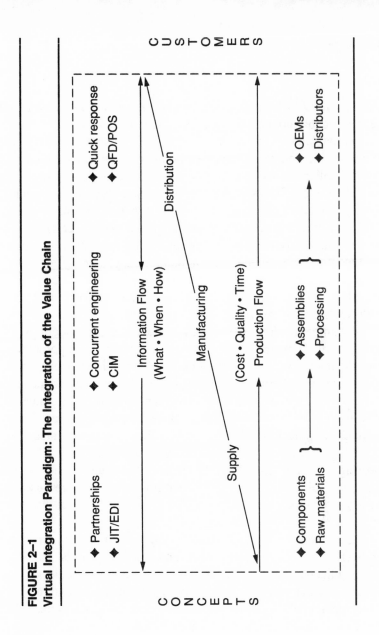

The significance of this diagonal line is that product and information flow are inextricably connected—product value added across the entire value chain is enabled via information flow. This information becomes more powerful when incorporated into contemporary methods such as quick response (QR), supplier partnerships, and concurrent engineering. The principles of quick response (QR) connect customers with distribution via quality function deployment (QFD) methodology and its execution through point of sale (POS) systems. Manufacturing and engineering manage product/process design simultaneously through the principles of concurrent engineering executed via computer integrated manufacturing (CIM) systems. Manufacturing establishes material contracts through partnership methods executed through just-in-time (JIT) principles and electronic communication found in electronic data interchange (EDI) standards.

A number of other issues are pertinent to the consideration of vertical and virtual integration strategies. The enterprise's approach to globalization may have a great impact on the decision whether to build or to supply product. Studies verify that higher margins are found at the top of the value chain—nearest the customer—where added value accumulates, customization occurs, and services are attached to products. There is typically more profit opportunity in final assembly, integration, and packaging than in raw materials or other, lower, supply chain parts that make up end products. Commodity products, found earlier in the value chain, typically operate in lower margins that are more susceptible to erosion by competitors who are making sustained capital investments in process technology.

This scenario has caused the original equipment manufacturers (OEMs) to outsource component and basic materials yet still exert strong influence with these key suppliers and distributors (from raw material to consumer contact), which represents the initiation of a virtual integrated model. In other companies, however, the value chain has remained vertically integrated, with the bulk of the supply chain owned by the final product producer. Even those products not owned by that manufacturer usually are provided by "captive" vendors.

An enterprise that is currently competing in global markets or is experiencing the trend of increased offshore sales should assess what resources are available in those markets. If the skills needed to supply, manufacture, and distribute are available, virtual integration will most likely be the option. If the skills are unavailable, vertical integration may be the most rapidly deployable option.

The Four Models: Vertical to Virtual

There are four fundamental models a company may employ, ranging from a traditional vertically integrated factory to a virtual disaggregated enterprise.

The Traditional Vertically Integrated Factory
In a vertical factory, final products, their subproducts, and associated fabrication are performed on a single colocated manufacturing site. Purchased products and components are generally either low-cost commodities or specialty components and materials. Colocation includes departmental and centralized support services to the factory—for example, planning, production control, purchasing, process/industrial engineering, and administrative support. Colocation may or may not include other major departments such as engineering, marketing, sales, systems, and finance. Communications are typically face-to-face, real-time. Capital investment is high in both physical and intellectual assets (e.g., industrial engineering). Total product cycle time is short, inventories are low, and product management is comprehensive. Typically, a vertical factory is a product-driven, focused factory.

The Traditional Vertically Integrated Company
The vertical company is characterized as a multisite operation that is often factory-process focused and that, in aggregate, builds a product from beginning to end. Decentralized technical support to each factory (site) is typically combined with centralized purchasing for basic materials, commodities, and specialty items. Communications are typically batch (e.g., daily, weekly, monthly updates) and seldom offer face-to-face meetings. Capital is also high in the introduction and maintenance of new technology or process advances. Product management coordination is more complex than in a vertical factory and often necessitates increased cycle time and high in-transit inventory. A vertical company is much less susceptible to external factors (e.g., supply fluctuations) than other models.

The Virtual Integrated Enterprise
The virtual integrated enterprise follows essentially the same manufacturing model as the vertical company, but with several enhancements. Communications are real-time or on-line as in the vertical factory; however, electronic connectivity substitutes for colocation to handle

communication flow. Virtual teams are supported by electronic conferencing, electronic networks, individual PCs, terminals, and central electronic libraries that emulate the distinct advantages and attributes of one-site colocated organizations. Product management is dramatically improved, coordination is high, and inventories are replaced with information; process capital remains high as new process technologies are introduced. Control also remains high, whereas flexibility remains limited and risks controlled. Profits from the firm's final product will be channeled back into lower level, high value-adding processes.

The Virtual Disaggregated Enterprise

The virtual disaggregated model requires a major strategic reassessment of the manufacturing (vertical) and business (horizontal) processes required to design and build products. This model emphasizes retention of critical proprietary manufacturing processes and potentially high-risk supply components and their associated processes. Outsourcing (not temporary subcontracting) of nonstrategic manufacturing processes is supported by a partnership or alliance formation, but support and co-ordination functions (e.g., scheduling, CAD/CAM, planning) remain in-house. Outsourcing of business processes is also considered (e.g., data processing, billing, transportation, warehousing). Communications are the same as in the virtual company, except that telecom standards (e.g., open systems) and data format standards (e.g., EDI) are required. Much less capital is required, yet process technology remains contemporary. Product management is more complex but much more responsive to product flux and/or geographic dynamics. The internal focus is on strategic or proprietary-added value and management of alliances.

The shaded area in Figure 2–2 depicts the company "owned" assets of a hypothetical virtual disaggregated enterprise named *The Flex Company*. Companies shown below *The Flex Company* (A, B, C, D) are all product producers along the supply chain beginning wih raw materials (A) and fabrication (B). Companies C and D are producers of nonstrategic or proprietary subproducts and accompanying products. All are directly connected vis-á-vis information to *The Flex Company*. Companies E, F, and G also are autonomous companies who provide value-added services deemed nonstrategic or nonproprietary business processes. They also are directly connected through information links. The entire virtual enterprise is encapsulated via dotted lines to illustrate that all companies within the added-value supply chain operate as if colocated.

FIGURE 2-2
The Virtual Disaggregated Enterprise

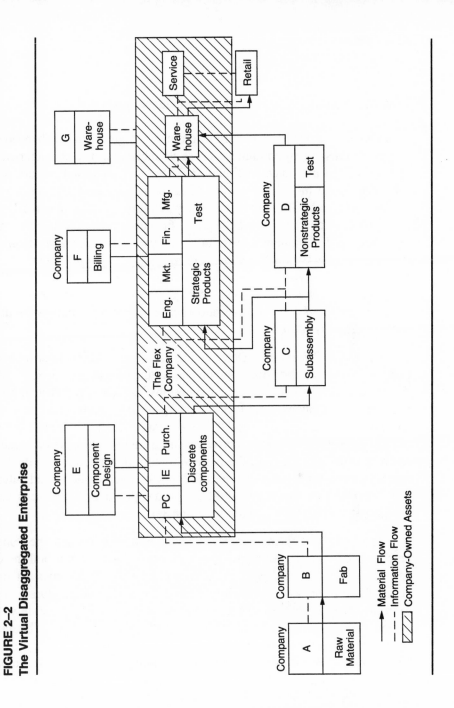

→ Material Flow
--- Information Flow
▨ Company-Owned Assets

Selecting a Model: Variables and Considerations

As an enterprise decides which model to use as a guide, tradeoffs need to be made across many variables. These variables and the characteristics of each model are listed in Figure 2–3. Several important factors will influence which models or combinations of models best support a corporate vision, including business strategy, culture, growth, new markets, technology, strengths and weaknesses, financial or capital health, and regulatory and compliance restrictions. *As pressures increase to introduce new products rapidly, respond in real-time to customer needs, and finance growth across the world, the virtual disaggregated enterprise will become the model of choice, offering a solution that balances physical ownership and process integration with cooperative management and process disaggregation.*

Customer Priorities.   Determining how important it is to customers that the company build what it supplies is a fundamental part of assessing the vertical and virtual disaggregated options. Building, rather than buying, some components may lock an enterprise into outdated technology and render it unable, for capital investment and depreciation reasons, to take advantage of impending advances in new materials, processes, or product designs. Further, the more vertically integrated a manufacturing organization becomes, the less likely it is that suppliers (and future suppliers) will be open and willing to share production advances and developments for fear of technology transfer.

"Built Here."   Another key element is how important the "built here" culture is to the company. For some organizations, "not built here" has the same connotation as "not invented here"—it becomes an unacceptable option—whereas some U.S. automobile manufacturers, for example, have concluded that selling a foreign sourced automobile with a Detroit logo on it is better than not selling a car at all. The fact is, when confronted with the option of shipping products through their competitors' revenue streams or having negative financial results, most manufacturers are able to identify and implement strategies that either reinforce their culture or that incorporate cultural change.

Supply Links.   For some companies, supply links in the value chain may be deemed so critical that the only choice is vertical integration. Many computer manufacturers (e.g., DEC, IBM, and Hewlett-Packard) have taken this approach with certain semiconductor devices

FIGURE 2-3
Summary Characteristics of Vertical/Virtual Models

	1. Vertical Factory	2. Vertical Company	3. Virtual Company	4. Virtual/Disaggregated Co.
Ownership	• Full	• Full	• Full	• Shared
Structure	• Single-colocated site	• Multisite process focused	• Multisite	• Multisite interdependent relationships
Production	• Start to finish	• Start to finish	• Start to finish	• End product focus
Functions	• Centralized	• Decentralized/Centralized	• Decentralized/virtual teams	• Only strategic functions retained/others outsourced
Communications	• Face to face, real time	• Batch communications • Seldom face to face	• Real-time, on-line • Electronic networks	• Real-time/telecommunications standards
Capital Investment	• High investment in physical assets	• High investment/maintenance of new technology	• High process technology investment • High information investment	• Information intensive
Cycle Time	• Shortest	• Longer	• Very short	• Very short
Inventory	• Low	• High	• Inventory replaced with information	• Inventory replaced with infomation
Product Management	• Comprehensive	• Difficult	• Easier	• Complex
Flexibility	• Lower flexibility	• Higher flexibility	• Higher flexibility	• Maximum flexibility
Predictability	• Highest	• Higher	• Very high	• High
Overall Cost	• High	• Low	• Lower	• Lowest

that are considered so strategic that component manufacturing could not be put at an arm's length, either for reasons of product quality and supply or because their product or system technological innovations were viewed as being driven by proprietary component advances. However, in nearly all cases the process technology was deemed so specialized that *remote* focused factories were built and virtually colocated through methodology and communication systems.

Managing Culture.   Managing culture becomes more challenging as the company evolves from a single location, to multiple locations, to inclusion of independent companies that are all members of the enterprise. Most managers are well trained in single location management. The skills gap widens as the enterprise model becomes more complex. Many managers lack the skills necessary to manage cooperative peer-to-peer relations with multiple facilities, functions, international cultures, and independent alliances.

Communications and Computing.   Low-cost communications and computing have enhanced the capabilities of organizations to deal with and coordinate activities in the enterprise. Although these advances may give greater enabling advantage to virtual integration strategies, they do not solve the cultural diversity challenge or system application choices that are essential to virtual enterprise performance.

Value Analysis.   Value analysis of the total manufacturing processes will reveal both critical and unimportant processes. Elements of the production process that produce more problems than they are worth may be candidates for disaggregation or outsourcing. Other processes may be difficult or impossible to outsource, necessitating vertical integration, even though such structure provides few benefits.

MANUFACTURING ARCHITECTURE FOR THE 1990s: THE VIRTUAL ENTERPRISE

The business and manufacturing architecture for the 1990s is one of a virtual enterprise, with no respect for geography. It functions as if colocated with its suppliers, its distribution channels, its alliance partners and, most importantly, *with every customer worldwide*. This new, virtual architecture compresses engineering/marketing, manufacturing, logistics, and administration functions so that each element of the value chain finds its relationships with all other elements expedited and optimized. *The architecture is populated by teams of fundamentally sound, contemporary organizations inspired by excellence, driven by results, and benchmarked by customers who value quality and service as much as or more than cost.* These organizations have earned the confidence of their clients and build upon a knowledge of customer requirements and what it takes to excel.

Clearly, the architecture is not a theoretical construct, but is derived from extensive experience with and analysis of the industry, market, and technological forces that affect manufacturing enterprises. Customers and vendors alike are alliance partners in this architecture, which, when properly implemented, operates as if it were an adjunct to each customer site, tangibly present and highly responsive to customer needs.

As depicted in Figure 2–4, the overall architecture of the virtual enterprise links vendors and customers with product definition, product building, order fulfillment, and sales and business administration activities. Strategic alliances are maintained with vendors and customers. Thus, each element of the enterprise is connected to every other element, with distance measured not in miles, but in minutes. There is no fixed colocation requirement, but manufacturing is no longer off-line, insulated and buffered by bureaucracy from suppliers and customers. It is the essence and center of the customer-supplier continuum and the medium through which demand becomes satisfied in real-time. Within the virtual enterprise, manufacturing joins engineering and marketing in planning for customer requirements and in developing products and services, feeding the customers' desires to vendors and, in turn, feeding vendor developments to customers. It also links them to sales and administration.

Real-time, on-line, customer-driven demands are the lifeblood of this virtual enterprise, and the full resource base of the virtual enterprise is available on call for each customer need. The successful virtual enterprise may conquer nearly insurmountable barriers to competition and will leapfrog competitors who remain content with simple linear improvements to standard manufacturing design.

Supporting Principles and Technologies of the Virtual Enterprise

Successful virtual enterprises know their customers well, exploiting proven methods and technologies that optimize customer satisfaction

FIGURE 2–4
Virtual Enterprise Architecture

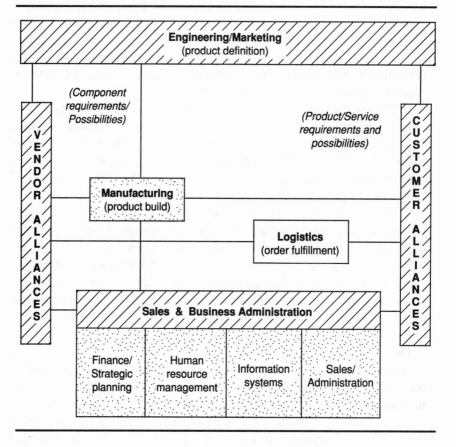

and eliminate the process risks prevalent in today's business environment. Knowledge of the customer will not come through purchase orders, contract negotiations, or fixing problems, as in the past, but through system-supported access to details of the customer's current and projected needs. Virtual connections between companies will serve as sensing devices to monitor and capture new directions or requirements. Figure 2–5 enhances the basic structure of Figure 2–4 to show the key practices, principles, methodologies, and concepts that are applied to major business architecture components of the virtual enterprise.

These practices, principles, methodologies, and guiding concepts form the infrastructure of the virtual enterprise architecture and define

FIGURE 2–5
Virtual Enterprise Architecture

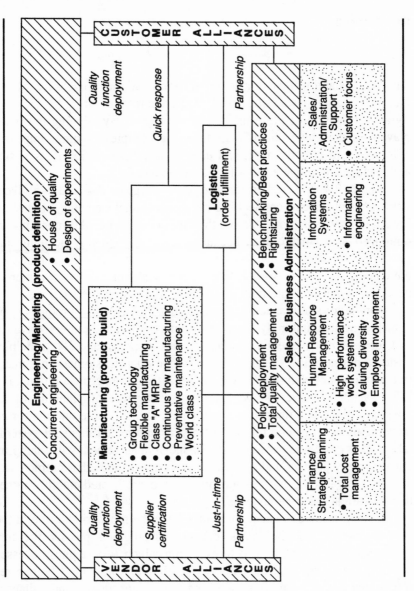

the channels and formats for communication and interoperability. Manufacturing again plays a critical and integrative role, ensuring the credibility and utilization of these many methodologies. By aligning the many players in the value chain, manufacturing compresses time, improves efficiency and effectiveness, and ensures that the benefits of its virtual architecture are delivered to all alliance partners.

Figure 2–6 is a further enhancement of Figures 2–4 and 2–5. Technology-based systems connect individual functional elements, orchestrating simultaneous activities across the virtual enterprise. All functions are optimized and synchronized because they share a highly accurate and integrated data base. Functional partnerships benefiting all members of the enterprise must be well defined, thereby forming long-term interdependencies that promote mutual investment and strategic sharing.

Parallel or simultaneous processes enable world-class products to be launched in breathtakingly short time frames, as manufacturers strive for that ideal of instantaneous products. Quick response and JIT principles ensure a nonstop flow of information and product. Customers, not materials requirement planning (MRP) systems, trigger enterprise production; MRP systems evolve to take on the primary role of planning rather than execution. The financial department is focused more on monitoring strategic plans than reporting on history, as automated financial systems take care of day-to-day accounting. Financial management will champion contemporary product and process accounting methods that promote *actual* costing, leading to strategic pricing and profit predictability rather than historical variance analysis.

Human resource management may have the most critical role in the new architecture for the 1990s, because its programs provide the corporate and compensation structures within which people and processes interact, grow, and evolve. Without superb and well-crafted human resource management, the framework will misorient, decay, and collapse. (These issues will be discussed in depth in Chapter 3.)

Sales and Business Administration

In some respects, sales and business administration have the steepest hill to climb, because most organizations do not have an integrated sales system, but rather numerous ad hoc systems and informal personal networks supporting the sales and order functions. These ad hoc systems and informal networks keep sales administration from expiring but fall short of methodically applying viable system-level remedies.

FIGURE 2-6
Virtual Enterprise Architecture Systems

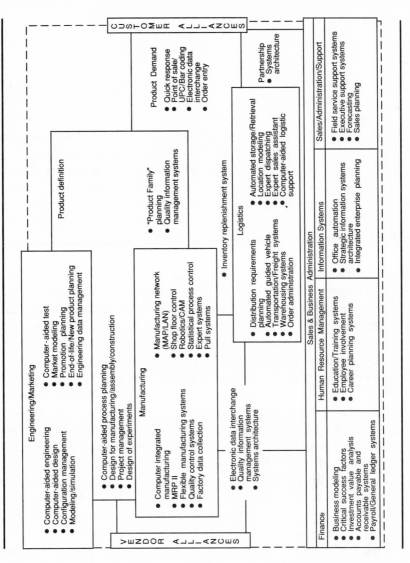

The virtual architecture and its supporting principles and systems are structured to provide for the needs of the sales staff so that they can focus not only on exactly meeting targets, but also on continuously establishing more demanding targets. The result is likely to be an *active* sales force that spends its time on customers rather than on reports and ad hoc administration. The sales department will be supported by far more effective, efficient, and informed information systems, which will serve as enterprise bridges for communication. Improved market intelligence will be aided by reduced cycle time, resulting in increased forecast accuracy; and, once cycle time has collapsed sufficiently, sales forecasting will be replaced by order taking.

Expert systems will supplement the sales force in designing and configuring product and service solutions. On-board product diagnostic systems will dispatch services before breakdowns occur and identify replacement parts along with service procedures. Examples of such futuristic diagnostic systems can be found today in Digital Equipment Corporation's computers, Xerox's document handlers, and both defense and commercial aircraft. All that will be left will be selling.

Logistics: A Leading Indicator of the Value of Virtual Integration
The intimate relationships and systems supporting rapid customer response must extend throughout the virtual organization. One consequence of this is that the role of logistics, which includes many order fulfillment functions, will expand. (Programs supporting such relationships with suppliers will be described later in the chapter.) Logistics, which has emerged as a professional and technical vocation, will have an increasingly critical role in the virtual manufacturing enterprise because it adds much of the value to the goods and services provided and because it may be the only part of the organization that has persistent, daily contact with customers.[1] Many of the key business drivers, including customer focus, globalization, cost, innovation, and quality, have significant impact upon or are principal objectives of logistics operations.

Logistics often manages the greatest percentage of inventory (and, in some cases, physical assets), manages the longest period of composite cycle time, and is making an increasing contribution to real added-value services. A variety of industry sectors, including consumer products,

---

[1]For further discussion of the role of logistics in manufacturing, see Christopher Gopal and Gerry Cahill, *Logistics in Manufacturing* (Homewood, Ill: Business One Irwin, 1992).

chemicals, apparel manufacturers, service companies, and others compete based directly upon their logistics capabilities, especially in customer service and responsiveness.

Not surprisingly, logistics is becoming increasingly complex and more reliant upon both technology and methodology. Logistics manages the operational activities that link manufacturers through JIT methodologies to vendors and manufacturers through quick response (QR) to customers. Electronic data interchange (EDI), an increasingly important facilitator of the flow of products and services, instantly connects value chain members and plays a key role in supporting logistics. The performance level role that logistics plays in both JIT and QR operations makes it either a primary enabler—or disabler—of world-class value chains.

Superior logistics performance is playing a significant role in helping companies develop innovative business strategies, and may be one reason that Procter & Gamble, Xerox, and Benetton are among those companies sustaining competitive advantage over their global adversaries. *In fact, superior logistics operations may displace multiple geographic manufacturing sites by, for example, creating highly responsive order fulfillment from a centralized product location. (Ironically, this kind of superiority also creates the advantage of sourcing components from the world's best vendor, regardless of its geographic location.)*

Table 2–1 shows how the logistics profession continually requires new competencies and expert knowledge in several technical areas. That

---

TABLE 2–1
Logistics Expertise

- Export/Import regulations
- Emerging compliance standards (i.e., ISO 9000)
- Transportation alternatives and cost/benefit tradeoffs:
  - Air   • Land   • Sea   • Express
- Warehousing
  - Equipment   • Systems
  - Material handling   • Packaging
- Systems/Technology
  - Hand-held computers   • Electronic data interchange (EDI)
  - Electronic libraries   • Pen-based systems
  - Point of sale   • Modeling
  - Bar coding   • Expert systems
  - Integration (i.e., with MRP)

---

is, in addition to the basic set of technology/systems shown in Figure 2–6, the logistics activity in many firms now necessarily incorporates the expertise shown in Table 2–1.

Logistics is clearly no longer simply a tactical activity; it plays a strategic and integrating role throughout the value chain. Along with superior engineering/marketing, excellence in manufacturing, and innovative alliances in sales and purchasing, logistics is clearly an investment imperative for leading-edge companies.

The Integrative Role of Engineering/Marketing and Manufacturing

Engineering/marketing and manufacturing must align and integrate with each other, and together they must successfully align and integrate with vendors, customers, and other alliance partners. The resulting aligned enterprise will provide the foundation for developing and delivering best-in-industry products and services. Manufacturing has the opportunity and obligation to really make a competitive difference, not by merely doing what it traditionally has done, but by playing an active and directive role as the integrator. Endowed as it is now with an impressive array of technology, manufacturing has never been in a better position to do this, since technical limitations disappeared long ago. In addition to the wealth of technologies in engineering/marketing and manufacturing, Figure 2–6 also shows computer aided process planning (CAPP), design for manufacturing (DFM), design of experiments (DOE), and project management as playing a key integrative role between these two activities. The only problem is that concurrent engineering—the seamless integration of these methodologies and technologies—has yet to be realized in many firms.

In many organizations, manufacturing continues to be the crusader for methodologies, technologies, and new exciting concepts. Despite the many changes in the business and manufacturing worlds, manufacturing is still the only part of the organization that actually *makes* things. In turn, the ability of engineering to sustain seamless, in contrast to more traditional departmentalized, relationships among value chain members will determine whether simultaneous product and process development occurs.

Manufacturing and engineering must look outside the narrow boundaries of what has been seen as their territories and collaborate with marketing, which through its strategic planning process, decides which new products are funded and developed in highly market-driven organizations. (Less market-driven enterprises may have alternative methods of merging marketing into product planning.) Because the market strategies have such a profound impact throughout the enterprise, any improvement to them must take into account a wide range of stakeholder perspectives. Strategy developers therefore have access to technology such as new modeling tools, simulation systems, statistical techniques, and worldwide market data bases in order to keep up with global stakeholder concerns. *Intuition and guessing, in turn, are being replaced by systematic, empirical market testing because being right the first time has never been more important.*

Manufacturing as the Core of the Virtual Enterprise

For the manufacturing enterprise, opportunities for competitive advantage must be derived from the core of the enterprise—its manufacturing processes. The more thoroughly integrated an organization's selection of people, process, and technology options, the more capable the organization. And, at least for the time being, the manufacturing component of the organization has the most informed perspective and the greatest impact upon this integrating process. It is therefore ideally positioned to lead in the process of aligning people, process, and technology strategies and tactics.

> Manufacturers that thrive into the next generation, then, will compete by bundling services with products, anticipating and responding to a truly comprehensive range of customer needs. Moreover, they will make the factory itself the hub of their efforts to get and hold customers—activities that are now located in separate, often distant, parts of the organization. Production workers and factory managers will be able to forge and sustain new relationships with customers because they will be in direct and continuing contact with them. Manufacturing will, in short, become the cortex of the business.[2]

Manufacturing can no longer focus internally at the expense of its emerging role as the company coordinator and champion of strategic competitiveness. It should take the lead in educating itself and its enterprise about this portfolio of people, process, and technology solutions to ensure that this integration and alignment takes root and is responsibly

---

[2]Richard Chase and David Garvin, "The Service Factory," *Harvard Business Review*, March/April 1989, p. 62.

nurtured. *Manufacturing must champion an enterprisewide commitment to world-class competitive advantage.*

The integrative role that manufacturing must play today is far more complex than the virtual enterprise architecture just discussed might suggest. As a result, evaluating options and developing strategies and programs requires a comprehensive and dynamic·analytical framework. The framework, oriented around business drivers, contains three basic building blocks (people, process, and technology) that emphasize the alignment and integration of its components, not their further technical advancement. The framework's goal is exceptional enterprise performance, enabled by the organization's superior capabilities. This framework is derived from a detailed analysis of the 10 key issues and business drivers for the decade of the 1990s (discussed in Chapter 1): globalization, innovation, time, customer focus, quality, environment, cost, financing growth, learning and managing change, and regulation and compliance. *The organization that results from this new framework is structured by advanced, yet standard, systems; by contemporary methodologies that embrace available technologies, tools, and process capabilities; and by the strengths derived from the manufacturing enterprise's culture and its people.*

As previously discussed, the architectures in Figures 2–4 through 2–6 are driven by customer needs and incorporate a portfolio of practices, methods, and systems. At the operating level, each company must decide on an integrated solution set that maps to the corresponding business issues of that market. This solution set is called the "framework" of the virtual enterprise architecture. The integration of these components is paramount to establishing a competitive advantage.

The complex, real-world issues that are of concern at any one moment involve an interplay among a very extensive set of interrelated drivers and subcomponents. Looking inside the framework, there are six people-oriented elements, seven process-oriented elements, and eight technology-oriented elements, all applicable to the current manufacturing environment, as illustrated in Figure 2–7. This three-dimensional matrix will be sufficient to structure and guide comprehensive analysis of most, if not all options. Selecting the relationships between each issue/driver with respect to any one matrix element requires extensive review and analysis, beginning with a review of each matrix selection in the context of the other elements in all matrices. For example, selecting an optimum organizational design requires aligning that design to the

FIGURE 2–7
The Framework of the Virtual Enterprise

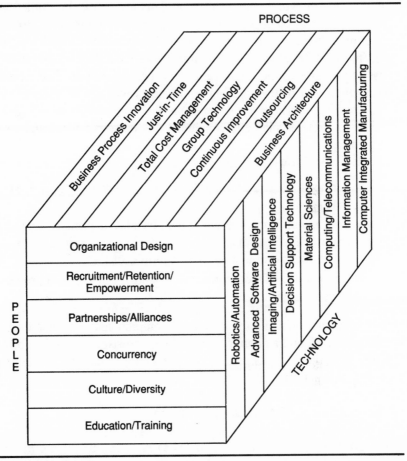

business architecture (and vice versa); selecting a business architecture requires aligning to the organizations computing and telecommunications infrastructure (and vice versa); and aligning this infrastructure to the organizational design (and vice versa). This is likely to be an iterative process.

Figure 2–7 is meant to be a guide for comprehensive exploration of the relationships between issues, people, processes, and technology and for confirming the alignment of selected options with each other. Although the specific elements of the people, process, and technology framework are appropriate for the state of the manufacturing industry today, systems, processes, and methodologies will emerge and mature, causing components of the three matrices to change, with some elements removed and others added.

The overall business strategy prioritizes the competitive drivers and determines which solution elements will require significant management and resource investments. Although some solution elements will have less importance to the organization and perhaps require fewer resources than others, all of the solution components will see some level of use. For example, consider a consumer products company that has just completed its strategic plan and concluded that customer focus and cost will be strategically important over the next three years. Based upon the integrated model illustrated in Figure 2–8, one can determine that

- Partnerships and alliances play a primary role in both strategic issues.
- Continuous improvement programs play a primary role in each issue, while information management plays a primary role in customer focus and a secondary role in cost.
- Computing, telecommunications, and JIT will play a primary role in both issues.

In theory, it is important to think comprehensively when evaluating the framework and its application to the enterprise. In practice, however, a few solution elements usually emerge as absolutely critical and should be worked with first.

The Benefits of Virtual Disaggregation

The goal of virtual disaggregation is to replicate or exceed the advantages of colocated processes without the disadvantages of multifocused, heavily capital-intensive, vertically integrated factories. When properly executed, virtual disaggregation expands the range of strategic options, enhances product diversity, and extends market opportunities. Products and processes that are peripheral to the manufacturers' strategically important products and services or key capabilities are candidates for outsourcing. The allies need to be aware of the strategy being followed by the enterprise with whom they are building a relationship, so that they can build in the same amount of flexibility as their customers and partners.

Another benefit of virtual disaggregation orientation is that it reduces fixed assets and expenses and often fine tunes and improves the

FIGURE 2–8
Alternative Responses to Business Issues

★★ = Primary
★ = Secondary

	Business Issues	
	Customer Focus	Cost
PEOPLE		
Organizational design	★	★
Recruit/Retain/Empower		★
Partnerships/Alliances	★★	★★
Concurrency	★	★★
Culture and diversity	★	★
Education/Training	★	★
PROCESS		
Process innovation	★	★★
Just-in-time	★★	★★
Total cost management	★	★★
Group technology	★	★★
Continuous improvement	★★	★★
Outsourcing	★	★
Business architecture	★★	
TECHNOLOGY		
Robotics/Automation		★★
Advanced software design		★
Imaging/Artificial Intelligence		★
Decision support		★
Material sciences		★★
Computing/Telecom	★★	★★
Information management	★★	★
Computer-integrated manufacturing		★

retained value-adding processes while still enabling an enterprise to focus on what it needs to do best. Thus, for most enterprises, any business support process or nonstrategic value-adding process is a candidate for an alliance, or in some cases for a joint venture developed specifically to produce an entire product or service. By viewing internal overhead functions or indirect costs as support services, an organization may be able to identify opportunities to improve delivery, quality, or costs of these services by outsourcing them as well.

There are some negatives, of course. A virtual outsourcing integration strategy may lessen a company's control of supply and production, unless carefully crafted virtual alliances are developed. Suppliers or alliances may even become competitors or an enterprise may find itself at an arm's length from critical design and manufacturing expertise. These concerns must be thoroughly understood and addressed to turn risk into maximum benefit.

Organizational Benefits

In the vertically integrated company, assets are owned by the company, which also directly manages the people and processes involved. This may mean that the organization does not have to bargain for capacity or deal with other side effects of shared manufacturing resources (particularly if all the factory capacities are in balance with each other). As a result, negotiation may not be a necessary element of managing the value chain, possibly reducing turnaround times.

Some enterprises consisting of multiple business units are structured so that each has a high degree of control and autonomy, perhaps even inclusive of engineering and support functions, which are likely to require redundant effort for production, systems, and management in the vertically managed business unit. This is particularly true when an organization finds itself revising or replacing systems and processes that are likely to be more commonplace in the future.

Clearly, one advantage of the virtual model is that process costs and associated overhead expenses are closely aligned, therefore offering more control and predictability. Another is that the responsibility for remaining abreast of developments in markets and technology is directly coupled to the focused product and/or process. When well executed, virtual integration encourages collaboration among member factories and suppliers, so that they play to each other's strengths rather than weaknesses.

The degree to which communication technology has been incorporated into an organization is likely to have a bearing on how aggressively virtual integration should be pursued. For instance, if a technologically lagging organization adopts a strategy that requires extensive linkages throughout the enterprise, its members will almost certainly require substantial technical, cultural, and educational resource commitments.

An Improved Introduction Process

One real advantage of virtual disaggregation has been a substantially improved product introduction process. Companies like Dell Computer, McKesson, and Sun Microsystems have become masters at leveraging alliances to work in parallel toward cooperative new product introductions. The virtual disaggregated enterprise, when properly aligned and managed, offers greater opportunities for rapid deployment through concurrent engineering. If it also extends through the distribution network of the value chain, it can respond better to customer feedback and reposition engineering, manufacturing, and field support along customer real-time priorities, enabling consumers to be more directly involved in product design. It is also likely to result in improved and more desirable products.

In this kind of enterprise, management of human resources is likely to benefit from more emphasis on teaming and collaboration—which develop employee empowerment and cross-enterprise communication— than on control. However, unless an enterprise can invest in and master these new skills for management of virtual factories, the benefits of such cooperation are not likely to be realized.

The ultimate goal of virtual disaggregation is, of course, the formation of a powerful network of independent yet virtually integrated companies that could have various levels of business and interlocking equity holdings among all its members. (This kind of symbiotic relationship across the value chain has already been achieved in Japan, where the *keiretsu* organization has proven to be a powerful financial force in the marketplace.) Networked members might coordinate closely in developing future products and could even share senior technicians and intellectual assets. Enterprises consisting of world-class companies are likely to find that their combined influence facilitates capital formation.

THE TRANSFORMATIONAL ORGANIZATION

Although many companies have worked rigorously to reduce the number of reporting levels while simultaneously delegating authority and broadening communications horizontally through and across functional departments, manufacturing companies are still, nonetheless, typically known for their multilevel, hierarchal structure. Many companies have experimented with hybrid organizational structures (discussed later in this chapter), empowerment of people, and peer-to-peer communications. (See Chapter 3.) However, even these forward-thinking companies still conduct business and develop and manufacture products along a generic functional/departmental framework that facilitates accountability and provides lines of vocational development and reward.

The Four-Level Manufacturing Structure

Those who have been involved in manufacturing since the 1950s have witnessed the evolution and maturing of manufacturing organizations into the four-level structures we find today: the factory, manufacturing, operations, and the enterprise. These four areas are the domains of the factory superintendent, the vice-president of manufacturing, the chief operations officer, and the transnational executive officer (see page 70). The first three of these have a history of responsibilities and activities that help to define their current state (see Figure 2–9).

The Factory Superintendent
Throughout most of the history of manufacturing, the factory floor was where value was added to products, mostly accomplished by "touch" labor, often by blue-collar workers operating machinery to convert raw materials into products. These labor- or machine-intensive operations were responsible not only for most of the value added, but also for the bulk of manufacturing costs. Keeping those costs as low as possible has been the responsibility of the factory superintendent, who also oversees manufacturing throughput and performance by managing the factory floor (including maintenance), labor, inventory, and stores. During the 1950s and 1960s, considerable effort was made to reduce the costs of manufacturing. Typically, this effort focused on tasks or departments to improve factory floor efficiency and to reduce labor costs.

The Vice-President of Manufacturing
The vice-president of manufacturing is responsible for the overhead and the infrastructure that the factory superintendent utilizes in production and for solving most of the problems affecting the factory, including materials management, industrial engineering, manufacturing systems support, human resource management, and cost accounting.

The vice-president has traditionally been responsible for cost performance throughout the entire manufacturing organization. When material costs as a percentage of overall cost were increasing, they were viewed as more germane to purchasing and materials management. As the manufacturing process became more complex, quality and time objectives began to warrant more attention. Whereas the superintendent focuses on cost reduction, the vice-president of manufacturing focuses on the contribution of costs to value and margin.

FIGURE 2–9
Responsibilities in the Four-Level Manufacturing Organization

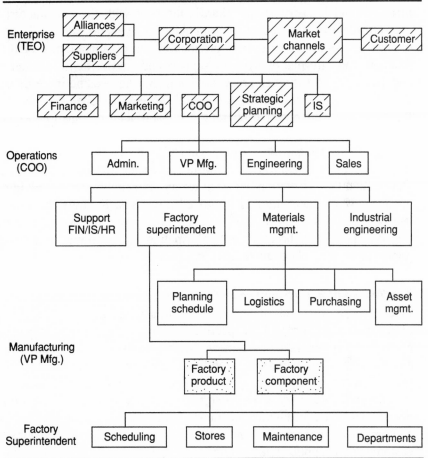

Since the 1960s, the spotlight, in the form of improvement and innovation, has been shared between the manufacturing organization and the factory floor, with the principal focus on quality rather than cost. The orientation has been horizontal, on functions and processes, rather than vertical, on department and tasks. Information and planning have replaced inventory and end-of-the-quarter heroic effort as key enablers of performance. Technology and methodology have played an increasing role in manufacturing flexibility and profitability.

The Chief Operating Officer

Because of the wide variation in operations among manufacturers, the role of the chief operating officer (COO) is less consistent among organizations and industry sectors than is the case with the manufacturing vice-president or the factory superintendent. In general, the COO coordinates all direct value-adding activities of the organization, including financial and information systems support and, most often, engineering and sales. These activities arose as manufacturing became more dependent upon, and involved in, the overall success of operations and as functions that were once peripheral to the manufacturing function became central.

Since the 1980s, the "bright light" of improvement and innovation has shone upon operations. The principal focus was time, as well as quality, and the orientation has been toward expanding market and introducing new products through improved processes. Synergy, innovative use of resources, empowerment, teamwork, and time-based competitiveness have been layered onto information and planning to produce unprecedented levels of manufacturing performance.

The Transnational Executive Officer

In contrast to the traditional CEO, the transnational executive officer (TEO) will bring a global perspective to manage the transnational value chain from suppliers to customers. With technology continuing to be an enabler of manufacturing capabilities and with competition intensifying and becoming more global, companies are being forced to consider manufacturing capacity at the enterprise level. They must attain levels of investment and coordination in transportation, infrastructure capacities, and employee management and training and develop broader visions of customer and supplier relationships.

Today, the emphasis is shifting from the factory floor to the global value chain, and the principal focus is on innovation throughout the chain, outside as well as inside the enterprise. This orientation toward the virtual enterprise has created a new management requirement: the need to manage intimate, strategic alliances and partnering with external organizations. This job falls to the TEO. The TEO also has the task of integrating the alliances throughout the organization—to *create* the virtual organization. He or she needs to provide guidance for this activity as well as an overall vision.

FIGURE 2–10
Focus Metrics for the 1990s for Each Level of the Enterprise

		COST	CAPACITY	QUALITY	DELIVERY	INVENTORY	NEW PRODUCT
Level 1 *Enterprise*	TEO	Value chain effectiveness across all dimensions					
Level 2 *Operations*	COO	Value	Flexibility	Customer satisfaction	To Request	JIT	TTM
Level 3 *Mfg.*	V.P.Mfg.	Margin	Resources	Process	To Commit	ROA	Concurrent engineering
Level 4 *Factory*	Superintendent	Cost	Equipment utilization	Product	Through-put	Turns	Prototype and Pilot test

The Focus Metrics for Each Level of the Enterprise

Manufacturers will focus on many of the same issues that have been concerns for decades, including cost, capacity, quality, delivery, inventory, and new product, but developments in methodology and technology have spawned a new and evolving series of concerns for each level of the organization just mentioned. Each of the four organizational levels has a different perspective on and different responsibilities with respect to these concerns. Figure 2–10 illustrates that while each level of the manufacturing organization focuses on the same basic issues (cost, capacity, quality, etc.), each addresses those concerns differently.

The Organizational Design of the Manufacturing Enterprise

The structure and design of any organization should reflect and support its purpose. That is certainly the case in a manufacturing environment, where the fundamental purpose is to create or add value to goods or services and to deliver these to customers in a timely and profitable manner. In the past, this value was largely aggregated around products; today, customers are valuing such intangibles as quality, service, and timeliness. As manufacturers strive to meet customer competition and global needs, they often find that the structure of their organizations is not up to the challenge and that organizational design and manufacturing strategy must go hand in hand.

Historically, manufacturers have been oriented around a *centralized* structure that has its roots in the smokestack era of industry when highly segmented and specialized tasks, each of which was repeated again and again, added incremental value to products. As organizations undertook a wider range of activities, this model became less advantageous. The scope of the task of staying abreast of products, markets, and production issues expanded to the point that it could no longer be effectively managed by any one person or group of people because of the flexibility, responsiveness to business challenges, and timeliness of service that customers demanded.

Thus, *decentralized* organizations, where management authority was delegated and policy authority remained centralized, evolved and gained popularity. However, in time, these organizations also became complex and cumbersome. Moreover, as efforts to improve performance shifted management focus from cost to margin to value, the capital inefficiencies of a decentralized operation became increasingly less acceptable. As a result of these inefficiencies, many manufacturing enterprises have been left with a mix of organizational structures, some centralized and some decentralized, and perhaps this is for the best. No single organizational form will be optimal for all enterprises or for any one enterprise all of the time.

For the 1990s, an extremely centralized or decentralized philosophy is not likely to be effective. What is needed is a pragmatic approach to enterprise orientation and design:

- Reflecting the overall operations and culture of the organization.
- Supporting top management's perspectives and capabilities.
- Accommodating the strengths and weaknesses of the company's employees.
- Taking into account the time required to convert vision and strategy into action.
- Acknowledging the limitations of the enterprise and its infrastructures.

In short, the organizational design should be closely aligned with the organization's strategy and should also be closely and consistently tuned to the organization's people, process, and technology.

The Hybrid Organization

Clearly, the traditional centralized or decentralized structures are either inhibitive or unaffordable as a single organizational approach when confronted by the challenge of the virtual model. The virtual model will look for creative new organizational structures—and the *hybrid* organization is one of them. It allows for shifts in responsibility within the infrastructure and for varying changes in focus. Typically, the infrastructure of successful hybrid organizations is planned or coordinated centrally, though most other issues are decentralized. Simply put, the hybrid design apportions responsibility among those who best understand how to do the job, allowing for both specialization and a broader team approach. To address overall organizational issues, representatives from various segments of the business work together to amalgamate their areas of expertise and perspectives. Think of the manufacturing organization as a human being: suffering some kind of decline, it will often constrict the flow of "blood" to failing or less critical areas, in order to pull back and consolidate. Because the hybrid design is more flexible, drawing life from several different sources, it is more likely to survive.

Perhaps the greatest dividend a hybrid design offers is that it taps the capabilities of individuals, accommodating and leveraging leadership and excellence, whether the source is the boardroom or the factory floor or both. A hybrid structure offers new and powerful opportunities for organizations to be more cost competitive, quality competitive, and time competitive, providing that the people making and implementing decisions are familiar with the details, have good judgment, and make sound decisions.

The Concept of Virtual Teaming

Teaming is a critical success factor for the realization of high-performing virtual enterprises. And perhaps nowhere are the differences between the hybrid and other organizational structures more apparent than in the concept of teaming: the use of ad hoc, project-specific teams and the assignment of the best person for a particular project, regardless of the worker's location or title. Teaming is required to support the extremely flat structure of the virtual organization, and although it is complex in design and requires strong personal leadership, the benefits derived from empowering teams of capable individuals are worth the extra effort.

A critical part of the hybrid design, teaming contributes significantly toward improved organizational performance, meaning that often there are more decision makers in the hybrid design than in either the centralized or decentralized architecture. By the same token, it means that there are many more alert people scanning for opportunities and problems—and, therefore, more people accountable for decisions. Together, this becomes a powerful incentive for workers to become much more personally involved in and committed to improving the organization's performance.

STRATEGIC ALLIANCES

There is an emerging reliance on a new relationship among enterprises that some call *partnerships*. The term *strategic alliance* (SA) seems more accurate, implying a strong, evolving, dynamic relationship among the organizations. Strategic allies co-invest in each other's success, sharing people, technology, processes, and proprietary information to enhance their individual and collective performance. This concept is key to the creation of the virtual enterprise. The basic goal is to deliver to the customer, in as timely a fashion as possible, the lowest-cost, highest-value product that the entire value chain—not just a single company—can produce. Partners in a virtual enterprise dont focus solely on controlling internal costs and processes. Instead, within the context of cooperative effort, the virtual enterprise manages the total value chain leading to the end-customer through a fabric of alliances with suppliers, manufacturers, distributors and others.[3]

Strategic alliances are structured relationships between independent firms that involve more than a contract to supply or share in the development of goods and services. Examples are

- Joint ventures, with mutual stock ownership.
- Minority stock investments.
- Extended supplier or distributor relationships.
- Joint product development projects.
- Informal intercompany arrangements.
- Combinations of the above.

Strategic alliances may be defined more formally as "organizational arrangements and operating policies through which separate organizations

---

[3]L. Scott Flaig, "The 'Virtual Enterprise': Your New Model For Success," *Electronic Business*, March 30, 1992, p. 153.

share administrative authority, form social links, and accept joint ownership, and in which loose, more open-ended contractual arrangements replace highly specific, arm's length contracts."[4] In other words, they are separate organizations working together to achieve common objectives, including growth, increasing profits, limiting strategic risks, and improving competitive posture. Strategic alliances often are also aimed at improving operational performance; in manufacturing, this would include improving quality, responding more rapidly to customer needs, lowering costs, and being more efficient in the use of financial and other scarce company resources.

In addressing this topic, it is important to remind ourselves of the fundamentals of the purpose of a business. Henry Kaiser once said: "Find a need and fill it." Perhaps more elegantly, Peter Drucker's dictum was that the purpose of a business is "to create a customer," which raises questions: Who is the customer? How should the customer be served?[5]

A progressive corporation knows that the customer is whoever has needs that can served by the products and services of the company, wherever the customer may be. The answer to the second question is that the customer should be served in the best possible way from its own perspective: the most fully and completely, most timely, and most economical way.[6] *In summary, the business should be customer-focused and its strategies should go beyond the notion popularized in recent years of achieving a sustainable competitive advantage. The purpose of a business is not to defeat a competitor but to serve a customer.*

Two Corollaries

From this perspective, based on customer needs, two important corollaries follow. First, profit is a derivative, not a fundamental objective. It is a measure of how well the purpose of the business is being served, assuming a reasonably healthy level of competition in the industry. Second, if a business services its customers very well, it will be rewarded not only with high current profits, but also with a high market share as more

---

[4]Joseph L. Badaracco, *The Knowledge Link* (Boston, Mass.: Harvard Business School Press, 1991), p. 4.

[5]Peter F. Drucker, *The Practice of Management* (New York: Harper & Brothers, 1954), p. 37.

[6]See, for example, Michael E. Porter, *Competitive Advantage* (New York: Macmillan, 1985).

customers are attracted. And as countless studies have shown, a high market share correlates very well with high future profitability. Thus, by this most important measure, if the business meets its aim of serving the customer, the company will be both currently and strategically successful, and it will be positioned to enrich its shareholders. It is within the context of servicing customers that supplying products or services becomes paramount and supersedes the paradigm of building products (vertical integration). Therefore, strategic alliances have become an attractive strategy in achieving this competitive advantage.

Many indicators suggest that the use of strategic alliances is accelerating and that they will be an increasingly important feature of the corporate landscape as the 1990s unfold. Strategic alliances are different from many of the subjects covered in this book in at least three respects: they are relatively new, especially to U.S. managers; they are not well understood as yet, in that surprisingly little research has been done on the issues they tend to generate; and they are controversial among some senior managers, in part because their track record has been mixed. Some strategic alliances have succeeded, but too many have not. Nevertheless, their use is increasing because they meet important corporate needs. In doing so, however, they also pose unique challenges for management.

Features of Strategic Alliances

In form, strategic alliances may have some or all of the following features: A merged ownership structure (via stock or partnership interests), a term of indefinite duration, and a dissolution arrangement. They may be formed for different reasons, as indicated in Table 2–2. Strategic alliances usually involve leveraging one or more business opportunities—product, market, technology, or process—or otherwise securing one or more significant strategic or operational competitive advantages for its parents. Sometimes they are entered into as a method of shoring up a competitive weakness. A manufacturing strategic alliance involves the manufacturing function as a dominant or important dimension of the alliance.

When they are undertaken, strategic alliances "blur the boundaries of firms," inherently challenging many of the fundamental assumptions that underlie traditional management approaches, including what a firm is, why it exists, and whom it serves.[7]

---

[7]Ibid. 4.

TABLE 2-2
Examples of U.S. Strategic Alliances

Strategic Type	Strategic Purpose	SA Partners	Products
Horizontal	Market access	Owens/Corning Fiberglass	Insulation
		Hercules/Henkel	Water-soluble polymers
	Technology development	Apple/IBM	Software
	Commercialization group	US West/Carnegie	Expert systems
		Exxon Chemical/JSR	Chemical processes
	Production	GM/Toyota (NUMMI)	Autos
		IBM/Matsushita	PCs
Vertical	Supplier distribution and franchising	Boeing/Weber	Seats, galleys
		Mercury/Yamaha	Marine engines
	Logistics	Sears/many manufacturers	Consumer products
Transitional	Market access	Inland Steel/Nippon	Steel
		Deere/Hitachi	Excavators, loaders

Why have strategic alliances become more common? Are they a fad? We don't believe so, because they have been long in coming and because there is abundant evidence that their driving forces seem to be strengthening. During the past 20 years the number of domestic U.S. joint ventures increased rapidly. They are particularly prevalent, for example, among manufacturers of electrical and electronic equipment, computers, and aerospace products.

The use of strategic alliances seems to be accelerating. During a recent 18-month period, some 1,800 strategic alliances have been formed in the United States alone. Of these, at least 20 percent have cited improved manufacturing effectiveness as a prime objective or feature of the strategic alliance. [8] In Europe, the number of cooperative agreements increased dramatically during the 1980s. Among the Japanese, strategic alliances have been a factor since before World War II and have increased in importance to the point where they are the norm for doing business. A survey conducted by Ernst & Young in 1990 among 750 CEOs in the electronics industry revealed that most believed that strategic alliances would become increasingly important in their corporate strategies in the 1990s, and that manufacturing alliances were expected to grow by more than one-third. [9] The 1992 survey further revealed that, on the average, electronics companies already held 20 strategic alliances.[10]

Drivers of Strategic Alliances

A number of changes or trends in the business environment have acted as drivers for strategic alliances. The four most important ones are the traditional competitive factors of cost, quality, and delivery, amplified by the time dimension, as well as the emerging drivers of globalization, technology transfer, and the increased difficulty of making acquisitions.

Competition
Every company is avidly pursuing competitive advantages in order to survive, if not prosper. Product life cycles have shortened, so today's cash

---

[8]Lionel Fray Associates research, consisting of an analysis of a database of all U.S. publicly announced SAs formed since January 1990.

[9]Ernst & Young, *Electronics '91: Framework for the Future* (San Francisco, Calif.: Ernst & Young), pp. 27–28.

[10]Ernst & Young, *Electronics '92: Strategic Alliance Outlook* (Cleveland, Ohio: Ernst & Young), p. 8.

cow turns into tomorrow's failure much faster. The intensity of competition is being felt in virtually all industries, including many in which competition was previously much more restrained, or regulated, such as the airlines or the telephone business in the United States. The result has been much stronger pressure on management to improve organizational and financial performance, areas where strategic alliances have shown themselves to be a natural extension.

Globalization

Markets are globalizing as they become more common in their characteristics and are more accessible to transnational suppliers. Consumer markets around the world are exhibiting more common characteristics, and although important differences remain, the result has been that consumer tastes, styles, and preferences for product features are converging, for example, in automobiles, diapers, and packaged foods.

Industrial markets have also become more similar because of the growing international standardization of products and supplies and the inexorable force of competition that puts increased pressure on the procurement function to get the best products and services available at the lowest cost, no matter where they are obtained. Also contributing to these basic changes has been the growing base of market information, which continues to become more accessible and useful through developments in information technology; and the fact that national barriers have diminished in importance with the reduction in trade barriers in Europe and in North America.

Technology

Both the pace and the rate of technology dissemination have accelerated. This change has been a major cause of the shortening of the life cycles of products and technologically based services. Information technology has a particularly strong effect. As amply described by many sources, information technology has literally transformed the operations of many companies and contributed directly to globalization by creating a single market where separate markets used to exist.[11] And, perhaps most importantly for strategic alliances, information technology has made it possible for individuals and groups to communicate, and thus work

---

[11] See, for example, Thomas H. Davenport and James E. Short, "The New Industrial Engineering: Information Technology and Business Process Redesign," *Sloan Management Review*, Summer 1990, pp. 11–27.

together effectively, even when they are widely separated geographically or functionally.

Acquisitions

In the late 1980s, companies sought acquisitions as a means of diversification or to shore up a weakness. But acquiring a company has become more difficult, and in certain parts of the world, acquisitions—especially contested ones—are discouraged. Strategic alliances often become the more feasible alternative, as financing is harder to obtain and prices remain high. Perhaps more fundamentally, many recent corporate experiences with acquisitions have demonstrated that while it is possible to buy 100 percent of the equity, it is impossible to buy 100 percent of the mind, spirit, and devotion of its people: acquisitions have often led to mass exodus of key entrepreneurial professionals.

Rationales for Strategic Alliances

There are two important rationales for the use of strategic alliances. We will label one *strategy* and the second *knowledge*, with each providing a different and useful perspective.

Strategy

This rationale views strategic alliances as the option that best meets a company's particular set of strategic requirements—for example, the need to diversify into less mature businesses, globalize one or more business operations or enter foreign markets, develop new technology, or meet major competitive threats by providing a higher quality product with better performance at lower cost from a different manufacturing base.

For example, if being the best at servicing the global customer is the aim, it is unlikely that the company will find the necessary resources within the boundaries of only one corporation. And, while corporations can be acquired, it may be difficult or too costly to do so, or may not have the desired effect, or may take longer than the strategic window of opportunity will remain open. Thus, strategic alliances become a strong consideration.

Strategic alliances in manufacturing have been used to achieve better production efficiencies through greater scale, better process technology, and less costly labor, while sharing capital and other risks related to higher fixed costs. The high-tech and pharmaceutical industries have been particularly active in this regard, with strategic alliances formed not only to achieve more efficient production economies, but also to offer worldwide customer service, manage fast-moving new technologies, sell into unfamiliar markets, and cut skyrocketing R&D costs. Additionally, the steel, footwear, and automobile industries have found highly attractive labor rates in the Far East and Central and South America through the formation of strategic alliances. On the downside, however, is the inevitable pressure to seek new, low-price (not necessarily low-cost) countries as the standard and cost of living rapidly accelerates in the initial strategic alliance countries (i.e., Korea and Japan). In summary, when they are a viable option, strategic alliances can provide the fastest, most profitable, and least risky way to meet the fundamental aims of the business, albeit only temporarily in some cases.

Knowledge

The second rationale for strategic alliances is based on the emerging importance of business knowledge.[12] In the context of business and corporate success, as we use it in this chapter, knowledge is the combination of know-how, creativity, and information that is critical to the operation and success of a business. Knowledge has become the most important factor accounting for business success. As a consequence, competition has become knowledge-driven.

Business knowledge is either migratory or embedded, although neither occurs in pure form. Migratory knowledge can move relatively easily from company to company—for example, product designs (which can be copied), machines (which can be purchased), and even individual minds (which can be hired). Although the flow of such knowledge can be slowed, it is prone to "leakage." Embedded knowledge—craftsmanship, teams of people with complementary expertise and highly developed ways of working with each other, and geographically or culturally based know-how—is less subject to leakage and can be used to develop and sustain competitive advantage. In manufacturing, for example, it may be the individual and collective skills in a plant that enjoy high productivity and produce high-quality products.

Many organizations realize that the means by which they have traditionally developed business knowledge (e.g., in-house R&D) are now insufficient and that successful firms have developed a different form of relationship with outsiders called *knowledge links*. (The strategic alliance

---

[12]Badaracco, *The Knowledge Link*, pp. 9–13.

is one such link.) Such firms are characterized by their ability to learn, an openness to ideas from outside, a dense web of relationships that extend throughout and beyond the firm, and a social network that absorbs, creates, stores, transforms, buys, sells, and communicates knowledge. They employ strategic alliances liberally because, properly used, such links can be a uniquely powerful way of accelerating and improving the development and utilization of embedded knowledge.

The best examples of firms operating in this fashion today are Toyota, Hitachi, and Nissan, members of *keiretsu*, groups of companies in Japan that have been formed as a galaxy of companies surrounding one major manufacturer. These groups, which have strong financial, organizational, and social connections with each other, pass and develop a great deal of business knowledge among them. European examples include Airbus Industries, Olivetti, and the web of parts suppliers in the automobile industry. In the United States, most such associations are still in the early stages of development. Corning and IBM, however, have formed dozens of strategic alliances and they seem to work well. IBM has established more than 30 (see Figure 2–11).

FIGURE 2–11
Big Blue's Long List of Link-ups (Since April 1988)

- Metaphor
- PCO (optoelectronics)
- Polygen (pharmaceutical/chemical software)
- Interactive Images (graphics technology)
- MSA (software)
- Computer Task Group (computer services)
- Image Business Systems (imaging software)
- I/NET (research and development)
- AMS (software systems integration)
- Policy Management Systems (insurance software)
- Bachman Info. Systems (software engineering)
- ROLM (distributor)

- KnowledgeWare (software engineering)
- Index Technology (software engineering)
- Spectrum Healthcare Solutions (software services)
- Geographic Systems (geographic information systems)
- CADAM (computer aided design and manufacturing)
- Early, Cloud & Co. (teleservicing software, services)
- Rational (software engineering)
- Valisys (computer integrated manufacturing)
- WCSS (retail software)
- ARDIS (radio service)

- Seer Tech. (investment management systems)
- Valid Logic Systems (design automation software)
- InterBold (self-serve banking systems)
- Hogan Systems (banking software, services)
- Advanced Network and Services (networking)
- Financial Technologies International L.P. (trust, investment software)
- Check Solutions (software)
- Intera Tydac Technologies (geographic data systems)
- Meritus Consulting Services (consulting)
- Lexmark International (information products)

Risks and Results of Strategic Alliances

Notwithstanding the power of the logic for the use of strategic alliances, they are not the answer to all corporate dilemmas because they do have risks:

- The objectives of founding partners may be less homogeneous than originally thought.
- Valuable technology or business know-how can leak out of, as well as migrate into, the corporation.
- There may be unexpected diversions of management energies because strategic alliances sometimes generate organizational tensions between those in and out of the strategic alliance.
- Litigation may occur.
- Partners can become future competitors made stronger by the experience of the strategic alliance.

Most importantly, perhaps, managing strategic alliances effectively is different from managing a traditional organization, and many executives have little or no experience with them.

Still, many companies find that manufacturing strategic alliances have led to substantial benefits. Examples of strategic alliances and their accomplishments are listed in Table 2–3. As indicated previously, the strong results achieved by these companies are not necessarily typical. Although many companies have compiled good empirical findings about the use of strategic alliances, the fundamental operations of strategic alliances and the means by which they may best be implemented are not yet widely taught in graduate business schools.

Making Strategic Alliances Perform Effectively

The two major rationales for strategic alliances—strategy and knowledge—pose fundamental quandaries for their management. The potential power of the knowledge rationale is usually limited by the fact that the objectives of the parents of a strategic alliance will seldom completely coincide.

A central challenge to the leaders of strategic alliances is to manage the process of knowledge development as a primary driver to the success of their ventures, focusing especially on embedded knowledge, which is more likely to become the basis for sustainable competitive advantages. The major implication of the knowledge rationale lies in the recognition that today's product battle may be only an episode in a longer war—the victor being the one with the ability to invent, make, and sell not just one product, but a continuing stream of products. This is what knowledge-based competition is about.

To be counted a victor, a company will need to continually develop its base of knowledge and supplement its development efforts with a well-chosen web of strategic alliances. This focus poses a particular

---

TABLE 2–3
Strategic Alliances of Large U.S. Corporations

General Electric	• In 1986, started or expanded 12 strategic alliances • Jack Welch (CEO): "strategic alliances...reduce the investment in time it takes to bring good ideas to customers." • *Results:* —Market value increased from $12 billion in 1980 to $65 billion in 1991 —Rose from 11th to 2nd rank among U.S. corporations
Wal-Mart	• Had reputation for toughness with manufacturing suppliers • Resulted in problems with quality, flexibility, and delivery • Converted to strategic alliance relationships with selected manufacturers; among other things, shared information systems with suppliers • *Results:* —Much better reported relationships —Cycle times for established products: 9 days —Cycle times for new products: 4-week target —Quality sharply improved —Wal-Mart has become largest U.S. retailer, very profitable
Procter & Gamble	• Has launched major strategic alliance program —Using multifunction experts —Using ordering and invoicing information technology system • *Objectives:* —Cut inventories —Smooth production schedules —Identify service and quality problems quickly • *Results:* —Expected savings of $1 billion for P&G —Expected savings of $1 billion plus for P&G customers

challenge to manufacturing strategic alliances, which are often established to provide lower-cost products and accelerate market expansion
and are often initially based on migratory knowledge. This inherently
poses risks to the partners because the older factories of the parent tend
to become less competitive, and they find it difficult to change well-
established, though less-efficient, patterns of operations. Often, they are
unable to modify established pay scales and structures because of union-
ization and the expectations of their labor force.

As an organization, a strategic alliance has a unique structure and
life cycle. After the critical stages of its birth and initial establishment,
it grows and achieves maturity. Though there are exceptions, the strategic alliance may be terminated when it no longer serves the purposes of
its founders. Although such cycles are found in all business organizations, they are more likely to occur in strategic alliances. This tenuous
longevity of a strategic alliance, together with the complexity of its role
in accomplishing the purposes of its founders, tends to generate some
unusual operational management challenges. The relationships between
senior managers of the partners are of critical importance; the more partners, the more complex the relationships become.

Major Syndromes and Typical Problems

As a result of their unique structures and the circumstances attending their
formation, strategic alliances exhibit a characteristic pattern of syndromes
or problems.

Senior Management Involvement.   One pattern often seen in large
organizations with strategic alliances is that CEOs and business unit leaders are deeply involved at the formation of the strategic alliance, but they
tend to lose visibility once it is started. Consequently, the focus of the
strategic alliance sometimes will drift away from the founders' inten-
tions. If the strategic alliance experiences a crisis, senior management
will often become involved again, but by then some options for action
may have been lost.

Expectations.   Another pattern develops when the purpose of the
strategic alliance was viewed as a solution to a narrowly defined strategic
requirement such as entry into a foreign market or plugging a weakness
in the production operation. Strategic alliances offer more than just rapid

solutions to such near-term performance problems and, consequently, tend to develop more slowly in early stages than independent ventures, needing time to achieve their potential.

Culture. A third pattern can be traced to significant mismatches between the corporate cultures of the two groups of managers and employees from the founding companies. For example, in transnational strategic alliances the expected differences between any corporate cultures are compounded by differences in national culture, language, and geography. Sometimes, when the parents are a large company and a small company, they have different expectations for the comprehensiveness and pace of decision making. Although this does not mean that parents with dissimilar cultures or of different sizes cannot form successful strategic alliances, it does provide another challege for management.

These and other typical problems experienced with strategic alliances can often be traced to the following:

- Inadequate strategic planning by one or more of the strategic alliance parents as to the direction and thrust of their core businesses and the expected complementary strategic role of the strategic alliance.
- Insufficient planning for the formation of the strategic alliance.
- Poor partner selection.
- Insufficient understanding of challenges the strategic alliance will face and an appropriate corresponding set of expectations.
- Insufficient knowledge and experience in operating and managing strategic alliances.

Candidates for Strategic Alliances

Finding candidates for alliance partnerships is not easy or simple. Criteria for selection will include synergistic enterprise strategies, both current and future; compatibility of corporate culture; efficient inter- and intra-organization communications; and world-class manufacturing performance. Effective enterprise partnering involves sharing strategic planning, R&D, marketing, sales, and support data. "In selecting alliance members for a world-class value chain, the architects of the virtual enterprise must find advocates of contemporary methodologies, technologies, and processes."[13]

World-class competitive enterprises cannot afford even one non-competitive partner. The effective enterprise alliance will be a powerful value chain of connected people, systems, and organizations that are motivated and directed by the voices of its end consumers. Leadership is key, but it is not enough; each and every employee must do his or her best in order for the alliance to achieve world-class performance.

Before Formation of Strategic Alliances

In general, strategic alliances seem to fare better when they build on strengths, rather than shore up strategic weaknesses like high-cost production operations. Before performing a strategic alliance, a company should

- Consider all the options for meeting its strategic needs, including internal development and acquisition as well as one or more strategic alliances. Particular attention should be given to the preference of the strategic alliance over an acquisition, which has more subtle issues in addition to the general problems of acquisitions cited previously. Most successful acquirers tend to be those that spot bargains, are good negotiators, and realize near-term improvements in operations, an approach that will not work with a strategic alliance and will, in fact, undermine its chances for success. As will be outlined below, the approach to properly structuring a strategic alliance begins with a different set of premises.

- Clearly set forth the objectives to be served for itself as distinct from those of the strategic alliance. Occasionally the greatest value of the strategic alliance will be in the form of contributions to the company's core business, which will not show up in the strategic alliance's financial statements. If that is likely, the company should make sure that this value is identified and considered.

---

[13]L. Scott Flaig, "The 'Virtual Enterprise': Your New Model For Success," *Electronic Business*, March 30, 1992, p. 155.

- Make sure that the business scope potentially being given up to the strategic alliance is not of primary interest to itself. A company should not use its truly core capabilities to form a strategic alliance.

The initial approach to a prospective partner and the onset of negotiations is a critical period because it has a major effect on the later relationship and culture and on the strategic alliances chances of success.

Effective Management of Strategic Alliances

When these partnerships are crafted into a well-conceived and well-managed team, they become "a set of independent companies that work closely together to manage the flow of goods and services along the entire value-added chain."[14] There are two basic approaches to managing these alliances:

- *Create an independent organizational element with responsibility for managing all alliances.* This entity must have intimate familiarity with the strategic goals and controls of the enterprise. Thus it will be in an excellent position to create and manage relationships with other organizations. Central authority makes this style of management lean and responsive to shifts in strategy.
- *Decentralize the management of partnerships, with operating directors responsible for those alliances affecting their operations.* Here, purchasing agents establish alliances with suppliers; logistics directors manage partnerships with transportation services; and engineering directors are responsible for product development alliances. Decentralized alliance management is more responsive to the changing needs of the factory, suppliers, and customers.

A third approach can be crafted from these two, whereby a central authority provides the strategic directives and the procedural and legal support for the alliances while the functional directors identify and se-

---

[14]Russell Johnston and Paul Lawrence, "Beyond Vertical Integration—The Rise of Value-Adding Partnership," *Harvard Business Review*, July/August 1988, p. 94.

lect partners and manage those partnerships for the life of the alliance in accordance with the enterprise's overall strategies.

Effective management across the value-adding supply chain is everyone's job, from the TEO to the stock clerk, across all the companies within the value chain. Outbound logistics at vendor organizations work with customers' inbound logistics, and engineers from one company work with engineers from other companies—directly, not through an "interpreter" in purchasing. Individuals and departments should have direct and effective channels of communication, not only with their counterparts but also with any others who can help improve the alliance's goods, services, or operations.

It is important to have clear criteria for the acceptable performance of the strategic alliance (from the company's point of view at a minimum), and to be prepared to terminate the alliance if it fails to meet them after an adequate period. When evaluating performance, a company should make explicit operational and strategic evaluations at selected times (a function of the life cycle of the strategic alliance, the nature of the business, and the nature of strategic developments). The frequency of these evaluations can range from quarterly to every several years. Termination may take the form of separation, liquidation, or a buy-out by one of the parties. The mechanics for accomplishing the termination should have been dealt with in the formation agreement. It is also helpful to have the outline of a termination plan to ensure that major issues have not been ignored.

Profound Changes

Strategic alliances have become important in recent years throughout the world and are likely to become more so in the future, particularly with the advent of the virtual model. By responding to fundamental changes in the business environment and in the way corporations are competing, they can help companies achieve strategic successes, although they will also create profound challenges.

Companies whose goals are to improve product quality and lower manufacturing costs need to break down the elements of the company's manufacturing operations and retain only those that meet world-class standards of quality and efficiency. They must use strategic alliances as a means to complete the rest of the product or service offering. The remaining task is to manage the strategic alliance so that it develops a strong, embedded knowledge base that serves its own needs and those of its parents.

SUPPLIER PARTNERSHIPS

One increasingly common form of strategic alliance is the supplier partnership. There is a growing trend among U.S. manufacturers to dramatically redefine the nature of their relationship with suppliers, from an adversarial relationship based almost entirely on price to a long-term partnership founded on cooperation, trust, and total-cost-based pricing. This is not a new concept among worldwide manufacturers, however. The Japanese have long relied on a select group of suppliers in order to ensure total quality across the entire value chain. And, in fact, much of the impetus for this change among U.S. manufacturers is a direct result of increasing worldwide competition, particularly from the Japanese.

Historically, U.S. manufacturers have relied on multiple competing sources in order to ensure low cost and uninterrupted supply. However, in the past decade, U.S. corporations have come to understand, mostly from their Japanese competitors, that the cheapest parts and materials are not necessarily the least costly in the long run—in fact, they are often the most expensive. In order to achieve the highest quality, and thereby reduce total cost, everyone in the integrated supply chain must work together as partners. This supply chain, which we now refer to as the virtual enterprise because of its electronic connectivity and partnering philosophy, has emerged as the competitive model for the future.

By focusing on price, manufacturers in the past provided little incentive for suppliers to improve quality, which resulted in higher costs for every link in the supply chain. Today, supplier partnerships have become an integral part of corporate quality programs, and customers and suppliers alike have reaped tremendous benefits from this partnering. Yet cost and quality are not the only benefits to be gained from these partnerships. Other improvements include greater flexibility, reduced cycle time, and gains in innovation as a result of technical collaboration and information sharing.

It is important to differentiate among the three relationships that have emerged out of the virtual model. Each has its own unique characteristics and expectations. When moving beyond a traditional vendor relationship into a partnership or strategic alliance, mutual expectations need to be made explicit.

Level 1 Vendors	Level 2 Partners	Level 3 Strategic Alliances
Commodities— class "C" parts	Commodities—class A/B parts	Custom parts
Price driven	Total cost, quality, delivery driven	Value driven
Inventoried	Forecast/schedule information	Flexibility
Electronic shopping	Electronic/face-to-face	Proprietary information sharing
Purchase orders	Release to contracts	Long term
Many vendors	Primary sourcing	Single/sole sourcing
Part certification	Process certification	Vendor certification
Outsourcing (temps)	Outsourcing practices (e.g., billing, warehouse, transaction processing)	Outsourcing (Application development)

Establishing true partnerships between suppliers and customers is not an easy task. It requires major cultural transformations to change the way the procurement game has always been played and to establish the foundation of trust upon which these partnerships must be built. A foundation of trust allows the customer and supplier to share information about overall strategy, long-term goals and product design. This communication is critical to building and maintaining these relationships across an integrated supply chain. One of the best examples of a corporation that succeeded in this endeavor is Xerox. In fact, it has often been said that Xerox is the "Western benchmark" for supply chain management and, in particular, supplier partnerships.

XEROX CORPORATION: A "WESTERN BENCHMARK" FOR SUPPLIER PARTNERSHIPS

Xerox, known as The Document Company, is a multinational corporation that serves the document processing and financial services markets. Document processing is its primary business, accounting for 76 percent of its $18 billion revenue (1990 sales revenue). Revenue in document processing grew from 1989 to 1990, which resulted in a 23 percent increase in income during that same period. "Their document processing activities encompass developing, manufacturing, marketing, servicing, and financing a complete range of document processing products designed to make offices more productive."[15] Its product line in document processing includes copy and facsimile machines, printers, scanners, networks, computer software, and other related products. It has over 110,000 employees and conducts business in over 130 countries around the world. Central to the current success of Xerox's document processing group is its materials management function. Yet things were not always this way. What follows is the story of how materials management turned itself around by focusing on a key component of its business—its suppliers.

Xerox's share of the worldwide copier market had shrunk by half, from 82 percent in 1976 to 41 percent in 1982. And it was not until 1981, after visiting Fuji Xerox and performing some preliminary competitive benchmarking in Japan, that David Kearns, then CEO of Xerox, realized just how good Xerox's competitors really were. "We were horrified to find that the Japanese were selling their small machines for what it cost to make ours," Kearns said. "Our costs were not only way out in left field, they weren't even in the ballpark. Let me tell you that was scary, and it woke us up in a hurry."[16] Xerox's manufacturing costs were, in fact, 30 to 50 percent higher than its Japanese competitors and it took Xerox nearly twice as long to develop new products. Xerox, like many other U.S. corporations during this time, had paid little attention to its competitors across the ocean, believing that they provided little, if any, threat. The harsh reality, however, was that the Japanese had dramatically improved their manufacturing capabilities by focusing on such concepts as total quality and statistical process control (SPC), and in many ways had left their American competitors in their wake. Thus, in 1981 Kearns called a high-level meeting with 24 of his top people and, in the first of two week-long sessions, asked each individual what it was that Xerox had to do to regain what it had lost and turn itself around—no holds barred.

---

[15]Xerox 1990 Annual Report, inside cover.

[16]Gary Jacobson and John Hillkirk, *Xerox: American Samurai* (New York: Macmillan, 1986), p. 6.

Since those critical meetings in 1981, Xerox has implemented count-less changes to regain its competitive position in the marketplace. Many of these changes occurred within materials management and have been instrumental in changing its organization, mission, and vision for the future. However, Xerox has also instituted major worldwide programs—perhaps the most published and successful of which has been its "Leadership Through Quality" program. An integral part of this program has been, and is today, its commitment to supplier partnerships. The evolution of materials management at Xerox spans the last decade, for it is within this time frame that Xerox has successfully changed the way it does business with its suppliers. As a result, Xerox has aligned itself with world-class suppliers along a worldwide integrated supply chain and has emerged as one of the first U.S. corporations to successfully regain lost market share from the Japanese.

Historical Perspective: Materials Management

In 1980 Xerox played the procurement game much like every other company; the name of the game was relentless competitive bidding. Their overall purchasing philosophy was based on many sources, multiple quotes, and inventory hedges. Quality consisted of receiving inspection at every plant, lots acceptance (AQL), and plenty of safety stock. During the early 1980s, Xerox took some initiatives to combat those preliminary benchmarking results, and although the results were dramatic, Xerox had only begun to build the foundation of supplier partnerships. It was not until the latter part of the 1980s, when Xerox formed multifunctional commodity teams, reduced its supplier base by over 90 percent, and instituted total quality that Xerox became truly committed to building a partnership with a select group of suppliers. Today, according to Ray Stark, V.P. of Materials Management, "Results through quality—that's our theme."

Early Initiatives

The first major initiative Xerox undertook as a result of those preliminary benchmarking studies was to focus on zero defects, and thereby reduce total cost. It concluded that too much time and energy was being wasted inspecting parts and materials from suppliers. Moreover, it couldn't inspect out defects, particularly if it wanted to offer competitive prices for its products. Its goal was for suppliers to ship directly to manufacturing sites and distribution centers. The removal of inspection and material handling became its vision to world-class cost competitiveness. To accomplish this, it needed to have quality built into the components rather than inspected out, so it began to focus on improving process. Its challenge for the 1980s became making its supplier processes capable of delivering quality at the source. The enabler of this vision was part certification via statistical process control.

After a period of introduction and training in 1981–1982, the number of certified parts increased dramatically—from zero in 1981 to nearly 3,000 in 1983. "In the beginning," according to Ray Stark, "there were three day forums." Today there are still forums and conferences, but training of suppliers is most often done on-site at supplier's locations. By 1990 the number of certified parts reached nearly 18,000. Moreover, the percentage of certified parts flowing directly to the production line went from 30 percent in 1981 to 80 percent by 1983. Today, 95 percent of all production material is consistently shipped directly to manufacturing assembly lines. The remaining 5 percent includes items for which there are unstable processes that make process control difficult to achieve. For these items, known problem parts are identified during assembly. The reduction in defects per parts per million was even more staggering— from 4,220 in 1982 to 1,342 in 1983. Today the figure is down to about 240, with a benchmark for the future of 125.

Xerox was not the only one to reap the benefits from training suppliers in SPC. Suppliers substantially reduced scrap, inspection, and rework costs. According to Ray Stark, "There was a lot of anxiety. A lot of suppliers really fought the idea in the beginning. But many of those suppliers became the greatest missionaries of the program after they experienced some of the benefits." During this time, Xerox also began a practice known as early supplier involvement (ESI) aimed at involving suppliers more in product design. This practice was an important step in fostering open communication and trust. Yet Xerox knew that these initiatives were not enough. It was merely the first step in building the foundation for a partnership and aligning itself with world-class suppliers across a worldwide integrated value chain.

The Formation of Commodity Teams and the Reduction of Its Supplier Base

Another strategic objective fueled by benchmarking Xerox's Japanese competitors was to dramatically reduce its supplier base from 5,000 to about 500. In order to achieve this objective, Xerox reorganized its materials management function around multidisciplinary, multinational commodity teams. The commodity teams consisted of engineers, quality assurance personnel, cost experts, and buyers. Today there are 11 commodity teams:

- Clutches/motors.
- Elastomers.
- Metals (machining and sheet metal).
- Optics.
- Plastics.
- Sensors and subassemblies.
- Printed wiring board assembly (PWBA).
- OEM/UIM.
- Power systems/interconnect.
- Packaging.
- Logistics.

The initiatives were mostly organizational, designed to establish a structure conducive to building partnerships. In the words of Dick Holcomb, the Electronics Commodity Manager, "You run your commodity team like a business." It was virtually impossible to build the type of relationship Xerox hoped to have with its suppliers if they numbered over 5,000. "When capacity permits, manufacturers are better off with single source suppliers. A carefully selected and managed supplier offers the greatest guarantee of consistently high quality, namely, commitment to the product. Suppliers who feel part of the family permit manufacturers to subject them to rigorous inspection, certification, and education."[17] Therefore, the primary mission of the commodity teams became the reduction of Xerox's supplier base through a rigid supplier selection process. They accomplished this task and originally pared the supplier base to 325. Today it is around 400 and is fondly referred to as the "400 club."

The priorities of the commodity teams were, and are still today, to focus on supplier-base upgrade and development and on the delivery

---

[17]David N. Burt, "Managing Suppliers Up To Speed," *Harvard Business Review*, July/August 1989, p. 128.

of supplier capabilities to the business units and product development teams. Their mission is defined as follows:

- To manage the commodity teams as a worldwide business and to provide corporate leadership and direction in the areas of supplier-base management and development, technology/engineering, materials, and tools.

- To focus on meeting customer requirements in terms of quality, cost, delivery, and service to the product development teams and the plants worldwide.

- To provide parts, tools, and materials at world benchmark quality, lead time, and cost, with the benchmark suppliers emphasizing continuous, ongoing improvement.

The formation of multidisciplinary commodity teams has been key to the development of supplier partnerships. The teams provided suppliers with key contacts at Xerox, whose responsibilities were to develop the supplier, provide accessibility to Xerox engineers and other key personnel, and share information about the overall strategy and future directions of Xerox (see Figure 2–12).

The Role of the Buyer

Also of significant importance to the development of supplier partnerships was the elimination of competitive bidding. In order to build a partnership based on trust and cooperation, it was essential to eliminate this practice and focus on total cost. This goal required a major cultural transformation for both Xerox and its suppliers. Perhaps the most affected by this transformation were the buyers, who were forced to completely change the way they had conducted business for years. The "line 'em up, beat 'em up and get the lowest possible price" mentality was no longer accepted. Today Xerox engineers work directly with suppliers to establish a target cost and work together to achieve this cost. Figure 2–13 illustrates the change in both the buyer's role and also in the way in which Xerox conducted business with suppliers.

This transformation becomes even more dramatic upon visiting Building 205 in Webster, New York, the heart of Xerox's materials management. You are at once struck by the absence of people—particularly if you had ever been there prior to 1986. There are few, if any, people

FIGURE 2–12
Commodity Teams at Xerox

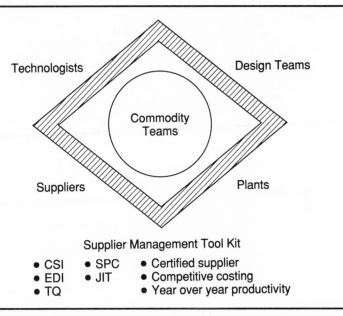

Technologists

Design Teams

Commodity
Teams

Suppliers

Plants

Supplier Management Tool Kit

- CSI
- EDI
- TQ

- SPC
- JIT

- Certified supplier
- Competitive costing
- Year over year productivity

Source: Reprinted with permission of Xerox Corporation.

in the lobby; and there are only a handful of Xerox employees at any given time in the building itself. The reasons for this embody a new era in materials management at Xerox—an era in which the customer is so committed to building a partnership that they spend the majority of their time at the supplier's location—teaching, learning, sharing information, and arriving at common goals and strategies.

Total Quality Strategy

In 1986, following the formation of commodity teams and reduction of its supplier base, Xerox began to implement a critical initiative—total quality. The goal of this initiative was to enable suppliers to meet Xerox expectations for world-class parts quality. It was designed to give suppliers the benefits of Xerox's total quality process—Leadership Through Quality. It accomplished this by helping supplier management internalize the principles of total quality and implement appropriate cultural

FIGURE 2–13
Strategic Alliances: Xerox Buyer's Role

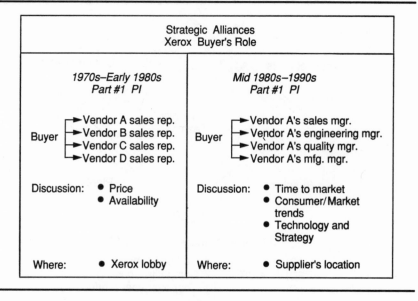

change. From 1987 to 1990, Xerox engaged 104 suppliers worldwide in a systematic total quality installation process. Some of the key elements of a total quality culture include the following:

- *Management behaviors*: Leadership and discipline; quality is the basic business principle.
- *Quality principles*: Vision, policies, and principles establishing a quality culture for the company.
- *Competitive benchmarking*: Targeting to be the "best of the best" for all areas of the business.
- *Cost of quality measurement*: Measuring the quality cost opportunities and reduction of quality costs through prevention.
- *Customer relationships*: Systematic process for the identification and meeting of all customer requirements.
- *Problem solving/employee involvement*: Systematic process for solving problems through teamwork and employee involvement.
- *Quality technologies*: Statistical tools, manufacturing technologies, and quality management techniques used to measure quality, minimize variation, and achieve continuous improvement.

Supplier Certification and Continuous Supplier Involvement

By 1988, Xerox had achieved many of its total quality goals, including world-class systems and processes, 100 percent conforming material, and adoption of a total quality philosophy by its suppliers. It was during this time that Xerox began to move beyond "certified parts" to the concept of "certified suppliers," who were given priority for new work. This was a crucial step in forming supplier partnerships, and in fact, as a result of this initiative and continuous supplier involvement (CSI), Xerox established a true partnership with its suppliers for the first time. The Certified Supplier Program went beyond the notion of an "approved supplier." It demanded new independence, new confidence, and new accountability. Continuous supplier involvement demanded open communication, honesty, and the inclusion of suppliers in virtually all phases of product development, from the preconcept phase through development.

A Focus on Building Partnerships

Xerox also understood that it could not simply establish guidelines and standards that suppliers had to meet in order to do business with it without establishing the same for itself. This is the essence of a partnership—a two-way relationship. So Xerox established guidelines for itself and its suppliers in the form of definitions of both the model supplier and customer. Xerox developed the profile of the model customer based on supplier input. These characteristics are subdivided into management attitude, quality, cost, delivery, and service. Some of these characteristics include the following:

- **Management attitude:**
  - To demonstrate honesty and avoid false promises.
  - To communicate openly regarding organizational responsibilities, strategies, business constraints, and expectations.
  - To be responsive to supplier requests.
  - To make every effort to understand suppliers' cultures and problems.
  - To be a significant customer.
  - To reward performance with business growth.
  - To be willing to change.
- **Quality:**
  - To share quality responsibility with supplier.
  - To develop universal quality metrics.

- **Cost:**
  - To establish realistic cost targets.
  - To provide benchmarking assistance.
  - To share costs of change.
- **Delivery:**
  - To strive for minimal schedule changes.
  - To develop realistic schedules and priorities.
- **Service:**
  - To recognize that continuous supplier involvement (CSI) is a two-way street.
  - To provide training (JIT, TQC, CSI).
  - To share design, commodity, and technical knowledge.

Strategic Initiatives in the 1990s

Today, it can be said that Xerox has truly established partnerships with its suppliers—and that, in many ways, it is the Western benchmark for supplier partnerships. Figure 2–14 illustrates some of materials management's strategic initiatives in the 1990s and the tools and enablers that Xerox plans to utilize in order to achieve these initiatives. Xerox has currently "certified" 100 of its 400 suppliers. It has also recently added cost and delivery to the certification process. Its vision of the future is simple: to be the best.

Conclusion

Xerox has learned many things as a result of this experience. Perhaps most important, however, is that it can never again become complacent. Even being the best is not always good enough. In order to remain competitive in the 1990s, Xerox knows that it must continually strive to be the best possible—to go beyond what is best today, so that it can continually improve and be the best in the future. It is a lesson many corporations are being forced to learn as a result of the increasingly global, competitive, and dynamic environment in which they now operate.

The evolution of materials management at Xerox provides a concrete example of the strength of integrative manufacturing and the tremendous power of transformation that is possible through the successful integration of people, process, and technology.

FIGURE 2–14
Strategic Initiatives for the 1990s

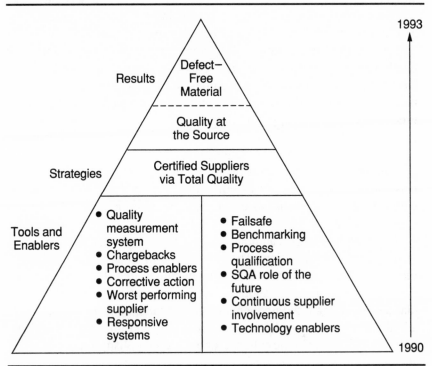

Reprinted with Permission of Xerox Corporation.

SUMMARY

Although the vertical enterprise—which incorporates much of the value chain under one roof—has long been a model for manufacturers, a new alternative has evolved: the *virtual* enterprise, which, through focused factories, supplier and distributor partnerships, and a variety of centralized and decentralized components, results in continuous-flow manufacturing as if all components were, as in the vertical model, in one location. This kind of change not only affects the manufacturing function itself, but also becomes central to the strategic advantage of the entire organization. Thus, it is vital that all strategic considerations are measured carefully before a change of this magnitude is adapted. For example, the scale of resource commitment called for must be considered—is the transformation too costly? But organizational advantages must be weighed as well. In the vertically integrated company, assets are owned, so that capacity does not become a bargaining point, and process costs and overhead are closely aligned, offering more control.

The virtual organization offers some other very strong benefits, including an expanded range of strategic options, enhanced product diversity, and extended market opportunities. It can also provide an improved product introduction process, where alliances can be leveraged, offering greater capacity and opportunities through concurrent engineering and the rapid deployment of off-the-shelf opportunities. There are negatives, too, of course: less control of supply and production, with the possibility of suppliers becoming competitors. While outsourcing peripheral products and services does have its downside, it does allow the organizations within the virtual "team" to concentrate on activities that add the most strategic value.

The best alliance candidates will pursue a similar strategy to that of the central organization. The importance of finding the *right* partner means the best candidates will be challenging to find, but it will be worth the effort—because they should either help meet the company's particular set of strategic requirements (e.g., globalization, diversification) or add the combination of know-how, creativity, and information critical to success. (If the strategic alliance doesn't accomplish either of these, it should be questioned seriously.)

The integration of people, process, and technology is essential to the success of the virtual enterprise—*the* model for the 1990s and beyond. This chapter should be regarded as an overview of the people-process-technology equation; the four chapters that follow provide specific discussions of each element of that equation. The vital role that people play will be discussed first, in Chapter 3.

CHAPTER 3
PEOPLE

INTRODUCTION

This chapter explores the human side of manufacturing today—the most crucial element of our framework of people, process, and technology. "Competing on science and technology means competing on the organization of information; invariably, one thinks of a battle of computers. But the machine is not at the center of competition . . . knowledge workers are the only corporate asset that lasts."[1] People are both the source of strategy and the means to achieving its goals—even a technology-based strategy has its foundations in people. Without the right people, the most streamlined processes make no difference to the bottom line.

Included in this chapter are three related discussions:

- Trends in human resources.
- Human resources in transnational corporations.
- Knowledge workers and the electronic work force.

TRENDS IN HUMAN RESOURCES

CIM, JIT, GT, MRPII, TQC—none of these systems, methodologies, or techniques serves as an end in itself. Each is just one part of a larger vision of a flexible and responsive manufacturing enterprise. Hitting it right in the marketplace means that firms must respond quickly to changing customer demand and customer satisfaction. Flexibility is necessary to make the changes required by customer demands and desires. Four trends are driving the current move towards flexibility:

- The mass markets of the past are giving way to customization. Firms need to fine-tune their products and product mix.
- Increased competitiveness is causing companies to be more

This chapter was written with the assistance of Hilary V. O'Donnell.

[1]Kim B. Clark, "What Strategy Can Do for Technology," *Harvard Business Review*, November/December 1989, p. 98.

customer-driven than ever before. Henry Ford's famous quip— "You can have any color car you want so long as it's black"—is used today to demonstrate how far we have come in our thinking about what controls product decisions.

- Powerful and pervasive telecommunications and computing power have increased the volume of information, transaction speed, and the rate of change. These, in turn, compress both the possible and the expected rate of response.
- Modern mobility and the politics of nationalism, regionalism, and immigration have created an unprecedented mixture of people. Population diversity is reflected in both the labor pool and the supplier/customer base. Companies are increasingly expected to respond to both the internal (employee) population mix and the external (supplier and customer) population mix.

It is the dynamic interdependence of these four trends that demands flexibility. Blindly sticking to the old ways or not developing an ability to change will result in lost business, missed opportunities, and increased employee turnover. The need for flexibility puts demands on firms in every single function and action. It requires that they respond more quickly, shorten their lead time to change, and develop corporate cultures that encourage change.

If we accept "shorten the lead time to change" as an operational definition for flexibility and then apply it to the human resources function, we can develop a model for human resources management that will support a systemic or enterprise-wide drive for flexibility. A flexible organization leads to an improved strategic position and a competitive advantage that help ensure long-term viability. A human resources department can realize its competitive advantage when it embraces flexibility as its strategic direction.

Making a Case for Change: U.S. Workers of the Nineties

Who are the people that will be in the U.S. labor force of the 1990s? Who will provide the talent necessary for U.S. companies to compete on a global scale? Data from the much-publicized "Workforce 2000" study reveal the following:[2]

---

[2]Mark L. Goldstein, "Tomorrow's Workforce Today," *Industry Week*, 15 August 1988, pp. 41–43.

- The work force will grow slowly, becoming older, more female, and more disadvantaged. Only 15 percent of the new entrants to the labor force over the next 13 years will be native white males.

- To maintain its present population, the United States would need a fertility rate of 2.1 percent. For the past 20 years it has held steady at 1.8 percent.

- The baby boom has been followed by a baby bust, which means that proportionally fewer young workers will be in the pipeline and eventually there will be more experienced workers than new entrants in the labor pool, with the number of 16- to-24-year-olds remaining flat. Overall, demand for labor will outstrip supply.

- 74 percent of all women between the ages of 25 and 54 held paying jobs in 1990 (up from 35 percent in 1948). The Bureau of Labor predicts that by 2000, women will constitute 47 percent of the work force.[3]

- Immigrants will represent the largest share of the increase in the population and the labor pool since World War I. Given that Europe is also experiencing a birth rate less than that needed to maintain population levels, it is unlikely that immigrants to the United States will be from the nations from which most came in the past. More likely, they will come from Asia and from developing countries, where cultures, values, and languages are vastly different from existing U.S. models.

- 50 percent of today's marriages end in divorce, and the children of divorced couples continue to live full-time with the mother. This, coupled with an increase in single mothers, means that the number of households headed by a single female parent is increasing. In addition, one in four children in the United States today lives below the poverty level.

- Women are having fewer children and at later ages in their lives and stages in their careers.

- 35 percent of the work force is made up of dual-career couples.

The combination of these factors indicates clearly that the typical workers of the future will be unlike those who populate the workplace today.

---

[3]Nancy J. Perry, "The Workers of the Future," *Fortune: The New American Century*, 1991, pp. 68–72.

Any firm's next employee is likely to be a Hispanic, a divorced or single mother of school-age children, or a 42-year-old woman who is pregnant for the first time and who is half of a dual-career executive couple. No longer is a 28-year-old white male college graduate the norm.

"Yet the great majority of companies, by all estimates, have done little to prepare themselves" for these eventualities.[4] Perhaps management does not believe that these conditions will materialize. Perhaps it feels overwhelmed contemplating change of this magnitude. Perhaps it is too perplexing to contemplate what will be required of U.S. managers and firms in the future. No matter what the reason, however, only a proactive approach will bring the needed results. These are the people that firms must call upon to deliver. These are the people who will shape U.S. workplaces. These are the people who will determine America's competitive ranking in the world.

What Progress Has Been Made So Far?

Over the past 25 years, the number of women doing paid work outside the home has been steadily increasing. Women have gained access to almost every career field and they are present in greater and greater abundance throughout the system. If we rate the United States on how well it has adjusted as a nation to this major work force shift, and if we use that rating as an indicator of how well firms may do in responding to future demographic shifts, firms will clearly need to do more and do it differently. Twenty-five years after the current wave of women entered the work force, many, if not most, are feeling disheartened and tired. They wonder why there has been so little progress. Many are leaving corporate America. In 1968 women earned 59¢ to a man's $1.00 earnings. In 1991 the figure was 65¢ on the dollar.[5] A generation of women graduated from MBA programs 20 years ago. In 1990, according to a *Fortune Magazine* study, only $\frac{1}{2}$ of 1 percent of the top wage earners (19 out of 4,012) in the companies on the *Fortune* 1000 list were women. And the men are still standing next in line for the promotions to the top jobs.[6] Where are the women? Over a third

---

[4]Goldstein, p. 42.

[5]Jaclyn Fierman, "Shaking the Blue Collar Blues," *Fortune*, 25 April 1990, pp. 203–218.

[6]Jaclyn Fierman, "Why Women Still Don't Hit The Top," *Fortune*, 20 July 1990, pp. 40–60.

of the female MBAs of the graduating classes of 1977 have already left corporations. They left not to have children but to find greater career satisfaction. Many have become entrepreneurs. Currently, women head three out of four new business startups. The message may be that if women do not feel welcome to join or remain inside corporations, they will use their talent to establish their own systems outside existing corporations.

The picture is no better for minorities. Lack of recognition for the many talents of blacks, Hispanics, Native Americans, and others means living each day with corrosive frustration. This frustration shrivels the soul, and powerlessness and lack of affirmation lead to aggression. How can America remain a world power if people drop out or turn on each other in frustration? This is a time when the United States needs to energize its very best talent—drawn from the *entire* population—and bring it to the forefront.

Two Bedrock Changes: Active Inclusion, Active Retention

The single biggest change that companies can make to stay competitive is to become *actively inclusive*—to seek effective means for involving everyone in the firm's workings and success. This means changes in recruitment, hiring, promotion, decision making, communication, appraisal, reward, recognition, and development. In the coming decades, firms should become so proactive that EEO and Affirmative Action will look as quaint and outmoded as the original room-sized Univac does in relation to a PC. The second necessary change is to fashion organizational cultures, structures, and benefits systems that will *actively retain* employees. Of course, these two changes need to occur simultaneously.

Firms that find ways to make these changes will be sought by workers and will be in the enviable position of being able to hire the best. The last two decades have been difficult and disheartening for employers and employees alike. In most cases, the reason that substantial change has not materialized is not lack of effort. The problem is that there is no linear progression. Expending more effort or money on relationships or programs is not necessarily the solution; rather, the goal should be changing the very nature of the relationship. To achieve flexibility, firms must practice active inclusion and active retention. Changing the nature of the employer/employee relationship is the way to proceed.

Moving the Employee-Employer Relationship toward Partnership

Henry Ford's mass manufacturing philosophy and Alfred Sloan's command and control hierarchical management of standardized products philosophies brought "a strict division of labor; a rigid, bureaucratic, militaristic management pyramid; an ethos of autocratic control by a managerial oligarchy geared to cost minimization. For nearly half a century, the North American automotive multinational stood as the ultimate role model for successful manufacturing operations. Several generations of managers and industrial leaders were educated and trained within these constraints."[7]

For a variety of complex reasons, women and minorities with different sets of values and experiences entered corporations in growing numbers. They pressured the system for inclusion. Corporations were unprepared and took a defensive position—merely reacting or, at best, responding quickly. This created a relationship with one side making demands and the other side reacting while no longer feeling wholly in control.

The employee-employer relationship started out as a zero-sum or win-lose equation. Power was seen as finite: "If I have power and you want some, I have to give up something for you to get something—and I'm not going to do so willingly." The parties quickly become adversarial. Since women and minorities had enforceable legislation on their side, firms had to make accommodations and attempt to satisfy these demands. This antagonism is analogous to the relationship that developed in the United States between unionized labor and management. The latter adversarial relationship did not change until competition from the Japanese caused labor and management to step beyond their constant conflict. They have begun to join forces, to work in a *partnership style*, in order to beat the stiff competition.

These lessons are applicable to many other workplace issues as well. Once firms got the hang of a labor-management partnership style, they adapted it to other situations. Suppliers began to link with the firm in partnership. Customers and stakeholders could be seen as partners. Functions or divisions inside the firm began to form partnerships. Even

---

[7]Roland G. Bertado, "A Reappraisal of Automotive Management and Organizational Deployment," *Journal of Automobile Engineering*, 20 November 1990, p. 275.

competitors could become partners. Some conceptualized a firm as situated in the midst of a complex and interdependent network of stakeholder relationships. Theoretically, firms that embraced this concept and acted on it progressed further, faster. Firms already skilled in partnering are at least ready for the next evolutionary step: they will be first in line to form partnerships with their employees.

Flexibility, or short lead time to change, implies constant negotiation. Negotiating parties acknowledge that each contributes to the relationship and that there is long-term value to both in preserving the relationship. Adult-to-adult relationships between employee and employer need to become the norm. Given the tradition of hierarchical organizational structures, and the information and decision-making flows that grow from them, the typical outcome has been parent-child or patriarchal relationships. In such a configuration, the firm sees itself as being one-up: it has jobs available and the employees have a need for work. Contrast this stance with that of a firm that views the employee as one-up: the firm needs skills and work performed, while employees have the supply of skills it needs. In the first instance, the firm has the supply of goods and is in an advantageous position. In the second case, the employee has the supply of goods and has the advantage.

The reality, however, is that both employers and employees have supplies and needs. They can establish a psychological contract based on reciprocity and negotiation. Both parties stand to gain, and both are prepared to compromise to achieve their respective gains. Both bring something of great worth to the relationship. This attitude sets the stage for contact, discussion, exchange of ideas, respect, compromise, mutual exploration, and mutual success. It is a win-win scenario that forms the basis for partnering. These are subtle and far-reaching changes, but the potential results provide pragmatic reasons for firms to move ahead.

Organizational Culture

A distinct organizational culture will grow from implementing a partnership style and the principles of active inclusion and active retention. Like the air we breathe, culture is around us all the time; it affects our functioning, the quality of our performance, and our views of what is worthwhile and normal. Culture is the sum of a group's identity, language, history, systems of nonverbal communication, material well-being, and accepted ways of doing things.

National cultures change at a glacial pace. Corporate cultures, on the other hand, can be consciously created, modified, and changed. People experienced in organizational change estimate the time frame as five years of systemwide, sustained, planned effort. To reach the goal of flexibility, firms need to create a culture designed to yield that result.

At the heart of culture is a set of core values. These values give rise to a system of beliefs, which in turn lead to certain behaviors and practices. Since the behaviors and practices are observable, they can be overtly transmitted as "the way we do things around here." In national culture, these form the boundaries between different peoples, regardless of where the lines are drawn on a map. Similarly, the corporate differences between "the Disney way" and "the IBM way" are apparent to both the insider and the external observer. Programs and practices in the organization are an outgrowth of a firm's corporate culture, and they help to institutionalize the underlying values and beliefs.

Reflecting these assumptions, the following discussion will progress from the values and beliefs that shape a culture, through the characteristics of the culture, and on to the behaviors, programs, and practices one is likely to encounter (see Figure 3–1). Remember that all are focused on producing flexibility, which will increase market share and revenue.

Values

There are three values essential to the corporation to move toward flexibility:

- Diversity.
- Discourse.
- Empowerment.

Diversity
Firms need to pay attention to diversity for several reasons. The demographic shifts, reciprocal relationships, and negotiation outlined earlier are the most obvious; others are less evident but no less important.

First, global competition means that customers and vendors are diverse. Companies need to understand their needs and wants, how to advertise and market to them, and how to form alliances with them. In short, companies need to know how to do business with them. Global outreach works in both directions. U.S. firms will be reaching into

FIGURE 3-1
Three Core Values of an Organizational Culture

Values of:	Lead to Belief in	Hallmarks of the culture	Behavior	Human Resource Practices and Programs
Diversity	• Inclusion of everyone is beneficial • Everyone has a unique contribution to make • Greatest innovation comes at the synergistic point where differences meet	• Participative • Mutual respect • Acting like partners	• Involvement • Constituent groups have voice, sit on committees, are at all levels of firm including the very top	• Flextime • Job sharing • Child care • Maternity/paternity leave • Diversity programs • Mentoring • Orientation • Succession
Discourse	• Information sharing • Listening • Ongoing learning • Spread of innovation • No one person has all of the answers	• Informed employees • Learn from experience • O.K. to take risks • O.K. to fail • Flat structure	• Dialogues in all directions • Work in teams • Human networks • Human scale • Entrepreneurship • Aligned system	• Workforce planning • Career planning • Training and development • Job enrichment • Performance planning and appraisal
Empowerment	• People are trustworthy • Motivation is a function of self-esteem and self-determination	• Meritocracy • Investment in people • Long-term perspective • Personal commitment and responsibility • Renewal and innovation	• High motivation/low supervision • People rotate in/out of active status • Loyalty	• Reward systems • Recognition • Compensation

other countries, and other countries will be reaching into the United States. This phenomenon is already becoming familiar. The British and Dutch have invested heavily in property, plants, and equipment in the United States for generations. For example, Holiday Inn and Burger King are both British-owned. Because of the intertwined histories of the United States and Britain, the adjustments were gradual. Presently there is increased Japanese investment in the United States, with some 1,400 Japanese factories currently in operation.[8] Due to greater cultural gaps, the distances to be bridged are much greater. Americans will be learning what it is like to have Japanese factories, banks, and other businesses in their communities. Later, businesses may be Mexican, Thai, Russian, or Romanian.

Secondly, business is increasingly complex. Work that individuals used to perform is now done in teams. For this reason firms may need to transform a collection of individuals of both genders and of different ethnic, racial, and religious backgrounds into a cohesive team sharing a common goal, trust, and interdependence.

Third, productivity is at stake. U.S. firms must attract and motivate the best and brightest people from every available source and coax the greatest contribution from each person. Companies can't afford to have people working at 50 percent capacity because they feel that certain of their abilities and attributes aren't welcome. By his own admission, one African-American Harvard University graduate earning $63,000 from his high-tech employer states that he works at "less than half capacity because I am always trying to figure out how to do things like a white person would. I wish I could just do things like I would. They are not getting their money's worth this way."

What should U.S. firms hope to accomplish by valuing diversity? First and foremost, companies will be creating an environment in which every employee can make his or her fullest contribution to company goals. This will boost productivity immediately and enormously. Second, diversity will change the psychological contract between employees and employer. When an employer works to create an environment in which diverse people and talents are valued, people get motivated and energized. They work at full capacity and get something back from the system in terms of career and personal growth. People will play hard if they know that they are truly on the company team.

---

[8]Perry, p. 67.

What does the diverse work force want? Susan Aaronson, a senior consultant at Digital Equipment Corporation in Maynard, Massachusetts, has worked on issues of diversity in the American workplace for over 15 years. She offers the following observations:[9]

- "People want to feel included, heard, valued, trusted, safe, treated like adults. They want to feel that somebody is willing to take a risk on them. In short, they want to know that they will be treated fairly and equitably."
- "They want to know that opportunities for jobs, recognition, promotion, and compensation are open to all; that these can be theirs, too. That if they work hard they can get the rewards the system has to offer."
- "They want responsive management."

These desires sound like what anyone would want from the workplace. The challenges for managers, however, are not to be minimized. They will need to find ways to utilize the full talents of this diverse work force, to practice management processes that are bias-free, and to have the personal comfort, knowledge, and skills to deal with people who are different from themselves. Managers will have to believe in the richness that comes from diversity and be prepared for continuous learning about themselves, others, and the organization. They need to model ways to value diversity and be unafraid to risk making the mistakes that often teach the most treasured and remembered lessons. This is a continuous improvement process akin to the underpinnings of quality education.

How will companies know if they are getting there? Women and minorities use two quick tests of whether an environment is inclusionary. First, are there minorities present in all levels of the organization, not only at the bottom, or in personnel? The importance of role models cannot be stressed too much. When women, for example, don't see women at the top of the management ranks, they know that this is a place to pass through, not a place to stay and make a commitment to. Second, do the norms and behaviors support diversity? If racist humor, for example, is acceptable, this is not a place where African-Americans will invest their talents. It's that simple.

---

[9]Susan Aaronson, interview held in July 1991 in Maynard, Mass.

In their book, *Workforce America!*, Loden and Rosener argue that "the cost of doing nothing to proactively manage employee diversity is already too high within the American workplace."[10] They identify some of these costs as:

- The substantial dollars that must be spent on recruiting and re-training due to high employee turnover.
- The number of discrimination complaints that are filed due to the mismanagement of diverse employees.
- The everyday conflicts that flare up and the tension created between co-workers over a comment, gesture, or joke perhaps delivered without malice but received as an insult.
- The deliberate acts of sabotage aimed at making co-workers who are different "look bad."
- The time and money wasted in corporate turf battles between members of different ethnic and racial groups.
- The cost of absenteeism associated with psychic stress.
- The time wasted due to miscommunication and misunderstandings between diverse employees.
- The enormous amount of personal energy and creativity that is wasted everyday on active resistance to this inevitable change.[11]

An organization that values diversity expresses these beliefs:

- Including everyone is beneficial.
- Everyone has a unique contribution to make.
- The greatest innovation comes at the synergistic point where differences meet.

As mindsets change as a result of valuing diversity, people who were previously outside the mainstream become important resources in the change process. Support networks (which minorities can form on the basis of their difference from the majority) can pinpoint and feed to upper management ways that policies and practices affect minorities. These resource groups have become important sources of feedback and

---

[10]Marilyn Loden and Judy B. Rosener, *Workforce America!: Managing Diversity as a Vital Resource* (Homewood, Ill: Business One Irwin, 1991), p. 13.

[11]Ibid., p. 12

information to management at corporations such as Digital Equipment, Xerox, Avon, US West, and Levi Strauss.

Diversity leads to a participatory culture full of respect for each individual. As a result, individuals get involved. In these workplaces, diversity is visible at every level and in every job category. People sit together with management on committees to solve company problems and promote company goals. Employees work with managers to create visions and strategic directions for the company. Constituent groups within the culture have a voice. There are celebrations of diversity, and conflicts are embraced as opportunities for change and learning. People successfully work conflicts through to resolution and new understanding. People act like partners.

Discourse
The second value essential to corporate flexibility is discourse. Communication too often becomes a one-way street, emanating from the top down. Discourse (which has the same roots as the word *conversation*) means that ideas can be shared in all directions. Both the spirit of discourse and the mechanisms for it to happen must be present.

Discourse gives rise to the belief that information sharing is right and necessary. Sharing the corporate vision, strategies, and goals is fundamental, as is getting input and reactions to refine them. People believe that listening is a way to learn and that ongoing learning keeps an individual and an organization vital. They believe that the exchange of ideas leads to innovation and discovery and that no one person has all the answers.

In the culture that grows from these beliefs, people are informed. They learn from their own experiences and from those of others. This is a culture in which it is acceptable to take risks and to fail. The most characteristic behavior in this culture is people working in teams. There is ongoing, multidirectional, honest communication. There are human networks and a human scale to the work, the processes, and the infrastructure. Internal employees innovate and create new business ventures through intrapreneurship. People work in concert with company goals, secure in the knowledge that what they do is connected to the larger picture. The organization is aligned.

More than any other variable, discourse drives flat organizational structures. Information that travels by the shortest distance and most direct route is the freshest, most accurate, and most relevant. Given the distance between the top and the bottom of organizations in pyramidal, hierarchical structures, it is not surprising that the top and the bottom are disconnected, don't understand each other, can't communicate, and (more often than not) are working on entirely different agendas, goals, and programs. They are literally living in different worlds. A flat structure, with its quick access, puts everyone back on the same team on the same playing field on the same day. It is a huge step toward a winning attitude and the success that results.

Empowerment

The third value essential to corporate flexibility is empowerment. Technically, to empower means to invest with legal power, or to authorize. In today's human resources vernacular, however, the word is used more for its connotative than literal sense. *Empowered people operate out of the passion and courage of their convictions. They have fire in their belly.* They do the right thing, live out their values and beliefs, behave authentically, and follow through on commitments. They are honest and fair with themselves and others, up-front and nonmanipulative. The definition of empowerment is difficult to pin down exactly because it deals with the elusive world of feelings. *People feel empowered when their head and heart and gut are synchronized and they are centered in the power that results.* Examples of empowered people include Rosa Parks claiming her bus seat on that day in Montgomery, Alabama, and Jacques Cousteau bringing his message that we are duty-bound to live in harmony with the oceans and all its creatures. Everyday people all around us are empowered as they accomplish their potentials. Empowered people develop and live out an ethic that changes the attitudes of others.

Beliefs that grow from valuing empowerment are

- People are trustworthy.
- Motivation is a function of self-esteem and self-determination.
- Recognition of good performance makes people feel good about themselves. All these feed self-esteem. Again, we see reciprocity in operation.

The culture that springs from empowerment is a meritocracy. It invests in humans and their growth and development, takes a long-term perspective, and supports personal commitment and responsibility. The behaviors in this culture revolve around high motivation with low supervision. This results from the combination of teamwork, shared vision, and self-determination. People rotate in and out of full-time status. They express loyalty and achieve quality and excellence in processes and products. They follow through on commitments and take initiative by signing up for work that contributes to company goals. They seek innovation and renewal.

Square D, a Palatine, Illinois, electrical equipment and electronics products manufacturer, has developed a sophisticated empowerment program. Its cornerstone is "Vision College," created to spread the corporate vision among its 20,000 employees. The college's director, Sharon Arvidson, "points out that 'hard-core empowerment' comes down to the three Ps: permission, power, and protection." She says Square D is attempting to "change the way people manage their work from a traditional base that's been around for 40 years to one in which we encourage people not to check their brains at the door."[12] Although you cannot simply empower people, you can change what they value. Those people then understand that they have power within themselves and can make a difference.

This is the foundation to the concepts of systems thinking and the learning organization, laid out so brilliantly by Senge in his work, *The Fifth Discipline: The Art and Practice of the Learning Organization.* He states that today, "more than ever we are becoming overwhelmed by complexity. Perhaps for the first time in history, humankind has the capacity to create far more information than anyone can absorb, to foster far greater interdependency than anyone can manage, and to accelerate change far faster than anyone's ability to keep pace. Certainly the scale of complexity is without precedent. Organizations break down, despite individual brilliance and innovative products, because they are unable to pull their diverse functions and talents into a productive whole."[13]

Human Resources Practices and Programs

This is the final link in the chain leading to flexibility. Unfortunately, there is no prescription outlining certain practices or programs for achieving flexibility. The situation is alarmingly similar to climbing the Himalayas, locating the guru, popping the "What is the meaning of life?" question,

[12]Joseph F. McKenna, "Smart Scarecrows: The Wizardry of Empowerment," *Industry Week*, 16 July 1990, p. 14.

[13]Peter M. Senge, *The Fifth Discipline: The Art and Practice of the Learning Organization* (New York: Doubleday/Currency, 1990), p. 69.

and being told that the answer is inside you. Believe it or not, this is the good news.

Earlier we stated that partnership comprises active inclusion and active retention and that an organization that values diversity, discourse, and empowerment, has five important features: constituent groups with a voice; teamwork; shared vision and informed employees; personal responsibility; and innovation.

Partnership is the means of challenging the members of a work force to create their own human resources practices and programs. Working with the coaching, support, coordination, and expert consultation of internal human resources professionals or external consultants, teams of employees are asked to develop the frameworks for the entire range of infrastructures. They must become informed about where the business is going and how it is doing, get accustomed to working in human networks, and understand the interdependent nature of employees and the success of the firm. As they grow in these respects, they can be trusted to deliver affordable, realistic suggestions that maximize business, competitive, and employee advantages. They will provide solutions that actively include and actively retain. The solutions of each firm will be custom made to suit its needs.

Implementation requires no sales pitch to convince employees of the benefits to them. The situation is analogous to what happened inside corporations when they began to ask for customer help in product design and for supplier help in inventory management. Management learned things that they could never have imagined on their own because, by definition, they lacked the customer or supplier perspective. Employees will tell management what they need, what they want, how to include them, how to retain them, how to build motivating cultures. Once a firm establishes the values and partnership, it only needs to create the cross-organization teams, ask the questions, reinforce the vision, set broad parameters, and provide its teams with expert resources. The greatest challenge then is to be receptive to the results, creativity, and the surges of energy, enthusiasm, and loyalty that the firm will receive in response.

In his book, *Productive Workplaces*, consultant and educator Marv Weisbord states from his wide experience that "companies get better when employees cooperate on joint tasks. When people meet across levels and lines of status, function, sex, race, and hierarchy, when problems are seen as systemic rather than discrete, wonderful (and unpredictable) things happen. Long-standing lockups, assumed to be intractable, are resolved.

Relationships improve, walls come down, problems are solved, norms change."[14]

Likely Outcomes
It is difficult to predict accurately just what programs and systems an organization will design. However, suggesting some criteria and possibilities may be useful: Overall, the people programs must be tied together into a system and must all be directed at achieving flexibility. Don't expect a traditional structure for personnel in which there are separate departments of compensation, benefits, staffing, training and development, and employee relations. Probably only parts of the previous organization will still fit. But it is critical to ensure that all the functions are mutually reinforcing.

Recognition and Reward Systems

These are the two most powerful tools that an organization can use. Reward systems, which include compensation, need to be designed to reward the values of the organization. There need to be rewards for quality, not quantity; for diversity, not sameness; for innovation and risk taking, not for staying in line and doing things by the book. The book should be thrown away. A company should look at what its system outcomes currently are, for that is what the company is rewarding now, whether it intends to or not.

Firms must close the gaps between what they say and what they do. They cannot say that they value diversity, but have no minority vice presidents. People see right through these inconsistencies. They will act in accordance with what is *really* rewarded. The greater the gap between what a company says it values and what it actually rewards, the greater the management credibility gap.

Recognition, power or mastery, and money are some of the great human motivators. Recognition covers everything from a nod and hello from a senior manager to an on-time and accurate performance appraisal; from verbal praise for a job well done to a plaque in recognition of performance; from a mention in the company newsletter to a stock grant. For the most part recognition is free, abundant, and easy. It is also

---

[14]Marvin Weisbord, *Productive Workplaces* (San Francisco: Jossey-Bass, 1988), p. 274.

consistently overlooked. Why? Perhaps it is the Puritan ethic—Americans are afraid of spoiling their children with too much attention. It is time to abandon this model. Recognition isn't just for children or for junior employees. All adults, including senior managers, need and want it. Recognition feels good. It stimulates people to perform well and to repeat good performance. Every organization needs more of it.

Consider the example of the director who gave an important presentation to some key customers. Word got back to his organization that he had done an outstanding job. One of his staff was in a perky mood that day and so cut a star shape out of cardboard, loaded it up with glue and gold glitter and taped it to the director's office door to replicate the backstage door of a Broadway star. Nearly everyone in the organization saw it prior to his return. Pride in the competence of the organization's manager spread. Upon his return, he showed his pleasure at being recognized. Then he had the genius to take it one step further. Each week thereafter, he was on the lookout for someone who had performed star-quality action that week. He would tape the star to their office entrance and it was left there for the entire week. People began to talk about the office stars, what they had done, and sharpen their own performances in hopes of having the focus of attention for a week and recognition from the director. It cost not one cent, yet what it bought is beyond measure.

A third variable connected to producing the results that a company intends is often overlooked in human resources discussions: its financial systems—how the company keeps score. The behaviors and decision patterns of managers are usually predictable if a close look is taken at a company's financial systems. Financial measurements must align with company values and people systems for maximum impact.

Benefits
Benefits are intended to reduce risks and protect employees from hardship. They should enhance an employee's ability to contribute. They include such elements as medical and dental plans, vacation, sick days, tuition assistance, maternity/paternity leave, disability compensation, leaves of absence, adoption assistance, and childcare. Companies need to hear from employees what coverage is relevant. The needs of a new college graduate, a single parent, and a disabled veteran are different.

If an employee has difficulty in any nonwork area of his or her life, the firm has trouble. U.S. organizations are not clean rooms that can keep out everything that contaminates the production or research process.

Companies are dealing with people; they have to take "the good, the bad, and the ugly." Firms take the childcare issues along with the leadership capabilities. Firms take the temporary instability and productivity drop during the crisis of divorce along with the excellence in closing sales. Firms take the request for leave of absence (to hike, photograph, renew, and contemplate) along with the innovative product development. People need to have options for benefits that are relevant to them as they pass through various life stages. Self-selection of benefits packages empowers employees because it puts them in control—they can take care of the important aspects of their lives.

Selection and Hiring

As stated previously, if companies are serious about achieving diversity in their work force, they will have to be proactive and creative in their recruiting. Firms will also need to get beyond tokenism into "critical mass" to get the benefits of diversity and to entice minorities to stay. When there is not a critical mass, the gains from diversity don't materialize. The few members of a minority will, for safety and survival, mimic the dominant culture. Their impact will be washed out. All minorities are, at a minimum, bicultural. They can survive in their own culture and in the dominant culture. They will choose the latter if there are not enough people of their own culture for support. Under those circumstances, everyone is still acting from the assumptions of the dominant culture. The synergy produced by interacting, testing each other's assumptions, and broadening each other's perspectives is lost.

Given the opportunity, the people of difference on your design teams will help devise excellent ways to recruit, select, and retain minorities. When companies become as serious about diversity as they are about cost containment, quality, increased market share, or inventory reduction, they will devote similar energy, focus, creativity, and funding to this issue.

Not enough can be said about the power of orientation to bond all types of people to an organization. Those first hours, days, and weeks are a window of opportunity that must be used to the firms advantage. People can be quite forgiving of later imperfections when they are starting from a good foundation. On the other hand, when a good foundation is absent, not much can be done to strengthen the structure built on it. The resulting weakness can damage everything thereafter. Firms must be sure to stress the importance of orientation to their design teams.

Human Resources Planning and Development

In addition to vision, values, and mission, another driving force behind human resources planning and development is a two- to five-year business plan, which serves to determine the types and numbers of skills needed to implement it. Also crucial is knowing the current state of the organization—what skills it currently has in what numbers and locations. Once a firm knows what it has now and what it will need, it can plan to bridge the gap by hiring externally and training current employees. A business plan enables a firm to change rapidly enough to achieve flexibility. With the future outlined, a company can be continually recruiting, acquiring, developing, and orienting the next wave of talent so they are ready, just in time.

Demographers tell us that 75 percent of the people who will be working in the year 2000 are already on the job, that scientists and engineers will be in short supply by the turn of the century,[15] and that the current trend is for people to move through three to four careers over the course of their working life.[16] In addition, "just 60 percent of the high school class of 1989 signed up for postsecondary training of any kind. And if history is any guide, only half the college bound will earn a baccalaureate."[17] These facts imply that companies will need to train and develop their current and future employees as a normal part of doing business, and that they will need to be creative in recruiting technical talent.

Why devote the considerable time and expense necessary for employee training? The answer is so obvious that it escapes many executives' notice. Current employees are a rich resource. They know the products, corporate culture, customers, other internal players, and the industry; they grasp company vision and strategies. They are context-rich. For many reasons they are an obvious choice for investment.

- Reading, writing, and empowerment are linked together. When a firm invests in and develops its employees, it is furthering their empowerment.

---

[15]Ibid., 68–69.

[16]Charles Handy, "The Coming Work Culture," *Lears*, January 1991, p. 58.

[17]Fierman, "Shaking," p. 214.

- Training and education sends employees the message that they are being supported to be successful. They have the means to do a better job. When a firm invests in and develops its employees, it is furthering its partnership with them.
- Increased productivity and improved quality are two outcomes of training a work force. When a firm invests in and develops its employees, it is furthering its business goals.

A company can ensure that the talent it needs in the future is trained by working with high schools, community colleges, technical and trade schools, and colleges and universities to establish appropriate curriculums; other options include work-study, apprenticeship, and similar programs. Selecting the right schools for collaboration can lead to new-hire feeder systems for people of difference. By investing in future employees, a firm can further its efforts toward diversity.

Management-sponsored and -supported career planning is the tool that creates a link between individuals' goals and the firm's current and future human resource needs. A well-designed program provides management with many opportunities. It can feed employees information about the future skill needs of the firm. Managers can collect information for the firm about the current skills and the employees' intended career directions. Plans and budgets can be drawn up about the types and costs of development required for both the short- and long-term.

With its value on discourse, a company will have employees informed about the current state and future direction of the business and indus' y. It will have mechanisms for communication and partnership building between managers and employees. These are the foundations for career planning. Since the firm also has empowered employees, the 51 percent responsibility for developing and implementing career plans can be given to the employee. The rest of the responsibility for successful career planning lies with the managers.

If a firm believes in the wisdom of investing in people for the long-term, other mechanisms may fit with and supplement its human resources systems:

- Performance planning and performance appraisal.
- On-the-job-training.
- Bias-free promotion processes.
- Coaching and apprenticeships.

- Job rotation.
- Job enrichment.
- Flexible arrangements such as job sharing and part-time work. (Firms may also consider mechanisms for people to rotate in and out of full-time status in much the same way that sabbaticals work in universities.)

Training and development solutions will be unique to each firm because they are responses to unique business situations and problems. At the same time, surveying what other businesses are doing may be helpful, for many of their ideas and successes can be tailored to a different company's situation. One firm can also learn from the experiences of others and possibly avoid some of their failures.

If information is provided on the business, work force, and skills/ training challenges, and if design teams are asked to get smart about current practices, they are likely to produce success stories. For example, Sears is working with a vocational high school in Chicago to train juniors and seniors so they are qualified to work right after high school as beginner Sears technicians.[18] And at Polaroid headquarters in Cambridge, Massachusetts, a program has started in conjunction with Cambridge Rindge and Latin School to train students for entry-level jobs.[19]

And what of on-the-job training efforts for current employees? Motorola is a Grade-A trainer, spending about $60 million a year on 104,000 employees worldwide. The payoff has been savings of no less than $1.5 billion over the past three years, largely because of improvements the training has made in its work force.[20]

GE Chairman Jack Welch has put in place cutting-edge, interdependent programs to encourage employee empowerment. The Work-Out program, which functions similar to a New England town meeting, is a three-day, off-site session attended by 40 to 100 employees who form groups to propose and debate solutions and propose changes in the way things get done at GE. Through this program, workers have gotten a taste of empowerment and scored some quick and big wins for the corporation. The process is now expanding to include suppliers and customers.[21]

---

[18] Perry, p. 68.

[19] Fierman, "Shaking," p. 216.

[20] Ibid.

[21] Thomas A. Stewart, "GE Keeps Those Ideas Coming," *Fortune*, 12 August 1991, pp. 41–49.

Management and Change Implications

As change consultants and organizational development practitioners know, and as experience in firms demonstrates, there is always a pull or regression toward the comfortable, conventional, earlier modes. Major organizational change must be supported from the very top of the organization, aligned with business goals, and seen as a long-term commitment. The top leader or top management group can sustain and maintain the forward momentum and must be deeply committed to overcoming regression or sabotage.

When a traditional hierarchical organization commits itself to a partnership style, the principles of active inclusion/active retention, and the values of diversity, empowerment, and discourse, the rules of the game and the power structure changes. An inevitable result of this shift is a drastic change in the role of middle managers. "In the organization of the future 'everyone' has to be a manager, but no one can afford to be only a manager. Communicator, strategist, motivator, facilitator, coordinator, goal-setter, adviser, and mentor—the 'new' manager will cease to be an expression of status and become a leader with a definable value-adding activity with specific skills, needs, and clear personal performance measures. This is a giant leap from managers who know one more fact than their subordinates to leaders with a clear vision, sharing values and objectives with their teams."[22]

These managers are facing the unknown. Like everyone, they will experience stress and a range of emotions that may include anxiety, fear, anger, loss, and sadness. They need support, reassurance, clear direction, communication, and training. They need reward, recognition, and career opportunities. With these supports, performance deterioration, absenteeism, illness, and turnover can be contained, although not eliminated. Change is personal work, as well as organizational or system work. The people involved react across a continuum of behaviors, and the bell curve applies.

Conclusion

If a partnership style truly has been established, discourse will continue until everyone is pleased with the people-systems and proud of his or her

[22]Bertado, pp. 279–280.

own contribution. The implementation will be much smoother and take less time than if experts had designed and then sold it to the employees.

In addition to the positive effects of the newly created people-systems, the firm has also created an environment in which the employees involved in the process have shared the valuable experience of true teamwork. It has taken the opportunity to do it in real-time, with real business issues. The firm will also have a team of people who can evaluate the program and revise it to reflect changes in business directions. They can coach others on teamwork, perhaps even author a quality approach for the company. They might be good candidates to design a participatory business planning process. They might even start a new revenue producing venture for the company, leading others in the industry to create flexible people-systems.

Once a company has changed the nature of the relationship and established a climate where people use all of their talents in the workplace, it has a group of involved and committed people working on its team. From here, the possibilities are unlimited.

To recap, there are five simple and basic steps for establishing a work force for the 1990s and beyond:

1. *Recruit and retain.* Companies must invest in retaining their best people. Cost-cutting measures such as early and voluntary retirement are examples of programs that drive out the best and and most experienced people.

2. *Value diversity.* Olympic teams, world-class orchestras, surgical teams, and university faculty are populated and led by people of all colors and all nationalities. Manufacturers must take an active approach to developing and maintaining quality people.

3. *Educate and train.* Knowledge is a more powerful tool than methodology or technology. Creating a knowledgeable work force is an investment in the organization's capabilities when knowledgeable workers are retained.

4. *Empower.* Empowerment should not be confused with delegation. Empowerment requires moving decision making as well as actions to the employee level.

5. *Create high-performance work systems.* When coupled with aligned and integrated technology, the four preceding steps create work systems that are synergistic and enrich the organization. These systems will be the foundation of the manufacturing work force for the year 2000 and beyond. Investments in education

and training empower an organization's culture and, in combination with focused HR policies, prepare the enterprise and its people to take advantage of high-performance work systems.

HUMAN RESOURCES DEVELOPMENT
IN THE TRANSNATIONAL CORPORATION

The second "people issue" in manufacturing concerns human resource development in the transnational corporation. As the world economy grows more and more interdependent, this issue becomes increasingly crucial to the manufacturing industry.

In the past, corporations expanded into foreign markets by focusing on considerations of labor cost, optimal manufacturing sites, strategic alliances, and market opportunities. During the 1980s, however, corporate executives realized that attention to these dimensions was no longer sufficient, that companies must become global corporations with global leadership to compete successfully on a worldwide basis—or even to maintain market share within its domestic borders. Yet before anyone could agree on the definition of "global," business theorists coined a new term: transnational. Drucker, Bartlett, Ghoshal, and other theorists believe that this transnational corporate form will carry us into and through the 1990s.

The terms *global* and *transnational* are used with increasing frequency in modern enterprises. But what do they really mean? And what are the organizational and leadership implications of each?

The Changing Corporate Model

Over the centuries, trade between nations has taken shape in terms of four different models:

- Multinational.
- International.
- Global.
- Transnational.

Multinational
Multinational firms grew out of the culture of two historically dominant European nations, the British and the Dutch. These nations' long history

of seafaring trade led them to establish colonies that were part of an empire, loosely managed from afar. Over centuries of commerce, this style became the paradigm for business organization; it was also adapted as the foundation of business culture. Many European firms have used this organizational form on a worldwide scale up to the present. What distinguishes multinationals is a management style in which a country headquarters, corporate headquarters, and subsidiaries located around the world all operate quite independently as a loosely organized conglomerate.

International

The international firm is a natural evolution of the American experience. U.S. firms developed growth models based on their history of expanding within the country's vast domestic market. In this market, language, money, and culture all were uniform. Recreating abroad what had been successful at home made sense. Executives used this same model when a firm planned an expansion into a foreign market. In the international organization, the domestic operation is cloned and transplanted to the overseas operation. Strategies and products conceived at headquarters are transferred lock, stock, and barrel to the international locations. These attitudes are provincial, but they worked well in the 1950s and 1960s, when the world was simpler and more insular.

Global

To a tiny, ambitious, heavily populated, and resource-poor island, trade and export are matters of survival. Combined with the unique, long-term timeline characteristics of the Japanese culture, the model for the global firm is based on the Japanese management and commerce styles. The hallmark of the global firm is a standardized product that can be marketed and exported anywhere in the world. The global firm views the world as a single, extended market and sees itself without geographic borders. To be successful, it looks at this total market and designs products with universal appeal; it then distributes these products on a worldwide scale. The global firm has a single, long-term strategy, with a focus on economies of scale, consistency, and efficiency.

Homogeneity and uniform standards are the organizational response to the demands of a global firm. Decisions and planning are centralized but, significantly, worldwide markets are kept in the forefront of considerations. A great deal of effort and resources are spent in designing products and strategies that translate well across national, cultural, and language borders.

Transnational

A transnational firm blends the best pictures of the other corporate models. Viewing the world as one market, it nonetheless tailors its products to the local economy, preferences, needs, and tastes. High-level vision, policy, and philosophy are centralized in the organization, but implementation and operational decision making are decentralized in order to responsively serve local markets. The heart of a transnational firm is a network of strong and flexible national organizations with fast and effective cross-border communications.

Transnationals exercise significant autonomy at the local or branch level. Managers have the power to determine what works best, and they are measured on their profitability as well as their overall contribution to the long-term success of the enterprise. They respond to the local foreground and the global background simultaneously. In the transnational enterprise, communication does not have to travel through the center, although a strong center does exist. Schematically, it resembles a computer network rather than the traditional pyramid of hierarchical models. Responsibilities of the center and the localities are clear and do not overlap. Different parts of the enterprise take the lead on different issues, depending on the technology, competitiveness, competence, or other areas of expertise that have developed.

Of the four models, the transnational mindset and structure can most appropriately respond to current cultural trends. Firms that see the globe as one market, learn to fine-tune to market subsets, and create horizontal structures will have the greatest opportunity for growth in revenue and profits.

Firms committed to valuing diversity will leverage their capabilities. They establish diversity in their employee pool to create effective strategies, and they are able to draw on and respond to local cultures and markets. Successful transnational firms are characterized by the following:

- A long-term perspective and long-term goals.
- A vision and plan to become a transnational firm.
- True international management teams.
- No geographic boundaries and a clear global identity.
- Management of people on a global basis.

Human Resources Challenges

All firms have unique human resources challenges arising from their size, growth curve, stage in the life cycle, markets, and products. The transnational firm, too, has specific characteristics that give rise to specific challenges. The characteristics of most transnationals are

- *A balance between centralization and local autonomy.* Firms should combine global vision and marketing direction with strictly local implementation.
- *Clear lines of authority, well-defined responsibility, and maximum freedom to execute.* To simplify the complexity of the global corporation, all managers must be clear about their responsibilities—the decisions for which they are paid and upon which their performance is measured.
- *Flexibility and responsiveness.* Transnational strategy planning provides one way to achieve these goals.
- *Visionary and inclusionary leadership.* The primary role of leadership is creating and communicating a vision of the firm in its transnational state and creating harmony and movement toward that vision among all its different parts.

Given these characteristics, what are the human resource challenges in a transnational corporation? For most firms there are nine.

Challenge 1: Creating and communicating the vision. To the transnational firm, the vision is the means for becoming global and the magnet holding all the decentralized parts of the system together. The vision keeps the entire system on track and serves as the beacon that keeps all employees and all bottom lines focused on the success of the overall enterprise. It is the only way to manage at the macro level and give the requisite autonomy at the local level. It needs to be overcommunicated and kept alive through daily use and continual reference.

Challenge 2: Values transmission. The values are the first-level means of accomplishing the system's vision. A broad-based socialization process is needed to transmit the values and the attendant business ethics across all the locations and cultures participating in the firm. It is unrealistic to rely solely on the global executive's charisma and energy to transmit the firm's values.

Challenge 3: Creating an organizational culture.   The organization's culture is the medium that carries the values. At the heart of creating the transnational firm's culture is helping people suspend their ethnocentricity, their insular feeling of what is right and normal, and supplanting it with a belief that all peoples from all cultures have worth and value. Education and training can help an organization establish and maintain cultural direction; human resources plays a critical role in designing and deploying education and training programs. One of the transnational firm's hallmarks is the nonjudgmental encouragement and acceptance of input from all relevant players. Other useful concepts in an organization's culture are embracing and managing change, and encouraging and managing debate or differing opinions.

Challenge 4: Transnational teamwork.   A firm cannot get beyond multinational, international, or global definitions without developing transnational teamwork as its mode of doing business. Through teamwork, everyone participates in the system. Without transnational input, there is no transnational output. This concept is rooted in the highly pragmatic realization that no isolated person or group can know the answers to complex global problems; transnationalism depends on the power of collective wisdom. This wisdom goes beyond polling for input from a wide audience and learning from the interaction of the teamworkers. It also requires mixed teams and cultural sensitivity. A solid foundation of cross-cultural education is a prerequisite in the transnational firm, with any resources allocated to intercultural development likely to be well invested.

Challenge 5: Encouraging local innovation.   To balance the global and the local, autonomy must prevail at the local level. Through local autonomy, the local markets are captured and local advantages are used in the transnational enterprise. The local units are like the ships in a fleet. All use the charts (values) and stars (vision) for navigation, but each must use its own strengths, resources, and knowledge of local waters to follow the best course at any given point. They must be constantly alert to changes and able to innovate, initiate, renew, and respond.

Challenge 6: Gearing the system to a global pace.   Participation takes time. Cross-cultural understanding takes time as well. So do internalizing information, incorporating wide views and perspectives, and making decisions with greater numbers and diversity among players. Obviously the firm's overall time frame needs to expand. Expanded time frames can lead to the longer-term perspective necessary for global competitiveness.

Challenge 7: Empowering the system. Lacking vertical hierarchies, top-down direction, and bottom-up reporting, the whole system needs to be tuned in, turned on, and ready to act. If everyone is clear on the vision, values, and ethics, then all parts of the system can operate for the greater good of the enterprise and move toward achieving its vision. Finding ways to empower everyone throughout the system without creating decentralized chaos is perhaps the greatest human resources challenge that the transnational firm faces.

Challenge 8: Metrics and rewards. A powerful technique for preventing chaos is to reward the desired outcomes and set up measurement systems to track them. This requires a great deal of creativity and can become an unnerving balancing act. Traditional rewards for individual performance or local unit bottom-line excellence produce outcomes opposed to transnational teamwork and global thinking. The resource mobility needed for transnationalism will not be achieved if foreign assignments and repatriation work against an employee's career or financial progression and satisfaction. The matrix will not work because only one part will be seen as having a positive consequence. The key is to reward people by measuring their performance against the shared values and to evaluate business performance by the accumulation of decisions consistent with achieving worldwide advantage.

Challenge 9: Human resources planning and development. More than in any other type of firm, the transnational needs people to work well on teams. They also need the right mix of people, in the right places, at the right time, with the right skills and cross-cultural experience. This will not happen naturally. It is the unusual person who willingly steps outside his or her comfort zone to venture into cross-cultural waters. Management must promote multicultural growth in order to determine individual needs, construct a plan that closes the gap between present skills and the future demands of transnational management. The firm must employ career and succession planning, rotational planning, cultural sensitivity and awareness training, and new models for management and leadership, along with plans for executive and management development, team training, and language training. It needs new models for assessing skills and potential. The planning and development function itself must be transnational.

Leadership of the Transnational Firm

Given our definition of a transnational firm and the human resources challenges facing it, a *transnational executive officer* (TEO) must be a worldview visionary and a catalyst who imagines, creates, and leads all the divergent parts and players forward. The challenge is daunting. To succeed, the TEO must possess a broad set of skills, experiences, and characteristics. Among other things, the TEO must have the ability to create a corporate culture. This ability results from translating values and theories into action while linking organization elements into a balanced system. The TEO must be sufficiently gifted to see the whole, to be clear about what is important, to understand the dynamic interaction of the parts, and to then build the cultural elements so that they support each other.

For example, a common major shortcoming in multinational companies is an inability to design reward systems that value and utilize expatriates' experiences to the benefit of both the firm and the expatriates themselves. A TEO knows the importance of intercultural management teams to the firm's success. With only 29 percent of U.S. expatriates reporting that their work experience abroad had positive career implications, the TEO will require a solution to this waste. In other words, the TEO needs to lead from a clear set of values, then close the gap between values and practices. He or she needs to translate the general agreement about the importance of people to a company's success into practices that provide all employees with the opportunity to be well informed, demonstrate initiative, and communicate meaningfully with management. Similarly, the importance of customer services and product quality must be reflected in new ways of including customer and supplier perspectives in decision making. Value placed on renewal, growth, and change needs to be supported so that people embrace change, rather than resist it. Perhaps just as important, people's performance assessments should be made consistent with the template of the firm's corporate values.

The ideal culture that the TEO builds in the successful global firm will be one in which

- No internal boundaries exist (e.g., among marketing, engineering, manufacturing, various wage classes, labor/management, genders, etc.).
- No geographic boundaries exist.
- All stakeholders—*especially* the customers—are included.
- Reliable communication flows as a result of effective delegation, trust, and partnership—not because of corporate control.
- Noncompetitive centers of expertise develop because no one person or group can understand all the complexities.
- All employees have the skills, information, confidence, and backing of management to do their jobs.
- People have a chance to win and feel empowered.
- Cooperation and teamwork are the preferred modes of operating.
- Clear lines of authority and responsibility exist.
- Competence as well as cross-cultural skills and experience are rewarded.
- Continuous learning is the norm.
- Leadership is accepted wherever it is found.
- Win-win solutions are sought, and decisions do not play one group or nationality off against others.
- The long-term interest of the enterprise is firmly maintained as the standard for policy decisions.

What professional attributes make it possible for the TEO to establish this sort of corporate culture? Of the many we could discuss, these are the most significant:

- *The TEO is a good listener and observer who is also decisive.* The leader must pay close attention to signals from the environment, yet not become paralyzed by excessive attention to the cultural boundaries present. He or she must be able to find, understand, and respect the cultural limits, then push them gently to prompt needed innovations. He or she must be able to make a decision even when confronted with a complex and bewildering array of options, or where there is great uncertainty about the outcomes. This ability is based on a clear and well-defined set of values that guide appropriate business action.
- *The TEO is a visionary and a good communicator who can package and send messages that unify.* Although this is an important

skill for any leader, it is especially important in a multicultural setting. Here the leader is asking people both to hold on to their national culture and to relinquish it to embrace a "greater commonality" for the success of the enterprise. Communication needs to be clear, direct, and simple.

- *The TEO is open to new ideas and wide participation, which leads to learning.* Openness can also keep a TEO's ego from getting in the way of greatness. It lets an executive understand that business is a team effort and that contributions must come from everyone, everywhere. The role of the TEO is not to provide answers but to frame the questions and encourage participation in finding the answers.

- *The TEO is organized.* Organization is valued not for its own sake, but because it is an outward manifestation of an inner understanding of what truly matters. In the complex environment of transnational companies, an understanding of priorities is basic.

- *The TEO is factual and neutral.* The global leader cannot afford to side with any group or idea, other than the long-term success of the enterprise, in order to keep everyone in the system committed and involved.

- *The TEO is flexible.* A TEO needs the agility to switch styles and meet cultural assumptions or expectations while being fully grounded in his or her own identity. Far from being a chameleon that changes to make itself look like its surroundings, the flexible executive is solidly rooted in a core identity. It then becomes easy for the leader to modify peripherals such as manifest cultural styles. Trust grows when the TEO and others can work comfortably together without compromising anyone's integrity.

- *The TEO is able to spot and nurture talent.* This is another general leadership trait that takes on more weight in the transnational firm. The TEO needs sufficient self-awareness and cross-cultural sophistication to spot talent across cultural gaps. He or she must be able to identify those with values and leadership qualities that will enhance the firm's future.

- *The TEO is adept at cross-cultural team building.* Building partnerships, tapping the talent of good people, bridging cultural gaps, and creating strategic interdependencies all help to execute a global strategy while empowering those at the local level to be in control of their own sphere. Working together in teams on common issues is the inescapable medium in the transnational firm. These can be in the form of permanent or semipermanent teams or temporary task forces and "ad hocracies."

The TEO and Teams

Building effective teams is important in any corporation, but it requires special attention in the transnational firm for three reasons.

First, members of teams in the transnational corporation will be, by definition, very diverse. The TEO cannot assume that team members start with shared skills, assumptions, values, or even a common language. These have been important obstacles to global teamwork since at least the time of the Tower of Babel.

The second reason that building teams is important is that in the world of global business, alliances and partnerships increasingly influence competitiveness. At least as many resources are required to manage, maintain, and expand the subsequent relationships as were required to negotiate a deal in the first place. In the transnational firm, with its decentralization and absence of a vertical hierarchy and reporting lines, people cooperate to the degree that they believe their self-interest is being served. The TEO must realize that win-win relationships are the glue holding the system together. Motivating people by identifying common goals is crucial. In addition, the TEO encourages interdependencies so that all parties must work together to reach group and individual success. Creating these strategic interdependencies is necessary for establishing effective teamwork.

The third reason why teams must be carefully constructed is the complexity of the task of asking people from different cultures to work together in teams. In these situations, people must relinquish deeply embedded, historically rooted, stereotyped assumptions about others— assumptions that they may not perceive or, if they perceive them, may believe to be justified. People must take the more difficult, energy-intensive route of working from differences rather than similarities. They are asked to grow and change and challenge themselves.

To address these issues, the TEO must have at least three significant attributes that facilitate team building in the transnational setting. The TEO must be

- *Competent with languages*. At a minimum the TEO needs to speak the basics of at least one other language, preferably the local language. This shows respect for people of other cultures and is a demonstration of good will and open-mindedness. New language acquisition generally requires one year of concerted effort before meaningful conversations can be conducted with native speakers.

- *Professionally well-rounded.* Given the broad scope of the job of the global executive, the TEO needs to have experience outside his or her own field. By gaining first-hand experience in a variety of disciplines, the future TEO can learn to appreciate interactions and tradeoffs, to deal with complexity, to understand the inter-connectedness of elements in a system, to operate despite great ambiguity, and to see the world from multiple perspectives.
- *Multidimensional.* A TEO needs to have lived and worked outside of his or her native culture, ideally for a series of two- to three-year assignments in two or more of the geographic trading blocks that comprise the bulk of the firm's current and future market share.
- *Mature in judgment.* The sophistication and breadth that result from international work experiences lead to mature judgment in social and geopolitical issues.

In addition to these more traditional leadership and management attributes, successful TEOs must also manifest the following:

- *Humility.* A humble TEO operates from the belief that combined knowledge and openness to experience lead to the best and wisest decisions.
- *Curiosity.* A TEO who asks "why" and "how," who wonders why people and things are the way they are, and who has an active and engaged mind, can facilitate innovation.
- *Persistence.* The successful TEO must be able to take setbacks in stride and push on.
- *Energy.* TEOs need to be able to travel extensively, tolerate long hours, synthesize masses of data, and adjust to different time zones, cultures, and styles.
- *A sense of humor.* TEOs must be able to laugh at themselves and their own mistakes.
- *A relaxed approach to problems.* Because of internally consistent metrics, a strong value system, a system that rewards competent performances, and consistent motivation, the TEO should trust that the job will get done well.

- *Ability to see oneself as seen by others.* Seeing oneself through the eyes of others allows for course corrections and second chances. This process of mirroring allows continued growth, openness, and flexibility.

Note that the foregoing description of a TEO differs from what is typical of a successful American CEO. The following composite of an American CEO highlights the differences.

> He or she is a benevolent autocrat who is very bright, trustworthy, and determined. He or she is sincerely concerned about the well-being, health, and future direction of the company. As a benevolent autocrat, he or she decides, mostly on his or her own, what's best for the company and the future course or direction the company should take. Once he or she decides on a course of action, he or she gains the commitment of constituents by using strong communication skills, especially persuasive or selling skills. He or she drives the organization by personal example and recognizes and rewards those who contribute to targeted goals. Their determination and persistence is fueled by a high energy level, a strong need to achieve and an assertive, aggressive behavior. The strength and power of convictions and actions lies in his or her extremely high level of self-confidence. He or she is a strong-willed, domineering driver who knows what he or she wants and how to get it.[23]

The preceding view of the American CEO came from a 1990 nationwide survey, and only one-third of the respondents saw the CEO as encouraging participation or being open to ideas and suggestions of other organizational members. Less than half viewed the CEO as being visionary. Since vision and openness to others' participation are critical to the TEO's success and to the global manufacturing enterprise, this divergence of vision with respect to leadership is indicative of the challenges ahead.

KNOWLEDGE WORKERS AND THE ELECTRONIC WORK FORCE

Finally, let's turn to the third fundamental human resource issue in manufacturing today: knowledge workers and the electronic workforce.

---

[23]Nationwide study conducted and published by Management Science and Development (a Pittsburgh-based management consulting firm), November 1990.

During the past several decades, as manafacturing has become more focused on adding value and satisfying customers, its success has become less dependent on developments on the shop floor and more dependent on developments in information management. Such information may concern products, customers, suppliers, or the business itself. An increasing amount of the work performed in a manufacturing environment focuses more on customer and market knowledge and less on production procedures. As the information content of products and processes has increased, the job of the manager—the traditional white-collar worker—has mirrored this rise. His or her position now includes managing that information as well as normal production. This shift has also been reflected as well in nonmanufacturing circumstances and is generally described as the rise of the knowledge worker, one whose job involves acquiring, exercising, or describing information and knowledge.

An estimated 80 percent of all workers in the United States will use intellectual rather than manual skills by the year 2000. Such people are commonly referred to as white-collar workers. Much of the white-collar worker's day is spent interacting with other people. In the past, these interactions involved face-to-face meetings, telephone conversations, or written memos and correspondence. As computers, workstations, and networks have evolved, a variety of desktop applications has emerged, and electronic messages now supplement face-to-face and voice-to-voice communications. The most popular of these applications is electronic mail.

The value of these applications is that they provide the benefits of the traditional types of communication without the constraints. The principal constraint of talking, whether in person or on the phone, is that all of the conversation must take place during the same span of time. Consequently, only those who are available during that span can participate. In addition to taking place at a single time, face-to-face discussions have the additional constraint of occurring in a single place. These limitations are becoming more and more unacceptable, particularly in organizations that have invested in computers and communications to loosen the shackles of time and space.

The constraints of time and space are mitigated by electronic mail, EDI (electronic data interchange), and computer applications often described as groupware. Each of these supports rich and meaningful communication among workers and organizations not sharing a schedule or location. Other benefits are found in improved efficiency of creation, storage, retrieval, and routing of messages and information. Taken together, these have made the sharing and use of knowledge over networks a key strategy for improving operations.

In addition to removing perceived constraints, electronic communications can enhance and enrich the communication process. Network-based communications are more frank, result in less self-censorship, bring about greater participation by all members of a group, and generally evoke more suggestions and options for problem resolution than face-to-face discussions. Also, network-based groups tend to be more innovative and contour the application of resources more closely to the problems being addressed. In part, these benefits stem from removing social interaction from the workings of the group.

Knowledge workers today are likely to use workstations or PCs and communications networks. They probably spend a significant amount of time in electronic connection with others' computers transferring documents, data files, and personal communications. The value that such workers add to the manufacturing process stems from their judgment, experience, and knowledge. And although knowledge work may or may not have direct impact on shop floor manufacturing procedures, such work has significant impact on the people, the processes, and the technology that form the organizational infrastructure of the manufacturing enterprise.

Improvements in overall organizational efficiency and effectiveness brought about by the application of process analysis and quality management programs stem directly from knowledge work and the skills of knowledge workers. More and more, shop floor changes, such as improvements in materials and equipment utilization, derive from knowledge work and the interaction of knowledge workers. In the past, the manufacturing enterprise was affected primarily by production developments on the shop floor. In the future, the organization will experience a similar degree of impact from developments of knowledge workers.

A lack of means for interconnecting knowledge workers and their knowledge bases dilutes the benefits that can be delivered to organizations. Developments in industry standard networks and network interconnections are continuing to improve local and wide-area network services. An additional benefit is that the same computing and communication networks required to link workers within the walls of an organization can also be used to link workers beyond its walls.

Significant demographic and technological trends will cause businesses to provide an infrastructure that supports off-site knowledge workers. The supply of qualified professionals is not keeping up with demand for technical resources to support increasingly complex products and services. Information technology can help improve access to this limited supply of knowledge workers by structuring new paradigms for white-collar workers and by providing new technologies to support group work.

U.S. Demographic Trends

As we move into the 1990s, several trends will affect the supply of knowledge workers and the ability of an enterprise to attract and retain good people. Staffing for engineering environments will be particularly difficult.

- *Shortage of future knowledge workers.* Demand for engineering talent and other technical skills continues to exceed the supply of available personnel. Competitiveness for key individuals will increase as corporate intellectual assets are sought to gain competitive advantage.[24] In addition, both work force population and the percentage of students entering technical professions are declining (see Figure 3–2).[25]
- *Slow work force growth.* The rate of increase of the overall work force is declining.
- *Aging population.* An aging work force will pressure businesses to accommodate its needs. These will include reducing travel time requirements, creating part-time work assignments, and providing incentives or support to maximize knowledge worker contribution. Workers aged 35 to 54—who now account for 38 percent of the work force—will represent 51 percent by the year 2000.[26]
- *Rising travel expenses.* Enterprises will find business travel and commuter costs increasing faster than inflation as the energy supply diminishes and environmental taxes increase. The cost of travel is starting to exceed the value of face-to-face networking for a global company. Between 1981 and 1990, domestic U.S. air fares increased twice as much as increases in the consumer price

---

[24]Thomas A. Stewart, "Brainpower," *Fortune*, 3 June 1991, pp. 44–60.

[25]U.S. Department of Labor, *Workforce 2000*, prepared by the Hudson Institute (Washington, D.C.: U.S. Government Printing Office, 1987), p. 78.

[26]Ibid., p. 81.

FIGURE 3-2
Three Significant Workforce Trends

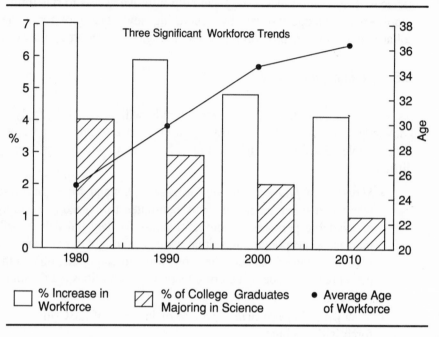

```
        % Increase in          % of College  Graduates      • Average Age
        Workforce              Majoring in Science             of Workforce
```

index (1980–1990). Runzheimer International, a consulting firm in Illinois, predicted that air fares will rise nearly 40 percent by 1995.[27]

- *Relocating employees less attractive.* The cost of relocating knowledge workers to a plant will continue to increase; relocation will be found less desirable by workers. In addition, companies will have to balance the costs of building new plants in highly desirable locations (based on tax incentives and environmental flexibility) against gaining access to a skilled labor force to operate the plants.

These trends will increase pressure for leading companies to rethink their strategies for hiring and retaining staff. The result will be the establishment of the electronic work force (EW). A combination of information system technology, business process redesign, and human

---

[27]"Smart Ways to Cut Travel Costs," *Fortune*, 3 June 1991, p. 79.

resource policy change will create a business environment for professionals in separate geographic locations to work together on complex projects.

Building an Electronic Work Force

In the 1990s, there will be some prototyping of the EW by leading companies. Large global enterprises will be the first to experiment with information technology on the viability of electronic meetings and project delivery mechanisms. Electronic mail is already heavily used by major U.S. corporations. However, unstructured work-group technologies alone will be inadequate to establish an effective EW.

Enterprises that lead in development of the electronic work force may find that they can hire and retain the best talent and in some cases reduce costs. Workers may be attracted to EW companies over more traditional commuter-enforced cultures. EW companies may need to spend less on white-collar office space.

Imagine this scenario. ABC company has spent millions on a lights-out manufacturing environment. Recently deployed technologies in manufacturing (e.g., CIM, CAD/CAM/CAE) diminish the need for on-site engineering and manufacturing support. Suppose that ABC identifies a potential new consumer product but lacks the necessary personnel to design and prototype this idea. ABC locates Ellen, the leading designer of this type of product. Unfortunately, she is taking a research sabbatical in a remote location. ABC offers Ellen the chance to design and build test products without leaving her location. In addition, ABC offers her an assignment to review similar products and make recommendations on changes. Ellen decides that this is an opportunity for her to produce an exciting new product without being obligated to travel or make significant lifestyle changes. She accepts the offer.

Cases like this example raise a number of issues, such as how to motivate and effectively manage an EW team. In addition, demand for more complex EW support (e.g., voice recordings, images, and motion video to supplement E-mail) will create new opportunities for IT vendors.

Future EW Technologies

As the corporate culture and technology evolve and benefits are tested, greater demand to support EW capabilities are likely. Several technologies need to mature and be institutionalized if enterprises are to link up with the emerging electronic work force:

- *Telecommunications.* With access to both satellite and optical fiber communication channels, past limitations of accessing voice and data will disappear. With satellite communication dishes becoming smaller, it will become more feasible to link homes and small offices, regardless of location.
- *Flex-management.* Manufacturing productivity has improved with the use of flexible tools and just-in-time inventory. The creative aspects of the enterprise could use productivity improvements as well.
- *Structured work group.* A structured work-group system could consist of some of the front-end capabilities found in project management, the graphics and dictionary support of computer-aided software engineering (CASE) or CAD/CAM, and the communications support now being introduced in the multimedia marketplace. This integration of multimedia with the formalism of project management methods could support an action-oriented work-group environment. The structured work-group system is different from the available tools on the market that support unstructured work functions (e.g., electronic bulletin boards, electronic mail systems).
- *Intellectual assets data base services.* A quicker match-up of knowledge workers with the tasks associated with new product development will be needed. This will require automation of both the internal and external intellectual assets available to an enterprise (e.g., consultants, academics). These names could be imported to a structured work-group technology that would then identify available resources to staff an important corporate initiative. Service firms (management consulting, engineering) would market access to their intellectual assets as a product.

Technology alone is not enough to create an environment that supports an EW. Corporations will have to rethink their business processes, benefits packages, and culture to take advantage of connecting to this new electronic intellectual network. Successful EW programs have demonstrated cost savings, improved morale, gains in productivity (often over 20 percent), and more effective communication among the work group.

The trust factor will be particularly important in early EW programs, since managers will have to build faith that nonvisible employees (telecommuters) are providing the necessary productivity. The organization may have to shift from management based on seeing employees to management based on seeing results. With this skill in hand, EW organizations are finding their programs straightforward to administer and manage.

In a variety of ways, EW status can be more attractive to prospective and current employees than either self-employment or more traditional employer-employee relationships. Employees often highly value an EW organization because it offers the opportunity for greater flexibility in their personal and professional lives. The high level of communication and the availability of information and computer-based tools in an effective electronic work force provide the raw materials that empower employees to be productive and creative.

In addition to worker support for the electronic work force, cost savings will provide additional incentives for enterprises to build an EW infrastructure. The EW paradigm will be prototyped in the early 1990s, gain momentum (e.g., standards, acronyms, seminars) in the mid-1990s, and be institutionalized in late 1990s and early 2000s.

SUMMARY

People are, perhaps, the most critical element in the manufacturing equation—the source of strategy, the means of achieving its goals, and the ultimate difference in success or failure. This chapter has explored three important issues associated with human resources.

Trends in the labor force show that, by the end of this decade, certain types of workers will be increasingly predominant, with women, immigrants, and dual-career couples playing more significant roles.

Existing shortcomings mandate a direction for corporation growth. Diversity ("everybody has a unique contribution to make"), discourse ("information sharing is right and necessary"), and empowerment ("motivation is a function of self-esteem and self-determination") will be essential, as will recognition and reward systems.

Although all organizations have human resources challenges, the transnational firm has specific ones, including creating a vision that keeps the entire system on track; creating a process to transmit the system's vision; creating a culture that reflects the entire organization; creating a solid foundation of cross-cultural understanding; and encouraging local innovation, among others. Critical to the success of this kind of company is the transnational executive officer (TEO), who must be a worldwide visionary, a catalyst, and a leader—decisive, but also a good listener and observer.

An estimated 80 percent of all workers in the United States will use intellectual rather than manual skills by the year 2000—we call them "knowledge workers" or the "electronic work force." They will not necessarily work on site but will often be tied to the organization electronically, transferring documents, data files, and personal communications. Improvements in overall organizational efficiency and effectiveness brought about by the application of process analysis and quality management programs stem directly from knowledge work and the skills of these workers. Enterprises that lead in development of the electronic work force may find that they can hire and retain the best talent and possibly reduce costs. But this will call for more than technology. Corporations will have to rethink business processes, benefits, and culture to take advantage of connecting to this new electronic intellectual network.

By its very nature of being physically disconnected, the virtual enterprise will depend on a well-articulated vision that pulls the pieces together around a common set of objectives and values. These values promote individual thought and contribution, which build on the strengths of diversity and enable a worldwide organization, through advances in technology, to have "hallway" conversations on the business drivers of each and every customer in their value chain.

In the two chapters that follow, we move on to the process part of the equation that is vital to our framework, and see further how their integration with human resources issues is crucial.

CHAPTER 4
MANAGERIAL PROCESSES

INTRODUCTION

This chapter focuses on the process component of our framework of people, process, and technology. Due to the wide array of processes present in a manufacturing enterprise, we have chosen to break these down into two types of processes—managerial and operational. The subject of this chapter is managerial processes. Chapter 5 focuses on operational processes, those processes that relate more to the day-to-day, hands-on operations of a manufacturing enterprise. Managerial processes discussed in this chapter include *business alignment*—how to integrate corporate and functional objectives; *information management*—how to manage and leverage one of the most crucial, yet least understood assets of an organization; and *total quality and total cost management*—how to implement superior value-added processes.

Central to the discussion of all of the preceding, and perhaps the most key managerial processes, are those related to strategy development and alignment. Strategy is a word that is often used but is difficult to define. It is derived from the Greek word *strategos* and is defined as the science and art of *military command* exercised to meet the enemy in combat under advantageous decisions. It has come to mean many other things since its inception. According to Hayes and Wheelwright, "The word 'strategy' has been used so extensively in the past decade that it has lost much of its unique meaning when applied to the practice of management. Most definitions of strategy, however, include such elements as establishing purpose, setting direction, developing plans, taking major actions, and securing a distinctive advantage. There are five important characteristics common to the use of the term in business, including time horizon, impact, concentration of effort, pattern of decisions, and pervasiveness."[1] Strategy development, implementation, and strategic controls are all key managerial processes that are discussed in this chapter. In sum, managerial

---

[1]Robert H. Hayes and Steven C. Wheelwright, *Restoring Our Competitive Edge: Competing Through Manufacturing* (New York: John Wiley & Sons, 1984), pp. 27–28.

processes, when effectively utilized and integrated with the key components of people and technology in our framework, can be a source of tremendous competitive advantage.

STRATEGY, A MATTER OF OPTIONS:
MANUFACTURING STRATEGY ALTERNATIVES

In the face of impending change in the 1990s, many organizations are establishing or reestablishing strategies that, for better or for worse, will position them for the years to come. A thoughtful and thorough review of alternatives is appropriate.

An enterprise needs to consider strategies within the context of its own organizational dynamics and core strengths and weaknesses. Assessments should be made as to how consistent a strategy is with current operations and culture. Although it is not advisable to choose strategies based solely on their compatibility with the corporation's current culture, it is usually advisable to implement strategies that do not provoke culture shock, unless "change management" methods are introduced to "grease the skids." (See Innovation Methods in Chapter 7.)

Selecting an appropriate strategy is an intensive process that will require executives to weigh the advantages and disadvantages of each alternative. Furthermore, input and leadership from executives firmly establish their support of the strategic direction and endorsement of the allocation of resources necessary to implement the plans. The active participation of senior management in the ongoing, strategic planning process provides important affirmation of the decisions made.

In assessing strategies, management should consider what is and what will be driving the organization. Is it driven by market, technology, customer, function, or a combination of these? What strategies and culture are currently in place, and how will these change over time? The chances for success are increased when the strategy is compatible with the existing corporate culture. In strategy selection, it is critical to either adapt the strategy to the culture, or, if necessary, to identify and address cultural barriers.

There are many other high-level strategy options requiring consideration and evaluation. Should a company be bearish on investments such as R&D, which creates new products, or software, which produces intellectual assets? Should it be bullish on production assets such as plant and equipment? Selecting the correct mix of investment is a challenge.

Should a manufacturing strategy orient more toward customization or standardization? What strategy will bear the most fruit when integrating new processes and products into the organization? Any one of these issues contains a variety of options and covers a wide spectrum of thought.

For many single-location businesses, the options are often mutually exclusive. A small, single-plant manufacturer would be hard-pressed to pursue strategies of customization and standardization at the same time. But in a very large or diversified company, a number of strategy alternatives might be successfully employed simultaneously, though not necessarily at the same site. All large companies today have some degree of virtual/disaggregated structure. As they diversify, they will ultimately select a hybrid approach in response to various marketplace realities.

Strategy Development

Strategy development is the search for an effective action plan that nurtures and compounds a business's strengths and competitive advantages. In the past, enterprise strategies have rarely included ideas from employees immersed in the manufacturing process on the factory floor. But in order for manufacturers to achieve business excellence, all levels of the enterprise will have to contribute to the formulation and realization of synergistic strategies. Senior management must seek out those with the best ideas and recognize those who come forward to contribute meaningfully to cost, quality, and time improvements.

During the 1970s and early 1980s, planning became formalized and corporate planning activities—and central planning staffs—expanded greatly, primarily in response to growth, diversification, and daily distractions inherent to line positions. Often, these staffs crafted detailed strategies that looked good on paper but were too distant from the realities of the line operations of the business. The corporate staff could see the grand scheme of things, but only the people who delivered the products and services—particularly those who serviced the customer—could see that more basic needs had to be looked after.

Today, most of those corporate planning staffs are gone, largely due to initiatives aimed at quick cost reduction, decentralization, or delegating decision making further down into the organization. Central planning has been largely eliminated in an attempt to align planning more closely with the operations of the business and reduce unnecessary layers of command throughout the organization.

Many of the initiatives of the 1990s that emphasize business process redesign and quality are long overdue, but they incorrectly assume that the organization has a clear sense of where its competitive advantages lie today and where they will lie in the future. The planning process must focus the organization on the basics: its customers, their needs and wants and the prioritization of programs to meet evolving customer needs. The strategy development process and the strategy itself (whether written or oral, formal or informal) provide an overall context for implementing changes that relate to people, process, or technology. These factors are the key levers for improving organizational performance.

Resource Considerations

Strategies enabled by technology and methodology, such as time-based competition, have established their merit and are evolving rapidly. When enhanced by a supportive corporate culture, these newer approaches offer operational alternatives and levels of performance unavailable in the past. Some strategies take more time to put in place than others. Some take more money. Some take more education; some, more training. An accurate assessment of where an organization stands with respect to its resources will provide the backdrop for strategy analysis and decision.

It is critical to consider the scale of resource commitment when developing a strategy. There is little value in exploring strategies that are too costly to be implemented. It is equally important to not let the resources overwhelm the strategy. General Motors, when it invested $75 billion in technology during the 1980s only to lose substantial market share, arguably let process technology take precedence over business strategy.

Just as 80 percent of a product's cost is already committed during the design phase, an organization's competitive capabilities are similarly determined via the selection of its strategy, though implementation is also important.

The number and complexity of strategies also needs consideration. If a few very powerful strategies deliver 90 percent of the objectives of a multiple-strategy solution set, the incremental value of the additional strategies must be carefully weighed against the resources required to deliver it.

A Template for Developing Strategy

The template for developing strategy has a variety of elements. Many are tightly controllable; others afford very little organizational control.

Internal factors affecting strategy include the organization's existing strategy; its current capital, both physical and intellectual; and the core strengths and weaknesses of the enterprise. The external factors having an impact are information technology; process and materials technology; competitor strategies; market opportunities; and "macro factors" such as social, political, and economic climates. Each of these internal and external factors is composed of a series of discrete subfactors. Figure 4–1 contains examples of these subfactors relevant to strategy development today.

FIGURE 4–1
Strategy Development Template

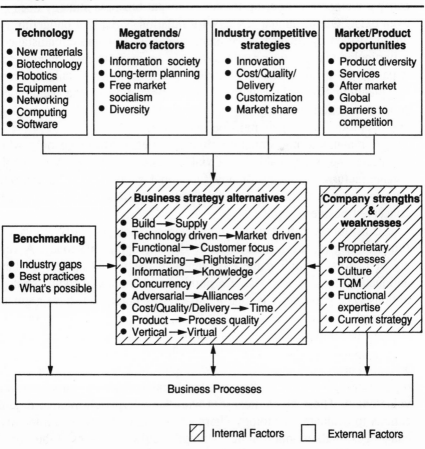

ALIGNING MANUFACTURING AND BUSINESS STRATEGIES

It is no longer reasonable, as it was in the past, to develop and implement a strategy with little more than a thorough understanding of the organization's capabilities and goals, a strong commitment, and common sense. As enterprises and their manufacturing organizations have become more complex and more dependent upon the richness of opportunity that information technology provides, developing a manufacturing strategy has become considerably more complicated and challenging than it was even a few years ago.

Yet, far too many companies still develop their manufacturing strategies in a vacuum, without regard for the market, the competition, or the organization's strengths and weaknesses. In some cases, this is done because a well-formulated, up-to-date, relevant business strategy does not even exist. Often, annual strategy formulation is really a budgeting exercise, driven by finance department demands. In some circumstances, a particular manufacturing technology is so exciting and enticing that it passes for a manufacturing strategy, while in other instances, strategic planning takes place without any appreciation of the technology-supported options. Clearly, neither situation is optimal, since technology and operational strategies must be integrated.

A manufacturing strategy delivers strategic advantage only when it reflects and is an enabler of a viable business strategy. Accordingly, a manufacturing strategy, or any functional strategy, will successfully leverage an organization's resources only in collaboration with a well-conceived business plan.

Unfortunately, past plans and strategies, though clearly relevant to future strategies, are not likely to be directly applicable today. A variety of factors, including the emergence of the virtual enterprise, have antiquated or made less viable a number of historically robust strategy options. The good news is that manufacturing enterprises have a greatly expanded set of strategies to select from, as highlighted in Figure 4–1.

As the organization and its environment have become more complex, so has strategy development. No longer just a matter of product and market issues, developing a strategy still starts at the top of the organization, but now it often involves alliance partners throughout the value chain. These allies must join with the enterprise's internal organizations to evaluate technology alternatives, industry trends, competitive challenges, market opportunities, strengths and weaknesses of the overall enterprise, and other critical factors. As key alliance partners join in the process of strategy development, the virtual enterprise begins to take form as the preferred organizational structure.

The virtual enterprise is broader, and there are more strategy enablers, because of developments in information technology, materials technology, and process technology, as well as in manufacturing and management methodologies. A manufacturing strategy that fails to leverage and account for these developments is likely to fall short.

Local and global trends—social, political, and economic—have more bearing and impact on strategy formulation and implementation than in the past, and the challenge is to take these trends into account and use them to the manufacturer's advantage. Global competition has had a dramatic impact on the level of competitiveness that most manufacturers face; and although there are more competitive strategies available today than a decade ago, there are also more competitors.

Careful assessment of the organization's internal strengths and weaknesses is the precursor to strategy selection and development, and identifying benchmarks and best practices can help an organization evaluate and assess the relative competitiveness of the strategies under consideration. In addition, judgments about the company's market opportunities and the capabilities and capacity of the organization's infrastructures must also feed into the enterprise's manufacturing strategy. With industry increasingly relying upon quality, time, and flexibility as metrics for competition, it is more important than ever that manufacturers develop strategies that serve the identified needs of their customers. Although successful manufacturers are likely to find that well-conceived strategies play to their strengths, enterprises should avoid the trap of doing only what they *know how* to do rather than doing what they *need* to do.

Matching Manufacturing and Business Strategies

The Boston University Manufacturing Roundtable found that for a two-year strategy horizon, manufacturing managers in the United States and Europe believe that their most important role in the early 1990s will be to effectively link manufacturing strategies to business strategies. The five most important improvement programs for U.S. manufacturers over the next two years were thought to be

1. Linking manufacturing strategy to business strategy.
2. Giving workers broader tasks and more responsibilities.

3. Statistical process control.
4. Worker and supervisor training.
5. Interfunctional work teams.[2]

Aligning manufacturing strategies with an enterprise's business strategy is a challenging, iterative, complex process in which business and functional strategies are compared, tested, and balanced. It is not a simple top-down or bottom-up, single-pass affair. Manufacturing strategy alignment requires assessing the strategy and its interaction with and impact upon five major organizational elements: the business strategy, the technology strategy, the manufacturing information systems architecture, the organizational infrastructure, and functional integration.

Strategy alignment involves assessing and balancing internal and external considerations. Information technology, materials technology, and process technology must all be reviewed not only in terms of the manufacturing organization and its capabilities but also in terms of the organization's competitors and the service and product demands of the market. The business strategy must be assessed in light of the manufacturing strategy, and vice versa. The organization's infrastructure and the information system infrastructure must be able to support the strategies adopted. Often, infrastructures must be revised in order to take advantage of strategic opportunities and, clearly, the opportunities must be evaluated in terms of the implications for the infrastructure.

In practice, alignment will converge upon a strategy that, though perhaps not optimal, is sufficiently optimized to warrant no further investment of resources in the alignment process. This convergence can be detected by a reduction in meaningful feedback among the organizational elements and a decreased value in improvements to the strategy. Establishing stability, balance, and harmony among business and manufacturing strategies is usually a complex process and rarely, if ever, accomplished by directive.

Developing business strategy is not simple; it is an iterative approach to aligning process, products, and functions. Benchmarking in each of these is now essential to developing strategies that truly move the company to a much higher competitive plateau. Ultimately, these

---

[2]Jefferson C. Miller and Jay S. Kim, "Beyond the Quality Revolution: U.S. Manufacturing Strategy in the 1990s," Manufacturing Roundtable, School of Management, Boston University, Boston, 1990, p. 12.

strategies and best practices will directly affect the way the company does business; in other words, they will alter the company's business processes, such as order fulfillment, new product introduction, and planning and scheduling. Successful strategic planning, whether centralized or decentralized, has three common development processes: visioning, goal setting, and defining objectives.

Visioning

Visioning is the effort of an organization and its leadership to identify the desired future state of the company, which depends on core competencies, or those "distinctive capabilities that have special value to a particular part of the marketplace." We define core competencies as being built around the integration of key processes, products, and functions.[3]

The demand responsiveness strategy of Benetton or The Limited (defined as having the right product, in the right place, at the right time, at the right price) and the on-time delivery focus of Jan Carillon when he took over Scandinavian Airlines provide clear examples of the value of a well-defined vision effectively driving strategy. Such a vision cuts across traditional functional perspectives and promotes an integrated business process orientation *focused on activities rewarded in the marketplace.*

Visioning, to be effective, must reflect the realities of the marketplace. There is no substitute for good analysis that focuses on customers and competitors to define the decision factors affecting purchases, such as, how products are differentiated from their competition. This analysis also allows an organization to anticipate and begin planning for marketplace change.

Perhaps the best approach is to continually strive to determine what an organization's customers and suppliers must do to improve their own competitive positions and then position the organization to serve those needs. Once the vision is in place, the emphasis shifts to a goal-setting process.

Goal Setting

If an organization chooses, as did Benetton, to orient efforts around a central core competency such as demand responsiveness, the challenge

---

[3]See C. K. Prahalad and Gary Hamel, "The Core Competence of the Corporation." *Harvard Business Review*, May-June 1990, pp. 79–91.

then becomes one of identifying the major components and initiatives to support that strategy. For Benetton, and for others who select demand responsiveness as a core competency appropriate to their circumstances, the initiatives become reasonably clear:

- Systems initiatives emanating from a point-of-sale (POS) environment to capture product movement data.
- Manufacturing flexibility to enable the company to respond to shifts in product, style, and color demands.
- Logistics and procurement management to shorten time-to-market.

Defining Objectives

Many of the more successful planning efforts actively and productively involve line management and line personnel, because those charged with implementing change will do so best if they have been involved in charting the course requiring that change. The process described outlines the necessary strategic direction, initiatives (goals), and metrics. The subsequent effort to develop the discrete strategies can and should include cross-functional or process-oriented teams working with management. But senior management remains responsible for defining and communicating a set of goals related to the company vision.

Once the goals concerning, for example, logistics and procurement improvements have been set, a team can isolate the discrete strategies necessary to achieve the goals and support the metrics. Such a process enables senior management to further institutionalize this critical event orientation and expand participation in the planning process. One note of caution, however: Strategies must be focused, simple, direct, and limited in number.

Strategy and Implementation

Formulation of strategy should be in balance with implementation. If a strategy is virtually impossible to implement, it is probably not the right one, at least for the moment. The simpler and less complex a strategy, the more likely it is to be implementable, all other things being equal.

Often, newer technology-based strategies offer the most adaptability. But many traditional strategies, when implemented with innovation, remain viable today. High-volume mass production and vertical integration are two such strategies. The challenge is to design and put in place goals and plans that are aligned with operations or to develop opportunities that adapt quickly and effectively to the rapidly changing conditions of production and competition.

For most enterprises, the issue will not be a choice between a vertically integrated factory and a virtually aligned factory or a choice between a high-volume commodity product factory and a custom-product factory. The issue will be matching several, if not all, models to the business units or geographic characteristics across the company in order to optimize performance across all major markets.

Many enterprises will be selecting and compounding strategies that are directed at a mix of products and operating environments. The majority of organizations will opt for strategies that are not to be found at the extremes of the spectrum. The final solution is likely to be an aggregate of strategies or hybrid of several strategies with the components being interdependent.

Once selected and initiated, a strategy needs to be maintained, upgraded, and updated. *It is the responsibility of management to persistently alter and modify the strategy, to keep it current, to keep it compelling and abreast of technology and methodology, and to keep it synchronized with the larger contexts of global competition, developments in the economy, and the circumstances of the industry.* This requires an ongoing investment in talent and resource. These activities include, but are not limited to, the strategic controls described later in this chapter.

Management Processes: IBM Canada

Often, in order for the strategic performance measurement system to be effective, key management processes must be redesigned to focus on these new measures. This requires orienting the agenda of management to these new sets of measures and redesigning the planning/budgeting process, reward and compensation systems, shareholder and employee communications, and the capital analysis and allocation processes. Such a project is ambitious, but it can be done. IBM Canada, for example, is perceived within IBM as a laboratory for new ideas. In the mid-1980s, it experienced eroding financial performance, with net income declining in 1985 and revenue flat and margins declining due to competition in 1986. Bureaucracy throttled both risk taking and time spent with customers. During this period, an initiative at IBM headquarters adopted a process-oriented view of the business and IBM Canada's organization and its management processes were redesigned.

Throughout the organization, IBM Canada adopted a common definition of financial and performance measures that focused on a dozen or so major business processes, supported by an executive information system that for the first time codified reporting across the entire organization. A program for developing performance metrics for each process was initiated, and the "Clean Sheet Management Team" was charged with redesigning the organization from scratch.

The team, composed of five functional managers rather than senior staff, developed a four-phase approach that was used to guide the reorganization. During Phase I, the CEO and the executive committee identified a clear direction for the organization. Phase II required the development of strategies in support of that stated direction. (This was done in group sessions using decision support software that helps prioritize tasks and analyze critical success factors.) In Phase III, discrete tasks were identified and linked to the Phase II strategies, which mobilized the entire organization and involved everyone in effecting the changes needed. Phase IV consisted of creating a communications plan to inform employees of the changes and their roles.

The vision established during Phase I had three components: providing total solutions to customers, empowering the work force, and providing a responsive management support system. The goal was to create a new approach to managing and measuring the performance of the business based on value-adding processes that cut across the organization, for example, reducing resource requirements and cycle time by more than 50 percent in major business processes.

The new organizational structure is based upon cross-functional teams (whose members typically allocate 10 to 15 percent of their working hours to their team responsibilities) that are assigned specific responsibilities. They are charged with identifying opportunities for change and improvement and with implementing those changes; team members are empowered with the decision-making authority of the executive committee for their specific expertise or functions.

The organizational restructuring has been completed, and the company is in the process of implementing education, measurement, and reward systems. Early results have been encouraging, with the organization going from eight or nine layers of management to five. The proportion of IBM Canada workers designing, building, selling, installing, or servicing IBM offerings (in other words, *directly adding value*) has increased from 40 to 60 percent. The CEO no longer attends meetings on topics that do not cut across functions, a measure of the heavy emphasis being placed on cross-functional integration in the organization.

Supporting Organizational Infrastructure

Changes in measurement systems and management processes require re-tooling the supporting infrastructure, whereas the infrastructure processes and the associated technology must be reconfigured simultaneously. The reconfiguration must include

- A process orientation to information management and systems development rather than a functional orientation.
- A focus on user-driven information rather than purely technology-driven solutions, which generate data but not information.
- An organizational culture that supports information sharing among a set of internal and external customers rather than "information politics."
- Analytical functions that effectively support decision making and organizational change.

Integrative strategies revolve around the processes, functions, and products that make up the core competencies of an enterprise. Strategic mapping and strategic control are key elements in facilitating communication (external and internal) and managing implementation.

Planning for Change Implementation

The best strategies are worthless unless implemented. Put another way, a grade B strategy with AAA implementation will win in the marketplace nine times out of ten over an elegant but poorly-instituted strategy. The key to success is continuing to drive the strategy planning process deep into the organization.

To plan for change, small teams are optimal, composed of staff who build or deliver products and services. The team will develop action plans in support of each strategy. For example, within a flexible manufacturing strategy, one metric might be process cycle time, with a corresponding goal of continually reducing it by a certain percentage each year. A small cross-functional target team of five to seven people, including a team leader, could be empowered and commissioned to plan for and achieve that goal.

Structurally, it is important to identify key events and supporting issues in the planning documents. These documents should include

---

Goal:	Describe the overarching goal.
Strategy:	Describe the specific strategy in support of the goal.
Events:	Describe detailed activities required to achieve the strategy.
Responsibility:	Describe who in the organization is best suited to champion the activity.
Timing:	Estimate elapsed time required to complete the activities.
Considerations:	Describe the resources required for implementation, including capital (people and equipment), training, expenses, etc. Describe barriers and critical success factors (culture, competing or complementary programs, etc.).
Priority:	Assign a relative importance to the activity—high, medium, or low.

These schedules, key elements of strategic control, can be summarized in the "performance statement" described on pages 156–157, which emphasizes that the strategy must be a persistent and iterative process.

Strategy and Strategic Control

Many organizations have invested considerable time and money in the strategy development process, only to fail at implementing the strategy. A critical component of strategy implementation is an effective strategic control process, which facilitates implementation by integrating a sufficiently comprehensive set of strategic measures with key management processes. Changes in the measurements or in key management processes, in turn, require retooling the supporting organizational and technological infrastructures.

New measurement and reward systems are critical, and they require substantial organizational change. Performance measurement systems often are used to link worker performance and compensation. "What gets measured gets attention, particularly when rewards are tied to measures," wrote Robert G. Eccles, in a *Harvard Business Review* article. "Grafting new measures onto an old accounting-driven performance system or making slight adjustments in existing incentives accomplishes little. Enhanced competitiveness depends on starting from scratch and asking: 'Given our strategy, what are the most important measures of performance? How do these measures relate to one another? What measures truly predict long-term financial success in our businesses?' "[4] Planning for and successfully implementing new systems is challenging, particularly because most organizations will find it hard to overestimate the degree of change required to implement effective, forward-looking systems.

Strategic control systems have three fundamental and common components:

- Performance criteria and metrics (above and beyond traditional financial measures) that provide accurate leading indicators of strategic performance.
- Management processes for allocating resources, communicating strategic initiatives, and evaluating performance. These must be consistent with strategic performance indicators.
- Organizational and technological infrastructures that efficiently support the new measurement frameworks and management processes.

Strategic Performance Criteria

At Ciba-Geigy, the Swiss pharmaceutical and chemical manufacturer, strategic control is seen as the connecting link between the development and the implementation of a strategic plan. The company has incorporated a formal system for tracking progress made toward strategic objectives. This system places continual pressure on business managers to take corrective actions if the process is deviating from key objectives and to provide early warning of problems to the company's executive committee.

Every four to five years, each of Ciba-Geigy's 18 business sectors (which may contain several individual business units) prepares a strategic plan consisting of long-term objectives, key strategies, and funding requirements, all in sufficient detail to allow the executive committee

---

[4]Robert G. Eccles, "The Performance Measurement Manifesto," *Harvard Business Review,* January-February 1991, pp. 131–132.

to review and appraise the plan. Particularly volatile sectors plan more frequently. Also every four to five years, a corporate-level team conducts a portfolio review of all sectors and develops a 7-to-10-year corporate strategic plan.

Each business sector's plan defines from 8 to 20 strategic control parameters and tracks these over a seven- or eight-year period. Annually, each sector prepares a two- to six-page strategic control statement that reports on progress made against the sector's control parameters, evaluating the validity of critical business assumptions, summarizing progress on strategic programs, and confirming or revising objectives.

These strategic control statements are key source documents in the annual budgeting process. They also feed into compensation programs, with a portion of senior managers' bonuses related to progress toward objectives. The goal here is not to place blame for planning errors, but to fine-tune strategies and the process of their development.

In order to be effective and predictive, performance measures need to shift beyond traditional financial information and take into account a variety of critical performance indicators related to quality, customer satisfaction, time-to-market, and relative competitive performance. The performance measurement system must also allow for consistent evaluation of performance against key strategic criteria, such as

- *Nonfinancial targets.* Indicators that allow measurement of customer satisfaction, quality performance, market share and product introduction, and process improvement.
- *Strategic initiative milestones.* Interim and final deadlines for strategic projects such as product rollouts, research and development efforts, and organizational development initiatives.
- *Economic and competitive factors.* Economic growth rates, market growth, competitive responses, demands for social responsibility, and regulatory activity—these and other external considerations that have bearing.

DRIVING NEW STRATEGIES

Shifting Strategy: From Physical to Intellectual Capital

Conditions in the 1990s are encouraging organizations to direct increasing amounts of capital into intellectual, rather than physical, assets. More often than not, this means investing in information resources and the methodologies and technology that keep information flowing into, out of, and throughout an organization. Figure 4–2 depicts the capital shift under the heading "Manufacturing Performance Enablers." It is in this context that intellectual capital (knowledge)—that is, the product of information technology and management in collecting, advising, disseminating, accelerating, and integrating people and processes—is having a profound impact. The MIT study, "Management in the '90s," which concluded that the impact of this technology is doubling every few years, implied that IT has provided manufacturers with eight times improvement since 1980; yet most companies today are conducting business on 1980

FIGURE 4–2
Manufacturing Performance Enablers: A Paradigm Shift

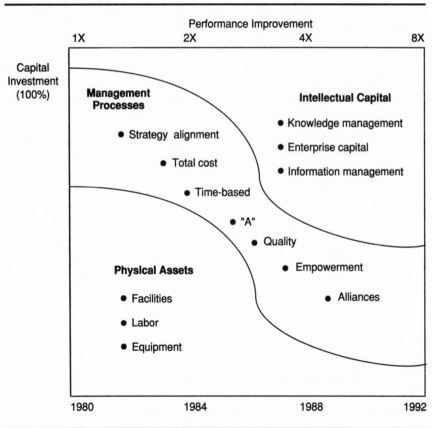

platforms and applications. Furthermore, when intellectual capital is applied within contemporary management processes and coupled with advances in facility design, labor productivity training, and process and equipment innovations, the aggregate performance improvement opportunity is even further magnified.

Companies such as General Electric, Merck, Federal Mogul (see Chapter 7), and Digital Telecommunication Group (see Chapter 7 case study) are widely recognized as well-managed and innovative enterprises. They use the knowledge base of their organizations to provide a steady stream of quality products, processes, and services. Inherent in this kind of strategy is the transfer of funds from the budgets of the industrial engineers to those of the chief information officers (CIOs), showing the reorientation of investments from site and plant toward the company's most important intellectual assets: information and knowledge.

Information has become the most valuable component of the value-added chain today, in stark contrast to the 1950s, 1960s, and 1970s. But while many manufacturing companies are very well-versed in evaluating facility and equipment investments, few have the skills and experience to make similar assessments of information and communication systems, or of the information and applications that such systems should support. Improvements in methods, processes, and products are the result of motivated, effective workers supported by well-designed information systems. With proper management, these improvements can be the source of competitive advantages that no manufacturer can afford to ignore.

Information Management

The need for more timely, relevant, high-quality information is being driven today by the increasing competitiveness of global markets and coincides with the meteoric emergence of the power of information technology. Although it is unrealistic to expect any technology to respond to the subtle and diverse needs that organizations have for information, computers are great enablers and highly efficient tools for storing, retrieving, distributing, and manipulating information. However, technology alone cannot manage information.

Information management is the relatively new practice of managing an enterprise's information resources as an asset that is as important as land, machinery, capital, or staff. Currently, few organizations apply traditional management disciplines to planning, controlling, and staffing their need for information. Instead, judgment concerning which information to provide is often unmanaged and decisions are made by default, with little leadership or guidance from an enterprise perspective. Thus, executives are more likely to receive historical, inward-looking financial and operating data than nonquantitative, forward-looking, externally-based information.

To observe how information management works in practice, here are three reasonably well-known applications whose focus is (or should be) the value of information: competitive information and environmental scanning; capturing organizational knowledge; and executive information systems. All of these applications can be viewed as steps toward the ultimate but distant goal of easy access to all the information the employee needs for superior job performance—a lofty goal that is still organizationally difficult in most enterprises, but technologically possible through better information management.

Competitive Information and Environmental Scanning

In a recent survey, at least 80 percent of *Fortune* 500 firms were found to have some sort of competitive information function in place, capabilities developed ostensibly to help corporate senior management and planners understand the policies, strategies, and products of the competition.[5] These capabilities are usually found in the marketing or planning departments (when not tied to an actual product or market group), which collect and distribute information from various sources, usually print based, and respond to user requests. The effectiveness of these endeavors, however, has been mixed for several reasons:

- The information is from well-known sources (annual reports, published articles) and therefore lacks a strategic edge.
- The information is not put into a meaningful context for the user.
- Relevant information is not distributed in a timely manner.

There are numerous ways to deal with these shortcomings. Examples include the following:

- At Polaroid Corporation, the news wires are continuously monitored by a preprogrammed scanning application. A story directly

---

[5]Society of Competitor Intelligence Professionals. John Prescott and Craig Fleisher, "SCIP: Who We Are, What We Do," *Competitive Intelligence Review*, Spring 1991, 22–27.

affecting the company's competitive environment is summarized in one or two pages, with a text added to explain what this incident means for the company, and is distributed within hours of the story's appearance.

- At a large regional telephone operating company, all employees attending industrial or academic conferences fill out a report concerning competitive information they have learned. These brief reports are distributed to a targeted audience. Knowledge of each employee's professional interests is crucial, so that nontraditional competitive information can be captured and used cross-functionally.

Learning Why Others Are Successful.   Often competitive information enters the company through competitive benchmarking (comparing one's own operations with like organizations for improvement purposes) or best practices reviews (how and why others have achieved their best rank for a function or process). Companies such as Xerox and General Electric, for example, put considerable effort into learning how other successful companies execute strategy, design products, manufacture their goods, perform customer service, and execute other key operations.

In the past, these studies were often done by outside consultants and the results were communicated only to senior management. However, in the past few years, GE has started to use best practice review findings at their own monthly courses for managers, and GM has set up a competitive war-room that permits the cars and components of chief competitors to be inspected and reverse engineered.[6]

Scanning for Maximum Usefulness.   Other information that all companies need is an understanding of the wider work environment, which includes regulatory, technological, political, and social development. Although the need for this type of information has been recognized in business for many years, it rarely is collected and used in a way that has maximum effectiveness for the company. It is generally agreed that scanning can help in effective intelligence gathering; unfortunately, most scanning results in historical information, which is received by management too late to take effective action. Also unfortunate

---

[6]Thomas A. Stewart, "GE Keeps Those Ideas Coming," *Fortune*, 12 August 1991, p. 41.

is the prevalence of scanning within a specific function (e.g., marketing, research and development, legal, etc.) without utilizing the information cross-functionally, or else using it in a serendipitous fashion (e.g., usually through random reading, conference attendance, and other informal channels).

There are instances, however, when scanning can be used competitively—for example, to gather information about an emerging technology from obscure sources and to disseminate it before it becomes common knowledge. "Knowledge about new technologies often first appears in public in odd little engineering journals," said the vice-president for development of a *Fortune* 200 high-tech manufacturing firm. He has a midlevel engineer on staff who issues a weekly report condensed from his electronic search of commercially available technology and government-funded research and engineering databases.

3M Corporation has another way of using scanning: information professionals continuously monitor the national and international patent filing data bases relevant to 3M's interests and distribute them to appropriate scientists, engineers, and executives. In some cases, all the patents of a specified firm are automatically retrieved and disseminated. Those who need information from the patent data base request it once and then continuously receive it as it becomes available.

Many Japanese companies have a strong belief in the value of competitive information, which plays a prominent role in many Japanese business processes. At the Toshiba Company, for example, the Business Information Center acquires competitive and market materials from diverse commercial and internal sources, which are scanned, formatted, translated, and distributed daily via local area networks (LANs), wide area networks (WANs), and faxes to corporate headquarters, branch offices, and factories. This system, which enjoys strong senior management support, has 600 daily users and is valued for its timeliness, scope of content, and the abstracting skill of the system's workers. Plans are underway to transmit this information via satellite to select non-Japan-based Toshiba facilities. All this information is also archived on laser disc.

Capturing Organizational Knowledge

Organizational knowledge is the sum of business knowledge possessed by a organization—its invisible assets—that is carried forward within the corporate culture and does not disappear when an individual leaves or a unit is reorganized. It is possessed by individuals, exists within both computerized and manual systems, and is embedded within corporate processes, procedures, and functions. This last characteristic is a double-edged sword, since ineffective or false knowledge can be perpetuated through "that's-how-we-do-it-here" commands.

For some time, information professionals have stated their goals as "the right information, to the right people, at the right time," but neither technology nor methodologies have been applied to the problem of identifying the information that everyone needs, because no one knows what to look for. Although technical developments like hypertext and hypermedia, object-oriented software, and very powerful data base management tools are bringing us closer to this elusive goal, ways to use information and knowledge effectively throughout the organization are still needed.

One way of better understanding the information needs enterprise-wide is to index the skills, background, and experience of all employees. Although this is a large-scale task, involving significant technical and management resources, it can pay substantial dividends for a company.

- At AT&T, for example, this resource is used to give managers a selection of employees who would have the experience necessary to work on a particular project.
- At one of the world's largest professional service firms, capturing expertise is called the *knowledge base* and the data in it is used to respond to requests for proposals (RFPs), fill openings for human resources, and to assist in general marketing.
- At IBM, information warehouses are being developed to solve problems of accessing company-wide operational data that is scattered over systems, geographies, functions, and divisions.

At a number of companies, including two Du Pont divisions, information is often clustered within functional units, divisions, and departments, as well as in cross-functional areas such as information centers and libraries or executives' offices. The company has started to map its information resources in order to create a dynamic inventory of company-wide information nodes—also a useful step toward increasing the flexibility of information management.

The Sumitomo Insurance Corporation of Japan offers another interesting use of capturing knowledge. Because in Japan it is considered vital to have a clear and fairly detailed knowledge of a potential client before making a sales call, Sumitomo has employed information workers at a central library to create profiles of potential clients from commercial data bases, reference books, and reports filed by the sales force. The profiles, which are continuously updated for company use, contain company news, financial and marketing data, and biographical material about the client's management team.

Executive Information Systems

Executive information systems (EIS) grew out of the earlier movement called decision support systems (DSS), but both approaches are founded on the observation that information is such an important executive tool that top managers should have their own system to deliver information that they determine to be valuable.

A sizable software and consulting business has grown up around EIS, developing and trafficking its specialized software and providing consulting advice for integrating the system into the organization. Yet, for all the money and effort spent on EIS, the results, as with the other systems discussed here, are mixed.

Although any number of success stories can be found, over one-half of EIS installations are not in use three years after start-up, according to estimates. Even at installations that justify themselves, organizations often express the opinion that while the EIS is valuable, it is not as valuable as was expected. For example, in many cases, it has become the electronic equivalent of a paper report, but with no change in content. It does not utilize the full power of the computer, even though it can provide communications and processing power that could prove remarkably valuable. In addition, executives get some of their information from sources that are external to the organization and are, therefore, difficult to structure for computer-based access.

Despite the literature of EIS success stories, recent research indicates that even the most successful systems need continuous rethinking and redevelopment. One issue that emerges in these studies is broadening access, to this choice data beyond senior management. This ties in with the current management trend of empowering managers with the information that they need, or might need, to be more efficient. Another emerging EIS issue harkens back to DSS days—that of using new categories of information and the more available and accessible power of today's computers to generate and evaluate more what-if scenarios for management.

At a *Fortune* 500 scientific equipment firm, the CEO has appointed a series of senior management information czars to see that internal information is used consistently throughout the enterprise and to uncover and develop new categories of information that can be used in the executive information system. This process creates a core set of universally accepted information and definitions that is seen by this company's executives as a necessity for implementing a strategic vision.

Managing Information as a Strategic Asset

Managing information as a strategic asset presents difficulties. Although the concept of information's value to the firm is rarely disputed, allocating resources for managing it can be difficult, because traditional management measurement tools and systems are not relevant for monitoring and assessing the value of the investment. "Take it on faith" is a difficult argument to make in current times.

Whereas much research has been done on methodologies to justify information technology projects, little has been done on valuing information management work. Recent thinking, however, indicates that organizational change involving new processes, policies, and procedures of information management will rely not on financial captial, but human and intellectual captial, which are often in abundant supply. What is needed is the management will and vision to implement information management practices.

As two information scientists recently wrote, "How could there be a revolution in information and knowledge going on? But the main point is this: look beyond the machines and the networks . . . the value is in the information and knowledge—that is the new prime enabler of change."[7] Clearly, information management is an important way for organizations to leverage their expertise, knowledge, and experience to gain a leading edge.

How must they go about it? As mentioned previously, a set of data (core information) that are vital to the enterprise's functioning should be identified and made available throughout the enterprise. This goes well beyond the organization's chart of accounts or typical MIS data and can involve such categories of information as quality, time-to-market, morale, progress towards strategic goals, and customer service. One of the key traditional differences between managers and employees has been the information available to them. By determining core information and

---

[7]Harry Tennant and John White, "Information and Knowledge: Prime Enablers of Change—Thoughts on Information in the 1990s," *Computing Technology*, September-October 1989, pp. 53–59.

making it broadly accessible, a company can enable employees in significant ways.

Total Quality

Much of the strategy development that has gone on in the last half dozen years has been driven by one of the vital priorities for manufacturers in the 1990s: quality. In this context, that means "continually exceeding customer satisfaction through attention to detail."

To be competitive in the global manufacturing environment of the 1990s, an enterprise must consistently deliver quality. It must permeate products and services and be inherent in design (product quality) and in production (conformance/process quality). A recent study of quality management practices at over 500 manufacturing and service organizations in the United States, Canada, Germany, and Japan found that an increasing percentage of their employees were becoming involved in quality-related teams.[8] This is not surprising, considering the variety of immediate business and shop floor issues that have fueled interest in quality.

More and more often, quality is a key point of competition, and many enterprises have developed effective quality improvement programs that also make critical contributions to other key efforts, such as cost containment and new product development. Extending the quality commitment to deliver "quality as viewed by the customer" can dramatically improve customer satisfaction. All in all, investing in quality delivers dividends today as well as in the days to come.

Total quality management (TQM) integrates technologies, methodologies, and philosophies and links form, function, and procedure. The key tenets of TQM imply a quality discipline that extends throughout the organization, which will be its best opportunity for gaining competitive advantage. World-class competitors realize the importance of total quality in their products and services because they have developed world-class organizations and mobilized them effectively.

Getting a total quality program in place and functioning well is an ongoing process consisting of the phases illustrated in Figure 4–3. As shown in the Figure 4–3, TQM starts with an awareness of and

---

[8]Ernst & Young and American Quality Foundation, *International Quality Study* (Cleveland, Ohio: American Quality Foundation and Ernst & Young, 1991), p. 30.

FIGURE 4–3
Implementing a TQM Program

Phase I	Phase 2	Phase 3	Phase 4
Top Management Awareness and Education	**Building a Critical Mass**	**Achieving Total Quality Control**	**World-Class Quality/ World-Class Competitor**
Understand need and benefits	25–50 percent of management committed quality	All employees in all departments introduced to basic tools/philosophy of total quality management (TQM)	Design quality dominates efforts
Learn and apply: • Quality improvement process • Problem-solving tools • Statistical thinking	Pilot projects (limited scope) Education in quality concepts/philosophy (20–30 percent)	Organization-wide commitment	Reorganization around key products/services, markets
Develop vision, change strategy, plans	Training in basic tools (10–20 percent)	Many cross-functional improvement efforts	Process institutionalized and self-sustaining
Form steering committee	Facilitation training (EI, team process)	Suppliers heavily involved	Totally consistent management practices
	Education in advanced tools (1–2 percent)`	TQC promotion organization/ upper management audits	50 percent plus trained in advanced tools
		Ways of life: • Customer orientation • Continuous improvement • Elimination of waste • Prevention, not detection • Reduction of variation • Statistical thinking/use of data • Adherence to best known methods • Respect for people and their knowledge • Use of best available tools	

focus on quality at top management levels. With a clear understanding of the measurable benefits and costs of quality, an education program can be undertaken. Next, senior management is trained in problem solving, statistical thinking, and quality improvement processes. Management's updated awarenes of quality opportunities supports the organization's pilot projects and builds a critical mass of commitment in the organization. Education programs concerning quality become more widespread, as does training in the basic tools and facilitating teamwork. Limited training in advanced quality management tools is available. During the next phase, TQM takes root in the organization and extends to suppliers. An enterprise-wide commitment to TQM is achieved and cross-functional improvement efforts flourish. During the final phase, people, process, and technology are highly integrated, and the use of advanced tools has penetrated deep into the organization. The organization is in a position to establish itself as a world-class competitor with ever-improving products and services.

Implementing TQM

Leadership of the enterprise-wide quality program must be capable and vigorous, because mobilizing an organization for a TQM effort is vital to indoctrinating the organization in the commitment to quality (see Figure 4–4). Change goes hand in hand with quality improvement and human nature resists change, even when the change is for the better and its impact is reduced by improved technology and methodology. Therefore, building the necessary interest, and necessary commitment can be a lengthy process, but success has its rewards for the organization.

One of the key tools of leadership is policy, which requires development and deployment; both these processes serve as excellent opportunities to fine-tune the policy to the organization and to make converts to the new policy. Policy deployment is the English version of the Japanese term *hoshin kanri* (literally, "establishing a direction"), a core system of management and total quality that combines strategic planning and implementation with daily management, cross-functional management, annual plans, management reviews, and diagnoses.

A process-oriented approach that also focuses on targets and goals is one of the key features of policy deployment, and is a major difference from traditional management-by-objective programs. Another important feature of policy deployment is the concentration of improvement actions related to quality, cost, delivery, schedule, and morale. Improvement activities are coordinated both vertically and horizontally through a total

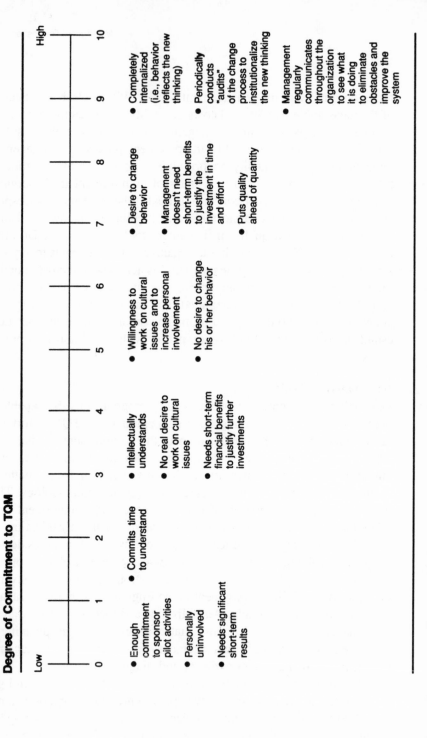

FIGURE 4-4
Degree of Commitment to TQM

Low — 0 1 2 3 4 5 6 7 8 9 10 — High

0:
- Enough commitment to sponsor pilot activities
- Personally uninvolved
- Needs significant short-term results

2:
- Commits time to understand

3-4:
- Intellectually understands
- No real desire to work on cultural issues
- Needs short-term financial benefits to justify further investments

5-6:
- Willingness to work on cultural issues and to increase personal involvement
- No desire to change his or her behavior

7-8:
- Desire to change behavior
- Management doesn't need short-term benefits to justify the investment in time and effort
- Puts quality ahead of quantity

9-10:
- Completely internalized (i.e., behavior reflects the new thinking)
- Periodically conducts "audits" of the change process to institutionalize the new thinking
- Management regularly communicates throughout the organization to see what it is doing to eliminate obstacles and improve the system

174

quality management system for daily control and cross-functional management. This forms a management network that allows the organization to react quickly to external threats and problems.

Policy deployment requires education in concepts, problem-solving techniques, individual and team roles, and the specific workings of the system. The organization's performance with respect to policy-deployment milestones should be tracked and reviewed meaningfully on a monthly basis. Performance measurement is important, not just for financial reasons but also because people want to know what they have gained from the change. Technology and processes cannot be improved without empirical assessments of performance. (Performance measurement and analysis is treated in more detail later in this chapter and in other books in this series.)

Linking reward and compensation to performance measurements requires confidence that the metrics are accurate indicators of performance. Indeed, an organization with well-founded metrics systematically rewards and encourages employee performance that leads to outstanding quality, productivity, customer satisfaction, or process improvements. Ongoing education and training programs leverage outstanding performance and provide the foundation for quick response across the organization as a whole.

Quality in Design and Manufacturing

Many quality control methods in manufacturing regard quality of design as an important determinant of overall product or process quality, effectiveness, and efficiency. Quality function deployment (QFD) is a popular methodology that formalizes and structures product and process design and analysis. "It is a planning, communication, and documentation tool that determines where energy, effort, quality improvement tools, and technology need to be applied in order to sustain the overall product plan."[9] QFD takes a strong customer orientation. "It provides a mechanism for determining customer requirements and translating them into relevant technical language that each function and organizational level can understand and act upon. It starts with the 'voice of the customer' at the concept stage and carries through manufacturing with highly detailed instructions for production process control or for how front-line

---

[9]The Ernst & Young Quality Improvement Consulting Group, *Total Quality: An Executive's Guide for the 1990s* (Homewood, Ill: Business One Irwin, 1990), p. 14.

employees will provide a service. The mechanism is generally presented as a series of related matrices and charts."[10] By using the customer to guide R&D, engineering, manufacturing, distribution, and sales, QFD increases customer satisfaction and loyalty while reducing costs and time-to-manufacture.

The benefits of a successful QFD program include

- Significant reduction in product development costs.
- Less time required to bring new products to market.
- Greater customer satisfaction, lower costs, and improved responsiveness.
- Increased productivity and market share.
- Earlier identification of conflicting requirements.
- Easier determination of key product and process characteristics.
- Fewer engineering changes before, during, and after start of production.
- More facts (real customer needs) used instead of opinions (perceived customer needs).
- Common language and common purpose among all organizational levels.

An expensive and time-consuming part of the design process is the experimentation and testing to determine, verify, and set the critical control parameters of the system. In general, with complex systems and large numbers of variables, it is neither practical nor viable to investigate all possible combinations of control factors. Design of experiments (DOE) provides a set of tools and techniques to efficiently and effectively analyze experiments to optimize product and process design/cost with minimum effort. Like QFD, DOE reduces the time to bring new products to market and increases customer satisfaction.

Design of experiments offers the following benefits:

- Brings new products to market faster than the competition.
- Encourages a team/consensus approach to design, resulting in earlier identification of potential problem areas.

---

[10]Ibid.

- Determines key product and process characteristics more readily
- Makes it easier to link design for assembly and design for manufacturing to manufacturing efforts.

Where QFD and DOE focus on the quality of design, statistical process control (SPC) focuses on the quality of conformance to design— of the manufacturing process. (Refer back to the Xerox case study in Chapter 2 for an example of the utilization of SPC. It is also addressed in detail elsewhere in the APICS CIRM series.)

Manufacturing reliability and performance are managed by SPC but are supported by total productive maintenance (TPM) disciplines. TPM, which reengineers the workplace from the perspectives of people, process, and technology, combines innovative approaches to maintenance with workplace organization and training to enhance manufacturing performance and reliability.

Much has been written about these methodologies and their practice. Each should be considered carefully when developing an enterprise's quality programs.

Total Cost Management: Process Value Analysis, and Activity-Based Costing

TCM allows companies to actively manage and control costs at every stage of manufacture, from product design through sales and service. It involves controlling tomorrow's costs, not just keeping records of costs already incurred, and it should include not only management of direct costs but also a strategic focus on overhead costs.

A successful total cost management program will

- Identify success factors critical to strategic goals.
- Establish performance measures that motivate and measure the progress of personnel, processes, and systems.
- Isolate cost drivers and costs of non-value-added activities.
- Identify activities and bases for accurate, simple product-costing methodologies.
- Align TCM information and reporting with strategic goals.

Administrative and management costs account for a growing proportion of all costs in manufacturing enterprises, making more comprehensive cost management programs a necessity. Cutting costs is not the goal of TCM programs; eliminating activities that are not added-value is the goal. The effectiveness of TCM will determine whether cost performance is a competitive weapon or a corporate millstone.

TCM is supported by two methodologies: process value analysis (PVA) and activity-based costing (ABC), which provide the foundations in methodology for process improvements.

- PVA enables an understanding of the details of each process and its associated components and attributes (cost, time, and quality).
- ABC builds upon PVA to detail and manage the costing of products, customers, regions, distribution channels, or other cost objects for profitability reporting.

Acquiring an in-depth understanding of business processes and continuing to improve those processes are the driving forces behind effective management of costs.

Process Value Analysis (PVA)

Process value analysis focuses on meeting customer requirements and minimizing cost and lead time. The customer focus drives higher quality and the reduced lead times drive the costs of processes and costs of managing those processes.

Cost management is a philosophy that belongs to everyone in the company, and it should capitalize on the knowledge and energy of all people at all levels. As a methodology, PVA provides

- A framework for understanding cost behavior.
- Support for the selection of activities within the process to which costs should be applied.
- Cycle time analysis for resources/cash conversion relationships.
- Identification of value-added and non-value-added activities.
- Identification of operational cost drivers.
- Opportunity improvement plans to link quality, operations, employee involvement programs, and systems that maximize value.
- Measurement structure for continuous improvement.

Since a business is a collection of interrelated processes, analyzing these processes and their interrelations is key to realizing business performance improvements. PVA uses several key orientations and concepts to ensure that analysis focuses on the underlying root problems rather than the symptoms:

- *Customer orientation*. Customer requirements of products and services must be clearly understood as the starting point for improvement efforts.
- *Internal and external customers*. The next person receiving the output of an activity is the customer whose requirements should be addressed; internal customers should be treated the same way as external customers.
- *Process orientation*. Focusing improvement efforts on work processes is a shorter route to optimization than focusing on departmental activities.
- *Ongoing and lasting improvements*. The causes of non-value-added work must be determined and eliminated; processes should be continually monitored to ensure ongoing improvement.
- *Employee involvement*. Involving employees in improvement efforts ensures high-quality recommendations, successful implementations, and widespread feelings of ownership.

Two overriding objectives are facilitated by process orientation and improvement: higher produce quality which manifests itself in improved quality of design and quality of conformance of products and higher service quality which can be measured in timeliness, accuracy, defects, and the ability of the products or services to meet or exceed customer expectations and requirements.

Reducing Overhead

Overhead can be reduced by eliminating non-value-adding activities and processes; by optimizing value-adding activities; by investing in activities that prevent rises in the costs of quality; by making processes more efficient and effective; and by redeploying underutilized resources whenever possible. The lower costs of managing the process are brought about by creating a leaner organizational structure, improving spans of control, delegating of decision-making authority, eliminating non-value-adding activities, and appropriately scaling management at all levels.

Each overhead activity must contribute value to the business processes of the company and be driven by customer requirements. To make lasting improvements and continuous cost reductions, the analysis of the business processes of the organization and the derivative recommendations for improvement must focus on the true cost drivers, the structural causes of cost.

Cost reductions and quality improvements can be realized immediately and on an ongoing basis through continuous improvement plans and cultural changes that

- Eliminate work activities that do not contribute to the value of the business process (i.e., unnecessary or redundant work).
- Decrease process times and minimize delay or other stagnant times of business processes.
- Improve work flows and procedures.
- Reorganize processing units.
- Configure processing areas to match the improved work flows and processing units.
- Provide additional training to employees.
- Design quality into the work process and minimize rework.
- Increase employee ownership of the process beyond those activities performed at their workstations (desks).
- Focus managers' attention on the completed successes of the whole process, not just the individual activities within the process.
- Redeploy personnel to higher priority operations and activities on temporary or permanent basis.
- Strengthen operating links and communications among process units.
- Increase the effectiveness of automation in the process once the waste has been identified and eliminated or reduced.

Costs Are Caused and Incurred
PVA begins with the premise that costs are caused and incurred in a process. Without accurate identification of the actual cost sources and process behaviors provided by PVA, the likelihood of optimizing processes is very low. The level of conversion costs (nonmaterial related costs) is determined largely by the complexity, configuration, flow design, flow flexibility, and other attributes of the process. Reduction in process costs is accomplished through improvements in process layout,

compacting design flow, synchronous processing, and the elimination of all forms of non-value-added (NVA) waste, such as:[11]

- Waiting.
- Overproduction.
- Process waste.
- Waste from defects.
- Waste of motion.
- Inventory waste.
- Transportation waste.
- Duplication of effort.

Complexity of process and impediments to flow are at the root of many nonproductive costs. When complexity or other forms of excess are automated, the NVA waste may be hidden from management attention, institutionalized, or even accelerated.

Cost is incurred at the process level and should be attached to the product as it flows through production. With the exception of a pure product-focused work cell, where the production process and product flow are virtually identical, product routings follow diverse process paths. Each process has a series of inputs, transformation activities, and outputs through which products flow. To be useful, product costs and performance measures must reflect the diversity of production, support, and management activities. The proper identification of economic consumption is accomplished by linking the operational/process focus of PVA with activity-based costing (see page 182).

Transforming Input to Output
An activity transforms input to product and service output through a process; the operational drivers are the facts, events, circumstances, or condition environments that cause the resource-consuming activities to be performed. This definition is important, for in practice there is a tendency to attempt operations and process improvement by attacking and reducing the activities performed rather than the drivers. This approach tends to

---

[11]Tom Johnson,"Activity-Based Information: Accounting for Competitive Excellence," *TARGET*, Spring 1989, pp. 4–9.

remove cost from the organization without differentiating value-adding costs from non-value-adding costs.

A necessary foundation for effective PVA includes a clear business strategy, known customer requirements, and identified critical success factors. Process value analysis has five basic steps:

- Develop a business process model.
- Develop activity definitions.
- Perform activity analyses.
- Define cost drivers and analyze them.
- Identify and develop improvement opportunities.

In sum, the basic goal of PVA is to eliminate non-value-added waste by removing the constraints to improved work flow. In practice, the perspective on improvement can be correct but the approach misguided. *PVA demonstrates that it is far better to eliminate as much as possible the causes of non-value-added waste, simplify the process, stabilize the inputs, and then, and only then, automate.*This is an important and strategic principle because it clearly demonstrates the goal of ridding the organization of non-value-added costs rather than just making production faster.

From a strategic perspective, an organization should be investing in new value-enhancing aspects of the business, divesting itself of value-subtracting areas, and optimizing the current value-added activities after eliminating non-value-adding activities in existing operations.

Activity-Based Costing (ABC)

An elemental part of any effective PVA program is activity-based costing (ABC), whose fundamental tenet is that costs are caused and that the causes of costs can be managed. Unlike other methodologies, ABC does not regard general or administration costs as fixed; all costs are attributable and allocatable to processes or products. This difference is an important one because the theory of activity-based costing has many uses beyond product costing. Much of the literature to date has confined itself to more accurate product costs without carefully studying why costs behave as they do and what can be done. Process-oriented ABC brings these all together by costing both the physical product and the process flow. The applications of processes costing in addition to product costing include

- Costing current and proposed processes as well as changes to processes.
- Costing the effects of part standardization.
- Assessing other cost objects such as customers, distribution channels, and geographic regions.
- Planning strategic product mix and business growth.
- Measuring performance and behavioral change.
- Managing investment.
- Budgeting with flexibility on activity cost.

Cost information, when available for both products and processes, allows analysis of the strategic implications of proposed changes. With ABC data, analysis of the "as-is" processes and the "could-be" processes is strongly grounded in fact and provides for accurate, more detailed, and more monitorable decisions.

There is great value to ABC analysis in designing process change and in controlling costs. If process improvements are engineered based on a flawed model of costs, there is little likelihood that the process will improve or that costs will go down. Often in such a circumstance, when the costs of the reengineered process do change for the better, costs elsewhere in the organization increase proportionally.

Integrating ABC with PVA

Some initial ABC project work can be performed concurrently with the PVA. The initial requirements for TCM (e.g., the preliminary diagnosis of the existing system and the conceptual architecture for the ABC system) can be done while the PVA is being performed, but a significant portion of ABC is built upon the foundation PVA provides.

Process value and ABC analyses offer an opportunity to educate those most familiar with the organization's performance in the PVA/ABC techniques and methods. This education is best achieved when someone with process flow or documentation experience is charting the PVA, guiding finance and accounting representatives and others in the analysis and in the learning experience. Such an approach will give the enterprise's personnel a better understanding of the process definition when it is time to determine activity costs. Likewise, during the costing segment of the exercise, the participation of nonfinance and accounting personnel will give the team a well-rounded understanding of the entire process and of the cost implications. This broadly based appreciation of methodology and organization-specific findings will pay dividends when identifying the drivers for costing output measures. For these reasons it is practical to overlap the PVA and ABC work.

The value in doing a PVA to support ABC will become more evident as the organization progresses through the methodology and confirms the postulated linkages through

- Understanding of cost behavior patterns.
- Segregating value-added and non-value-added activities.
- Defining the relevant activity cost pools based on the PVA detail activities.
- Linking PVA drivers to ABC output measures.
- Improving costing consistent with the resource consumption.

Continuous Improvement

TCM is not a program or project: it is a never-ending journey. A third principle of TCM is continuous improvement, which is critical to the sustained achievement of business objectives. A good acid test for the effectiveness of cost management systems is the level of support for this ongoing quest for improvement.

As is presented here, continuous improvement includes good performance measurement and decision support capabilities. Performance measurement is required to define the starting point (through benchmarking), to identify the route and the distance that must be traveled (gap between existing and target performance), and to gauge progress (pattern of actual performance). Decision support assists the effort by providing additional tools and techniques to assist in the design of improved systems and in the analysis of these systems' performance.

Performance Measures

Changes in the business environment and newer technology have altered how business is conducted and managed. Traditional measures are typically financial or labor-oriented with an emphasis on short-term results. Thus, such measures force decision criteria with short-term perspectives, which can lead to individual function or department optimization at the expense of enterprise or long-term performance. Short-term financial measures have been rendered less useful by changes in technology, process, methodology, and by an increasing level of competitiveness.

Businesses are moving toward continuous improvement through quality- and time-based competition, but traditional measures are not supportive of today's strategies at most companies. For example, those that tend to rely on labor-based measures make the implicit assumption that labor is (1) highly correlated with other support costs and/or drives the support costs and (2) is a highly significant cost item within the business. In most manufacturing companies, these assumptions are no longer true (or becoming less so); even in service companies, labor may be a significant contributor to costs, but it rarely drives costs.

Because they are inaccurate gauges of performance for the enterprise, traditional measures often send misleading signals to management. Increased process orientation, simplification techniques, automation, and systems integration, all of which have reduced the reliance on the touch labor, have changed the way in which we must look at our businesses.

Performance Measure Orientation

Measuring organizational performance has never been more critical and is key to improving performance for several reasons:

- It focuses attention on factors contributing to achieving the organization's mission.
- It shows how effectively an organization uses its resources.
- It assists in setting goals and monitoring trends.
- It provides the input for analyzing root causes and sources of errors.
- It identifies opportunities for ongoing improvement.
- It gives employees a sense of accomplishment.
- It provides a means for the organization to know whether it is losing or winning.
- It helps monitor processes.

"As important as measurement is, by itself it is worthless," wrote Dr. H. J. Harrington in *Business Process Improvement*. "Unless an effective feedback system exists, measurement is a waste of time, effort, and money. Specific feedback enables an individual to react to the data and correct any problems."[12] Performance measures should encourage people to modify behavior in ways that support the goals of the organization

---

[12]H. James Harrington, *Business Process Improvement* (New York: McGraw-Hill, 1991), p. 166.

and must encourage people to perform effectively (do the right things), efficiently (the right way), and in a value-adding manner to support customer requirements (for the right reasons).

A performance measurement system must

- Provide value and be responsive to customer needs.
- Improve the flow of work throughout the business processes.
- Consolidate and focus goals on the entire process rather than on subprocesses or departments.
- Move the organization toward continuous improvement.
- Manage process activities, not financial accounts.

The Performance Measures Link to CSFs

In order to ensure that the performance measures are in concert with the goals of the organization, the measurements must be specifically tied to the critical success factors (CSFs) of the business. Those measurements that are not supportive of CSFs stand a high likelihood of maximizing one area of the business at the expense of the whole and should therefore be challenged. All CSFs developed should have supporting analyses to ensure that tracking mechanisms are in place to measure progress toward the company's goals.

The Need for Financial and Nonfinancial Measures

Financial measures alone don't satisfy the objectives of performance measurement and care must be taken to adjust for any distortions attributable to Generally Accepted Accounting Principles (GAAP) reporting procedures. Incorporating nonfinancial measures linked to financial measures in order to show the effect of operational process change on the finances of the business forms the basis of a good performance measures structure.

No single measure will satisfy the needs of a business, although the total number of measures should be kept to a manageable level. Each metric will be dependent on the level in the organization at which it is reported. At the highest levels of the company, metrics such as long-term shareholder wealth, cash flow, and return on investment (adjusted) are appropriate. These financial measures will require the attention of the top management, who will also need nonfinancial measures such as market share, market image, and competitive analysis.

At the middle management level, the mix of financial and nonfinancial measures tends to be about equal. Relevant financial measures at this level include total cost, target cost, cost of quality, and product profit velocity. Meaningful nonfinancial measures at this level are considered customer service, cycle time, days in inventory, and asset deployment.

As we approach the operations level, the need for financial information is more limited. Examples of the financial measures that may be of particular interest are total process cost and activity-based costs. The majority of the measures at this level will be nonfinancial and could include setup reduction, schedule attainment, cycle time, process downtime, and non-value-added time reduction.

Within the nonfinancial performance measures at all levels of the organization, there is need for a balanced perspective with respect to efficiency, effectiveness, productivity, utilization, and quality.

Efficiency metrics address the question, "How am I doing at what I am doing?" The efficiency measure relates the planned input (i.e., standard material, labor hours, time, energy, etc.) to the actual inputs. Caution must be used in assessing efficiency, since an organization can be very efficient without being effective.

Effectiveness compares the anticipated output (specific products/ service performed, delivery time, quantity produced/delivered) to the actual output, in essence measuring what the organization has accomplished versus what we should be accomplishing. For optimal effectiveness, an organization must produce the right product or service in the right quantity at the right time to the right specification.

Productivity measures the actual output compared to the actual input consumed in the process of providing that output (material, labor, energy, capital, etc.). In other words, "What did it take for me to produce this good or service?" Productivity is similar to efficiency in that it evaluates how well an organization did at what it did and focuses on the output. In essence, productivity measures the efficiency of converting the physical inputs to outputs.

Utilization measures the use of assets in processes used to do business. Time, inventory, supplies, cash, working capital, and other inputs to the process are measured. An organization can be effective, efficient, and have high productivity but still be using excessive assets in production.

Quality addresses customer requirements and measures value-adding resources invested in the products or services performed in support of customer requirements and waste. Customers should be thought of as both internal and external.

SUMMARY

In order to be successful in today's dynamic business environment, a company must continually examine itself—sometimes simply fine-tuning its strategies to account for change, other times reinventing itself dramatically. In every case, however, its manufacturing strategies must be aligned with its general business objectives, so that company resources—human, technological, and financial—are used to the best advantage. This chapter has discussed both the selection and ongoing maintenance of the organization's strategy, as well as some of the more recent developments in strategic controls. Furthermore, we have examined the critical program elements of the process component of the framework: namely, functional alignment, information management, cost and quality management processes, and performance measurement.

In the past, strategy initiatives rarely came from the factory floor; today, it is acknowledged that leadership must come from wherever good ideas originate. For example, in the 1970s and 1980s, the strategic plan was often provided by a central planning function. Today, however, the planning function plays a key facilitation role that engages the line operation in initiating, preparing, and implementing the strategic plan.

The framework for developing strategy consists of a variety of elements, a series of internal/external factors that range from physical and intellectual capital to competitors' strategies and market opportunities. Successful planning has three common processes: visioning, the identification of the desired future state of the company (e.g., to be the best "service" widget manufacturer in the world); goal setting, which translates the vision into what expectations are implied (e.g., to have the shortest delivery time, highest quality, and broadest distribution); and defining objectives that indicate what is needed to reach the goals that have been set (e.g., to implement statistical process controls for quality).

One critical component of strategy realization is effective control—facilitating implementation through key management and measurement processes. These controls require performance criteria and metrics, management processes for allocating resources to new measures, organizational and technical infrastructures to support new measurement framework and management processes, and a reward system that recognizes behavior modification and milestone achievement.

Sometimes, the result of these measurements is the realization that manufacturing and business strategies are not aligned, and that bold action, through a strategy shift, is required to improve the organization's performance. In some companies, for example, this means a shift from physical to intellectual capital—a change in orientation from capital investments in plant and equipment to manufacturing information and knowledge (e.g., information systems that keep information flowing throughout the organization). A vital element in the success of this kind of shift is the use of information management, to ensure that the result of this intellectual investment is disseminated to whom it would be meaningful. This dissemination proceeds through tools such as executive information systems (EIS).

Another shift—but one in the course of being institutionalized over the last decade—is total quality. "Continually exceeding customer satisfaction through attention to detail" has become mandatory in the competitive global manufacturing environment. One of the most essential quality control methods is quality function deployment, which formalizes and structures product and process design integration with a strong customer orientation.

Identification and the control of costs before they have been incurred is the theme of total cost management, which enables manufacturers to proactively manage costs at every stage of the manufacturing process, from product design to sales and service. Total cost management consists of two methodologies, process value analysis and activity-based costing. These methods help organizations identify critical success factors; establish performance measurements that monitor the progress of personnel, processes, and systems; and isolate cost drivers and elements of non-value-added services. Total cost management also provides a framework for understanding cost behavior and a measurement structure for continuous improvement.

In summary, each managerial process (strategy development, strategy alignment, information management, total quality, total cost management, and performance measurement) share a common theme—that of integrating people, process, and technology in support of business vision. Because they have common characteristics and procedurally attack performance improvement, there is great synergy. An organization must be aware of these common threads in order not to duplicate effort and tax critical resources by driving independent programs. By integrating at the strategic level, the unique focus of each can be realized while sharing common resources.

The next chapter will discuss the role that operational processes play in the success of integrative manufacturing.

CHAPTER 5
OPERATIONAL PROCESSES

INTRODUCTION

To explore the issues involved in operational processes, this chapter considers the following topics:

- From factory focus to mass specialization.
- Product and process integration: concurrent engineering.
- Group technology.
- Just-in-time.
- Continuous flow manufacturing.
- QR/POS.

FROM FACTORY FOCUS TO MASS SPECIALIZATION

Many successful manufacturing strategies and organizations have built on the industrial revolution's foundation: mass standardization. They took production volume as the key to profitability; experience had demonstrated that the higher the production volume, the higher the utilization of resources.

Recently, however, competitive and customer pressures have pushed most manufacturers toward flexibility far beyond the capacity of their production facilities and organizations. To maintain or increase volume, many industries have had to diversify. Diversification has created competing demands for resources and made managing the manufacturing process much more challenging. This has brought about an examination of how to maintain mass production's economies of scale while remaining sensitive and adaptive to demands for greater product versatility and variability. One method of meeting these apparently conflicting demands is the agile factory.

The agile factory allows an organization to exploit economies of scale inherent in high-volume production while maintaining product responsiveness normally associated with focused factories. In many ways,

This chapter was written with the assistance of William B. Krag.

agility and focus are compatible. The focus could be on product type. Take a Ford Taurus, which could be blue, white, black, two-tone, four door, custom interior, standard interior, etc. The focus gives emphasis to a product line within which maximum agility is designed. By focusing on a major process (i.e., a glass factory versus a glass, metal, and plastics factory) the process design seeks out maximum agility in glass materials, size, and shape, therefore providing "one-stop shopping" for *all* glass products.

Factory Focus Alternatives

Typically, product-focused factories are manufacturing plants whose primary customers are relaters or consumers. These plants are often skilled-labor, final-test, and quality-assurance intensive, encompassing not only the more traditional labor added-value aspects, but also final customer configuration and packaging knowledge. Product-focused factories need to be very SKU flexible, combining high volume with high variability. In the automotive industry, for example, progressive factories are working toward filling customer orders, including variable features or options, directly from the factory. This provides greater customization and flexibility than the current system of prepackaged options. Often, such factories are oriented externally toward consumer satisfaction needs, distribution channel requirements, logistics, packaging specifications, and material supply availability.

In the past, a factory's orientation and degree of focus were largely driven by internal, product-related issues such as cost, quality, and delivery. Today and in the future, factory focus will also take into account external issues such as globalization, environment, financing growth, change management, and regulatory compliance. The focused factory is more likely to be responsive to customer and market needs and to employ product-specific production and business systems that optimize service-ability. It can concentrate technological expertise to benefit both products and processes. Although the focused factory standardizes equipment and infrastructure, it does so in order to create more flexibility in product output.

Implementing a focused-factory strategy often means creating many smaller factories within a larger manufacturing facility. This can be accomplished by organizing the shop floor into cells (modules) based upon the manufacturing process flow for sets of products. What once was a factory organized into sets of similar machines with conveyors supporting the flow between machines is transformed into sets of dissimilar machines physically grouped based on the steps in the manufacturing process. This approach is usually found in facilities that do not have extremely large or extremely capital-intensive equipment, either of which may limit the flexibility of shop floor configuration, or simply prove too expensive to duplicate across several product lines.

Mass Specialization

In the markets of the 1990s, manufacturers who are agile enough to produce customer orders profitably one lot at a time will lead those that can produce only in high volume. Since this is a tall challenge, an enterprise needs to examine itself and its goals carefully before committing itself to high-variability manufacturing.

To the extent that a company values product diversity and wants to extend and proliferate its product lines, and to the extent that it needs to be customer-driven at the retail design level, then mass specialization is an attractive manufacturing strategy. There are a number of circumstances where mass specialization as a target method of doing business will position an enterprise for market leadership, even if it is unable to fully achieve the goal. In general terms, being customer-driven will give a manufacturer advantages over others who are not customer-focused with respect to total costs, response time, quality, and customization. Without successful movement toward mass specialization, an organization will probably have to make redundant and perhaps prohibitive investments to deliver a broad range of products in a timely manner.

A strategy of mass specialization requires operational agility, often referred to as flexible manufacturing systems (FMS), to produce a rapidly changing mix of products in large, medium, and small lots (even as small as one item) in a consistent, timely, and efficient manner, with all products exhibiting high quality with competitively low costs per unit. These production efficiencies must be enabled by a flexible, highly integrated order entry and design system linked as seamlessly as possible to production facilities through networked manufacturing automation and information systems. Furthermore, although a variety of computer-based systems supporting mass specialization strategy are available today, mass specialization also requires the blending of business methodologies, manufacturing automation, and information technology.

Several organizations that have chosen to compete on the basis of manufacturing flexibility have implemented less aggressive strategies by decoupling major functions or services from the factory. This has often been done by moving the final order configuration and features selection closer to the customer. This strategy enables the manufacturing facility to concentrate on a high volume production of standard products that can then be configured or packaged with other selected products and services provided by other factories or value added retailers (VARs).

An organization might choose a strategy of outsourcing those aspects of the manufacturing process to manufacturers that specialize in producing the custom or integration/packaging elements. Such an arrangement would require far less manufacturing flexibility than performing the specialized manufacturing function in-house.

True mass specialization requires the careful design of a knowledge-intensive infrastructure. This can be accomplished by group technology to support the multiple interfaces and functions entailed. As illustrated in Figure 5–1, manufacturing complexity has evolved through five

FIGURE 5–1
Toward Mass Specialization

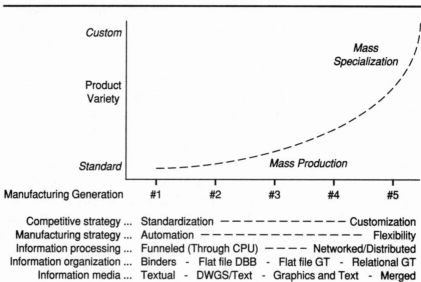

Competitive strategy ...	Standardization — — — — — — — — — — — — Customization
Manufacturing strategy ...	Automation — — — — — — — — — — — — — — Flexibility
Information processing ...	Funneled (Through CPU) — — — — Networked/Distributed
Information organization ...	Binders - Flat file DBB - Flat file GT - Relational GT
Information media ...	Textual - DWGS/Text - Graphics and Text - Merged

generations, beginning with simplicity (#1) and moving slowly to low-volume standard products, through higher volumes of product variations (#2-4) to today's most complex generation, that is, mass production of custom products (#5). Market expectations centered around custom design/service and manufacturing flexibility, coupled with the information technology enablement revolution (networking, group technology, and media capabilities), have provided the reason and the infrastructure to adopt these advanced manufacturing strategies.

Mass specialization also requires accurate, descriptive, technical data bases for all major aspects of the production universe. These include

- **Product**
  - Raw material
  - Commercial items used in product
  - Proprietary designed finished piece parts
  - Features (attributes/entities)
  - Subassemblies
  - Models and options
- **Process**
  - Machines
  - Material handling equipment
  - Measuring equipment
  - Computer equipment
  - Tools
  - Gauges
  - Fixtures
- **Support**
  - Maintenance items
  - Machine repair parts
  - Supplies (shop, medical, stationery, computer, etc.)
- **Technology**
  - Design rules (including product validation technologies)
  - Process rules (include manufacturing validation technologies)
  - Process capabilities (including speeds/feeds, precision, work cube size, etc.)

- Computer-generated time standards and standard data
- Device control programs and program modules

Note that this universe of production data extends well beyond physical items to include major categories for such product-related attributes as features and technology.

Very few companies have taken their group technology classification and coded data bases beyond the product category. But to effectively move to mass specialization requires, for instance, reuse of a computer-based library of part designs to rapidly produce new parts based largely upon previous part parameters. This approach enables piece-part designs to be created from predefined, standardized elements, with technology being leveraged to create an infinite number of end products from a finite number of inputs. Data-driven companies will not only distinguish finished from in-process states in their data bases, but will also control design and manufacturability by item and item revision level to ensure the production of high-quality, desirable, economical parts and products.

PRODUCT AND PROCESS INTEGRATION: CONCURRENT ENGINEERING

Successful world-class manufacturing companies are attacking the complex and highly competitive global market by employing time-based strategies and tactics. In the last chapter, Figure 4–1 provided a template to facilitate the development of manufacturing strategy alternatives. However, the alignment arrows between business and manufacturing strategy travel both ways; that is, it is an iterative process. Thus, advanced manufacturing capabilities, like concurrent engineering, offer a business strategy alternative that would not be considered if the process of strategy development between business and manufacturing were only unidirectional. The time-based approach to the marketplace has resulted in documented benefits, including 30 percent reductions in product development costs, quality improvement of 200–600 times, and 60 percent improvements in time-to-market. These kinds of benefits can be traced to a key tenet of time-based management: front-end loading in the product development life cycle using concurrent engineering.

A traditional product development cycle is linear: One thing leads to the next, and any changes induced downstream have to be passed back upstream to be reprocessed. The traditional product development process transforms first the product definition, and then the manufacturing process definition and the support definition. In concurrent engineering, however, the product process and support definitions are simultaneously developed by multidisciplinary, often colocated teams of experts. Concurrent engineering is built on a framework that includes integrated design and manufacturing processes, a cooperative multifunctional organization, and supportive enabling information technology. Concurrent engineering focuses on horizontal business process integration across functional lines. The product, process, and support product definitions are developed in an environment characterized by collaboration and careful multitask phasing.

In this cooperative setting, sales and marketing, engineering, procurement, manufacturing, and information technology departments all collaborate and work in parallel throughout the product life cycle to deliver high-quality, timely products and services to the marketplace. For example, marketing identifies a demand or need; in collaboration with engineering, marketing prepares the product specification. Manufacturing works in tandem with marketing and engineering in the planning stage to assess product producibility and costs. With engineering and manufacturing cost estimates available, marketing can better develop product cost and performance parameters. As a result, the design process captures the customers' requirements more completely and more precisely identifies and translates the requirements into manufacturing process design. Technology enablers can actually increase the speed with which engineering changes can be evaluated and incorporated. Thus, the use of leading-edge technology design iterations can be significantly increased in any given period of time. This enables the more careful exploration of a greater number of design/process alternatives during the early phases of the design/launch cycle time. Such work, planned and executed through the efforts of highly capable people, results in much improved launch programs from competely validated products and processes.

Timely information flow among the engineering, tooling, and manufacturing functions is a key proponent of the success of a concurrent engineering environment. The role of information technology (IT) is to provide underlying infrastructure in tools, techniques, and analysis for decision support and analysis. Accurate and accessible information is essential in the concurrent engineering process. The integration of computer-aided engineering, design, and manufacturing (CAE/CAD/CAM) data, test analysis, and simulation tools cumulatively contributes to the product and process definition. The ability to manage this heterogeneous data in a manner supporting the ultimate delivery of products, processes, and services is becoming a definite competitive advantage and a prerequisite for effective agile manufacturing.

Over the past decade or so, companies have invested significant capital resources in automation. These technology investments have improved the productivity, flexibility, and efficiency of their operations to varying degrees. Often, these automation investments have been referred to as islands of automation because they have been focused on single functions and lack readily implementable linkages to other systems and applications.

Companies implementing these independent and functionally based investments (e.g., order processing, CAD, and MRP) anticipate achieving orders-of-magnitude improvements in productivity and efficiency. Experience has often shown, however, that the gains have fallen short of expectations. This shortfall in productivity and efficiency occurs because the bottleneck in the product life cycle that the system was intended to remove simply shifts to a function that is downstream or upstream from the automated application.

Optimization of one function in the process does not necessarily lead to optimizing the overall process. The problem is not that selected functional investments are unworthy; automation is still necessary for improvement. Companies that are redesigning comprehensive business processes must, however, fully understand how changing a particular function (i.e., order fulfillment versus order entry, or product introductions versus design automation) will change the overall process, thereby optimizing the enterprise.

Simply put, concurrent engineering collapses the aggregate time-to-market by executing the product and process steps in parallel instead of sequentially. Figure 5–2 illustrates the concurrency of the business processes in the product development life cycle. In the concurrent engineering environment, product development and manufacturing processes are aligned with the way the enterprise conducts its business.

As illustrated in Figure 5–2, several tasks need to be performed in parallel or be overlapping. These tasks will surface constraints and client success factors that will serve as rallying cries for problem resolution. Information technology will serve as the medium upon which these

FIGURE 5–2
Concurrent Engineering Approach

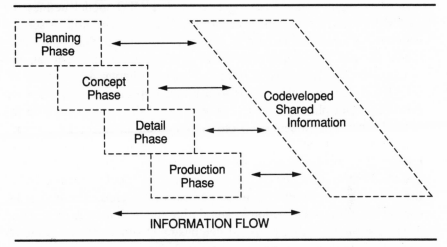

functionally separate organizations may collaborate to achieve product development. The information sharing illustrated here is the technical enabler toward implementation. However, the organizational behavior for sharing information so essential to the virtual enterprise must also be pervasive across manufacturing as well as among new product vendors for concurrent engineering to be successful.

Since the competitive imperative is customer satisfaction, the ability to translate customer requirements into specifications that the enterprise can understand and execute is the critical first step in the concurrent engineering process. Marketing, engineering, and manufacturing all have roles in formulating the product characteristics derived from the customer needs. The concurrent efforts at this early stage result in a better understanding of needs by the key departments of the enterprise. This improved product definition understanding translates into

- Better defined product specification and performance characteristics.
- Fewer design iterations due to improved interdisciplinary communication.
- On-time, predictable delivery.

The horizontal functional communication is focused on the customer. To facilitate this customer focus, a technique known as quality function deployment (QFD) should be deployed. The QFD model, also referred to as the "house of quality," establishes the baseline product understanding for manufacturing efforts. The QFD model defines the customer requirements, which in turn directly influence product specification development. The product specification is the initial control document that sets into motion the engineering, manufacturing, and support processes. (QFD is discussed in more detail in Chapter 4.)

Translating customer needs to a product specification is often the most important phase in the total life cycle of the product because the other downstream process decisions are based on this control document. Once the product specification is released, the transition to the concurrent product and process definition stage is initiated. It is during this first stage that the greatest influence on costs in the total product life cycle is made. Industry data reveals that 70 to 80 percent of the product cost is influenced by decisions and actions taken during the design stage (see Figure 5–3). A separate study by CAM-I demonstrated similar results: 60 to 80 percent of product unit cost is committed during the design engineering stage. These findings highlight the need for efficient execution of the early design and cost optimization stages of the product development life cycle. The time and cost necessary to perform this engineering optimization, procurement development, and manufacturing process streamlining early in the life cycle may actually increase with the simultaneous product and process development required by concurrent engineering. However, the benefits to be gained when considering the total product life cycle far outweigh these front-end incremental expenditures of time and money.

The Phases of Concurrent Engineering

Concurrent engineering's part in the transformation of the customer requirements throughout the manufacturing enterprise will be discussed by segmenting the engineering and production processes into the four categories of planning, concept, detail, and production. This framework will provide a structure for reviewing the concurrent engineering process approach and the applicable technologies for creating products and engineering processes in a concurrent environment. The examples used to illustrate the phases of concurrent engineering will be for discrete products; however, the models, tasks, and techniques are common to process-oriented products as well.

FIGURE 5–3
DESIGN Influence on Cost

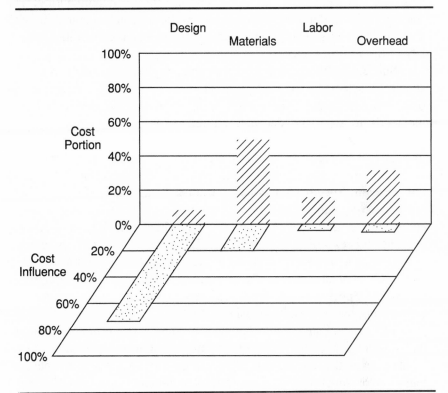

Planning Phase

The initiation of a concurrent engineering team begins with the planning phase. In this phase, the following four major activities are conducted:

- Select a multidisciplinary team.
- Develop integrated master schedule.
- Commit resources.
- Identify performance measures.

In selecting the multidisciplinary team, a strong leader must first be designated to head the project. This leader should be someone with extensive knowledge of the enterprise who is respected across the organization. He or she must be a doer and must understand what is required to deliver high-quality, reliable products and services in a timely fashion. The leader must have excellent team management and communication skills and will usually come from R&D, industrial engineering or manufacturing. The selection of a leader should focus more on these management skills than on technical skills. The project leader's management capabilities will be key to the project's success.

Subsequently, the core concurrent engineering team members should be selected. The core team should consist of six to eight members maximum; the participation of more than this number of people tends to slow the decision-making process, stifle creativity, and make project logistics more difficult. Team members should remain through the project. Marketing, engineering, information systems, procurement, manufacturing, and field support representation make up a typical team. Specific functional specialists form a second tier that supports the core team. These specialists are people with specific technical competencies that may be called on at times throughout the product and process definition process. Examples of specialists include finite element analysts, simulation modelers, NC programmers, process/equipment specialists, and materials specialists (i.e., composite, ceramics). Specialists are often assigned to support several concurrent engineering teams simultaneously.

The master integrated schedule identifies major project milestones and resources required to meet concurrent engineering team commitments. Since the concurrent engineering team requires horizontal integration of functions (i.e., design, procurement, manufacturing, and distribution), coordination of functional milestone activities is necessary. Also necessary is a level identification of the facilities and equipment required for the project, including the team's facility and equipment requirements and a high-level estimate of actual production requirements for the project.

To bolster effectiveness, the concurrent engineering team is often colocated in office space close to the production process. The team will need to have access to product and process information (i.e., specifications, geometry, analysis, process plans, and material requirements), which will often require an electronic network of terminals, PCs, printers, and plotters with the appropriate servers and software tools. Specifying these equipment requirements at the onset will help set the level of expectations for management and will speed project decision-making processes. In a similar fashion, the production facility and equipment requirements should be estimated. These processes help bring schedule-support requirements to the surface early in the product life cycle.

In this early planning phase, estimates for tooling and make-versus-buy decisions that would affect the master integrated schedule should be developed. Having these estimates early in the cycle is necessary to ensure the commitment of appropriate resources by management. A properly prepared, accurate budget—including personnel, facilities, and equipment requirements for the total life cycle of the product—helps facilitate investment decisions by project and corporate management during the critical early phases of the project.

Concept Phase

The concept phase begins when the concurrent engineering team is authorized to proceed. This phase specifically identifies the product and process domains by performing three activities:

- Evaluate customer requirements.
- Identify technology position.
- Determine design envelope.

With authority to proceed and product specifications in hand, the concurrent engineering team can then evaluate customer requirements in greater detail. The QFD model developed earlier will begin to take on more detail and help the team to refine the quantitative engineering characteristics of the product and process. Engineering's design parameters and manufacturing process requirements are discussed collaboratively. Design decisions are weighed against manufacturing's ability to produce. For example, machine tolerance capabilities are reviewed to ensure that quality parts can be made with available facilities and equipment. Design engineering is required to confirm design parameters and to identify alternatives if problems develop.

Project performance metrics should be developed by the concurrent engineering team at this time. For example, marketing may be measured on the number of contract and order entry errors made during the project. Design engineering might be assessed using measurements such as the number of engineering changes after document release, and manufacturing may be graded on first-time yield, scrap, and rework.

The QFD model, representing the customer requirements and engineering characteristics, is used as the framework to determine producibility, manufacturability, and supportability. As the concurrent engineering team works through this stage, it is in reality identifying the operating envelope and validating the manufacturing process. Even at this early stage, the concurrent engineering team (especially the leader) will have to begin maintaining a balance between engineering creativity and production capabilities. The leader must weigh engineering's ability function to stretch the product design features agains production's desire to keep new design decisions within the parameters of manufacturing capability.

Identifying the company's technology position with respect to products and processes comes down to making trade-off decisions. In the most basic of terms, the decisions are predicated on personnel skill base, facilities, and equipment, balanced against budget and timing. A technology baseline should be determined early to quickly surface needs for acquiring any necessary new technology through in-house development, acquisition, or merger. The outcome of this activity should be a formal statement of technical feasibility and technical risk exposure.

The traditional product conceptual development phase now begins in earnest with the application of computer-aided engineering, design, and manufacturing technologies (CAE/CAD/CAM). The conceptual design process should include trade-off studies and simulation analyses. A host of technologies and applications, such as finite element analyses, failure mode effects analysis, and computational fluid dynamics, may all begin to contribute to a more complete product and process definition.

Front-end loading of the planning phase and concept phase requires a shift in resources toward the earlier stages of the project. Taking the effort during planning to more fully explore design alternatives and optimize the design and resulting models pays substantial cost and time dividends in the downstream detail and production phases.

Detail Phase
The detail phase is where concurrent engineering provides the most benefits to the manufacturing enterprise's bottom line. Since concurrent engineering is a relatively new concept to most companies, many are tempted to begin to experiment with pilot programs and begin to apply concurrent engineering at this detail phase. From a total product life cycle perspective, beginning at the detail phase disrupts overall program continuity. Nonetheless, introducing concurrent engineering at this junction still improves product and process quality, reduces costs, and increases market responsiveness.

The five major activities in the detail phase are

- Product definition development.
- Process definition development.
- Product-planning definition development.
- Integrated product and process database development.
- Supplier selection and contract negotiation product definition development.

Production Phase—Computer-Aided Engineering, Design and Manufacturing Applications

Physical Part Definition Development. Creating product definition in concurrent engineering translates into geometry for parts, tooling, and fixtures, as well as associated definitions found in specifications, documentation, and analysis. Part definition can be thought of as a table of attributes that provide a robust description of the physical part. Managing these part attributes can be a formidable task. Data management will be more complex if part definition resides in both electronic and manual formats. If the definition is in electronic format and linked through an integrated computing architecture, data is much more accessible, updatable, portable, and requires less maintenance. That is why one of the hottest topics today is integrated data management.

As in the concept phase, a host of technologies are employed across multiple enterprise functions to create a product definition. The definition is comprised of parts, processes, operations, tools, fixtures, and so on. The following scenario describes how the blend of technologies supports the product/process definition.

The design engineer initializes the integrated product data base by creating a solid geometric representation of a part. A solid model is a geometric and mathematically complete representation of the part to be manufactured. In this scenario, the CAE/CAD/CAM system is a model-based system. Surface, wireframe, and flat geometry are automatically derived from the solid data base. Part data are interrelated at all levels within the data base. Thus, if changes are made to any of the geometry levels, all levels are updated to reflect the change.

The solid model is assessed using the single data base by the finite element analyst, who performs a detailed static/dynamic and thermal analysis on the solid geometric model. The solid model is a source for a wide range of analyses:

- Calculation of
  - Weights and centers of gravity
  - Surface areas.
  - Radius of gyration.
- Finite element analysis:
  - Stress.
  - Vibration.
  - Thermal.
- Mold flow.
- Optimization.
- Simulation.
- Kinematics.
- Group technology coding and classification.

The results of these analyses are stored in the integrated data base associated with and defining the part. Accessibility is controlled through a data management infrastructure.

The marketing department should remain involved during the design stage. The ergonomic characteristics of the product, identified in the QFD model and through market research, are likely to be critical to success so marketing should make sure that these details are incorporated. Simultaneous to the analysis effort, the engineering department develops several versions of the solid model on the design systems so that the marketing department can assess product ergonomics. Each electronic version illustrates different color and light schemes to depict part appearances.

Perhaps the marketing department likes what it sees on the CAD system. If a prototype model were available in a day or so to show target clients, a sale would be almost certain. Engineering creates a solid model CAD file and transfers it to the stereolithographic machine (a rapid prototyping machine). The solid model CAD file drives the machine, which typically uses three lasers to create a plastic prototype model. The turnaround for the marketing department to obtain the model is less than 24 hours. In addition the engineer tells marketing that, if necessary, the plastic model can be processed through a metal deposition process to produce a mold, which in turn can be used to create a powder metal prototype. As might be expected, marketing accepts the offer. In less than five days, a full-scale working prototype is available in this concurrent engineering environment.

Early in the design cycle, tools and fixtures are designed around the single source solid model. The resulting tools and fixtures data become a segment of product definition that is logically linked through the integrated data base to manufacturing engineering for data stream use. Manufacturing engineering has previously developed electronic data base design rules for machinability (i.e., milling, drilling, surface finish, material, feeds, and speeds), which are accessed and directly linked to the product model. This information becomes part of the product and process definition data for use in process planning, NC programming, and group technology.

Group technology is used in the engineering design effort to locate similar parts and/or part features that may currently exist. A search of the product data base is done, based on specific part characteristics. A list of candidate parts having similar geometric features is generated. With this list in hand, the designer can access the appropriate part configurations and work from a different perspective. If no matches are found, the designer starts from scratch.

Automatic generation of group technology coding and classification data is also obtained from the base solid model. The group technology characteristics are based on geometry parameters; since the model is mathematically complete, automatic generation of group technology data is straightforward. Numerous other advantages flow from the group technology capability. Output from the group technology data base will assist in determining part rationalization and identifying existing products and processes for like applications. The data base is also a source of process plans and shop floor control and plant layout data.

Simultaneously, the product design team representatives apply technologies such as design for assembly and design for manufacturability. These methods assist the engineering and manufacturing concurrent engineering team to maintain a systems focus for the design. These methods provide quantitative and qualitative analyses for design and process decisions to maintain the validity of the manufacturing process. The methods provide data that allow analysis and comparison of number of parts, assembly processes, machining rates, and assembly times.

Process Definition Development. The transition to creating the process definition begins soon after product definition. Many activities are taking place during this phase of the engineering process. Engineering data, such as parts geometry and procurement specifications, are readily available to downstream functions by virtue of the teamwork among the concurrent engineering participants and the supportive information systems environment. Additional process definition data developed include

- Fabrication plans.
- Assembly plans.
- Operator instruction sheets.
- Assembly layouts.
- Shop floor visual aids.
- Critical path analysis.
- Simulation.

Planning Definition Development. To produce planning definition data, the base product solid model and data created to this point in the product development life cycle are used in an automated computer-aided process planning (CAPP) environment. CAPP technology is used to automatically generate process plans based on product definition data and knowledge of manufacturing procedures. Artificial intelligence (AI) systems may be used to capture and leverage the manufacturing knowledge in a rule-based system that contains machine and tool information. Process planning output is linked to product definition data and to the NC programming application package, resulting in a powerful, integrated planning package for production.

During this process, the bill of materials is further refined and detailed to reflect how the part will be produced. The parts lists, bill of materials, and material requirements are developed to download directly into the MRPII procurement systems. The generation of bills are synchronized and planned, resulting in material requirements that are aligned with scheduled needs. Associated with these bills is a bill of materials generated for support tooling, equipment, and preventive maintenance. These segmented bills of materials are associated with each other. Item master data are also created for the bill segments describing

- Part number.
- Description.
- Unit of measure.

- Lead time.
- Lot size.
- Group technology classification and code(s).

Planning definition data is used to assess optimal processing time. The concurrent engineering team uses simulation software applications to validate the manufacturing process and balance operations. The CAE/CAD/CAM systems facility layout application packaging has the factory floor layout stored in the integrated data base. The data is downloaded to a simulation package to animate the work flow (i.e., robotics, material handling) of the product in the manufacture sequence.

Parameters for uniform workload, setup, lot size, and process floor layout and synchronization are accounted for in the simulation model. Analysis of optimized flow in-house and out-of-house is tracked. Preventive maintenance issues are accounted for, based on rate capability, equipment maintenance profiles, and capacity plan. They are then reflected in the preventative maintenance bill of materials that is logically linked to the as-designed, planned, and support bills.

Many of these activities are fleshed out well before final product data release. The benefits of this approach over more traditional ones are enormous in terms of eliminating non-value-added waste associated with engineering change notices, part shortages, procurement change notices, and quality assurance reports. The additional time and resources spent at the front end of the design phase results in significant savings.

Enterprise management will have to undergo a significant cultural transformation to accept the perceived risks of the concurrent engineering way of doing business. This is one crucial reason for management to be fully involved up front in the concurrent engineering process.

This change to "cooperative computing" forces change in the business process and enables an organization to become very agile (i.e., to go from "art" to "part" quickly and accurately). The opportunity lies in the ability to turn product design geometric, mathematical, and textual data into manufacturing production data rapidly. A large amount of product data is refined during this phase. Figure 5–4 illustrates the types and diversity of part data to be managed.

Initiate Integrated Product and Process Data Base. The fourth activity—initiating the integrated product and process data base—begins with creation of the first piece of geometry and associated existing data. These data come from many sections of the manufacturing enterprise, which

FIGURE 5–4
Concurrent Engineering Participation Relationship

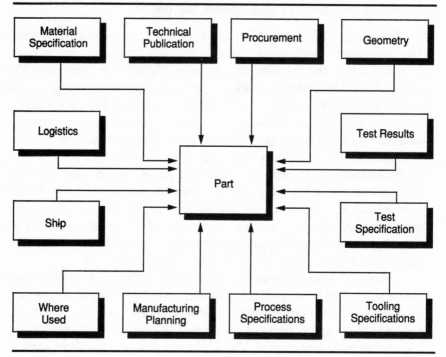

usually means that the data reside in many different forms, on different computing platforms, and under different automated and manual architectures. Effective management of the information has a direct impact on quality, cost, and responsiveness to the market. The higher the degree of horizontal integration among the functions creating and maintaining the data, the greater the opportunity for improved effectiveness and efficiencies.

A 1990 survey by Boston University indicated that the number one improvement program that Japanese manufacturers targeted for 1990-1992 was integrating information systems in manufacturing and across functions. In Europe, such improvement programs ranked fifth. U.S. manufacturers surveyed did not identify information systems integration as one of their top five improvement programs.[1] U.S. companies must

---

[1]Jeffery G. Miller, Jay S. Kim, Arnaud DeMeyer, Kasra Ferdows, Jinichiro Nakane, and Seili Kurosu, "Factories of the Future: Executive Summary of the 1990 International Manufacturing Futures Survey," Boston University, 1991, p. 6.

pay serious attention to this information systems (IS) component or risk further competitive disadvantages.

Data management is not a trivial task, but can be accomplished through an integrated and interfaced concurrent product and process data base. Companies have developed a number of systems to support the business, each designed to help manage particular elements of the business. The investment in this legacy of support systems is significant and cannot be discounted. This is why the information technology function plays a key role in the data/information integration scheme. It is important that a company leverage the ability to integrate where possible and that it interface, if necessary, all product and process definition data that have been created throughout the product life cycle.

Product and process data definition, storage, retrieval, translation, and communication is a major focus of factory technology efforts. Significant resources have been brought to bear by industry over the past several years. Standards groups are addressing the communication and translation of graphic, mathematical, and textual data across heterogeneous platforms, employing various computer applications. Several standards organizations and communication technologies have been established to help facilitate interconnectivity. Among them are

- MAP—manufacturing automation protocol.
- TOP—technical office protocol.
- OSI—Open Systems Institute.
- GOSIP—Government Open Systems Information Protocol.
- ANSI—American Natural Standards Institute.
- CALS—computer-aided acquisition and logistic support.

An overall computer architecture for managing dispersed data would allow disparate systems to communicate to provide accurate, accessible, and timely data. A conceptual architecture framed around an information engineering model is illustrated in Figure 5–5.

Select Suppliers and Negotiate Contracts

The information developed in the conceptual and detail process phases enables the procurement department to initiate the material acquisition process. During the process of creating product and process data, the procurement representative on the concurrent engineering team simultaneously interacts with the engineering, manufacturing, and

FIGURE 5–5
Concurrent Engineering Environment

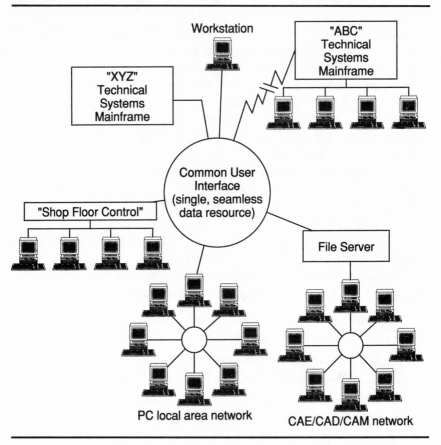

supplier base. Selecting suppliers and negotiating contracts is done in parallel with the phases previously discussed. Suppliers are evaluated on performance criteria such as technical capability, material quality, delivery performance, cost, responsiveness, and the quality improvement process on-site. As part of the manufacturing enterprise total quality management (TQM) process, a supplier certification program may have already identified primary and secondary sources.

Increasingly, new products are more dependent on embedded proprietary value in their vendor components and materials, which often requires that key suppliers play a direct role on the concurrent engineering teams rather than be represented through procurement. Furthermore, product enhancements and future innovation will also originate with suppliers rather than at the customer or marketing level, making it even more imperative that strategic suppliers be deeply entrenched in the concurrent engineering process. Moreover, the active inclusion of suppliers at the design stage establishes the customer/supplier relationship that is critical to a virtual enterprise, where customer-perceived value is the summation of speed, quality, and cost throughout the value chain.

In the procurement process, technologies such as electronic data interchange (EDI) accelerate the pace and reduce the total costs of doing business. With EDI, communication of purchase orders and payment is done electronically, thus minimizing costly paperwork and handling. But the supplier can also be an integral part of the product and process definition process. The manufacturer can use the supplier to help identify technical alternatives in the product and process definition, calling on the supplier's inherent expertise. The integrity and speed with which information is obtained and shared will establish the required technical infrastructure for suppliers' inclusion in concurrent engineering and the virtual model.

For example, a casting supplier can suggest geometry configuration alternatives that can improve cost. A materials supplier may suggest different alloys exhibiting mechanical or behavior properties better suited for the target application. The ability to share this kind of information at the earliest possible stages in design and development is worth the up-front investment required. For a supplier to be able to work in this arrangement, it is paramount that the supplier's quality standards are as high as those of the manufacturer and its customers.

Under these terms and with knowledge of the design intent, a concurrent engineering procurement representative can execute the negotiation of contracts with suppliers more efficiently.

Production

At the end of the detail phase, a build-to-production package is complete. This package—the basis for the product build cycle—contains all information required for production to begin. *The core concurrent engineering team should remain intact until full-scale quality production is validated.* If there is one point where the concurrent engineering team can be said to have completed its primary mission, it is at this juncture.

What makes concurrent engineering projects successful is their implicit recognition that the traditional business processes can be significantly improved through cooperative and simultaneous product, processes, and services developments. Moreover, concurrent engineering projects view systems and technology as common enablers to the process. Finally, they incorporate teamwork as an integral force in shaping and supporting new products and processes deployment.

Teamwork

To properly leverage the current and future systems and technologies, traditional hierarchical/functional/vertical styles of organization will not suffice. Concurrent engineering is one of several operational processes within the manufacturing enterprise that depend upon horizontally integrated teams. At a minimum, concurrent engineering teams comprise part of third or fourth generation organizations merely by the fact that they are multifunctional and integrated. Product teams have been used for years in the engineering domain; however, the revolutionary aspect of concurrent engineering is the multifunctional makeup of the team. For it to be the most efficient, though, a concurrent engineering team requires certain attributes that fall into two categories: empowerment and team rules.

Empowerment	*Team Rules*
Accountable.	Assume project ownership.
Responsible.	Mutual respect for point of view.
Authorized.	Feedback and clarify points until
Free to take risks.	accepted or understood.
Multiskilled.	Support team priorities over
Free to communicate.	individual priorities.
Possess the required resources.	Define and carry out action
Trained, educated, knowledge-	process.
able.	Submit value added and relevant
Team oriented.	information only.
Rewarded for true improvement.	Set time limit on meetings.

Teamwork is the key to the success of a concurrent engineering project. Colocating the team enhances the project's success; interacting on a day-to-day and face-to-face basis allows for quick problem resolution, synergy, and team spirit. Companies with strong traditional, functional organizations often have a difficult time working across disciplines. The long standing, arm's-length relationship between engineering and manufacturing in these companies gives meaning to the phrase "throwing the design over the wall."

Providing team-building education and training at the very beginning of a project will facilitate developing the teamwork aspects of concurrent engineering. Trained facilitators can help initiate and accelerate the team-building process. The group's dynamics and team chemistry become familiar to all players during this initiation period. This process provides an excellent example of how discourse and information sharing can lead to innovation and discovery as outlined in Chapter 3. In particular, teamwork is essential in the product and process concept stage of concurrent engineering.

To improve the product development process and the bottom line, companies need to improve their quality, cost, and time-to-market. Using concurrent engineering is an initiative that many world-class companies are taking. Further into this chapter we will visit Federal-Mogul and learn about a high-level concurrent engineering implementation.

GROUP TECHNOLOGY

Group technology is a broadly used term that refers to a concept, a methodology, a classification and coding scheme, and various analysis techniques. It is a fundamental tool for organizing products and production into families of similar characteristics, such as size, weight, material, process operation, and tooling type.

Simply put, group technology is based on two principles: (1) things that are alike should be manufactured alike, and (2) organizing parts and processes by their similarities highlights their differences. This approach brings information to the forefront for making decisions concerning product designs and production issues such as make/buy, tool selection, machine capacity requirements, process validation, and plant layout.

An extended form of group technology—organization of technical information (OTI)—broadens the purview of group technology to include organizing product-related objects such as raw materials, commodity components, proprietary-designed piece parts, subassemblies, product models, and process-related objects such as machines, tooling, and supplies. Once product and nonproduct elements have been organized, data bases can be constructed to support a variety of critical applications, including

- Rapid design retrieval to use similar items in future designs.
- Organization of computer-aided design (CAD) features by family.
- Identification of preferred drawing formats by family.
- Establishment of typical manufacturing costs by key characteristics within each family.
- Development of preferred manufacturing processes (routing) per family for both higher- and lower-volume parts.
- Development of computer-aided process planning (CAPP) systems that use data bases during the product design cycle to drive process rules to generate: (1) in-process documentation (i.e., drawings, instructions, and setup charts); (2) computer-calculated work measurement standards; and (3) manufacturing costs.
- Creation of material handling standards and practices by family.
- Introduction of job sequencing by specific production order to minimize setups, especially initial operations.
- Establishment of an analytical basis for identification and automation of manufacturing cells and flexible centers.
- Development of technical definitions of part families and features to establish NC program macros for similar machining cuts, robotic manipulations, and to coordinate measuring machine (CMM) motions.
- Provision of the data base required to develop production-balanced shop floor layouts.
- Creation of composite envelopes by families of similar items that enable the development of universal tooling, thereby significantly reducing setup time and setup support (crib packaging and delivery) activities.
- Reuse of obsolete or excess inventory for the manufacture of needed, similar items.

The combined effects of these applications enhance competitiveness and enable companies to increase employee satisfaction and product and service quality; they also reduce inventory costs and lead times.

First formalized in 1937, group technology was essentially a technique for manufacturing small to medium lots of similar parts using a small group of machines. It soon evolved into a methodology for classifying and coding parts and processes. Classification is the process of grouping similar elements; coding is the process of using symbols to identify those elements and their groupings. Since 1948, various classification and coding schemes have been developed: functional and descriptive, quantitative and qualitative, design and process-oriented, hierarchic and chain-type, and monocode and polycode.

All of these schemes share four principles:

- They must include all existing and new items.
- They must include like items and exclude unlike items.
- They must be based on definable or easily confirmable, permanent, characteristics of items.
- They must be easy to use by end users, not just specialists.

In product design applications, for example, group technology is used to identify such features as size, exterior and interior shape, composition, material, outside dimensions (location and length), and special characteristics such as precision and thread type, location, and length.

Computer-Aided Process Planning

Computer-aided process planning (CAPP) applies group technology to automatically generate the information typically found in process plans, including shop floor routings, work instructions, machining methods, tooling, cutting parameters (feeds and speeds), engineering illustrations, bills of material, time standards, cost estimates, quality control instructions, reference documents, and work center management data. In short, CAPP depends upon data-based information about products and production environments, combines this with processing science logic, and automatically generates all information needed to process and cost a product.

Today's CAPP systems are a fusion of five applications: word processor, data base manager, graphics, group technology, and artificial intelligence (AI). Two basic types of CAPP systems exist: variant planning and generative systems. Variant planning, the more common of the two, alters existing process plans to result in new plans. This type of system is similar to a word processor that alters a document found through a keyword search of a data base of process plan documents. Generative systems create new process plans from scratch using data about the workpiece, machining, tooling, routing, and other operations parameters.

Early generative systems were based on decision tree logic to organize the product and process data and to generate the new plan. Current generative systems use AI algorithms both to capture the knowledge of an expert—the process planner—and to automatically create new process plans from computer-aided design (CAD) data. AI-based CAPP typically uses object-based programming tools, structured query language, and other programming tools to retrieve, analyze, and organize production data easily and quickly, and to generate process plans. One immediate benefit of these fourth-generation tools is that operators can interact with AI-based CAPP systems using natural language, rather than alphanumeric symbols, to encode individual production characteristics and then find process information.

Future CAPP systems will feature graphical user interfaces, speech recognition input/output, and more sophisticated AI algorithms to model and simulate production scenarios. On the horizon is the fusion of CAPP with hypertext technology and multimedia documentation (including text, graphics, audio, and video). This CAPP system would enable operators to use a mouse cursor and point to any operation in a process plan to get additional information, such as operation instructions and referenced specifications (military).

CAPP is typically implemented after other fundamental engineering and production scheduling systems are in place, particularly CAD, group technology data bases of product and process, material requirements planning (MRP), and shop floor control. These other systems capture the fundamental design and production data used by CAPP; group technology and CAPP help organize, standardize, and leverage that data once it has been captured.

Implementing Group Technology and CAPP

At a minimum, creating and then implementing a combined group technology/CAPP system involves these steps:

- Determine the purpose of the classification, including type of user and application (design retrieval or process planning).

- Define the scope of the classification, including departments using the system, data to be classified, variety of data, and complexity of parts or processes being classified.
- Collect data. Initially begin with newly released parts or processes. Later, backtrack to include existing parts or processes (eventually, may wish to include prototype designs).
- Analyze the collected data to determine preliminary classifications.
- Quantify the distribution of data.
- Develop classifications that account for the entire universe of parts and processes; ensure that enough classifications exist and that each is unique.
- Optimize the classifications to distribute evenly the population of parts or processes.

Once classifications are determined, a coding system can be developed using numeric, alphabetic, or alphanumeric symbols. The coding system itself should be compact, recognizable, and adaptable to computerization. However, these three requirements can sometimes conflict with each other. For example, although a compact code is easy to enter into a computer, a human-readable code may require long descriptive strings of text and numbers.

Group Technology and CAPP System Considerations

Group technology and CAPP are still considered nonessential relative to (for example) CAD, MRP, and SFC. The reasons are many. First, implementing group technology and CAPP requires major time and labor commitments. Classification, coding, and data base building take up to two years and typically employ from two to over a dozen people. Implementation costs include internal staffing, computer hardware, applications software, and consultant services. Software alone typically sells for $50,000 to $100,000.

Second, group technology and CAPP systems have typically focused on part design applications, not manufacturing. Thus, users have been reluctant to apply these systems to process plans and production. Furthermore, a poorly designed classification and coding system for either part design or process planning helps no one. In the past, ill-conceived and poorly implemented systems have caused companies to drop group technology and CAPP implementation efforts altogether.

Third, group technology and CAPP are typically viewed as a computer system, and thus not considered managed by engineering or (especially) by manufacturing. Unfortunately, although the computer makes group technology and CAPP data readily available, implementation, ongoing data entry, and everyday use are still very much manual operations, since people are required to classify and code elements, as well as to determine what data is to be retrieved.

Fourth, natural resistance to change leads people to view these systems as tools that limit creativity in producing new designs or process routings. Users also might view group technology and CAPP as threats to job security. Both systems make data readily available to all—data that are often viewed as experiential. In addition, many users view coding as added work.

Finally, two goals of group technology and CAPP are to simplify operations and enable cellular, flexible manufacturing. Both of these goals, although consistent with today's just-in-time, shortened time-to-market and continuous flow production methods, may be threatening to traditional manufacturing shops. Thus, implementing group technology and CAPP represents a true business process redesign.

Group Technology and CAPP Benefits

By contrast, companies that have implemented group technology and CAPP systems swear by them. By grouping and easily retrieving design and production data, group technology and CAPP aid decision making, simplify and organize production, and reduce the duplication, confusion, and overall waste of time and paperwork associated with designing new parts, generating new process plans, and retrieving information. The result is reductions in overdue orders, throughput time, industrial engineering time, setup time and costs, production queue time, raw material stock, new shop drawings, production floor space, work-in-process, design costs, as well as increases in product quality, process planner productivity, and existing equipment capacity. Both group technology and CAPP promote standardization and optimization, document control, and provide foundations for paperless operations.

As a design retrieval system, group technology eliminates duplicate part designing and helps reduce the variety of parts. At an industry average of $2,000 per part introduction, eliminating duplication is profitable. For example, the group technology system at Morgan Construction Company, a manufacturer of rolling mill equipment in Worcester, Massachusetts, found about four duplicated designs per week out of approximately half a million parts and products. This saved the company about $400,000 per year in reduced design time alone, not including savings from reduced inventory and duplicated manufacturing effort.

For cellular manufacturing applications, group technology helps identify families of parts suitable for production by groups of dissimilar machines contained in flexible manufacturing cells (FMCs) or flexible manufacturing systems (FMSs). Similarly, group technology helps engineers identify common tooling, fixturing, tolerance, and setup requirements for families of parts. Together, group technology and CAPP reduce the time involved in determining part families, as well as help optimize the use of FMCs and FMSs, thus simplifying operations, increasing production, and reducing engineering and capital equipment costs.

For example, General Dynamic's Pomona Division in Pomona, California, used group technology to classify and code 4,600 machined parts, then rearranged its machine shop for cellular manufacturing. The rearrangement immediately reduced material handling requirements from 2.5 miles of part movement to less than 200 feet. Before group technology, parts required 51 machines and 87 paths; now the same parts stop at 8 machines along 31 paths. Throughput time was cut by 55 percent, scrap was halved, total process planning time was reduced by 44 percent, and direct planning time was reduced by 60 percent. The efficiency improvements let General Dynamics more than double the number of parts manufactured in the cell—yielding an overall average productivity increase of 70 percent for three cells.

In addition, CAPP in and of itself closely links design to manufacturing. That is, it institutes concurrent engineering by taking CAD data (both graphics and features) and returning accurate and validated production data, particularly process plans and bills of materials. Accurate bills of materials help ensure more accurate MRP operations; accurate process plans also help ensure more accurate shop floor control and product costing.

FEDERAL-MOGUL CUSTOMER-DRIVEN PRODUCT DEVELOPMENT PROJECT

Federal-Mogul is a diversified manufacturer and distributor of vehicular parts and fastening systems, primarily for original equipment manufacturers and the after-market support industries. With headquarters in Southfield, Michigan, the company employed 15,000 people worldwide in 1991 and had annual revenues in excess of $1.5 billion.

Federal-Mogul (F-M) has transformed itself into a truly world-class company. As was stated in its 1989 annual report, "We can only achieve this status through ceaseless improvement across the board—in our timeliness, our quality, and our service to customers." Among these objectives, time compression appeared to be the most important and was articulated as the corporate strategy. The company believed that time had become the key differentiating factor for success in the 1990s. High quality and low cost had become standards in the automotive industry through various supplier programs.

In 1989, Federal-Mogul set some aggressive, quantifiable, three-year goals:

- Reduce inventory at current cost by $150 million.
- Improve company-wide productivity by 30 percent.
- Reduce the cost of scrap and rework by $11 million.
- Double the company's ROI to shareholders to 17 percent.

These goals reflect Federal-Mogul's adoption of Japanese "pull"-style manufacturing, or "lean production" techniques. The company also recognizes that significant organizational and cultural change will be required to reach these objectives. Furthermore, the senior management team understands the value of a process perspective. They recognize that process integration is an essential aspect of improved customer service and time compression.

In 1989, Federal-Mogul had a complete turnover in the senior management ranks. Dennis Gormley became chairman and CEO of the company. He formed an Office of the Presidency and reorganized the company into four operating business units, each headed by a president. There are also a number of staff functions reporting to the CEO.

Fred Musone is president of Chassis Products Operations. When Musone assumed the presidency of the unit, Boston Consulting Group had recently completed a strategy assessment and identified a number of pressing issues facing Federal-Mogul. In certain product lines, competitors were able to bring products to market in half the time that it took Federal-Mogul to respond. Musone decided to attack this time-to-market problem head on and selected oil bath seals as the product for a pilot improvement program.

National Oil Seals

The oil seal division of Chassis Products, or National Oil Seals (NOS), manufactures seals for the original equipment and for after market. Revenues in 1989 were several hundreds of millions of dollars and are divided evenly between these two segments. Oil bath seals are a core product at Federal-Mogul, with a large customer base. In 1989, sealing devices represented 17% of total Federal-Mogul sales.

As just mentioned, a critical problem facing National Oil Seals was that the response time for its sample product development was no longer competitive. Competitors were able to provide a sample within 6 to 10 weeks following a customer inquiry, whereas it was taking Federal-Mogul 18 to 20 weeks. Moreover, the longer development time failed to yield a superior level of quality. This lack of responsiveness was threatening Chassis Products' most profitable product line. Furthermore, the product development process was like a "black hole" from the customer's perspective. Once a customer had placed an inquiry, there was no feedback and no way to determine the status until the sample product was in development.

The division's long-term strategy is to be the premiere provider of value-added solutions. This goal is articulated in the unit's mission statement: "To be the most responsive supplier and problem solver in the world in those segments we choose to compete in."[2] To fulfill this mission, National Oil Seals envisioned working more closely and interactively with customers to understand and anticipate their seal requirements. The division has now become customer driven, and National Oil Seals has integrated its product development process with that of the customers. National Oil Seals views itself as a service company

---

[2]Alan Johnson, General Manager, National Oil Seals division, in a presentation at Ernst & Young Manufacturing High Technology 1990 Current Matters Meeting.

that happens to manufacture products. It anticipates that customers will pay a premium for high-quality solutions (in terms of both product and service) to their sealing problems.

Product Development in National Oil Seals

New product development in the seals business is primarily driven by customer requirements, although advances in performance characteristics can lead to new development as well. Five categories describe the new product development requirements at National Oil Seals:

- Catalog look-up: the part already exists.
- New part/existing components: the requirements can be addressed through a new configuration of existing components.
- Same as existing part except for characteristics (e.g. dimensions).
- New application (new part and tooling).
- Iteration on above: based upon additional customer input.

For the most part, a customer request triggers the product development process for a new seal. This process is competitive, because a customer will submit the same request to each seal supplier. After receiving the specifications, product engineers design a seal to meet the customer requirements. The application engineers pass the new design along to manufacturing engineers in the plants, who design the manufacturing process. A design of the seal is delivered to the customer along with a price for the seal. The customer makes the decision based upon price, quality, and response time. Therefore, the objective for National Oil Seals is to develop the highest-quality, most cost-effective solution within the shortest possible time frame.

Product Development: Before

The former product development process was serial, with each step performed by a different department. The seals division was a typical hierarchical organization, with little capability to manage the process flow across the division. There was no overall "ownership" for the product. Each functional area was responsible for the product only during the time it passed through the area. Product development involved the following functions: applications engineering, product engineering, cost estimation, tool design, sample production, and sample testing. Each of these functions was performed at a different location. The completion of each activity and the subsequent hand-off to the next function were unscheduled and therefore unexpected by the receiving function. This process structure resulted in queues at each step along the way, creating the excessive cycle time.

Most of the cycle time problem stemmed from an inefficient communication between functional groups. After a sealing systems salesman sent in an order for sample, the form would end up unnoticed in an engineer's in-box. Blueprints sat for weeks in manufacturing. Since there wasn't any shared knowledge regarding manufacturing's capabilities, the sales force would often sell something that was impossible to make. In addition, the tool rooms and test facilities were unable to satisfy demand for their resources. The tool rooms needed to divide resources between production and sample work, which typically had conflicting priorities. The tool rooms had functioned independently in the past. Each plant acquired equipment to meet its own requirements. There was no effort made to optimize tool room usage throughout the division. The test facility received a constant flow of unscheduled and unexpected parts from various plants. There were a limited number of test stands, and it was almost impossible to assign a stand on short notice.

Federal-Mogul was using computer-aided design (CAD) systems at the time, but these systems did not improve engineering productivity. The CAD systems lacked the necessary level of numerical precision and document control. The engineers were using the systems primarily as electronic drafting tools. Although design standards had been developed, they were not being used on a wide basis and had become obsolete. Furthermore, communication between design and tool making software was inadequate to quickly machine parts. Engineers sometimes revised the wrong document, and these errors were not discovered until much later in the process. There was no way to share drawing images electronically. Communication between the application and manufacturing engineers meant shipping paper documents back and forth.

Customer-Driven Product Development Project

As discussed previously, the sample product development process in the seals division took on average 18 to 20 weeks. The inability to respond quickly to customer requests was resulting in a substantial loss of market share. Customers were often coming to Federal-Mogul as a second choice, only after one of its competitors had failed. Fred Musone knew that the lack of responsiveness was not merely threatening the division's competitive position, it had become a matter of survival. According to Larry Smith, MIS manager, "We saw that if it continued the seal group would be out of business."[3]

Management knew action was necessary to rectify this situation. Therefore, a "Customer-Driven Product Development" (CDPD) project was initiated. The goal of the project was to improve all aspects of the product development process. Specific project objectives were to:

- Reduce design time to be better than that of competitors.
- Enhance responsiveness to customers.
- Track sample process.
- Generate price estimates for customers in a short time frame.

Musone looked externally for assistance with this effort. He recognized that Federal-Mogul did not possess all of the skills needed to quickly execute the project, and where they did exist, it was not feasible to reploy them from other important assignments. He also recognized the value of using a consulting firm as a change agent in challenging projects. He selected Ernst & Young to assist with this project, partially because the firm was familiar with the current product development process as the result of a network architecture project. The analysis from that previous project was used for the Customer-Driven Product Development project and came to be known as the "AS IS" model.

Federal-Mogul managers had originally envisioned that an information technology solution would address the majority of the product development problems. They thought that the installation of a network would solve the cycle time problems by enabling electronic transmittal of various documents. However, based upon discussions of other companies' experiences in similar situations, the group began to understand that technology was only the enabler and that technology changes needed to be coupled with process work flow improvements and organizational changes in order to yield the improvements that Federal-Mogul wanted.

The Customer-Driven Product Development project was implemented over the course of 19 months, from May 1989 to December 1990, and was implemented in six phases:

---

[3]Stephen Kreider Yoder, "Putting It All Together," in "Workplace Higher Tech," supplement to *Wall Street Journal*, June 4, 1990.

- Preliminary analysis—the objectives of this phase were to identify short-term improvements to the process and develop a high-level depiction of the future process.
- Requirements definition—the goal of this phase was to add the detail to the high-level future model and develop systems requirements.
- Tool room rationalization—the objective of this phase was to analyze current tool room operations and suggest a more appropriate operating process.
- Package selection and contract negotiation.
- Installation and training.
- Pilot.

The core project team was composed of Federal-Mogul personnel, external consultants, and an automotive industry researcher from the University of Michigan. Staffing of the key Federal-Mogul roles was accomplished by an interviewing and screening process. Federal-Mogul selected a number of candidates, who were then interviewed before being selected to join the team. In most cases, this project provided a unique opportunity for some Federal-Mogul employees to step out of their everyday roles. The core project team possessed a number of skills, most prominently product engineering and systems development.

A number of other cross-functional teams were formed to develop requirements for the various information systems. The division's senior managers were asked to pick their top people for these teams. The time commitment for these team members was approximately six two-day meetings. The core team members served as facilitators for these team meetings. The core team was also responsible for issuing high-level technology guidelines to be used by these teams in their work.

The overall solution combined enhancements to the process structure, organization, and information to meet the desired objectives. The next sections discuss the specific project outcomes with respect to the redesigned and improved process, changes to the organization, and enabling information technology.

Process

As part of the project, the product development process was redesigned. First, the process was pared down to essential activities through the elimination of non-value-adding tasks. Then the team focused on improving the remaining process activities. The configuration of the entire process was also examined. Wherever possible, activities that had previously been performed sequentially were redesigned to be executed concurrently. It is interesting to note that the new process actually contains a few more activities than the original process.

Part of the solution also focused on improving the product design activities. In particular, the core team looked at how Federal-Mogul had been using CAD technology and found that they could reduce design time by making some changes. National Oil Seals had been using a CAD system for some time but had implemented the system without taking advantage of its capabilities. Since the company hadn't altered the process, the CAD system was essentially being used as a computer-aided drafting tool. The core team was able to improve the design process by developing a generic model containing the CAD parameters and the relationships between the parameters for each product family. In this way, they were able to automate as much as 80 percent of the design work.

A manufacturing/process review step was added to the process prior to issuing customer part prints and price quotes. In the past, the plants and manufacturing engineers were not included in the product development loop because the product engineers were measured on throughput. Because the product engineers are located in Southfield, it took too much time to send the design out to the plants to have it reviewed. As a result, sometimes the products that were designed could not be manufactured. With the installation of a network connecting the plants and the groups in Southfield, the product engineers can now quickly and easily share the designs with the manufacturing engineers. This new step ensures the manufacturabilty of the resulting design.

Another aspect of the new process design was extending the process beyond Federal-Mogul's organizational boundaries into the customer's organization. Although this aspect of the new process design was not implemented during the first phase of the project, customers will soon be able to access a Federal-Mogul data base containing product performance specifications and design information to perform "same as except" inquiries. In essence, the customer can then assume responsibility for one of the first steps in the product development process, a task now performed by design engineers. No other company provides this capability at the present time. It is anticipated that this feature will provide Federal-Mogul with considerable competitive advantage.

Interestingly, the changes in the oil bath seals product development process have eliminated the need for sales forecasting. According to the

Federal-Mogul 1990 annual report, "Our lead times with this product line are so responsive that we can link our manufacturing processes directly to our distribution network. In other words, product is made as it is needed for replenishment."

Another aspect of the process redesign and improvement was the creation of a "virtual tool room." Federal-Mogul was interested in increasing the capital utilization of NOS's three domestic tool rooms, all geographically separated, and all performing relatively similar work. First, the team analyzed the products produced, the skill sets and systems utilized, and the machining capabilities employed. They determined which tool room skills were unique and provided competitive advantage, which were widespread, and which fell somewhere in between. To validate tool room pricing accuracy and explore potentials for using outside tool room services, an extensive outsourcing analysis was performed to study the division's other tool rooms, other tool rooms within Federal-Mogul, and commercially available services.

The total capacity analysis resulted in a refocusing of tool room missions to minimize capital and human redundancy and better focus technical and fabrication expertise. The tool rooms were combined into one organization and are now scheduled and controlled centrally. One tool room was refocused from full service to maintenance only. As part of this conversion, tool development previously performed at this tool room was transferred to the other two full-service tool rooms. Libraries of common tool path NC programs were established to further increase responsiveness. Operator skills were enhanced by training in problem solving, computer operations, and NC programming areas. The final result was a tool room network that minimized capital and human redundancy while dramatically improving production throughput from 50 days to only $4\frac{1}{2}$ days.

Organization

The organizational enablers in the Customer-Driven Product Development project are the formation of Business Unit Teams and the change-oriented culture.

Business Unit Teams
One of the project outcomes was the formation of Business Unit Teams. These cross-functional teams are an organizational solution for dealing with the ineffective communication across functions. The teams are also

a mechanism for pushing decision making down to the operating level. Each team services everything associated with one product family. They are responsible for responding to customer inquiries and sample requests through delivery to the customer, and they are also held accountable for sample quality. A Business Unit Team makes the pricing decision, and is responsible for completely responding to a customer inquiry for a new product. In many regards, the teams act as autonomous businesses.

These teams are essentially self-managed, although in almost every case the team has selected a team leader. The teams typically chose one member who possesses leadership skills and talents. The Business Unit Teams exist within the hierarchical reporting structure in National Oil Seals. As with the other components of the project, the Business Unit Teams were introduced on a pilot basis. There are now eight Business Unit Teams in the division.

The teams are cross-functional, with representatives from sales, product engineering, manufacturing engineering, distribution, and testing. The teams are also "diagonal," in the sense that the members are at different levels within the organization. Yet, all members are peers on the teams. Some of the division's functions, such as design, plant layout, and costing, are not represented on teams due to limited resources. These groups support all of the teams. Due to the scarce nature of these shared resources, teams have to negotiate among themselves to have their work scheduled.

When the Business Unit Teams were first implemented, they met on a monthly basis. The frequency of formal meetings has since decreased, but team members do communicate very frequently, through phone conversations and the like. Each Business Unit Team has a quarterly business review with Fred Musone and Alan Johnson, general manager of sealing systems, to evaluate progress relative to the team's business plan.

Teams did not receive any special team-building training, although most had previously attended problem solving skills classes. These classes were not offered in conjunction with this project, but were part of Federal-Mogul's normal education curriculum.

Change Culture
Federal-Mogul senior executives have been creating an atmosphere of change for some time. Chairman Dennis Gormley often urges employees to start with a "clean sheet of paper" when attempting to solve critical business problems.

User ownership/involvement was a key aspect of the CDPD project. The entire seals organization was informed of the project and its importance to Federal-Mogul. At the beginning of the project, Fred Musone visited each factory and spoke with the employees on all shifts about the importance of the project to the success and survival of the oil seals business. In addition, senior managers were asked to place their best people on the teams, and everyone responded in kind.

Information Technology

Information technology (IT) was viewed as an enabling tool in this project. The technology components were one way to facilitate the process communications that needed to occur in order to reduce overall cycle time. The major systems were a CAD/CAM system and an Engineering Data Manager, as well as a scheduling system and a cost estimation system. Another important aspect of the enabling technology was the installation of a communications network linking the plants and headquarters.

The requirements for the various aspects of the IT solutions were developed by a number of technology teams, as mentioned previously. These teams were responsible for developing requirements, contributing to the RFP, evaluating vendor responses, and participating in the vendor selection for various components of the technology. The project team believes that a critical success factor in this area was establishing standards and guidelines on hardware to be used in software selection to ensure eventual integration and connectivity. These guidelines represent a technology architectural vision based upon heterogeneous open systems, workstations, UNIX and X.25 wide-area networks. The Engineering Data Manager successfully employs technologies from a variety of hardware vendors: IBM-compatible PCs, Sun and HP workstations, and Macintoshes.

Federal-Mogul has dramatically reduced the time it takes to design a die, from 8 hours to 15 minutes. The key to the time reduction is that the old process involved designing everything three times. With the new system, all functions share a model and modify it as needed.

The Engineering Data Manager is comprised of several components that all share an Informix data base. The applications include

- Storyboard—a process manager.
- Vault—used for drawing control.

- Status—used to monitor the status of an inquiry/sample order.
- Inquiry and sample order entry.
- Part and product data base.

Storyboard is the process management, or work flow software. This software routes the inquiry to the appropriate individual at each step of the process. For example, the salesperson receives an inquiry from the customer. Although some salespeople enter inquiries directly into the system via PC and modem, most complete an inquiry form that is faxed to headquarters, where a sales clerk enters the inquiry. Once the inquiry is in the data base, Storyboard picks it up and routes it to the correct person over the network. First, the inquiry goes to the design engineer, who develops a CAD drawing. After the CAD drawing is completed, Storyboard prompts the cost estimator and a manufacturing engineer at a plant. In fact, the system automatically sends the completed CAD drawing to the plotter at the plant. If changes need to be made to the design, the design engineer and manufacturing engineer usually confer via phone while looking at the same image on the system. Once the design and price estimates are completed, the salesperson is notified. This process used to take 3 to 6 weeks. The target is now 8 business days and the average cycle time is 12 business days.

The process is defined in Storyboard using rudimentary tasks, some of which are predefined by the software. As part of the CDPD project, each Business Unit Team defined the specific process for its product line using the high level "TO BE" model as a guideline. For each process, there are also subprocesses. The task is the lowest unit of work. For each task, the inputs, outputs, and role that is responsible for the task were identified. The Business Unit Team roles are defined generically — sales, design engineer, manufacturing engineering, and so on—and there is a table identifying the individuals filling those roles. The Storyboard tracks information about the process, such as inquiry number or drawing number, but does not contain the electronic inquiry or design.

When a person logs on, Storyboard lists the tasks pending for that individual. When the individual has completed the task, he or she enters the output identifier into the task information. This action triggers the Storyboard to proceed to the next task and sends a message to the appropriate individual(s).

The Vault maintains document control. It only allows access to those authorized to work with the document. The software also maintains the correct version of the design.

The status information is derived from the task information. The status information can be used by managers and Business Unit Team members to determine when a department plans to work on an inquiry or when the actual work occurred. There are also a variety of graphs and charts produced from the information for managers to use when monitoring the process performance.

Product Development: After

Federal-Mogul met its goal of reducing product development lead time. In fact, it now sets the standard for the industry. There have been other, unanticipated benefits as well, including

- *Increased market share:* Federal-Mogul asserts that its oil seals market share has improved three points as a result of the new customer-driven process.
- *Highest new application success rate ever:* Before implementing the new process, its hit rate on new application development was approximately 2 out of 10 . The rate has increased to 8 out of 10.
- *Repeat business:* The oil seal capacity is now filled with high repeat business. This achievement puts the division solidly on the path to meeting its strategy of developing a partnership with the customer. The vision here is to have customers come and say "help me design a solution."
- *Increased employee morale:* Employees throughout the division were proud of the clear results of the project. Since senior management had taken the time to inform everyone of the project and involved as many employees as possible, all employees shared in the success of the effort.

Lessons Learned

"Technology is the enabler, not the total solution," states Fred Musone. "It is extremely important—and we have selected outstanding systems to enable the project to work—but we had to change the process, the organization, and the culture in order to be truly successful. Our goal was to optimize the whole, not the pieces."[4] Larry Smith, Federal-Mogul

---

[4]Reuben Slone, "Shortening Product Lead Time," *Computer-Aided Engineering*, March 1991, pp. R24–26.

project manager for this effort, attributes 80 percent of the improvement to the organizational changes and 20 percent to the technology.

Federal-Mogul has begun to apply the new production process to other product lines. In addition, continuous improvement objectives have been established for the sample product development process to ensure that they continue to maintain their advantage in this area.

The key success factor for the Customer-Driven Product Development project was the obvious commitment of senior management to the initiative. Fred Musone's role in the project and his part in the communication activities contributed significantly to its success. Musone was able to effectively communicate his vision of the future to every employee throughout the organization. Other critical success factors included achieving a high degree of user ownership and taking advantage of the talent and skills of the core project team.

Another factor contributing to the success of the project was limiting the scope of the project to one process for a single product line. By focusing on the product development process for oil seals, Federal-Mogul was able to introduce a more process-oriented perspective on a manageable scale. Other characteristics working in its favor were the relatively small size of the seals organization and the relative simplicity of the product.

Federal-Mogul was able to achieve dramatic improvements with a limited degree of organizational structural change. The pre-project functional organization remained intact, but Federal-Mogul used the Business Unit Teams and information technology to transverse and coordinate the process.

Conclusion

For a traditional manufacturer to remain successful, it must become an enterprise consisting of world-class members that cumulatively produce high-value, low-cost products wherever markets emerge across the globe. Time-to-market, response time, and innovation will be targeted on a framework of parallel tasking performed by internal departments and external alliances/partnerships whose common good exceeds that of any individual member.

The strategy and ability to mass produce custom products (mass specialization) anywhere in the world will separate the big winners from the pack. Intellectual capital—that is, knowledge-based enterprises that add value through information and link the enterprise through communication networks—will be best positioned for the preeminence in their markets and create a truly customer-driven company.

The strategic alternatives are limitless and infinite in their configurations. The strategic imperatives, however, are absolute! This section has attempted to provide insight by listing multiple and diverse manufacturing strategies—many that have evolved and stood the test of time, others that have recently emerged fueled by the accelerated pace of technology. A new and compelling set of business drivers is forcing companies to invest their best resources in developing a powerful and largely customized set of strategic options.

JUST-IN-TIME

The concept of just-in-time (JIT) is simple to comprehend but difficult to implement, for it usually requires significant changes from tradition. Once implemented, however, the capabilities of manufacturing are so vastly improved that it is relatively easy to sustain.

The concept is this: allow the consumer of a product or service to trigger the authorization for the supplier to rapidly replenish what has been consumed. The customer and supplier are tightly linked, with very little inventory anywhere in the system. Uncertainty in forecasting is minimal because demand is known. To achieve this level of performance, quality must be defect-free, people must be capable, and processes must be simplified, effective, and valid.

JIT is not a discipline for moving inventory down the value chain; rather, it is a discipline for moving inventory *out* of the value chain. In some respects, JIT is a way of replacing inventory with information. For this reason, JIT is an enterprise-wide activity. It cannot be undertaken solely at the factory level, the department level, the company level, or even the enterprise level. All levels of the enterprise must be involved and aligned if JIT is to minimize costs and lead time and maximize quality. JIT is another way of expressing demand-pull, produce-to-order, or synchronous manufacturing. JIT tightly links customer demand to replenishment assembly and supporting component manufacturing. This leaves little pipeline inventory and no tolerance for error or incompetence.

Perfect quality requires a complete transition from after-the-fact inspection, compliance, and failure orientations to prevention and before-the-fact detection, including on-line, real-time process controls that monitor and manage processes so well that imperfect production is not possible. Capability of people implies a supportive and well-designed organization, a willingness to work together, the motivation to act positively, with sufficient knowledge and skills to do the right things properly. This goal requires years of steady discipline and modernization to achieve. Controlling processes to ensure perfect production instead of measuring parts after production is a revolution in process improvement—not an easy goal to achieve. Taken together, these visions lead to world-class levels of performance. In the largest sense, JIT becomes a vision that drives continuous improvements in an organization's people, processes, and technologies.

Short of this optimum state, however, real-world trade-offs do exist. Supplies sometimes come from very long distances in very large containers (sea containers). Ice storms, brownouts, and hurricanes cause power interruptions. Nonetheless, purchasing and manufacturing must provide assembly with a continuum of piece parts before assembly can begin. Consequently, depending upon the industry and the overall value of raw materials, it may be prudent to plan for significant surge capacity in raw materials and redundant, non-value-adding, standby reserves in other areas such as power conditioning equipment.

Relative to these precautions, different manufacturing strategies can be taken for various families of similar items, depending on item value. Recognizing this span of circumstances, it is reasonable to identify situations where it is strategically and economically prudent to "produce-to-order" and other situations where it is best to "produce-to-forecast." If these rules have been defined for a business, then many scheduling and releasing activities can be economically controlled in the shop.

A variety of techniques can be used in JIT production environments to keep the flow of goods optimal and prevent blockages resulting in inventory-in-process. These include work load balancing, preassembly kitting, prototype and production support, crib and stores support systems, maintenance systems, reconfigureable work environments, and continuous improvement programs.

Work Load Balancing

Two general circumstances typically occur whereby employees can be reassigned work within the continous flow manufacturing (CFM) environment. To balance work or keep employees busy providing value-adding work, while not violating the JIT philosophy, reassignments can be made to manufacture alternate parts. Additionally, work load balancing can be used to combat boredom and low production by designing job rotation schemes into the daily routine. For example, electronic assembly almost always requires preassembly steps (wire cut, strip, mark, terminate, and attachment into lights, switches, etc.). These repetitive tasks can be performed in a "sewing circle" setting to promote relaxation and communication, as an alternative to more rigorous paces on assembly lines. Moving people back and forth from the "circle" to the "line" helps balance work loads, relax muscular tension, and add variety to work tasks.

Preassembly—Kitting

Industry at large is very poor at kitting parts prior to assembly and/or kitting tools prior to setups. This is not because the technologies and methodologies do not exist, but rather because the kitting function is rarely recognized as important. Consequently, it is not supported by systemic coordination between information systems and material handling systems. Only recently have off-the-shelf bills of material automatically formatted pick lists (including item location notations). Moreover, only recently have these automated pick lists been interfaced to random access machines (automatic storage and retrieval systems, carousels, etc.), "pick-to-lights" systems, and other flexible assembly systems.

Within material handling systems themselves, economic nesting trays can easily be fabricated for each kit using common foam-in-place packaging materials, but this application has yet to be widely deployed. Moreover, the kitting of tools is often poorly handled (i.e., still in the "get a flashlight and look under the bench" stage). The growing awareness of the importance of setup reduction is, fortunately, putting some emphasis on the need to organize tooling prior to setup. Much more work needs to be done in the area of blending information systems, material handling systems, and JIT containerization and workplace layout schemes. This blending must occur before effective kitting can be accomplished so that assembly lot sizes of one (including prototypes) can pass through assembly as efficiently as larger volume orders.

Rapid Prototyping

The recent combination of three-dimensional solid-modeling CAD systems, machine tool NC axis controls, new liquid and powder materials (usually plastic) that solidify when energized, and precision lasers has suddenly given birth to CAD/CAM-driven rapid prototyping processes that can immediately postprocess a CAD image and produce a solid form on a stereolithography apparatus. This then can be extended to NC-controlled water jet cutting and NC machining of dies and/or parts, as well as electrochemical machining and electrodischarge machining. All these relatively new processes are enabling the rapid development of unique piece parts having exotic functional and esthetic shapes and surfaces.

By establishing computer communication networks that can download design data, graphic illustrations, and text explaining how products should go together, the rapid assembly of prototypes can also be accomplished. The technologies exist; if supporting documentation is sufficiently clear (a big if), then existing operators can easily switch back and forth from production to prototypes. As lot sizes shrink toward single units, there is in fact little difference between manufacturing processes and procedures for prototype production of fabrications and assemblies.

Crib Support Systems

Manufacturing operations have two key support elements—production control and tools control. The former plans, schedules, and tracks purchased and manufactured items. The latter plans, schedules, and tracks production support items such as tools, dies, gauges, fixtures and maintenance, tool room, and general supply items. With the heavy emphasis in the 1960s, 1970s, and 1980s on bill of materials as the core of material requirement planning (MRP) systems, production control has been inundated with sophisticated software products, theories, and procedures. Tools control, by contrast, has largely been ignored. This lopsided emphasis is unfortunate; for every product item released, it is common to track at least 10 to 20 tooling/support items needed to make the item. Linking parts to operations, tasks, and tooling is often very weak, even in the most modern MRP systems.

Maintenance Systems

The historical development of maintenance systems has been functionally oriented. This has given rise to financial data bases of assets for appropriation tracking and depreciation accounting, cube size, speeds, and feeds for machining; tolerance capability data bases for process planning by manufacturing and/or industrial engineering; and finally, maintenance data bases about machines, lubricants, and service schedules. Having separate data bases only invites redundancy of information, format inconsistency that frustrates integration, and multiple data maintenance efforts that are rarely performed rigorously. This leads to an eventual degradation in confidence levels in all the data bases. This functional view thus often leads to unnecessary system costs and dubious system utility.

The true effectiveness of maintenance systems relies not so much on the level of technology employed, but on the willingness of a company to grapple constructively with this fractured situation, to reorganize support staff to maintain data integrity, and to assure the long-term maintenance of the information. Given a new base of high-confidence information, any number of functional programs can be generated that satisfy accountants, engineers, and production and maintenance personnel all based on high-confidence technical data contained in one asset data base.

Reconfigurement

Over time, flexibility can be observed by the degree to which manufacturing operations are reconfigureable. For example, old companies have gone out of existence and new companies have reoccupied the old space to set up entirely new operations. Plants have been rearranged from functional layouts to cellular layouts. Product mixes have changed from ferrous and mechanical to plastic and electronic. In the past, these changes occurred at enormous cost. With the advent of short-cycle, agile manufacturing, it is necessary wherever practical to occupy manufacturing space with equipment designed to be portable. In effect, this creates an infinitely reconfigurable plant that is easily adjustable to accommodate changing product and sales demands. This high degree of reconfigurability can be designed into the plant at the component manufacturing level, at the process level (heat treat, plate, paint), and/or at the assembly level.

In addition to gaining flexibility by moving equipment around, a group technology strategy known as "composite configurations" can give a manufacturer an apparent or virtual flexibility. Supposing that a company has developed a classification system to identify families of similar parts and has rearranged the plant into a more cellular configuration, it would then be in a position to develop "composite parts" for each cell. These parts do not really exist; they are merely design or engineering envelopes (which could be CAD-based) of all the features embodied in all the components of specified families of parts. Having designed the composites, the next step is to tool the equipment to be able to manufacture a composite. In doing so, the tooling complement will be able to manufacture any part in any assigned family without setup. This is virtual reconfigurability at its best.

Continuous Improvement

Although continuous improvement (CI) is receiving much attention at functional and process improvement levels, it is at the process control level where the greatest quality gains can usually be made. To this end, it becomes essential to recognize the difference between the more traditional view of quality (in which compliance to specifications was the goal) and the newer perspective (which stresses the importance of converging ever closer to target values that have been calculated to best satisfy the customer). It is easy to understand how a strategy minimizing variation by converging on target values motivates continuous improvement efforts. In fact, maintenance in the traditional view no longer exists—it has been replaced by "perfection," with all efforts focused on continuous product and process improvement.

CONTINUOUS FLOW MANUFACTURING

Continuous flow manufacturing (CFM) represents the ultimate in flexibility and responsiveness. CFM means being agile enough to consistently produce—without disrupting manufacturing flow—products and services of high quality and low cost that meet the customer's requirements and demand. Many planning approaches, techniques, and tools are available to assist in reaching this level of manufacturing performance.

Within any one organization at any point in time, a wide diversity of opinions may exist regarding how much change should be attempted and how rapidly. A faster rate of change often entails having a team of experts undertake rapid problem identification and solution development, handing off the results to a user team. This form of change management does little to build internal capability or the conviction that ongoing performance improvement is necessary. It does, however, put solutions in place rapidly.

By contrast, slower and internally facilitated approaches are designed to build strong conviction deep within an organization—conviction that organizational performance improvement is a prerequisite to long-term survival. This approach provides a much stronger basis for ensuring that significant and continuous performance improvement is sustained.

Mission and Vision Critical Success Factors

The initial planning steps—ensuring that the organization has a clear understanding of its current role in the marketplace, of the level of performance expected in the marketplace, therefore prescribing the performance improvement necessary to succeed require much more attention than they typically receive. Their importance stems from the fact that the mission/vision/critical success factor development serves to drive all further performance improvement programs in consistent and coordinated directions. For example, this deployment sequence ensures consistent strategic plans for marketing/sales, product development, manufacturing, personnel development, and financial and working capital deployment. All these strategic plans must be consolidated, or at least coordinated, with respect to timing, direction, and implementation resources. Only by beginning with this type of clear, uniform, consensus-based direction can an enterprise achieve the improvements needed to sustain competitive advantages within a reasonable time and cost.

Item Popularity Generator

Whether any one particular item happens to be "popular" or not has further implications regarding how that item should be treated during the procurement and/or manufacturing process. For example, popular items should be promoted for sale; preferred as carry-over parts within new designs; processed on newer, more capable machines; incorporated into any automated procurement systems; and considered as candidates for material handling automation. Likewise, preferred parts ordered by preferred customers that have an increasing backlog could be produced to forecast in limited amounts (one-month amount), in order to assist with level-loading manpower in the shop. Conversely, nonpreferred items (sold to occasional customers and having no or declining backlogs) represent a combination of unfavorable situations that suggests they should be produced only after having received a confirmed order. Thus, a computer-generated popularity indicator can be used as part of an ongoing planning and shop scheduling rationale to determine which parts should be made to forecast and which should be made to order.

The development of computer-based expert systems to generate such item preferences is a planning and operational tool that is missing from most manufacturing enterprises.[5] Nevertheless, it is relatively easy to create, since it depends upon already existing information (group technology family numbers and MRP volumes and costs). Item preference can have a tremendous impact on standardization and deproliferations program effectiveness, both for product-related items (raw materials, commodities, and piece parts) and process-related items (tools, gauges, dies, fixtures, and supplies).

Production Flow Analysis

Ongoing manufacturing businesses often have a tremendous investment in tooling already in place. Thus, the challenge is to plan transitions toward JIT that properly acknowledge this existing base of tooling and set the stage for continuous performance improvement. Production flow analysis (PFA) is a key planning tool in this process. It finds the most efficient way to utilize the existing base of tooling, minimizing the implementation costs of converting operations from functional to cellular layouts. In forming cellular layouts, PFA sets the foundations for cell-by-cell continuous improvement. The heart of the analysis is three successive frequency analyses that look at the number of occurrences in which parts travel through the same paths as specified on manufacturing routings (the way the parts are tooled).

The three successive frequency analyses investigate and identify those parts that flow in similar fashion and in the same sequence through

---

[5]William Krag, "Dynamic Standardization using Expert Systems," Society for Manufacturing Engineers Technical Paper M5 89–389, 1989, pp. 1–15.

departments, machines, and operations. Those parts that can be nested into similar groups can immediately be placed into group technology cells without any tooling changes at all. This rapid planning approach to achieving cellular layouts, although only a beginning step, can be used to reduce in-process inventory, required floor space, and required number of machines dramatically, and to increase shop throughput and thus inventory turns and customer responsiveness. Ultimately, however, planning for cellular-based continuous flow manufacturing should be developed from both a PFA and a group technology perspective, which includes the identification of composites of all part family features and standard setups for each composite.

The PFA approach is shorter term in focus. It takes complex existing situations and quickly develops cellular layouts that require little retooling. Group technology, by contrast, builds information capabilities that will improve performance much more significantly across many functions and over a much longer time span.

Definition of Work Elements

Definition of work elements is a prerequisite to minimizing variation in process, and, hence, in quality improvement. Nonetheless, industry in general pays too little attention to the importance of accurate, clear, and current in-process work instructions. In the past, this area of definition has focused on setup charts for cycle-paced operations and time studies for labor-intensive work. In the United States, little effort is currently focused in these directions; yet the aptitude and knowledge levels of U.S. workers has been steadily decreasing as the natural language proliferation within the country has been increasing. These two trends combine to make work definition even more important than ever—particularly as a measure for quality improvement.

Two new technologies that can have an immediate, positive impact in this area have been developed, although it remains for an industry to recognize and adopt them. The first is computer-aided work measurement coupled with scaled illustrations of the workplace environment displayed on a graphics computer screen. Given this tool, changes to a workplace layout can be shown in the graphic illustration of the job site, and the system can immediately generate appropriate changes to the work standard. The second planning tool illustrates in color (on computer screens) the exact tasks required within a given operation or process. This can also be coupled with gauging, measurement, and/or diagnostic tests to ensure that a task is properly performed prior to proceeding to the next task. This latter tool can even be programmed to communicate to users in their natural language.

Both of these approaches to work definition have been implemented in industry and have contributed to tremendous increases in quality, productivity, and flexibility. In fact, the flexibility gained has enabled one assembler of electronic items to run prototypes through the shop simultaneously with production items; moreover, the assemblers generally do not know which items are prototype and which are production.

Adjacencies (Functions/Processes)

The relative physical location of functions and/or processes is critical to the overall effectiveness and efficiency of a manufacturing process. Adjacency chart planning is a simple, nonemotional, rigorous, and easily communicated method for determining the proper adjacencies as a preparatory step to optimizing plant layouts. A list of all value-adding (press, machine, heat treat, assemble, etc.) and non-value-adding (maintenance, cribs, metrology, production control, etc.) functions is made. Then, using a consistent coding scheme to indicate which functions should be close to each other and which should (or must) be remotely located, function locations are assessed and optimized. This exercise is an excellent assignment for two or three independent small, multifunctional teams. Comparisons of their results can then be made and areas of disagreement rectified in a larger group setting. Thus, an adjacency chart can be developed using facilitated approaches for achieving consensus. This is important because the chart is next used as a planning guide for the development of plant layouts.

Space Conversion (Non-Value-Adding to Value-Adding)

When existing manufacturing facilities start their transition to JIT-oriented, world-class layouts, the initial state is typically cluttered with space previously used for excess inventory, obsolete equipment, fixtures, tools, dies, molds, and/or space allocated to dedicated operations that may not really require dedicated space. As space inventories are made, the "space war" begins and departments tend to inflate their needs in order to acquire contingency real estate. It becomes critical to inventory the as-is space for each function carefully without including aisle space (note all aisle space separately) and to proof the total space inventory against the total building area to assure wall-to-wall accountability. Many areas will thus be identified as wasted space, unassigned space, or space that can eventually be converted from non-value adding use to more productive use.

Estimates must be made of realistic conversion rates. For example, excess inventory areas can be reduced significantly over time, but it is difficult to predict how rapidly this can occur. Dedicated space can be converted to flexible, shared space, but this process may be paced by tooling and setup improvements. Again, predicting timing may be difficult. As a planning task, space conversion must be recognized, and dealt with, on an individual basis. As a layout strategy, shrinking operations should be collocated with growing operations to facilitate the effective reutilization of released space. In this way, growth of value adding operations will put pressure on excess non-value-adding operations, encouraging their minimization.

Containerization Planning

Ideally, a manufacturing process should be designed so that part containers are not needed. Nevertheless, experience suggests otherwise. In fact, it is a little-recognized fact that entire plant layouts can be designed around a central core of modular containers.

Container elimination has successfully been accomplished in some assembly environments by utilizing shipping container dunnage as a holding pad during final assembly. With this strategy, the packaging must accommodate the needs of assembly and incorporate those needs into the packaging system design. Normally, however, most parts are stored in containers, fixtured to precision pallets (for machining), or held in bulk containers made of a special alloy that is resistent to hostile environments (acid etching, heat treating, etc.). It is this large universe of containerized, or racked, parts and materials that can be cleverly housed in containment systems to significantly assist in controlling inventories, orienting parts, protecting parts, and transferring parts within JIT demand-pull systems.

A great effort to redesign containers has been recently completed jointly by the U.S. automotive companies to achieve standard designs that promote reusability between supplier and consumer and gain handling efficiencies with respect to container sizes, stackability, nestability, durability, and label presentation. A plant modernization project team should become aware of the particulars of efforts of this sort. With knowledge of the full range of commercially available containers, it should be possible to develop an integrated containerization program that supports world-class manufacturing, including accommodations for eventual automation such as robots, automated guidance vehicles (AGVs), and automated storage/retrieval systems (AS/RSs).

Staffing Strategies

How people are factored into the planning process is extremely important, for this may well effect general acceptance of the final manufacturing operation. As automation levels increase, larger and larger blocks of space become more and more dangerous for people. This requires designating people-intensive areas and keeping them separate from automation-intensive areas. Likewise, within the actual workstations much can be done to accommodate the employees communication and social needs.

Work areas can be clustered and U-shaped to bring people closer together. Cells can be U-shaped or J-shaped to accomplish the same result. Glass walls can separate people from dangerous areas and yet providing comfort and convenience. Untended operations need monitoring, which can be done from elevated platforms, walkways, and offices. Companies are starting to recognize the strategic marketing value of manufacturing operations as technical showplaces with which they can impress customers. This results in the need to accommodate a steady stream of visitors through the plant without significantly disrupting operations and employees. Many plants have added visitors aisles, wall graphics, and even prerecorded process explanation stations to help sell the capabilities of their manufacturing operations.

New trends in the area of health and fitness are also influencing facility and layout design. Cafeterias, wash rooms, and employee stores are not uncommon. Some enterprises have added fitness centers, jogging tracks, and reception areas. Halls of history showing the evolution and accomplishments of a company help remind employees and customers of its steady progress and accumulated knowledge. Conveniences such as decentralized parking, security, attractive rest areas, close attention to ambiant and task lighting, and function- and comfort-oriented furniture are additional strategies for satisfying employees and impressing customers.

Layout Design

The overall design of a layout for a manufacturing process combines all of the considerations and planning issues previously mentioned. Furthermore, it is not until a detailed layout exists that accurate implementation costs can be estimated. Thus, detailed layout planning tools must be incorporated into larger appropriation requests for significant modernization programs. They also serve as planning tools for scheduling all move sequences, reporting progress, scoping responsibility, and scoping subcontractor contracts.

Layouts can be developed by a small team of inside experts, by the employees themselves, by consultants, or by any combination of the three. This multifunctional approach helps ensure that facility layout adequately reflects the needs of the people, processes, and technologies. It is equally important that process and building system experts be involved to avoid costly mistakes. The entire site—including land, building, and building systems—must be considered when developing a layout. This level of scope helps ensure that fire apparatus access, people flow, traffic, parking, trucking, docking, water retention, chemical processing, and all activities around the building perimeter are considered in addition to those within the building itself.

Using computer graphics-based systems to capture each machine's footprint to establish a graphic data base is the most effective approach to illustrating the layout. In this way, layers of the layout can be designated for each building system, and detailed layouts can easily be created for the "as-is" condition, the "to-be" condition, and any number of interim layouts showing move sequences and temporary move locations.

Justification Strategies

The more successful CFM modernization programs—those with the greatest overall performance improvements—have occurred when the *entire* modernization program was authorized to take place. Failure threatens when each subproject within the overall program is challenged in detail and required to be self-supporting. The major sources of cost savings in a typical modernization program come from inventory reductions, elimination of waste due to material handling and inefficient processes, improved staffing efficiencies, and a reduction in the cost of quality. The program costs, by contrast, should be built up by process, function, or system, such as receiving and inspection, machinery, automation, AS/RS, containers, and assembly stations. Thus, the real categories of cost usually do not line up with the categories of cost reduction. This justification format should be allowed to help ensure that the entire modernization program is held together.

The following case study highlights an unusually effective JIT implementation that relies upon established technology for plant and process modernization.

GENERAL DYNAMICS LAND SYSTEMS: PLANT REENGINEERING FOR WORLD-CLASS COMPETITIVENESS

The Sterling Modernization Program is part of the General Dynamics Industrial Productivity Program, which was launched in the early 1980s. General Dynamics, one of the top three U.S. defense contractors, is known for production of the Tomahawk cruise missile, the F-16 fighter jet, the Trident submarine, the M1A1 Abrams battle tank, and other electronic and space launch products. The firm, headquartered in St. Louis, Missouri, had sales over $10 million in 1990, most of which were to the U.S. government.

The General Dynamics Land Systems Division (GDLS) manufactures the M1 A1 tank. The division has two plants in Detroit, one known as the Detroit Arsenal Tank Plant (DATP), where they assemble machined components and vehicles and then test the vehicles on a test track, and the other known as the the Sterling Heights operation, which produces the electrical optical assemblies for the "brains" of the tank. The Sterling Electro/Optical Assembly Plant, 200,000 square feet in size, assembles components that go into several products, the largest of which is a periscope device known as the "Gunners Primary Sight." In addition, the plant assembles and wires the hull and turret network boxes, which are a maze of high-density wired network systems that were designed in the 1950s and 1960s.

Objectives

During the modernization program, the Sterling plant changed from a station-oriented assembly process to modern JIT assembly lines with integrated in-process inspection operations incorporated into key assembly tasks. Key objectives of the process and productivity improvements were accomplished through careful problem identification and involvement of employees in both planning and implementation. The planning and analysis phase uncovered many opportunities for improvement, including facility layout, equipment, material handling modernization, process streamlining, and workspace ergonomics. In responding to customer needs (U.S. government) and a divisional mandate, the Sterling Electro/Oprical Assembly Plant achieved many measurable performance improvements and savings.

The Sterling plant is an excellent example of a well-balanced modernization program involving people, processes, and technology. It has an unusual message, in that it demonstrates the importance of excellent in-process engineering documentation and technical communications to its people. The technical requirements were communicated in a paperless environment, such that the plant can now introduce new products just as easily as it produces existing products. The result is expanded capability, as well as new dimensions of flexibility.

Analysis and Planning Phase

Establishing the Need for Change
The Sterling Electro/Optical Assembly Plant was built in the 1970s as an annex for design engineering and as a prototype machining and assembly center. It quickly became overloaded with machining from other facilities. Like so many manufacturing/assembly facilities in the early 1980s, the GDLS Sterling plant was suffering from unplanned growth. The building was originally constructed and utilized for prototype assembly of large, tracked, self-propelled vehicles (M1 tank). This mission gradually was converted to a mix of machining and electro/optical assembly, utilizing many makeshift work stations, fixtures, and processes. Simultaneously, during the 1970s, the Army was placing great emphasis on modernizing its manufacturing base. Using structured analysis methodologies such as I-DEF, hundreds of government and contractor operated facilities studied their operations, including processes, methods, levels of waste, throughput times, cost, accuracy, material flow, supplier performance, employee attitudes, incentives and compensation systems, information systems, and strategic planning approaches.

Originally developed under the U.S. Air Force program for integrated computer-aided manufacturing (I-CAM), I-DEF (I-CAM definition method) is a methodology for developing and representing manufacturing-systems architectures. Structured analysis, which underlies I-DEF, is based upon the following concepts:

- A model that graphically illustrates why equipment, information, and activities that can build understanding of the system must be created.
- Clearcut distinctions should be made between the functions the system is expected to perform and how the system design will address those functions.
- A hierarchical model displays critical functions on top with lower-level functions underneath. Each submodule should have well-defined boundaries and be able to be decomposed to reveal greater levels of detail.
- Disciplined teamwork, including an informed review cycle, is critical in building an accurate system model that can guide implementation and operationalization.

By the 1980s, extensive analysis had been initiated at Sterling as part of a large GDLS-wide industrial productivity improvement (IPI) program. The results of the IPI study dovetailed with the willingness of the Army to extend the M1 contract to a "multiyear" profile, allowing contractors to stabilize operations and better concentrate on improving performance. Thus, the Sterling modernization program was formulated and funding was appropriated.

Planning for Success

The project leader for the modernization project, Mr. Richard Kreitz, was particularly proud of the fact that all the changes were implemented while the plant was fully operational. One of the key lessons to be learned from this case is the importance of broad employee involvement in the planning process to correctly identify roadblocks and to build widespread support for the challenging implementation phase. At Sterling, the plant manager and representatives from all departments attended weekly meetings for over two years, developing and executing over 200 action items.

When the modernization program was begun, employment was in excess of 600 people. Employment is now on the order of 370 people. Overtime is controlled and is less than 5 percent. The scrap and rework is very minimal, so almost everything they have done has worked. The time/quality/cost performance indicators demonstrated dramatic improvement through the modernization of layout and work methods. During the methods improvement process, workers had significant input in terms of suggesting and evaluating the features and options for various purchased workstations, fixtures, tools, seating and lighting approaches.

IPI Analysis Results

As detailed analysis and planning progressed, the full extent of operational improvement opportunities at Sterling became evident. Poor and inconsistent work methods and methods documentation were found. Hastily designed and worn tooling and fixtures contributed to quality variation and wiring mistakes. Nonergonomic workstations, lighting, and seating were frustrating assemblers, and their attitude suffered accordingly. Inadequate in-process work instructions and paper-based, handwritten instruction booklets contributed to inaccuracies, slow change implementation and esoteric documentation. Substandard environmental conditions contributed to contamination on critical surfaces (mirrors and lenses), and long cycle station build approaches to complex products having hundreds of wiring connections contributed to omissions, mistakes, and variation. From a material flow standpoint, there was much room for improvement.

Inefficient product flow through the shop, inadequate containerization of parts, and poor part protection contributed to constant item shortages whereas inventories (raw, WIP, and finished) bulged. "Make it, inspect it, fix it" processes contributed to very low quality yields throughout the complex processes. This resulted in recirculating inventories for rework ("eddy currents"), which absorbed a tremendous amount of unreported effort. In fact, almost three times the standard labor went into each certified end product. Given this base for operational performance, significant investment was required to modernize the building and processes, but it was relatively easy to justify this investment from savings in quality improvements, productivity improvements, and inventory reductions.

Program Justification Approach

The detailed planning was completed and included computer-graphic-based plant layouts, a carefully prepared list of required capital and expense items (mostly for material handling, workstations, fixtures, and building modernization items, including a clean room). In a very different order, the program savings were tallied. They included savings from reductions in scrap and rework and other costs of "unquality," elimination of waste and variation from much improved methods, and significant inventory reductions. Although the actual cost of inventory was not available, especially for government furnished material (GFM), order of magnitude estimations were used to "rough in" the extent of financial impact on performance of reduced inventories. The fact that costs were accumulated one way and savings another turned out to be a wise justification strategy. It prevented "cherry picking" the program and enabled the overall program to be orchestrated in its entirety. Now, at least six years after the beginning of the IPI program, every expectation has been surpassed. It was an outstanding financial and performance improvement success.

Implementation Solutions

The remaining comments will describe the more significant improvements that were implemented. Individually, they sound simple and basic. Collectively, however, they add up to an extremely successful JIT implementation. JIT must take place within an environment of increasingly enlightened employees, who, by education/training, demonstrations, and meaningful decision-influencing participation, have been informed and involved closely throughout the entire modernization process. The following program results involved all employees in the design and implementation phases.

Materials Management

Receiving and Receiving Inspection. The former state of receiving was one of tremendous confusion, huge incoming inventories, and stolen parts (to make up production shortages) from uninspected merchandise. In addition, sloppy receiving inspection areas exposed to extreme weather conditions further hampered the process. Today, GDLS Sterling is a CP^2 ("Contractor Performance Certification Program") contractor, which means that it has now been exempted from receiving inspection of incoming material. This large supplier development success, together with the internal receiving improvements of weather separation walls, flow-thru conveyors, modernized receiving validation equipment, environmentally secure coordinate measuring machines (CMM), and current sampling inspection procedure files, resulted in a "hospital clean," orderly and highly responsive function. The end result is a FIFO (first in, first out) system for receiving supplier certified material just in time.

Purchased Material Storage Areas.   Due to its relatively small size, the Sterling plant needed to optimize its storage spaces. Through specific changes in handling small items and a stacker storage and receiving system for bulky items storage capacity within existing floor space was increased by 35 percent. Where it once took 6 months to handle 800 lots, the plant now can handle 100 lots in a week. The overall backlog in receiving and inspection was reduced by an impressive 88 percent. This was accomplished through several changes.

The raw materials used at the Sterling plant are largely wire switches, plugs, machine castings and government furnished material (GFM). GFM comes from such sources as Hughes and Singer, both of which supply thermal and laser "black boxes." The commodity parts are broken down into small boxes and unit packs, so that controlling inventory is simplified. Many of them are stored in automatic carousels with "pick by light" features to minimize any errors from picking incorrect part numbers.

As might be expected, the former areas for storing "OK for use" purchased material now occupy approximately a quarter of the former space. The existing racking, however, is still reminiscent of the original needs and will be downsized in the future. Besides shrinking inventories, two other highly successful programs contributed to the improvements of this area. First, all as-received goods are repackaged into very small "issue size" packages with the internal part number and quantity clearly marked on the box. This container down-sizing, formerly performed during receiving inspection and now done by the supplier, enables Sterling to easily inventory its stock and quickly and accurately dispense material. Secondly, random access machinery is being used for small items. Two vertical carousels, side by side, give the shop order filling attendants random access and rapid retrieval of a very large number of stock keeping units (SKUs) within a very small space.

Process Improvements

Wire Prep Area.   Wire prep consists of unreeling a large variety of insulated wire types, cutting, marking, and packaging wires for the next operation. Formerly, a variety of wire types and lengths were processed and then kitted into ziploc-type bags. Wire type and quantity inaccuracies occurred, and this problem was exacerbated by assemblers who, short on various wires, would sneak back and raid the bags. As a result, everyone was running around, wires were incorrectly cut, almost a scrap barrel a day was produced of wire alone, and much time was wasted by many people trying to do the best they could given a very poor processing layout and methods.

In order to solve these problems, wire processing was split from kitting and JIT wire tubes were installed between cutting and kitting. These fairly simple process modifications, not especially technical in nature, have yielded significant gains in time and quality. Wires are now automatically cut, stripped, pinned, and placed in a JIT queue.

Currently, the wire goes to a wire cutting station, where the normal wire-cutting stands have been integrated with tools for wire marking and wire end preparation, such as crimping terminals on the end of the wires. The completed wires are processed and placed in vertical plastic tubes by part number. These vertical plastic tubes are placed in elevated boxes, so the wire-cutter operators can easily look at the ends of tubes to spot the nearly empty ones—the paperless signal to manufacture refills. So it is a just-in-time, demand-pull situation for creating wires. In addition, the wires hang vertically so they remain straight.

Pre-Wired Kits. Today, the wire cutter keeps the approximately 200 tubes full, while the kitter pulls the correct wires in the correct quantity from the tubes and places them into special wire kit trays. These trays are in turn placed on sloping, flow-through racks that feed the (wire) trays to the "first-end" assembly areas. No more scrap, no more looking for wires, no more inaccurate kits, no more raiding, and no more running around, and all this is accomplished without paper work orders. The benefits of the kitting improvements were twofold: employees are no longer wasting 40 percent of their time reconstructing kits, and part shortages are rapidly discovered and effectively eliminated.

Equipment and Ergonomics

Workstations. During the IPI program, 11 vendors brought sample workstations, seating, lighting, and tool racking systems into the Sterling plant for evaluation. The IPI team made up a weighting and scoring evaluation sheet and assigned the weights. The assemblers then brought their work to the display area, used all the equipment to their satisfaction, and completed the scoring after handling the equipment for several hours. In this way everyone affected was meaningfully involved in the selection and purchasing decisions relative to workstations, task lighting, tool racking, and seating systems.

Computer Graphic Work Instructions.   The subassembly stations are used to wire a variety of complex plugs, switches, and relays. Wire kits are selected from the flowthrough racks and put in the proper place at the workstations. On a CRT screen a computer graphic color image of work instructions appears after having bar code scanned the router, the work order, and the operator's identification badge. The system checks a data base to make sure that this person is certified to do the work. Once that front end check is complete, the graphic image will change from a general landscape scene to a picture of the specific plug to be wired and the instructions illustrating which wire goes where. Just to further emphasize which wire to pull, the system contains a "pick by light" system, using small bright red lights that go on under the appropriate wires. The operator reaches up to the kit, pulls the appropriate wire, and puts it in the plug. This completes the first-end connection.

Preventative Quality Measures.   Traditionally, wiring multiple wires into small, complex military-type plugs or circuit devices is performed using the first end of a wire at the start and then attaching the second end much later in the process. Usually, it is not until the second end is attached that circuit testing is done. In the past the first-end connection was occasionally inaccurately located in the plug and subsequent wires buried in complex assemblies. These mistakes were very costly to find and fix.

Now, once the first end of the wire is put in the plug, the operator touches the other end of the wire, the free end, with one hand and touches a button on the work station with the other hand. Using a commercially available first-end continuity tester, a low voltage is applied to complete the circuit to validate that the wires have been inserted into the right hole. At this point, the image on the CRT changes from a little yellow dot on the plug illustration to a green dot, indicating that the wire was inserted into the correct plug hole. The operator then pushes a foot switch to index to the next CRT picture with no keyboard input. This procedure essentially eliminated all miswires—one of the most costly and prevalent quality problems at Sterling.

Each workstation was equipped with a computer and CRT screen (but no keyboard). Using commercially available networks and commercially available color graphics software, the content of all the paper-based work instruction sheets was converted to color graphic math model format. Using bar codes, the operators scan the production "traveler," their own ID badge, and the station/operation identification label. The system checks the operator's certification status and then very clearly displays the various wiring tasks on the CRTs. As wiring tasks are completed and quality checks validated, the operator activates a foot switch that indexes the graphics to the next pictorial and text task instruction image. Thus, it is important to realize that this system not only ensures quality by the excellence of the in-process documentation, but does so in a very efficient manner. Of particular interest is the fact that the system was designed to define work at a *task* level within any given *operation* for any given *part number*. This added resolution could have a large impact on more traditional MRP systems, which usually only enable the definition of work at the *part number/operation* number level.

Human Integrated Manufacturing (HIM).   HIM is the realization of the belief that people are the most important asset a firm has. It is a combination of ergonomics, information technology, and quality process documentation. HIM ensures that all employees have the tools they need, a comfortable work environment, and clear documentation regarding what needs to be done and how to do it. Sterling today is a good example of HIM.

Facility Improvements

Clean Room.   To ensure that a level of cleanliness was maintained during final assembly, a 7,500-square-foot-clean room was designed and installed. Although the room was officially a class 100,000, additional air-change capacity and a HEPA filter expansion room were provided to be able to easily modify the facility to class 1000 in case future generations of product demanded this level of cleanliness. Recent clean room calibrations have indicated that the clean room can reach a class 3,000, which is not an official class, but on a scale of 100,000 to class 1,000, it gives some idea of how clean it already is. In addition, from the standpoint of electrostatic discharge (ESD) protection, safety systems have been installed throughout the plant. For example, all the columns in the plant have been grounded and connected, and all the work stations have been grounded to the column system, so they are currently in a position to implement complete ESD protection across the entire plant.

Each end of the clean room features vestibules for "gowning" and tack mats for cleaning shoes and rolling cart castors. Inside the clean room, a medium duty bridge crane was installed for flexible handling of heavy product assemblies. Pass-through windows were constructed for introducing lense items from an adjacent lense calibration area. Many windows were incorporated, as were light-colored floor, walls, and ceiling and very good lighting systems.

Automatic Material Handling Systems. Both an automatic guided vehicle (AGV) and an automatic flexible conveyor system were installed to handle product flow from central storage areas to production departments, between departments, and within departments. In addition, a horizontal carousel system was installed between two similar departments to provide random access to a wide variety of partially assembled items. A 20 percent increase in productivity has been attributed to these systems.

Status Room Including a Model of the Plant. Central to the plant is a status room, which is used for plant meetings as well as customer tours and new employee orientation. In this room is a scale model of the plant showing all workstations and equipment. Surrounding the model on the walls of the status room are pictures of products, with one entire wall devoted to performance charts. At the beginning of the project, this space was viewed as a luxury. Now, its true value is widely appreciated.

Conclusion

This, then, is the story of the Sterling modernization program. In summary, these programs take commitment, money, patience, and time. Nonetheless, the results are highly gratifying, and many times they have proved to be absolutely critical. The Gulf War proved this!

Lessons Learned

Several important lessons were learned from the modernization program at the Sterling plant. Soliciting and maintaining the active support of senior management throughout the project was critical to the program's success. In order to justify the project initially, management was shown videotapes of work in process from different shifts, to demonstrate the diversity of methods in use at the plant. This convinced them of the need for a step-by-step process analysis and major revisions. The value of keeping management informed during the implementation phase was confirmed by the positive response to 3-D sketches and color graphics used for reporting progress at monthly meetings with senior management. In fact, some of these managers regularly walked through the plant during the modernization process to monitor the changes taking place. Occasionally they brought customers along, indicating their high level of interest and support. Finally, managers and staff at the plant learned that with this level of support from above, they were able to accomplish more than they had thought possible.

The importance of people in the modernization process cannot be overemphasized. Soliciting input and participation from various departments and functions proved to be essential in pooling their knowledge and ensuring effective planning as well as consistent implementation. During the implementation phase, team meetings were held every week to keep people informed and to coordinate various aspects of the project. One striking outcome of the modernization success was a turnaround in GDLS management's attitude toward their employees—they learned about the power of their people. Other attitudes changed as well, and those managers who could not adapt felt increasingly out of step and, in some cases, were replaced.

Based upon experience learned from other modernization programs, the team conducted a cost/benefit analysis intentionally designed to look at the total program. Management had to support an all-or-nothing modernization. Another insight gained was the importance of setting goals and establishing ongoing measurement procedures. Central objectives, such as halving inventory, doubling throughput, and eliminating excess labor, were made explicit. They were measured on a monthly basis, and results were posted. This visual dimension of the project served to further involve and motivate participants.

The value of technology enablement in the modernization process was another important lesson learned by team members at all levels. Finding appropriate new technologies and integrating them with the procedural and other less technical changes was a challenge that paid off very well. The continuity testing equipment and networked work instructions were new technologies located by diligent searching that included reading relevant publications and attending trade shows. In addition, the networking and downloading of graphics was a big contributor to the in-process documentation, which set a new standard in process innovation. The resulting operational improvements speak for themselves.

Sterling Today

The plant features a U-shaped flow, where the raw materials that are now coming in are all vendor certified with no need for receiving inspection. This is a mega-leap in performance for General Dynamics, which used to have adversarial relations with government inspectors and suppliers. Nobody trusted anybody. Now, the modernization of the facility has been so complete, and the improvement of quality so dramatic that the company has won quality awards and has been exempted from receiving inspection procedures. Analysis by statistical process control found that before modernization 7,000 hours per year were spent on fixing defective parts. In addition to all the economies and productivity improvements mentioned above, an estimated $189,000 a year is being saved by eliminating the cost of defective parts and related expenses.

This system is a very fine example of human integrated manufacturing (HIM). It represents a complete computer-distributed in-process engineering requirements documentation system. It is of such great interest to General Dynamics that the PC-based system is now being converted to a mainframe file server network environment for use at other sites. Thus, the whole idea of excellence in in-process documentation, as demonstrated at the Sterling Electro/Optical Assembly Plant, is a very important (yet largely unrecognized in industry) aspect of promoting quality throughout its operations.

Today, the Sterling Electro-Optical Assembly Plant is a source of great pride and one of the most human integrated manufacturing (HIM) operations within General Dynamics. It is used as a source of ideas for other plants and continues to improve. Often visited by customers, it has become an impressive marketing tool, especially for foreign visitors.

QUICK RESPONSE/POINT-OF-SALE SYSTEMS

Quick response (QR) is an operations approach supported by point-of-sale (POS) systems. It is similar to IT in two ways. It is based on continuous forward movement of the product from manufacturing through the logistics network to the retail outlet without delay. Order fulfillment is driven by consumption, which is triggered by point-of-sale information at the retail location. Cash register entry serves as the I/O device that captures all relevant store product detail, including pricing, inventory balance, size, color, packaging, inventory policy, and more, and feeds that information electronically back through the logistics, sales administration, and manufacturing network, culminating in appropriate responses by all parties involved. Leading retailers, such as Wal-Mart, Kmart, Sears, and JCPenney, and a host of distributors are establishing QR as the new standard for doing business. Manufacturers are hustling to be recognized as industry leaders by developing this leading-edge capability. Walgreens offers an excellent case reference.

WALGREENS REDESIGNS INVENTORY MANAGEMENT

Founded in 1901, the Walgreen Company operates a chain of approximately 1,800 Walgreens retail drug stores in 30 states across the United States and Puerto Rico. Walgreens has 54,000 employees and 31,000 shareholders. Its drugstores serve approximately two million customers daily. They average $3.9 million in annual sales per unit, or $400 per square foot, among the highest in the chain drug industry. Walgreens drugstores are served by eight distribution centers and five photoprocessing studios. Although it is guided by a conservative fiscal policy, the Walgreen Company is dedicated to aggressive growth. Dividends, paid in every quarter since 1933, have been raised 17 times in the past 15 years. Walgreens is the nation's premier drug chain in sales and profits and second in number of stores. Sales for fiscal year 1992 exceeded $7 billion, with prescription drugs accounting for about 37 percent of sales.

In the late 1980s, Walgreens challenged itself "to maintain its profitability and investment levels in the face of fierce competition from technologically sophisticated mass merchandisers and grocery retailers." The key to competitiveness was defined as optimizing responsiveness to the marketplace through radically improved merchandising, logistics, and store operations.

In 1987, Ernst & Young was engaged to assist Walgreens' management in developing the technical framework and systems to support an improved inventory management strategy. Out of this challenge grew a new strategy called Strategic Inventory Management System (SIMS). With SIMS, Walgreens was building the infrastructure to support future growth and maintain a competitive position within the marketplace. SIMS is a highly sophisticated inventory management system that integrates merchandise management functions, from the store selling floor through the distribution centers and back through to corporate merchandise planning. Although technology has always been a cornerstone of Walgreens' strategy, its inventory control systems had evolved over a number of years. Management felt that the technology in certain areas had advanced sufficiently for Walgreens to gain a real competitive advantage by using it to provide information that had been previously unavailable. At the same time, the new systems would take advantage of new software development technologies so that they would be easier to maintain and change as the business continued to respond to the changing competitive environment. In the following case study, JIT principles and the key enabling technologies have been implemented to improve information and product flow, saving time and resources.

Establishing the Need for Change

Walgreens' motto, "Respected employees will offer quality customer service, which in turn builds value for our shareholders," offers insight into the direction the company took in the late 1980s. For Walgreens to attain its motto in the 1990s and to remain the drugstore industry leader, it needed a competitive advantage. The 1980s saw a blurring of competitive format within the retail industry. As a result, Walgreens found itself competing with nontraditional rivals such as grocers and discounters such as Wal-Mart. Walgreens looked to retail technology for the answer. Any computerization, Walgreens believed, must make the stores more efficient, less labor intensive, better able to anticipate customer needs, and ultimately, more profitable.

Walgreens faced many challenges in the implementation of SIMS, and it has taken several years' effort to manage the changes in new technology, organizational change, and fragmented management information system (MIS) resource management. The new technologies included the IBM mid-range computers (AS/400), a new development language, a new methodology, relational data bases, and the movement from a centralized processing strategy to distributed systems. Since the systems resulted in new practices and procedures throughout the organization, there were a large number of changes to implement. Finally, the fragmented MIS resource management, with two different systems development organizations needed to be overhauled.

Innovative Inventory Management

SIMS was designed to reduce the overall inventory investment while maintaining high service levels. By providing better information to support the buying decisions, it was believed that the overall cost of purchases could be lowered. The original, unsophisticated (monitoring) system, although it was successful at manual inventory control, might not have been sufficient to handle increased sales transactions, adversely affecting future sales and customer satisfaction.

Since Walgreens' growth investment comes primarily from internally generated funds, inventory control would improve its cash flow to meet its expansion policy. By investing in SIMS, Walgreens was building the infrastructure to simultaneously support future growth while enabling itself to maintain a healthy cash flow position.

Walgreens has historically carried substantial levels of safety stock inventory. By lowering its inventory investment while still maintaining shelf presence, Walgreens felt that it could significantly increase its inventory turn rate. This would require company coordination from the stores, distribution, management information systems (MIS), and purchasing functions. Furthermore, the new system would require closer ties with manufacturers through wider use of electronic data interchange (EDI) and the application of forecasting models.

SIMS is an on-line, JIT system that manages Walgreens' inventory from item forecasting to the actual sale of the item within the store. SIMS addresses the inventory requirements of three major business areas within Walgreens: distribution and logistics, marketing and merchandising, and store operations. Within these functional areas, processes were identified, analyzed, and redesigned into SIMS. SIMS integrates and incorprates all modules of an inventory management system. The components that make up SIMS are distribution management systems, corporate merchandise management systems, and in-store systems.

Distribution management systems control the movement of merchandise from the vendor's shipping dock through the final delivery to the store. The systems include enhanced visibility into the inbound pipeline and use of advanced technologies such as bar coding and wireless terminals to manage the physical operations of the distribution centers. The distribution and logistics systems are essentially distributed systems running at each of Walgreens' distribution centers. The distribution functions incorporate such systems as receipt priority planning, EDI, receiving and put away, slot management, order processing, wave planning, and shipping and billing. Most of these systems interface directly with computerized conveyor and picking systems within the warehouses and make extensive use of radio frequency devices for management of inventory across all stocking and picking locations. The overall objective of the new Distribution and Logistics SIMS is to provide greater visibility of the inventory pipeline, reduce stock-outs and shipping problems, improve the management of space within the distribution center, and to increase inventory productivity through the distribution center using improved planning and merchandise management systems.

Corporate merchandise management systems are used to help determine which items should be purchased to support the stores, along with the optimal quantities and source of supply. Once items are ordered, the corporate systems are used to monitor the flows from the vendors, through the distribution centers, and stores to the final consumer. The corporate business functions include such systems as promotional merchandise management, purchase order management, EDI, forecasting, deal management, promotional order management and several merchandise performance reporting and analysis systems. The focus of the marketing systems is to greatly improve inventory performance within the company through JIT techniques and to substantially lower the cost of goods using time-phased inventory management techniques and sophisticated purchasing alternatives. The marketing-based merchandise planning and management systems will use actual POS scanner data from each store in the chain rather than rely on warehouse withdrawals. The new SIMS will provide buyers with an extensive view of the entire inventory pipeline, projected inventory net requirements, and the performance of purchases as measured by item profitability.

In-store systems manage the merchandise within the four walls of the store. They assist the store manager by providing suggested orders to be filled from direct sources or the company's distribution centers, based on inventory balances and store specific forecasts. Point-of-sale scanning is an integral part of these systems. Cash registers record data by units, sales dollars, and averaging costs (gross margin) per SKU. Although the development effort associated with the systems targeted for store operations is somewhat smaller than either distribution or marketing, these are the cornerstone systems for achieving the overall inventory performance goals sought for Walgreens. The various inventory management systems that have been developed to execute at store level include item maintenance and price management, advertising, basic and promotional merchandise order processing, item movement processing, forecasting, receiving, perpetual inventory control, and direct vendor order processing. The objective of these systems is to substantially reduce inventory in each store, significantly increase inventory turns by maintaining reduced inventory levels, and improve overall customer service through reduced stock-outs. These objectives will be achieved in several ways.

- Store orders will be generated for both warehouse and direct vendor merchandise using an automated ordering system running against inventory balances, which reflect the result of all receipts, adjustments, and sales from the 4680 POS device. Automated store ordering will remove most of the inaccuracies that exist in today's ordering techniques.
- As excess store inventory is removed, the cost-of-goods-to-sales ratio will be lowered and maintained in each store. Using JIT concepts, less inventory at each store level will allow buyers to purchase less overall merchandise, thus resulting in lower inventory levels at the distribution centers.

Anticipated Benefits of SIMS

SIMS changes the roles of the store manager, distribution center, and purchasing. This sophisticated inventory management and control system is critical to retailing in the 1990s. Integrated software linking the warehouse management system, purchase order system, and point-of-sale scanning is sufficiently advanced and cost efficient to be an adjunct to a network of store managers. Walgreens has provided its store managers with strong merchandising tools, but it has also empowered managers to make a variety of relatively independent decisions by giving them access to the information they need to make those decisions. Rather than acting as a barrier, technology enables the merchant to get closer to the customers in the aggregate. In addition to acting as an enabler, specific SIMS benefits include the following:

- *Improved inventory control*—The system will aid in tailoring the merchandise to the unique needs of a given location. This may relate to age, income, or ethnic mix. Walgreens believes that better data on individual stores will enhance sales performance and/or margins. The store manager will have control over minimum/maximum shelf quantities by SKU. Walgreens has already achieved substantial savings in warehouse inventory using SIMS.

- With the *purchase order management system,* Walgreens can potentially increase its gross margin. Increased purchasing power will enable it to negotiate more effectively with vendors. With better data on product movement, promotional planning can assess productivity and/or gross margins. Also, tighter planning graphics should enhance gross profits per linear foot of display. Since over half the items in the store sell less than one unit per week, there are opportunities in merchandising control.

- With *cash register scanning,* life at the store level becomes simpler. The store employee has an incentive to work at a Walgreens store, because many repetitive chores have been eliminated. Due to reduced priority activity, it is estimated that 20 hours per employee will be saved at each store.

- In addition, more information is at the hands of store managers facilitating *decision making.* They will have the ability to override the automatic replenishment of merchandise at their stores. Another advantage is that automatic ad price checking and faster, more accurate checkouts will increase customer satisfaction.

- Walgreens' *shrinkage* will decline because it will know shrinkage by item and product line. This will enable the company to devise appropriate measures to respond to such problems as display, packaging, and theft.

- *Automatic replenishment* of warehouse-delivered items and *direct store delivery* of merchandise will eliminate 8 to 10 hours per week in store ordering time.

What is the Future of SIMS?

For a retailer, a missed sale due to product not being on the shelf can have a lasting effect if the customer shifts loyalty to another outlet. Furthermore, if the supply is late, the retailer must resort to markdowns, reducing profitability and diverting time and space from more profitable items. When implemented, SIMS will help Walgreens avoid these problems.

The future of Walgreens rests in its ability to provide superior customer service. It will stay competitive in the future by developing the entire supply pipeline from the manufacturer to the final consumer. In other words, after a customer has left the store, data collected when the cashier scanned the purchase is being used to order its replacement. The order system will then notify the vendor who, in turn, will notify the manufacturer. There is no room for late deliveries, missed pick-ups, or other delays. The tolerance levels for lack of quality service are low and are going to get lower. SIMS has been designed to keep up with these evolving competitive standards.

SUMMARY

Chapter 4 discussed the ways in which managerial processes can help a company improve its success. In this chapter, we saw how operational processes have helped manufacturers who have been forced by competitive and customer pressures to seek strategic alternatives that provide greater product versatility and variability.

Among the alternatives available to manufacturers today are (1) to focus manufacturing on one or two specific geographic markets (the agile factory); (2) concentrate their manufacturing sourcing efforts on the world consumer with operations that emphasizes Multi-processed-skilled-labor, product-process colocated vertical integration, and cost/quality assurance (the product-focused factory); (3) mass specialization, a term that describes the orientation of companies that emphasize product diversity, want to proliferate their product offerings, are customer-driven, and require a rapidly changing mix of products, with consistent high quality and competitive pricing. In all alternatives, the virtual enterprise model will enable companies to quickly adopt and implement lower cost, rapid response and high quality initiatives throughout the enterprise value chain.

Time-based model strategies, currently gaining popularity and driven primarily by increasing customer expectations, focus the company on improving time-to-market and quality while reducing development costs. These strategies rely on concurrent engineering, which thrives on an environment characterized by the integration of people, process, and technology.

Another important method increasingly appealing to manufacturers is group technology, which is a fundamental tool for organizing production and information into families of similar characteristics. It is based on two principles that also highlight product/process/component characteristic differences: (1) like products should be manufactured in a like manner, and (2) parts and processes should be organized by their similarities. One methodology that applies group technology is computer-aided process planning (CAPP), which aids decision making by simplifying and organizing production layout, as well as reducing duplication in both product and process design and increasing component standardization.

Key operational principles that manufacturers have been using (albeit independently) and continue to find successful are (1) just-in-time (JIT), which tightly links the manufacturer to the supplier by allowing the manufacturer's work-in-process to trigger replenishment of supplier materials; (2) continuous flow manufacturing (CFM), which facilitates optimum throughput and asset management; and (3) quick response/point-of-sale systems, in which retail companies' order placement/fulfillment is driven by point-of-sale consumer transactions. Together these three principles establish a consistent operating philosophy that ties the virtual paradigm together.

Both managerial and operational processes rely heavily on technology, which will be discussed in depth in the next chapter.

CHAPTER 6
INFORMATION TECHNOLOGY
IN MANUFACTURING

INTRODUCTION

A manufacturing strategy is only as good as the vision it reflects and the people and technology enabling that vision. This chapter examines the key roles that technology and people play in developing and implementing effective manufacturing strategies for the 1990s and beyond.

These manufacturing strategies stem from three principal foundations of technology: information technology, material sciences, and equipment tool innovation. Many effective strategies today are built upon one or more of these technological foundations. Often, however, rapid change and increasing competition make strategies obsolete. In many instances, little effort is made to keep the enterprise's strategies current or to integrate them to take advantage of available synergy.

Figure 6–1 depicts a balanced process for implementing strategy. At the conceptual level, an awareness of strategic possibilities supports the formulation of a business vision. At the strategy level, specific manufacturing technologies help define and enable manufacturing as well as business strategy alternatives. This bottom-up and top-down alignment of vision and strategy makes for a highly integrated, implementable, and effective strategy and, therefore, greatly improves the likelihood of business success.

Technology enablers have an indirect impact by shaping the strategic options available to managers and a direct impact by providing the actual implementation tools and capabilities.

To address these issues, this chapter covers the following topics:

- The evolving strategic role of information technology.
- MRPII in a world-class manufacturer.
- Manufacturing applications.
- Factory floor computing.
- Computer-integrated manufacturing systems.
- Current and emerging technologies in manufacturing.

This chapter was written with the assistance of Mark LaRow.

269

FIGURE 6–1
Integrated Strategy Implementation

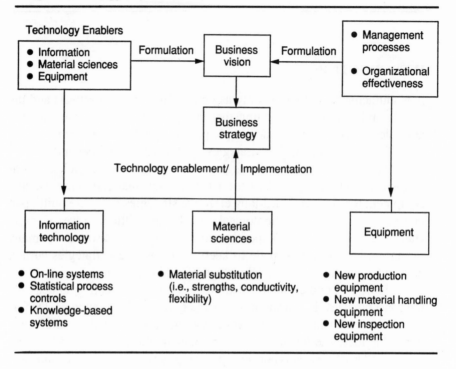

Information technology (IT) is challenging many fundamental and historical assumptions of manufacturing strategy and operations. IT pervades virtually every facet of a manufacturing organization. In some cases, IT automates existing business processes; in other instances it enables wholly new types of processes. IT can even create new markets and change the basis of how companies compete. The new opportunities created by information systems are playing a growing role in competitive positioning, and they are contributing to new ways of planning, managing, communicating, and working.

It will be increasingly difficult to define and implement an effective manufacturing strategy without relying on information systems. Unfortunately, only a few manufacturing executives have a sufficiently detailed technical foundation to be comfortable making policy decisions about information technology. This section is intended to help manufacturing executives gain a better appreciation of the power and limitations of information systems.

Contrary to the perspective of many computer technologists, hardware vendors, network designers, programmers, data base experts, and telecommunications specialists, a computer is not an information system. Information systems existed before the invention of the computer and will survive the next generation of high technology. An information system goes beyond computing technology to include the formalization of processes, procedures, data, and human roles and responsibilities as a structured mechanism for the execution of business operations. The computer and associated technology exist primarily to provide efficient mechanisms for systems enablement and control.

Unfortunately, the preoccupation with the technology component of information systems has hidden their true business orientation. Many business executives have delegated responsibility for systems and have thus surrendered control of the heart of the operations of their enterprise. This control has been transferred to the computer technologists, who often have little appreciation for the non-IT components of the overall system. As a result, management has often received technology-focused solutions for problems that were primarily operational or strategic, thereby adding to the organization's complexity and overhead without solving the original problem. Most technology-based solutions fail to take into full account the nontechnical elements of people and policy, and add unnecessary rigidity and expense. Properly applied computer-based information systems will be virtually transparent to the organization's higher objectives; such systems will address the problem at hand without imposing new constraints on the organization. Properly designed and applied IT-based systems permit users to focus on the conduct of business and the delivery of a product or service, not on the media for interacting or communicating. MIPS (millions of instructions per second), memory, disk drives, and networks rarely create value for the user in and of themselves. They are a means to an end—that of providing a platform for applications that support business processes. Successful systems employ a variety of computing and noncomputing elements. Hardware and software work in concert with logical processes and human-executed procedures to provide timely and efficient operations.

Information Technology and Intellectual Capital

Technology has always exerted powerful influence over manufacturing, and information technology (IT) has been the most powerful agent of change in this century. IT provides the underlying resource to develop a most important asset of the manufacturing enterprise: its intellectual capital. Intellectual capital—the knowledge of who the customers are, how to design a product, and how to build it, distribute it, and sell it—is now considered at least as valuable as the traditional land, labor, and capital resources of standard economic theory. Intellectual capital has risen to its high level of importance because it is now feasible to be a major manufacturing concern with very little investment in land, labor, or capital. "The new role of management in manufacturing is to create and nurture the project teams whose intellectual capabilities produce competitive advantage," according to Dr. Ramchandran Jaikumar. "What gets managed is intellectual capital, not equipment."[1] An increasing percentage of the value added to products and services stems from information. For example, a major producer of athletic footwear owns none of the raw material, none of the manufacturing facilities, and almost none of the retail outlets in its value chain and yet is a major and highly successful "manufacturer."

How is it possible to be a major manufacturer without owning manufacturing capacity? The answer lies in owning the knowledge, and thus the control, of the manufacturing function—in owning the mechanisms by which nonowned entities can be coordinated into a virtual manufacturer as described in Chapter 2. Many companies, particularly in high technology and biotechnology, are placing greater emphasis today on owning the intellectual capital and on using information technology to harness that capital for strategic purposes. There are many smaller examples of how intellectual capital affects the intrinsic capabilities of the manufacturing enterprise. Just as the sergeants in the army maintain the institutional knowledge necessary to keep the army running, so the plant forepersons maintain the institutional knowledge that keeps the plants functioning.

Information technology—in the form of computers, networks, application programs, and data bases—is absolutely essential for operating complex organizations, including virtual organizations. Information technology extends a company's ability to harness intellectual capital beyond the limits of individual human beings and organizational structures. IT can

- Capture and store large amounts of data.
- Process that data into higher forms of information suitable for decision making.

---

[1]Ramchandran Jaikumar, "Postindustrial Manufacturing," *Harvard Business Review*, November/December 1986, p. 69.

- Monitor, control, and execute many of the functions of an enterprise.
- Help make rudimentary decisions using the evolving technology of expert systems.
- Perform these operations faster, with greater capacity, and with greater consistency than any human-based or institutional-based intellectual capital resource.
- Share the organization's intellectual capital among many people in ways not possible without information technologies.

Information technology is closely coupled with business innovation and competitive advantage. Successful IT programs can result in simultaneous improvements in quality, cost, and delivery of goods and services. IT enables intimate and informed relationships with a manufacturer's customers and suppliers. As open systems gain momentum on a global scale, IT will provide backbone connectivity for information flowing throughout the larger manufacturing enterprise. As IT broadens its role, computer-integrated manufacturing support will become computer-integrated enterprise support, enabling manufacturers to add "full service" value throughout the value chain. IT primarily makes more information and makes it more accessible. When coupled with well-managed organizations, IT will produce superior results. In poorly managed companies, IT will only accelerate the inevitable.

It is alleged that information technology is reinvented every three to five years—a fantastic rate of advance. Moreover, the advances in information technology over the past ten years (starting with the introduction of the personal computer and the advanced microprocessor) and the progression expected over the next five years represent truly novel uses of information technology. Indeed, computing will continue to automate functions, but it will also be used as a medium for communications and coordination among people; it will be used to "generate information" rather than simply store and retrieve data; it will be used to extend and share individual intellectual capital rather than to simply store and retrieve institutional intellectual capital.[2] IT will rank on the same level as excellence in quality, service, and process in defining the world-class enterprises of the 1990s.

---

[2]For a complete discussion of this topic, see Shoshana Zuboff, *The Age of the Smart Machine* (New York: Basic Books, 1988).

A Historical Perspective of Information Technology in Manufacturing

Today, the typical manufacturing company's information technology is characterized by an extraordinary array of totally incompatible computers and networks. IT functions are supported by a very large collection of sometimes gigantic and intricate applications that have been substantially modified and patched over the years in an attempt to support the firm's changing needs. This process has been a losing battle. In many instances, the very information systems put in place to improve business operations are actually hindering its ability to adapt to the rapidly changing environment and are reducing its competitiveness. To understand this problem, we must first put information technology into historical perspective.

Initially, IT was introduced into manufacturing firms in much the same way that it entered other vertical industries—as an aid to the accounting function, owned by the financial arm of the enterprise. However, fundamental differences between the unique needs of manufacturing enterprises and those of other vertical industries soon caused manufacturers to use computers much more aggressively and in a wider set of roles.

From the early 1960s through the mid 1980s, an uncoordinated approach to IT investment was the natural outgrowth of the prevailing methodologies and the basic limitations of information technology. No computer was powerful enough to support the application demands of all functions across all operating units. No software programmer was capable of integrating all the diverse manufacturing functions into a single application. Networking technology did not allow distributed applications or computers to work effectively together. The result was the appearance of many distinct and incompatible information systems. Such disjunction was found not just between business units or even between functional areas within business units; in some instances, incompatibility existed between departments within a single functional area and between engineers within the same department. Incompatible "islands of automation" have become a standard operating condition for IT in virtually all major manufacturing concerns. Were it not for the expenses of duplicate personnel and maintenance, there would be little justification for consolidating or standardizing on a limited set of information technologies.

By the early 1970s, the first integrated applications began appearing in the manufacturing enterprise. These applications were extensions of existing applications and integrated some limited set of cross-functional processes. The initial impetus for these integrated applications was to reduce the tremendous amount of duplicate information being maintained by the multiplicity of information systems. The duplicated information would very quickly get "out of sync" with the various versions of itself, corrupting organizations' knowledge bases and often resulting in interrelated decisions being based on differing sets of data. Furthermore, employees spent a tremendous amount of time maintaining duplicate data stores.

These first integrated applications were monolithic in nature. All functions were written by the same software developers; the interactions between the functions and the format of the data stores were completely proprietary. Most attempts at software modularity were sacrificed for the sake of remaining consistent with an installed base of nonmodular code and for the sake of optimizing performance. Without modularity, it became exceedingly difficult to add new functions to a growing jigsaw puzzle of tightly integrated code. Eventually, the software vendors went back to the drawing board and reengineered the primary "integrated manufacturing software" MRP systems. These MRP applications were still not modular, and thus could not easily accept new functions, but they did integrate many fundamental functions of the planning operations area, including inventory management, production scheduling, materials requirements planning, capacity requirements planning, bill of materials, and warehousing.

Next-Generation Software

The biggest change in next-generation manufacturing software will not be new features or functions; rather, it will be in the form of an entirely new architecture for the application. The new architecture will be based on open systems (allowing the programs to be run on a variety of different computers); on modular applications code (allowing different modules from different vendors to be pieced together to form pseudo-customized applications); and on network computing standards (allowing the application to be broken into pieces, each one potentially running on a different computer in the network but working as one logical computer).

Manufacturing's massive need for computerization stems from its need to control its diverse data-intensive and activity-intensive functions and processes: managing and tracking inventory, labor tracking, machine maintenance, quality, costs, shipments, receivables, design changes, configurations, marketing changes, cash flow, and so on. In no other industry does information *automation* offer such significant power to improve operational performance. Automation by itself, however, rarely offers complete control over these activities.

As with any complex system, the many diverse components of the manufacturing system affect each other in highly complicated ways. For example, design decisions affect manufacturing decisions, manufacturing decisions affect marketing programs, marketing programs affect sales strategies, sales strategies affect financial decisions, and financial decisions affect customer/supplier relations, which in turn affect design decisions. *Integration* offers stunning possibilities; whereas computerization can monitor and control individual activities, application integration can begin to control the overall process in a coordinated manner.

The strategic concept that describes the integrated control and operation of the primary manufacturing processes is computer-integrated manufacturing (CIM). In the grand CIM vision, all diverse groups within the manufacturing value chain (including the traditional entities of engineering, operations, and business, as well as the less traditional entities of supplier, fabricator, distributor, retailer, and customer) should be linked in a "computerized forum" to coordinate and optimize their aggregate functions in the value chain. In other words, the best way to optimize any piece of the value chain is to optimize the entire value chain. The reason that "computerized" is part of "integrated manufacturing" is that there are no human systems capable of coordinating the complex and multidimensional interactions needed to support this scale of integration. In truth, however, even the computerized version of integrated manufacturing has not lived up to its promise.

In most CIM implementations, the information systems (IS) managers report limited long-term value because the CIM packages (principally MRPII packages) are so complicated, intricately integrated, and customized that no one can keep them up to date. A company's business processes and products change much more rapidly than the information systems can be modified to support these changes. Information technology today is barely capable of providing the high degree of integration necessary to achieve a static implementation of the CIM vision. The sophistication needed in IT to accommodate the dynamic nature of the real world of manufacturing is only beginning to emerge.

The overall value of a firm's IT investment is additive when the individual systems are operated independently; it becomes multiplicative, however, when the systems are integrated. The whole becomes greater than the sum of the parts when linkages are formed among the parts. This realization spurred the shift from an "automation strategy" in the 1960s to an "integration strategy" in manufacturing IT in the 1970s and 1980s. Ironically, those firms that invested most heavily in automation were least able to shift to an integrated environment. The reason is that systems developed without integration in mind are difficult or impossible to integrate after the fact. Automation without integration creates an intrinsic barrier to later integration.

Figure 6–2 describes the strategic role of information technology during three somewhat overlapping eras. During the first era, 1960s–1970s, the strategic role of IT was automation. Achievement of the goal was based on measurable changes in factory throughput and labor costs. Technology replaced people (robots replaced factory labor, accounting systems replaced bookkeepers). Information technology was also implemented to increase speed and efficiency in isolated workflow areas.

The importance of integration was the theme of the second era, which was identified in the 1970s when integrated information technology

FIGURE 6–2
Role of Information Technology in Manufacturing

	1960s–1970s	1970s–1980s	1980s–1990s
IT Emphasis	Automation ⟶	Integration ⟶	Flexibility
Primary IT Objectives	• Factory throughput • Labor costs	• Speed-to-market • Quality control • Customer/supplier coordination • Global efficiency	• Adapt to changing markets • Adapt to changing organizations • Accommodate new products • Adapt to changing business relationships
Principle Results	Islands of automation	Integration	Flexible integration

was still very immature. However, the 1980s witnessed the appearance of integrated MRPII packages that ran on very large mainframes or sets of midrange computers and were capable of integrating many fundamental manufacturing support processes. Because of the state of the art in several key IT disciplines, however, these new integrated systems lacked the flexibility to accommodate change.

The Flexibility Imperative

During the 1980s, one of manufacturers' fundamental concerns became flexibility—the ability to adapt to changing markets, changing product specifications, changing strategic relationships, changing economic and market conditions, changing competition, changing quality expectations, and changing business processes. This concern is the basis of flexible manufacturing systems (FMS) discussed in Chapter 5. Unfortunately, IT integration efforts had focused on setting up static models for integrating functions and processes. What we have learned through the 1980s is that one of the primary measures of competitiveness is adaptability. Business processes are changing at an ever increasing rate. Software applications embody those processes and therefore must change at the same rate in order to enable rather than inhibit change. The complex integration of already complex applications created an environment that limits and even throttles change. Just as very large investments in stand-alone automation hindered the move to an integrated environment, so too have large investments in monolithically integrated systems hindered the move to flexible systems. Thus, in many cases, integrated information systems that were installed to enhance competitiveness are now hindering it.

One might argue that the entire *raison d'être* of the current generation of monolithic integrated applications is to accommodate change in a coordinated fashion. On closer examination, one realizes that this flexibility is in tactical areas, representing only perturbations on the steady-state operating processes. For example, MRPII applications are designed to accommodate changes of product mixes, adapt to variations in materials delivery and machine throughput, and even to adjust to some changes in product design. But these kinds of tactical changes must all occur within the confines of the current business processes that have been "hard coded" into the MRPII system. Strategic changes—bringing a new product to market, establishing an electronic relationship with the customer, reorganizing into a flatter structure, and merging with another enterprise—are completely outside the range of current MRPII flexibility.

Information technology has historically been incapable of achieving high degrees of both integration and flexibility. The more complex something became, the harder it was to change it. Fortunately, two major trends in information technology will alter this situation. The first trend is toward a more infrastructure-oriented view of IT investments, and the second is toward a set of distributed and modular technologies that are designed to act in a unified manner. These trends represent profoundly different ways of thinking about computing as well as profoundly new technologies with which to implement ideas.

THE EVOLVING STRATEGIC ROLE
OF INFORMATION TECHNOLOGY

Creating Competitive Opportunities

Can a competitive manufacturing enterprise really move in a single direction with unified purpose? As top management charts business, service, and product strategies, it must have complete confidence that the organization is willing and able to respond to the challenges and opportunities of an often turbulent market. *Information technology can act as a powerful integrating force in the manufacturing enterprise.*

A recent information technology study predicted that fully 50 percent of new corporate investment will be in technology and that CIM will be at the core of competitive manufacturing.[3] This forecast underscores the transition of manufacturing from a physical capital orientation to an intellectual capital orientation. Reflecting this change, information technology is expected be the principal agent of change and enabler of productivity for the next decade and beyond. It can shrink time and distance and support new channels for distribution.

By shrinking time and distance, information technology significantly alters two of the most fundamental business processes: the conversion of customer orders into shipped products and the basic design of new products and processes to meet the changing needs of customers. Long-distance telecommunication of orders, detailed product engineering information (including design schematics and other graphics), and

---

[3]Ernst & Young, "The Landmark MIT Study: Management in the 1990s—Executive Summary," Cleveland, Ohio 1989, pp. 14–15.

the electronic transfer of funds support multinational supplier networks and worldwide customer markets.

New competitive opportunities emerge through ad hoc partnerships in markets that may span thousands of miles and multiple political boundaries. According to Ramchandran Jaikumar, "Firms can now operate as virtual entities with relationships and business processes particular to each situation, product line, market segment. . . .The shift from adversarial relationships with upstream and downstream players, to partnering is critical to effective network operations."[4]

Just-in-time materials management is often facilitated by alliances among manufacturers and by a reduction in the number of suppliers. *In such virtual partnerships, sharing information, tracking inventory, and timing deliveries will depend on comprehensive electronic communication.* Nothing can replace the telephone; increasingly, however, nothing can substitute for electronic networks that tie computers together, give them a common language, and allow them to query one another as well as respond to queries from enterprise personnel.

Information systems frequently offer hidden opportunities for competitive advantage that can potentially redefine a business or a marketing and distribution system. For example, large real estate agencies have developed interstate networks to relocate corporate employees into distant markets. And manufacturers are outfitting their sales forces with portable computers that can dial into corporate networks to configure customer orders, determine current prices, and assess product delivery dates—all at the customer's site. Electronic markets provide new business opportunities and will continue to prosper in the 1990s. These networks support new ways of buying and selling, especially when products are standardized and are easily described. Here, *the network becomes the key enabler, allowing trading within the enterprise and across the value chain, regardless of geographical boundaries.*

Manufacturers need to be aware of these new competitive opportunities created by information technology. Management can choose to pursue technology leadership or fast followership, but by ignoring these opportunities, organizations run the risk of being blindsided by information technology. As Ramchandran Jaikumar states, "It could well be that the opportunities for new and improved ways of doing work in business

---

[4]Jaikumar, p. 69.

can only be realized by those who have strategically established the requisite information technology infrastructure, . . . if so, then the sustainable information technology based competitive advantage that was so elusive in the '80s could indeed be attained in the not too distant future."[5]

Improving Processes and Linkages

The simplification of business processes, coupled with the sophistication of information systems, presents powerful opportunities for manufacturers. Bureaucratic business processes and archaic computer systems and applications create information-in-process that has the same clogging effect on the enterprise as work-in-process has on the factory. *Industry Week Magazine* noted recently, "It's ironic that many of today's products are designed and analyzed in a matter of days thanks to CAD/CAM, only to be held up by old-fashioned review processes that can take weeks or even months."[6]

Integration is key to overall productivity and should lead to shortened time-to-market, lower development costs, and increased product quality. Integration, however, is multidimensional. The potential of technology to act as an integrating agent can be maximized only when applied in concert with aligned business strategies, appropriate culture, trained people, focused organizational structure, and tightly coordinated business processes. With all these in place, integration can be pursued through slow, deliberate evolution or through revolutionary innovation.

The MIT Study, *Management in the '90s*, identified five levels of business integration. Two are evolutionary, three are revolutionary.[7]

Evolutionary:
1. Localized exploitation to optimize an existing function (e.g., order processing).
2. Internal integration and optimization.

---

[5] Jaikumar, p. 69.

[6] "Breaking Down the Barriers to Integration: CAD/CAM Planning: 1991," in John Krouse, Robert Mills, Beverly Beehert, Laura Carrabine, and Lawrence Berardinis, *Special Supplement to Industry Week Magazine*, Penton Publishers, July 1991, CCI.

[7] Michael S. Scott Morton, *The Corporation of the 1990s*, (New York: Oxford University Press, 1991), pp. 128–150.

Revolutionary:
3. Business process redesign using information technology.
4. Business network redesign, restructuring of the value chain of an industry or market, enabled by information technology.
5. Business scope redefinition based upon information provided by IT (competitors, suppliers, customers, etc.).

The importance of concurrent business process redesign through process value analysis cannot be overstated. "Companies invest heavily in the latest CAD-to-CAM hardware and software to automate as many jobs as possible in their operation," states Robert H. Hayes. "And soon after these systems are installed, separate groups and departments may issue glowing reports stating how user productivity is improved, in some cases dramatically. Many of these same companies are often puzzled and disappointed, however, when they see no appreciable gains in their overall operation. It takes just as long to get products out the door. Costs are about the same. And quality is hardly any better."[8] The reason is that these manufacturers implement CAD-to-CAM on a spot basis, with work flowing through the same old channels, usually in the form of paper documentation thrown over the wall from one group to another. So no matter how impressive individual gains are, they are overshadowed or mitigated by much larger problems in the organization. Integration must be pursued on all dimensions concurrently and management must ensure that integration efforts are closely linked to business strategies. Otherwise executives may find themselves creating expensive solutions to the wrong problems or spot solutions that provide strictly localized improvements.

Time-to-market can be a primary objective of technology-enabled process improvement. Eastman Kodak Co., for example, utilized cross-functional teams from marketing, engineering, and manufacturing to design and produce its entry into the single-use camera market in response to a major competitive threat. Groups of engineers worked on different components of the product simultaneously and kept abreast of other groups' progress through a common CAD/CAM repository that was updated daily. New ad hoc organization structures, teaming, and technology combined to deliver this new line of products to consumers in record time. Similarly, Federal Mogul reduced its proposal time from 20 weeks

[8]Ibid, CCI.

to 20 days using integrated CAD/CAM aligned with integrated business and organizational design.

The efficient sharing of information is central to improving and linking business processes. This sharing requires well-structured data that is accessible through properly designed networks. Information technologists must cooperate with manufacturing executives to design information infrastructures that promote sharing. Frequently, shared information will prompt company thought-leaders to ask unexpected but highly relevant questions that may result in new products and new processes. It is difficult to calculate the value of one good idea. Through information sharing, organizational restraints can be removed, ad hoc cross-functional teams can flourish, and new measures of performance can effectively focus on quality, timeliness, and cost of the product. Training in the new skills related to teamwork and group facilitation are essential. "Once feared as a force that would depersonalize the corporation, information technology has in fact begun to bind corporate employees into a more integrated whole."[9]

For manufacturers, improving business processes through multidimensional efforts, including information technology, is no longer an option. It is essential to survival. Computer-aided design, computer-aided manufacture, and the linking of processes through the computer-integrated enterprise are more than attractive options. They are core techniques that will define competition well into the next century.

Information Technology's Role in Enabling New Organizational Structures

Integration implies the bringing together of diverse ingredients into a unified whole—or at least into a tightly interwoven fabric. This description also defines the process of centralization. This similarity would suggest that the way to achieve integration is through centralization. Conversely, however, flexibility implies independent adaptation to a changing environment, which defines a decentralized structure. Is it possible to achieve integrated-flexibility if centralization and decentralization are opposites? Apparently enterprises can indeed achieve much higher levels of integrated-flexibility by decentralizing their organizational structures, to gain flexibility, while using IT to provide the integration "glue."

---

[9]Jaikumar, p. 69.

Information technology itself must first achieve much higher levels of integrated-flexibility so that the glue can be easily melted and reformed as needs change. This is now possible using the new technologies of network computing combined with decentralized IS organizations.

For the centralized organizational model, IT could conceivably provide the level of communications and control that would enable top management to change courses quickly and dramatically, which is the classical strategic promise of information technology. For the decentralized model, IT could provide the linkages between individual entities such that integration is obtained despite considerable autonomy. As a matter of course, both centralized and decentralized organizational models are likely to persist through the 1990s. Several major advances in technology will affect the ability to set up enabling IT infrastructures that can integrate disparate business entities without forcing monolithic structures. These advances are in the areas of computing technology, networking, and applications development. Underlying these advances are industry trends—the move toward open systems and the linking of an infrastructure approach to IT architectures—that affect the impact of IT as much as the advances in the technologies themselves.

Manufacturing Alignment with Information Technology

Like many terms in everyday use, "information technology" can mean different things to different people. Before presenting IT strategy alignment in detail, it may therefore be helpful to define the technologies included. Because IT strategy ought to consider the broadest possible scope, the definition of IT includes

- Transaction processing applications.
- Information processing and reporting applications.
- Decision support systems.
- Executive support systems.
- Professional productivity and groupware tools.
- Knowledge-based systems and artificial intelligence.
- Process automation and robotics.
- Voice and data communications.
- Design and manufacturing automation.
- Embedded computer technology, such as microprocessors in autos or security tags.

- Computing platforms.
- Data base management.
- Automatic identification, such as bar code readers.
- Imaging and multimedia.

This definition comprises a range of technologies somewhat broader than the transaction processing and management information systems that are the traditional focus of information systems planning. This wider definition reflects the accelerating integration of information systems with telecommunications and the bold new applications of IT in areas such as manufacturing, design, and control.

Information technology has traditionally been deployed in support of already formulated manufacturing strategies and processes, rather than playing a critical role in shaping those strategies and processes. Positioning IT in a proactive role—where manufacturing strategy is not viewed as given, but rather as something developed in light of emerging information technologies and applications—is a much more powerful approach. This is especially critical given the increasingly central position IT occupies in most organizations. As Terrence Paré observes, "Whether companies make potato chips or computer chips, intellectual capital is increasingly becoming their most valuable asset. Tomorrow's winners will be those best able to exploit the brains of their researchers, the power in their proprietary software, the data from their market research, and the management systems they use to link this all together."[10]

In most manufacturing enterprises, an explicit definition of IT's role in manufacturing strategy (as opposed to manufacturing processes) does not formally exist. Instead, so-called strategic information systems plans, with supporting application/data/technology architectures, are developed in response to the manufacturing strategy. Thus, manufacturing strategy is developed without explicit consideration of the ways in which IT might fundamentally alter the basic philosophy and approach to manufacturing.

To compensate for this shortcoming, John Henderson and N. Venkatraman suggested one approach to considering the relationship between Information Technology use and strategy.[11] Their alignment approach to IT strategy is based on the common-sense premise that the effective use

---

[10]Terrence Paré, "Who May Thrive Now," *Fortune*, 22 April 1991, p. 58.

[11]John C. Henderson and N. Venkatraman, "Understanding Strategic Alignment," *Business Quarterly*, Winter 1991, pp. 8–15.

of Information Technology requires consistency between the organization's business strategy and its IT strategy. In other words, a set of IT principles are established that align the opportunities and limitations of the technology marketplace with the company's competitive strategy so that the overall strategy is facilitated.

As we move into the 1990s, however, relegating IT to a supporting role is becoming increasingly outdated. Leading firms are now seeking ways of exploiting IT to remake their basic manufacturing processes and strategies. The most effective and sustainable examples of IT use are found when IT has been woven into the very fiber of the firm.

The Traditional Role of Information Technology in Strategy Formulation

If the objective is to incorporate IT into every aspect of the firm's strategic thinking, the traditional approach (depicted in Figure 6–3) is inadequate on three dimensions. First, the rapid evolution of IT itself is not explicitly considered a lever to change either the manufacturing strategy or the manufacturing processes and infrastructure. It is often said that IT represents the single most powerful tool for redesigning the enterprise, but the way IT is typically planned and implemented rarely allows for this higher-level discussion. IT considerations are usually tactical, introduced only after the general strategies have been developed.

Second, the competitive environment and manufacturing strategy are not defined in terms that are helpful for identifying opportunities to use IT strategically. At best, a short list of critical success factors that help to focus attention on important areas is developed, but little effort is made to describe how the firm will use IT to change the manufacturing process and its relationships with customers, suppliers, and competitors. Because IT is not really considered in this strategic context, there is little chance of identifying a best practice for a particular business process, either within the industry or in other industries.

Third, in most of the important examples of strategic IT use, the overall technology architecture, rather than any single application, provides the real competitive benefit. Traditionally, however, the architecture is considered only as an internal issue to be addressed after determining which applications and data must be supported. To take full advantage of the emerging technologies likely to be important to the firm, architectures providing the framework for future IT use and evolving manufacturing strategy must be developed.

FIGURE 6–3

Traditional Relationship Between Competitive Strategy and Information Technology

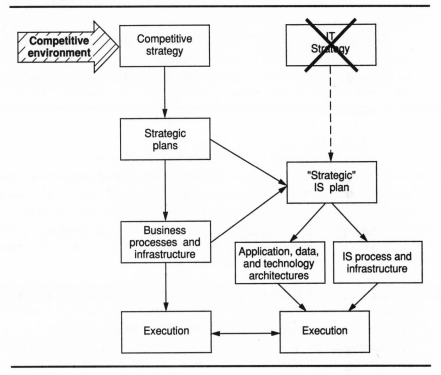

In many instances, the linkage between the firm's manufacturing strategy and its use of IT is developed through multiple independent planning, analysis, and design efforts; consequently, the likelihood is small that IT will have meaningful strategic impact. There is no strategy touchstone for manufacturing executives to use in making decisions about new applications, technology, and process. Because no overarching principles guide the hundreds of detailed decisions made yearly, each is independent of the others. Although these decisions may be optimized locally, there is no conscious and careful alignment of the firm's use of IT with its manufacturing strategy to optimize the overall strategy.

In an ideal world, there would not be a need for a separate IT strategy alignment exercise, since each component of the company's strategy would already incorporate and account for IT. For most firms, however, this is not yet the case. Therefore, IT strategy alignment can be a very useful exercise when undertaking strategic IT planning, architecture development, and other far-reaching, necessary tasks.

Strategy versus Planning

At the simplest level, an IT strategy expresses the firm's basic beliefs about its use of IT. This is not an action plan or a set of decisions, but a collection of fundamental principles that guide future decision making. For example, an IT strategy might include such directives as

- "All new product development will explicitly consider ways to embed IT capabilities into product design and delivery."
- "Because integrating our design teams located around the world is so critical to us, we will invest in leading edge groupware CAD systems. We will aggressively pursue new and experimental applications without requiring formal cost-benefit justification."
- "All product divisions will have responsibility for application development and acquisition, but all decisions about technology platforms and infrastructure will be made by corporate IS."

An IT strategy helps managers define the boundaries for deciding on future actions, but it stops short of determining the actions themselves. This is the fundamental difference between IT strategy and IT planning. IT strategy sets the priorities that govern decision making by users and data processing professionals. It forms the policy framework for the firm's use of IT and describes what senior executives can expect the IT infrastructure to deliver. IT planning, on the other hand, focuses on the execution of the IT strategy. Timing also plays a key role in distinguishing between IT strategy and IT planning. Business and IT strategies have time horizons that extend many years into the future. In contrast, IT plans typically focus on the next two or three years.

Information Technology Strategy Alignment Process

It is useful to draw a distinction between the content of an IT strategy and the process by which that strategy is developed. Three particularly important aspects of IT strategy content are

- Positioning and scope of IT activities.
- IT resource requirements and constraints.
- IT management and partnership.

Figure 6–4
Information Technology Strategy Alignment

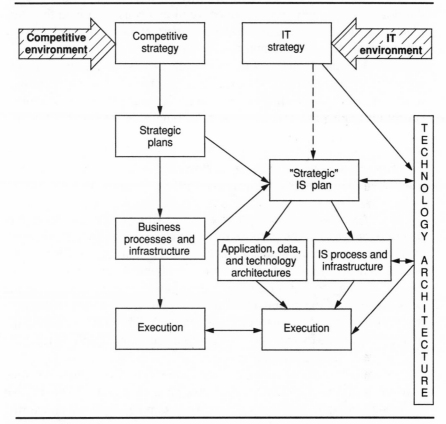

The fundamental difference between IT strategy alignment and traditional strategic IT planning is the use of IT as a formative driver of the firm's strategy, rather than just as a response or enabler. (See Figure 6–4.) IT strategy alignment can be thought of as the firm's linkage between a hostile competitive environment and the available technologies that position the firm for success. The technology architecture represents the infrastructure of that technology as applied to the specific opportunities of the business.

Effective Implementation Is Essential
Effective implementation clearly matters more than clever strategy. A consistent and focused program of innovation can make almost any strat-

egy a huge success, whereas even the most promising strategy will fail if processes, plans, and organizational behavior are not consistent. Therefore, the objective of the IT/manufacturing alignment approach is to develop an IT strategy that is supportive of and consistent with the manufacturing strategy, focused on a few important missions, and feasible given prevailing resources and constraints.

The IT/manufacturing alignment approach is not designed to uncover the single best IT strategy for any enterprise. Rather, its purpose is to identify the best match between a particular company's manufacturing capabilities and enterprise strategy in keeping with the possibilities that emerging IT presents.

The Four Phases of the Alignment Process

The actual IT/manufacturing alignment process consists of four phases.

PHASE I: Assess Alignment Between Current IT and Manufacturing Strategies.   The purpose of this phase is to document the firm's existing manufacturing strategy and existing IT strategy in a format conducive to analyzing the alignment between them. At one level, the purpose of strategy formulation and strategic planning is to ensure that the organization has the means (resources, organization, and processes) to reach its ends (goals, objectives, and mission). Therefore, one measure of alignment is the extent to which the organization is capable of reaching its goals with the existing IT principles.

A second measure of alignment is the extent to which the time horizon is consistent with pace of change anticipated by the IT and manufacturing strategies is consistent. For example, if the manufacturing strategy includes the goal of adding a significant new product every quarter for the next few years, then IT resources must provide for this goal.

A third dimension is objectives and values. A common form of misalignment occurs when the objectives and values of those responsible for the strategy domains are inconsistent. This frequently occurs when IT executives are not considered part of the senior management team and thus are not privy or contributing to the overall direction of the firm. At higher levels, there may be a lack of consensus, especially between IT executives and senior management, over the appropriate role of IT within the firm. For example, a chief information officer can consider himself or herself part of senior management but be excluded from acquisition or diversification decisions that involve the rest of the senior management.

PHASE 2: Identify Potential Impacts of IT on Manufacturing Strategy. In this phase, the frame of reference for the analysis expands to include the external IT environment. Alternatives to the current IT strategy are identified by investigating existing or emerging information technologies with relevance to the firm and by reviewing efforts of other organizations that have developed IT approaches applicable to the firm's strategic direction.

These efforts uncover IT options derived from the latest developments in technology and management approaches to IT that are relevant to the firm's strategic situation. The level of effort expended on this stage is determined by such factors as the degree of importance of leading-edge technology to the business strategy, the firm's willingness to accept IT-related risk, and the project team's industry knowledge and experience.

PHASE 3: Draft Aligned IT Strategy Alternatives. In this phase, the team creates a first draft of the organization's revised information technology strategy based on the alignment assessment of the current strategy and the candidate business practices and technologies identified through external scanning. The alignment assessment report provides a baseline for developing the new IT strategy. It highlights those areas of the existing IT strategy that must be revised because they inhibit or are ineffective in enabling the achievement of business goals. It also identifies areas in which there are currently no supporting IT principles. The revised and aligned IT strategy incorporates the findings of the external scan of industry practices and technology, ensuring that the strategy reflects the current state of the art and is not based solely on an internal review and perspective.

PHASE 4: Refine IT Strategy. In this final phase, the project team formalizes the draft IT strategy by documenting it in detail, refining and confirming it with senior executives, and devising a structure and plan for its implementation.

Information Technology Strategy Forces a Competitive Perspective

An IT strategy should encourage the organization to focus on activities with the greatest competitive impact. These may or may not be activities with the largest short-run financial benefits. In fact, a simple test of the effectiveness of an IT strategy may be whether an organization rejects otherwise attractive projects, such as those with a high ROI or low risk, because they are not consistent with the strategy.

Unlike strategic IT planning, information technology/manufacturing alignment takes a proactive approach to strategy formulation. Here the manufacturing strategy is not viewed as a given, but as something that should be challenged and, perhaps, modified in light of emerging technologies and applications. At the simplest level, an IT strategy expresses the firm's basic beliefs about its use of IT. It is not an action plan or a set of decisions, but a collection of fundamental directives and principles that guide future decision making.

Having examined the issues of IT and strategy, we will now explore some historic and current manufacturing applications.

MRPII IN A WORLD-CLASS MANUFACTURER

Historical Perspective

Manufacturers historically have attempted to use manufacturing systems as a means for mirroring segments of their operations. Originally, the focus of such efforts was on narrowly defined manufacturing functions such as inventory planning and production order scheduling. Over time, these material requirements planning (MRP) techniques evolved into the now familiar closed-loop manufacturing resource planning model MRPII. MRPII provides a comprehensive set of techniques that permit direct linkage between business, sales, and operations. Further, it permits monitoring actual versus planned performance and gauging manufacturing's financial impact on the business, thus providing the opportunity to close the loop with corrective action.

MRPII is an excellent example of a system that serves both an interdepartmental and an intradepartmental function. Launched in the late 1960s, it elevated the role of manufacturing management to planning and performance accountability. MRPII emphasizes the integrity of information, not simply its availability, and links individual applications through their common data. Futhermore, class "A" MRPII recognizes the optimal and consistent execution of all the critical modules, data integrity and performance objectives. This is rarely accomplished, but when done so, it reaps incredible rewards. (For an example, see the DEC case in Chapter 7.)

Three factors emerge as critical to maximizing the benefits from MRPII in this environment:

First, World-Class Companies Must Employ MRPII Techniques across the Entire Organization.   Time-based competition dictates that planning must focus on all segments of the company's logistics chain, not just on the manufacturing segment. Further, planning must incorporate all stages (including preproduction and postproduction) of the product cycle. This level of planning implies an awareness of operations both upstream and downstream from production that few companies have in place. Achieving this awareness requires a thorough understanding of the underlying business and operational processes, their outputs, and their impact on subsequent processes. Before MRPII techniques can be utilized to maximum effectiveness, the execution of underlying business processes must first be synchronized all along the logistics chain.

Second, Business and MRPII Performance Measures Must Be Directly Linked.   Performance measurement begins at the strategic level with the definition of the business objectives and the critical success factors (CSFs) necessary to achieve these objectives. A distinguishing feature of world-class companies is that factors affecting operational performance are clearly linked to business objectives.

Third, Technology Enablement Becomes a Critical Element in Gaining Timely Access to Critical MRPII Information.   The information requirements of a world-class manufacturer drive the need for highly integrated information architectures, often supported by network and communications technology. Direct linkage with CAD and CAM applications can significantly improve the integrity of product and process data while radically compressing design-to-production-volume cycle time. Forecast, order management, and distribution requirements planning applications can be integrated with MRPII. Simulation tools can be linked directly to a company's core MRP application, permitting management to conduct multiple MRP regenerations within a very short time span. This allows management to evaluate the impact of many variables on the manufacturing/materials plan without actually having to change it. This type of flexibility provides a more comprehensive basis for informed decisions—affecting both responsiveness and the integrity of operational plans. Output from one MRP application serves as input to another within the same organization or value chain partner. However, direct linkage requires standards, consistency of data, and common approaches to planning if the process is to function effectively.

The complex organizational structures and the diverse information requirements of today's world-class companies demand a broader, more comprehensive MRPII model. World-class companies cannot rely solely on traditional Class A measurements of performance. Rather, they must define their own unique variations on performance metrics. These metrics should be linked to each company's objectives and based on an in-depth understanding of the underlying business processes being measured.

MANUFACTURING APPLICATIONS

The interface between the technological elements and the human elements of a system is accomplished through application software. Application software provides high-level logic, along with the means for accepting new data and delivering the results of computation to users. Application software controls the technology portion of an information system, whereas the human component controls the organizational and interpersonal portions of the system.

A manufacturing enterprise is a very complex environment and typically requires a broad range of software applications. These applications operate in all levels of a manufacturing organization: factory, operations, manufacturing, and enterprise (see Table 6–1). Through software applications, massive amounts of data and information become accessible to users, who are now able to make critical decisions more accurately and quickly than before. Advances in technology also permit entirely new methods of pursuing, capturing, and applying knowledge. These new approaches can, if employed effectively, bring competitive advantage. Unfortunately, these contemporary technologies can usually be mimicked or copied by competitors, often resulting in short-lived advantages and necessitating an ongoing pursuit of even more advanced capabilities.

Major user groups within an enterprise often develop applications independently. As a result, these applications take on characteristics that reflect the unique needs of their developers, without respect for value added elsewhere in the organization. For example, factory systems were designed for the often hostile physical environment of the factory floor. Their ruggedness is intended to survive such hazards as flying metal chips, grease, electromagnetic interference, excessive heat, and rough handling. Information technology for factory systems reflects a mixture of real-time machine and process control requirements based on rapid

TABLE 6–1
Manufacturing Applications

Business Level	Business Applications	Applications Software
Factory	• Equipment control	• CAM, FMS, DNC
	• Material storage/Retrieval	• Warehousing, AGV, AS/RS
	• Equipment maintenance	• Maintenance management
	• Process planning	• CAPP
	• Quality control systems	• CAT, CAI
	• Process control (QA)	• SPC
Manufacturing	• Logistics	• DRP
	• Purchasing	• MRP
	• Human resources	• Manpower planning and development
	• Business systems	• MRPII
Operations	• Engineering	• CAD, CAE, engineering data management, configuration management, CAD/CAM
	• Integrated manufacturing	• CIM
	• Market modeling	• Simulation, product-management
	• Sales support	• Sales/order management, POS
	• Finance and administration	• Product costing
Enterprise	• Asset management	• Investment value analysis
	• Business modeling	• Sales forecasting
	• Business control	• Executive information systems (EIS)
	• Human resources	• Computer-integrated enterprise (CIE)
	• Finance	• Career planning, training aids
		• AP/AR/GL

input/output processing, with transaction-oriented factory data collection systems that track quality, production, and labor. Engineering and business systems enjoy a more controlled physical operating environment and often have specially designed computer rooms. Engineering systems support creative and analytical processes and are typically highly interactive and graphical, making heavy use of computer-intensive simulation and

TABLE 6–2
Characteristics of Manufacturing Applications

Environment	Factory	Manufacturing/ Engineering Operations	Business
Personnel and focus	Blue-collar	Technical professional	Management, professional
	Machine control	Office/lab	Central or remote
		Creativity support	Structured processes
Information technology	Control software	Graphical, geometry	Transaction
	Real-time control	Simulation	Batch
	Input/output	Analytic LANs	Data oriented LANs, telecomm
Sample data	NC programs	Part geometry	Customer/ supplier data
	Ladder logic programs	Configuration	Financial/cost data
	Scheduling data	Bill of materials	Payroll data

modeling. Business systems support repetitive, structured procedures that are primarily data and transaction oriented, either on-line or in massive batch programs, which often run during off-hours. The characteristics of manufacturing applications are depicted in Table 6–2.

Manufacturing Applications Integration

The highly competitive nature and expanding geographic markets of manufacturing have fueled the development of innovative application solutions. As these applications have evolved and matured, the need to interface and integrate applications has become more critical. Integration permits ready sharing of data for a more fluid flow of information. Unfortunately, many applications were developed to stand alone and thus employ differing technologies, standards, and user interfaces. This often makes integrating applications extremely complex and time consuming.

As shown in Table 6–3, information systems for manufacturing have been evolving over a 30-year period toward the elusive goal that

TABLE 6-3
Manufacturing Systems and Technology Trends

	1960s	1970s	1980s	1990s
Factory systems	Manual	NC/CNC Relay logic Inspection	DNC/CAM Programmable process control robotics	Flexible manufacturing cells Intelligent device control Product design cells
Engineering systems	Drafting board	Drafting board Prototype	CAD drafting Finite element	CAD design modeling
Business systems	Serial MRP Purchase orders	Fragmented MRPII Blanket orders Standard costing Suboptimized	Interfaced CIM EDI Product costing Reengineered	Parallel Enterprise integration Value chain management Activity based costing Innovation
Information technology	Manual Task Paper Decentralized	Automated point solutions Telephone Centralized Operational Data Mainframe Batch	Interfaced Suboptimized Local networks Decentralized Tactical Information Minicomputer Personal computer On-line Software packages Protocols Screen text Data base	Integrated enterprise Telecommunications Centralized/decentralized Strategic Information Network Workstation Real-time CASE (models) Open systems Graphical Relational/object Fourth generation language Object orientation
	COBOL	PL/1 Basic	PASCAL	

might be characterized as flexible integration. IT that is flexible allows applications to evolve gracefully over time to respond to business change. However, the overall integration goal requires multiple levels of integration in several dimensions, one of which is the technology. Tightly coordinated business processes, an aligned and supportive corporate culture, and streamlined organization structures are also necessary if integration is to deliver the full benefits that the technology has to offer.

The primary objective of flexible integration is to enable the enterprise as a whole to respond to the competitive environment with unity of purpose and maximum efficiency and effectiveness. Many companies possess the creative energy and financial resources to accomplish their manufacturing objectives, but market leaders go beyond this level of performance to mobilize corporate resources toward an integrated and aligned set of goals. As enabled by information technology alignment, enterprise integration supports goal congruency and maximum utilization of resources in competitive battles. Some industry experts have termed this ideal the computer-integrated enterprise (CIE).

Packaged Software Support—Past and Present

In large organizations, the demand for systems has far outstripped IT production. As a result, more users are developing their own applications. In addition, the enterprise continues to require larger and more integrated systems. Since IS has limited resources, these trends have forced the purchase of large enterprise-wide systems from software vendors, with development costs shared by all their customers. Unfortunately, packaged software vendors face the same dilemma as IS organizations: they must choose whether to build their next generation products on AD/Cycle, UNIX, or Windows. Thus, large complex packaged software releases (e.g., MRP, Integrated Financial Systems) will always be a step behind the latest hardware advances.

Manufacturing software vendors are retooling their applications to provide more distributed, flexible, integrated support for their customers, which will lead in the future to several manufacturing software capabilities:

- *Distributed manufacturing systems.* As data base vendors provide better capabilities for distributed on-line data bases (e.g., improved support for UNIX workstations), manufacturing software package vendors will port their products to these new platforms. This will provide the manufacturer with a less expensive hardware platform and the user with a more responsive workstation.

- *Structured workgroup applications.* These new technologies will incorporate more project management and scheduling support over work processes. Such systems will integrate the creative information contained in CAD, word processing, and imaging with the discipline of project management and methodology (i.e., procedures).
- *Virtual manufacturing.* Virtual manufacturing infrastructures will allow engineering and operations not only to design and build new products, but also to review the manufacturing status, processes, and technologies in an on-line, off-site fashion.

To take advantage of these impending changes, the manufacturer must plan now. Technology decisions and investments made over the next five years will significantly affect the costs of incorporating these advanced manufacturing software packages.

Manufacturing IT—Critical Success Factors

This shift toward distributed, flexible architectures requires information executives to rethink their allocation of resources. Three critical areas need to be managed if a manufacturing enterprise is going to be able to implement the foregoing systems:

- *Architecture and standards.* Data standards, network standards (LAN, PC, Phone), PC standards (platform and application), and hardware platforms all need to be standardized if integration of data, imaging, and voice communications is to be accomplished.
- *Business engineers.* The increasing pressure on human capital to build more complex systems on new technology architecture, sometimes in highly volatile business environments, will create software or the demand for a new breed of IT professionals. Computer-aided software or systems engineering (CASE)[12] tools will provide the technology leverage that, when combined with education, will enable future professionals to run this new IT network.

---

[12]For a definition and further explanation of CASE, see p. 322, subheading "Application Development Technology."

- *Technology transfer.* Training business users and IT technicians to take advantage of these new technological opportunities may be the toughest barrier to full implementation. Practices such as total quality management help by providing a better climate for technology use and productivity gains. TQM in the IS organization is now emerging as a powerful enabler for rapid, high quality, low-cost information systems.

Manufacturing IT executives need to review their strategies for managing IT if they are to successfully implement systems in this changing environment. Planning properly for new IT architectures, new business practices, and ongoing cultural change will mean lower cost and greater competitive advantage for those who do it well.

Barriers and Solutions

Barriers to implementing advanced information systems are similar to barriers to other major projects requiring significant investment. These hurdles involve financial and economic risk, people's general resistance to change, and the viability of the technology itself. Table 6–4 lists the barriers to implementing technology. A recent report concluded that in general, top management's minimal understanding of advanced manufacturing technologies was the primary obstacle to implementing systems.[13] Among advanced users of CIM, however, capital justification was found to be the most significant obstacle. The report identified three key capital justification practices that are often deficient:

1. Revenue benefits associated with various initiatives are not quantified. Because market research has not been performed to study the relative value customers attach to doing things better, the price/volume impact of a proposed change is not known with enough specificity to be admitted as evidence in the proposal.

2. Cost savings usually represent the backbone of an appropriation request and, even here, not all savings are captured. Because processes are not sufficiently delineated, real cost drivers are unknown and many of the savings associated with cost/working capital improvements are overlooked.

---

[13]Ernst & Young, "The Adoption of Computer-Integrated Manufacturing: Messages from More Experienced Companies," Cleveland, Ohio, p. 11.

3. No satisfactory mechanism exists to understand the strategic advantages of making an investment versus the consequences of not doing so. Competitive benchmarking and market research help businesses gain a better sense for this important but difficult area.[14]

When properly applied, CIM technology has proven its worth in countless applications; yet many companies are uneasy about the extensive investment in hardware, software, integration services, and training required. Simplifying and streamlining business and manufacturing processes prior to information automation permits more immediate identification of potential financial return and provides a strong foundation for systems implementation without the pain of major capital investment.

FACTORY FLOOR COMPUTING

The factory floor has been a laboratory for the use of IT in manufacturing. For the vast majority of manufacturers, the factory floor is well populated with equipment, more and more of which connects to a

---

TABLE 6–4
Barriers to Critical Success Factors in Adopting Technology

Financial/economic	• Capital justification • Overlooking the strategic benefits • Uncertainties of economic condition • Financial risk • Short-term incentives
People issues	• Top management lacks vision for long term • Top management does not understand benefits • Inadequate education of management, technical staff, workers • Middle management resistance
Technology issues	• Fear of technology • Insufficient attention to planning • Insufficient in-house technical support • Technical standards for integration

---

[14]Ibid., p. 12.

computer, is controlled by a computer, or has a computer embedded in it. At first glance, discrete manufacturing and process plants appear to be a mass of tools, devices, systems, materials, people, and movement. Upon analysis, almost all equipment on the floor falls into one of the following four categories:

- *Production and process equipment* for transforming materials into work-in-process (WIP) or finished products.
- *Materials handling equipment* for moving materials.
- *Computer-based controllers and software* for controlling materials and equipment.
- *Monitoring equipment* for checking the movement, presence, and status of materials and equipment.

Many machines, tools, and devices fall into more than one category. For example, a robot can be both an assembly machine and a materials handling device. The trend today is to combine heretofore stand-alone machines into systems capable of automated, continuous, high-volume production. As systems become increasingly integrated, these categories become increasingly blurred. This trend exists in both the discrete manufacturing and the continuous process industries. Thus, materials in discrete environments are moved by conveyor, and materials in the continuous process world flow through pipes. Likewise, programmable logic controllers (PLC) in discrete manufacturing monitor the activities as discrete events (such as on/off, presence/absence, or above/below a setpoint), and analog controllers in the continuous process world measure variable events (such as temperature, pressure, and flow). In almost every manufacturing environment, computers play an increasing role in coordinating and controlling ever-more-complex manufacturing processes.

Production and Process Equipment

There are several ways to transform material into products: manipulation, assembly, and blending. Manipulation involves machines tools such as lathes, milling machines, cutters, punch presses, and blow molding and injection molding machines. Each one changes the shape, rather than the composition, of the raw material stock. Assembly is a manufacturing process wherein parts are put together to form larger components. Assembly tools include robots, automatic insertion equipment, wave soldering baths, and adhesive applicators. Blending and process applications involve mixing, injecting, molding, or cooking solid or liquid ingredients (or both) into some other material. In these applications, the finished material does not resemble the constituent parts. Typical process equipment includes vats, mixers, cookers, and extruders. Nearly all of this equipment relies more and more on computing components to enhance the flexibility, reliability, and functions of production.

Materials Handling Equipment

Materials handling equipment provides the physical framework for moving and managing materials throughout a plant—from receiving (and before), through WIP, to shipping (and beyond). Here, too, there is increasing use of embedded and networked computers. There are numerous types of automated material handling equipment and systems, including

- *Diverters*. Diverters move material, fixtures, totes, and other items from one path to another. Diverters may have computer-based vision and item-handling capabilities.
- *Robots*. Robots vary in intelligence and capability, but almost all are based upon an integrated or embedded computer. Some robots are connected to networks and other computers. Robots can be stand-alone or attached to the machine tool served. Robots can be simple, inexpensive, pick-and-place devices, or relatively expensive, complex, multifunctional devices with multiple degrees of freedom.
- *Shuttles*. Shuttles carry material while they move on tracks, are towed, or follow a guidepath. Depending on the sophistication of their computing capabilities, some shuttles can pick up and discharge materials at special delivery stations. Of particular note are automated guided vehicles (AGV), which typically follow a wire or painted path on the floor.

Computer-Based Controllers and Software

A hierarchy of computer-based devices control both equipment and the data to run that equipment. Within the equipment itself, there may be microprocessor chips and single board computers (SBCs). The chips typically perform single tasks. SBCs are essentially personal computers (PCs) minus the case, hard disk, and power supply; they typically perform multiple tasks. SBC operating systems include DOS, Macintosh, and nowadays, even UNIX.

External to the production and materials handling equipment, device controllers include general-purpose industrial controllers, typically programmable logic controllers (PLCs); computer numerical controllers (CNC); production monitors; industrial PCs; and integrated PLCs. PLCs, the blue-collar computers, were developed as general-purpose replacements to electromechanical relays. As a rule, PLCs have limited logic functions and do not perform major data processing tasks. CNCs are dedicated machine tool computers; they translate numerical data into positional data and motion control. CNCs are generally application specific; the CNC used for injection molding, for instance, would not be used for a punch press. In terms of data processing capabilities, production monitors are situated between microprocessors and industrial PCs. These devices include a microprocessor-based data collector, programmable read-only memory (PROM), and digital and analog interfaces, all in a box suitable for harsh industrial environments. These devices perform simple control tasks, production and process monitoring, data display, reject and downtime tracking, and time stamping. Industrial PCs are mostly a repackaging of the same PC bought for home or office use. PCs are excellent at general-purpose computing but slow in machine or motion control applications compared to PLCs and CNCs. Industrial PCs have access to a wealth of applications, including spreadsheets, statistical process control, graphics, cost estimating, plant management, process optimization, design, and production monitoring and control.

Some PC-based office applications are gaining an industrial perspective. For example, on the market today is spreadsheet software that will automatically collect data from PLCs directly and plug those data in the appropriate cells of the spreadsheet. Operators can then use other applications to analyze and chart the data already in spreadsheet format.

Operator interface software is just as important in the industrial environment as it is in home and office PC-based computing. More and more manufacturing software is being rewritten to include graphical user interfaces, mouse point-and-click ease of use, pull-down menus, and high-resolution graphics. Through dynamic data exchange (DDE), many new applications are being linked to each other, thereby reducing manual data collection and rekeying efforts, increasing accuracy, increasing the quality of data analysis (now that the data are readily available), and speeding the time for analysis and decision making.

Industrial PCs can also provide the communications gateway between shop floor computing devices and higher-level supervisory computers. A similar gateway-type device is the integrated PLC. These devices combine standard PLC architectures with standard computer architectures on the same bus. The result is a device that connects real-time factory control with management information systems (MIS).

With the addition of 32-bit processing and bus communications architecture to PLCs, CNCs, and PCs (together with parallel processing, artificial intelligence algorithms, laser-based noncontact gauging systems, and sensors), computer-based controllers can perform feed-forward production and machine control, as well as virtually real-time diagnostics and fault tolerance. At the MIS level, there are supervisory computers, which generally control the other controllers. Supervisory computers include cell controllers and work center minicomputers; direct (or distributed) numerical control (DNC) in discrete manufacturing environments and distributed control systems (DCS) in process environments; and plantwide minis and mainframes.

Monitoring Equipment

Monitoring equipment falls into two broad categories: inspection and data collection. Inspection equipment includes both devices and systems. In particular, hundreds of types of sensors are available for measuring countless quantities, including mechanical, electrical, optical, chemical, positional, and thermal characteristics. Inspection systems include vision systems, coordinate measuring machines, and laser-based systems. For data collection, a variety of automatic identification equipment is available, including bar code readers, optical character recognition systems, and radio frequency identification systems, as well as simple photoelectric and mechanical contact sensors. Monitoring and sensing systems rely more and more upon their computer component to provide intelligence and programmability, thus providing flexibility as well.

System Design Considerations

Manufacturers used to install automated production technologies without a plan for integrating them into a larger system. The resulting configurations are often called—disparagingly—islands of automation. The fact is, a flexible manufacturing center or system and even an entire automated factory will always be an island. The extent of the isolation depends on how the automated system is integrated with the entire production enterprise as well as its customers and vendors. Four levels of integration exist:

- *Mechanical or physical integration*—such as between a robot and a conveyor system, where the height of both devices (as well as the orientation of the parts being moved) is critical.

- *Electronic integration*—such as the current, voltage, and frequency requirements between sensors and controllers.
- *Informational integration*—specifically, the transfer of data among applications running on different computer-based systems; this is the crux of the trend toward open systems.
- *Enterprise integration*—the linking together of not only multiplant operations, but also suppliers (and their suppliers) and customers (and their customers).

The configuration of equipment in the automated system depends on a variety of factors, the least of which is the type of product being produced and the product options. In addition to technology and system issues, labor issues must be evaluated when implementing factory automation. For example, the level of computer literacy required to run an FMS is substantially greater than that needed to run a stand-alone NC tool. However, increasing numbers of production control and scheduling software applications incorporate features to make them user friendly, thereby actually lowering the computer literacy requirement to run the application.

Employees' capabilities must meet or exceed the requirements of the manufacturing process and the technologies used. *Education and training are thus a continual requirement both in academia and daily shop operations.* Underqualified people can ruin the results of an otherwise perfect manufacturing process. Conversely, overqualified employees can cause irreparable harm to information systems and manufacturing processes if their boredom breeds carelessness. Avoiding these problems requires proper system design coupled with curricula that meet the learning needs of the organization and cover the advances in technology and production processes. Information technology is playing an increasingly critical role in education, training, and methodology support.

As higher and higher levels of automation are attempted, the physical configuration, flexibility, and adequacy of the support systems within the production facility can become more important. Ultimately, the people, the production facility, and the production processes themselves must be simultaneously optimized, aligned, and integrated to achieve the highest levels of automation within a sustainable, controllable manufacturing environment. *Information technology is the primary enabler and supporter of this alignment, integration, and optimization process.*

COMPUTER-INTEGRATED MANUFACTURING SYSTEMS—BALANCING THE TECHNOLOGY WITH HUMAN SYSTEMS

For almost two decades, the technological revolution called computer-integrated manufacturing (CIM) has captivated the manufacturing world. Technologies for modernization, productivity improvement, and quality enhancement have proliferated. From the perspective of many would-be users, however, these technologies are obscure, arcane, and costly, and they require an extraordinary transformation of a company's organization, operations, and systems. Recently, a profound change has taken place in CIM: software and hardware developers are now addressing and resolving the critical integration issues facing today's manufacturing enterprises.

Organizations that have already joined the ranks of CIM implementers have often had to deal with multiple systems that have evolved autonomously. It is not uncommon for a manufacturer to have 4 MRP systems, 12 or more order entry systems, or 17 purchasing systems. *Integrating these systems is a challenge, but it is a prerequisite to partnering, strategic alliances, and management of the value chain in a virtual enterprise.*

The CIM Challenge

One of the more controversial topics in manufacturing is the definition of CIM, in part because CIM systems are more than a set of integrated computer tools and processes. To deliver its potential, CIM must properly contour to and support the business environment. CIM systems have three fundamental integration elements: data architecture, technical architecture (hardware, software, network communications, and operating systems), and control architecture. Data architecture allows tools and applications to share information across the overall integrated environment. Technical architecture allows computers and application software to work together to solve common problems. Control architecture provides services, such as security and procedural enforcement, to manage all information used in the CIM environment.

Implementing CIM is primarily an issue of integrating the information (data architecture) and the information technology required to manufacture products. The ultimate goal of information integration is to increase the flexibility and performance of each manufacturing and business process. A practical example is a bill of materials. Product and manufacturing information is generated during product design and engineering and is then transformed to meet other functional areas' information needs (i.e., current product costs to accounting, raw material needs to procurement, pricing and feature update to marketing, inventory utilization against scheduled receipts to materials management, and so forth). Each area requires a different representation drawn from basically the same information. Thus, the critical factor for CIM systems is how to address and remove barriers, both technical and organizational, to information integration. These barriers have two sources: people and technology.

People and CIM

Clearly, one of the predominant people-oriented challenges in successfully applying CIM is to create an information architecture that allows an organization's staff to use CIM to its best advantage. The interdependency of the information used by CIM systems poses challenges to every aspect of the enterprise, including organizational structure, culture, policies and practices, and reward systems. Therefore, the CIM environment must accommodate the need for new skills, new knowledge, new forms and locations of decision making, and new reporting and accountability relationships.

The management of the changes associated with the introduction of CIM systems requires much the same level of design effort as the management of the technology itself. Challenges include devising an individual skills development plan, creating programs that build consensus and commitment to the CIM objectives, and developing an empowered team structure throughout the organization and the CIM life cycle. All individuals involved in the CIM environment need to understand how their particular commitments and obligations fit the strategic plans of the company.

Technology and CIM

Technology-driven systems issues cluster around computer hardware and systems software. Many CIM systems are based on proprietary hardware and architectures that have been customized for optimum performance. This often results in incompatibility of data and communication protocols when attempting to transfer data between unintegrated systems. In addition to differences in system architecture and data structures, network services often differ, presenting another set of problems.

Developers and vendors who independently construct applications in proprietary environments rarely use a common data definition or communication scheme. Even if the information is defined using the same scheme, the grouping and processing of data elements are likely to be different, necessitating customized translation software.

Systems and CIM

Removing barriers to cooperation, achieving agreement on objectives, developing cross-functional collaboration, and managing change across all levels of the enterprise are crucial to an effective CIM installation. In the past, CIM development has often been a highly specialized, or even mystical, craft. The traditional approach has been to churn a segment of a CIM structure through multiple iterations of the basic design-construct-implement cycle until the new segment matches the overall architecture.

There is a certain discipline required in CIM development. Development initiatives must recognize and adapt to the organization's limitations if they are to be not only technically and financially appropriate, but also culturally correct. Personal attitudes, existing culture, bases of performance evaluation, cross-organization structures, working methods, and foundations for interenterprise relationships all require alignment or customization to the specific CIM development. Likewise, the CIM must be designed and managed to accommodate and support the enterprise.

In any organization, there are three sources of direction and information for designing a CIM:

- Those responsible for the CIM's orientation and goals who will authorize the CIM systems: top management.
- Those who will design and construct the CIM systems: the CIM program team.
- Those who will use the CIM systems: plant management, operators, technicians, support groups, and alliance partners.

Each CIM system must be designed to fit the attitudes and working modes of the organizations and key players using the system. If effective use of the new technologies requires new skills and new roles, then education and training must be a priority of the CIM implementation.

In the last few years, the technical aspects of CIM have received considerable attention and development. Vendors such as Hewlett-Packard (with Open CIM and SOCKETS), IBM (with Distributed Automation Edition, POMS, and Plant Works), and Digital Equipment Corporation (with Network Application Support) are quickly closing CIM's technological gaps. Each of these vendors offers proven products that successfully reduce the technical impediments to cooperative and integrated CIM.

These cooperative computing solutions make the needed information and resources from CIM available to the appropriate users as easily as if the information were maintained at the users' workstations. Vendor-supplied integration tools provide information transport and manipulation capabilities independent of the business application platform and the information format. The result is that CIM applications can run hand-in-hand on various hardware platforms, communicating through standard network protocols (TCP/IP, SNA, Ethernet, OSI) and support tools.

The ideal CIM system combines planning, orders, product, performance, shipment, and other information with integrated product design, manufacturing operations, and corporate management activities. *It links suppliers and customers with activities upstream and downstream from both.*

Today, most manufacturing business systems are fragmented, with little interaction from one subsystem to another. The primary reason for this fragmentation is that most corporations are not prepared for a full life cycle CIM program and prefer to develop CIM components sequentially over time. This fact will continue to challenge an organization's ability to implement CIM in environments where multiple generations of technology coexist, a common circumstance in manufacturing environments.

Open CIM

The major CIM technology providers continue to contour their products and services to open systems architectures. This approach expands equipment and applications choices, and it provides users with the realistic anticipation that components will be able to function as part of a single integrated whole. However, this expectation is highly dependent on the vendors' product offerings, the efforts of the vendors' strategic development partners, and the degree of each customer's acceptance of the open systems strategy.

Open systems capable of operating on multivendor platforms require accepted standards and rules. These must address such issues as languages, data bases, operating systems, user interfaces, and networks. Over the last decade, federal users and other large-scale CIM users and developers have pushed to establish computer, controls, and communication standards. Computer providers to the U.S. government will be required to comply with IEEE 1000.3, the Portable Operating Systems Interactive Executive (POSIX) standard. Further, several key vendors have succeeded in establishing de facto standards with their products, such as Digital has done with DECnet.

The process of and commitment to developing integration standards has been laborious and slow, primarily due to incentives for vendors to incorporate evolving technologies and a lack of cooperation among vendors, users, and standards bodies in developing and establishing standards. As difficult as standards are to predict, the solution is not for prospective CIM users to just stand still. CIM applications built on industry standard protocols (UNIX, RDBMS, networks) can be isolated from platform technologies and can be initiated at any point in the CIM life cycle. With this strategy in place and development underway, companies can take advantage of both existing and emerging CIM systems.

The technologies described in this book exist and can be effectively used today. Some of these technologies still require increases in cost/performance before they can be readily implemented. However, for the majority of manufacturing enterprises, available CIM technology far exceeds the capability of the organization to use it in a fully integrated manner.

The greatest challenge today lies not in the technical barriers to applying CIM, but in overcoming the organizational barriers and resistance to changing the fundamental way the company is run. The organizational structure, company policies, reward systems, performance measurements, and communication processes must be revised and reestablished in parallel with CIM integration. This coordination will require middle and senior-level management first to recognize this necessity, and second, *to refocus their efforts away from better utilization of technology-oriented tools and toward improved management practices and organizational integration.* These changes are imperative if CIM is to help manufacturing enterprises achieve or sustain world-class status. In the following section, we discuss the future of information technology in manufacturing.

CURRENT AND EMERGING TECHNOLOGIES IN MANUFACTURING

The following overview of the most important trends in information technology focuses both on major technology advancements and on how developing IT is likely to be used in a manufacturing enterprise. These technologies have been grouped into four technology areas, each embodying some overall trend in the use of IT. The areas that will be discussed along with their primary technologies, are

- Computing platform technology.
- Networking technology.
- Application development technology.
- Specialized application environments.

In Figure 6–5, specific technology products have been positioned according to general hardware and software categories. The figure illus-

---

FIGURE 6–5
Information Technology Use Today

	Technology category	Technologies
H A R D W A R E	Computing platforms	Terminals, desktop computers, notebook computers, servers, mainframes, and supercomputers
	Networking technologies	Local area networks, wide area networks, mobile networking, interoperability protocols, and network computing
S O F T W A R E	Application development technologies	CASE, application style guides, data management, and object orientation
	Specialized application environments	Imaging technologies, expert systems, simulation, and modeling

trates a highly complex set of choices and alternatives offered. To choose correctly, a company will need to match software with hardware choices in order to optimize the solution against its strategy and its cost constraints.

Computing Platform Technology

Computing today is no longer restricted to large computers and the terminals that access them. As Figure 6–6 shows, there are much more varied selections of computing platforms and end-user devices today. This variety of platforms allows users to buy systems scaled precisely to their requirements. It is not necessary to buy more computing power than required; incremental power can be added as needed. There are two primary trends in computing technology: increasing computing power and increasing portability of the computing system.

FIGURE 6–6
Range of Computing Platforms

Least Powerful ← → Most Powerful

Device	Terminals	Windowing terminals	Personal computers	Work-stations	Servers and Super Servers	Midrange	Mainframe data base engineering	Super-computer Parallel processor
Sample vendors	IBM DEC	NCD NCR	IBM Compaq Apple	Sun HP Apollo NEXT IBM DEC NCR	Compaq Parallon	DEC HP DG Prime Wang IBM NCR	IBM Amdahl Unisys Terradata	Gray Hitachi NCR Thinking machine KSR
Micro-processor	None	Micro-processor	Micro-processor	Micro-processor RISC Processor	Micro-processor	Propri-etary processor	Propri-etary processor	Propri-etary processor or micro-processor
Operating system	None	None	DOS Windows CS/2 Macintosh	Unix	Netware OS/2	VMS MPE OS/400 Unix	MVS VM Unix	Unix

Trend 1: Increasing Processing Power

With the introduction of parallel processors, computer processing power will jump dramatically over the next several years. The impact of parallel processing goes beyond running applications faster or supporting larger terminal populations; the primary revolutionizing benefits will be in the ability to search massive data bases—data bases far larger than practical with mainframes today. As a result, wholly new forms of trend analyses will be feasible. We will surpass our current capabilities to analyze and categorize data. We will be able to track inventory to the finest level of detail, to perform extraordinarily detailed market analyses and correlations, and to develop trend monitoring applications for precise demand prediction. Other major advantages of this vastly increased processing power are

- *Performing complex calculations in real-time.* Prime uses include engineering applications that entail visualization, solids modeling, and finite element analysis. MRP applications can benefit from dramatically increased processing power by allowing continuous product sales data to alter warehouse shipments, production schedules, product mix, supplies deliveries, and financial operations in real-time. It is impossible to even consider such a system today because of the limitation of processing power.

- *Minimizing complexity through highly structured systems.* The current limitations in manufacturing computing do not stem from an inability to run "bigger applications," but rather from an inability to manage complexity (of application code, process control, intergroup coordination, network connections, and data base management). Increased processing power can be applied to subduing this complexity by accommodating more modularity without sacrificing overall system performance. Design emphasis will change from highly efficient systems to highly flexible systems.

- *Affecting application development.* The more powerful the processors, the less efficient the application code needs to be. This translates into two fundamental conclusions: (1) code can be written more quickly, since efficiency can be sacrificed, and its corollary (2) CASE application generators may be used more often to write applications. This second point can be taken one step further to imply that end-users may soon be "writing" their own applications through very simple point-and-click visual programming environments. Examples of this today are Microsoft's Visual Basic language, Apple's HyperCard, and a host of data base management access "front-end" products.

Trend 2: Computing Portability
Whether through laptop, handheld or the new notebook computers, portability promises to bring information systems directly to where data is created or actions are taken. Portable computing thus enables salespeople to execute purchase orders and contracts while at a customer site. It allows factory workers to scan parts lists or on-line assembly instructions while on the factory floor. It allows service personnel to refer to on-line repair manuals while on site and allows warehouse personnel to track inventory through bar code scanning and real-time data base access. *In short, portable computing technology allows sharing of an organization's information inventory with mobile users.* Bringing computing to the point of action also means that data bases can be more accurate, since data is verified at the source.

Of equal importance is the added dimension of increased communications capabilities. In fact, part of the evolving computing paradigm is the changing target of computerization. As Thomas Malone and John Rockart of MIT describe it:

> "The core of the new technologies is the networked computer. The very name 'computer' suggests how one usually thinks of the device—as a machine for computing, that is, for taking in information, performing calculations, and then presenting the results. But this image of computing does not capture the essence of how computers are used now and how they will be used even more in the future. Many of the most important uses of computers today are for coordination tasks, such as keeping track of orders, inventory and accounts. . . . In short, computers and computer networks may well be remembered not as technology used primarily to compute but as coordination technology."[15]

Portable computing, combined with radio-based networking, promises to extend the reach of coordination technology to mobile users. These technologies can allow

---

[15]Thomas W. Malone and John F. Rockart, "Computers, Networks and the Corporation," *Scientific American*, September 1991, p. 128.

- Service personnel to assist one another in troubleshooting problems by tying them into an electronic forum.
- Salespeople to access experts anywhere in the firm to answer questions on pricing strategies or configuration.
- Factory floor personnel to discuss a manufacturing problem with the engineers who designed the product being built, or with the equipment vendor whose machine is building the product.

Portable computing is expected to offer other benefits that enable manufacturers to improve quality and efficiency, to decrease manufacturing cost and duration, and to increase customer satisfaction.

Important Technology Advances
In addition to these two trends, there have been significant technological advances during the past several years. These advances involve

- Terminals.
- Desktop computers.
- Pen-based computing.
- LAN servers and superservers.
- Supercomputers and parallel processors.

Terminals. The primary advance in terminal technology in the past several years has been the introduction of the intelligent graphical networking terminal, also known as the X-window terminal, or X-terminal. The X-window terminal can perform complex screen and graphics manipulations without requiring exorbitant processing power from the host computer. The X-terminal's embedded microprocessor provides the computation required to generate the advanced graphical interfaces. X-windows represent a quantum leap in ease of use and in navigating through more and more complex information systems.

Desktop computers (personal computers and workstations). The major desktop computing advances have been in the convergence of desktop computer technologies and in the rapidly increasing processing power available in microprocessors. Desktop computing is comprised of personal computers and engineering workstations. The traditional distinctions between PCs and workstations have been price, processing power, and operating system, but these distinctions are gradually disappearing. Powerful PCs provide processing power from 2 to 6 MIPS, whereas the workstations start at 1 MIPS of processing power and go up. Today, the primary distinction appears to be not computing power, but operating system support. Workstations, almost by definition, run one of the many variants of the UNIX operating system and do not support DOS. PCs (with the exception of Apple Computer systems) support DOS and may support UNIX.

These changes are having considerable impact of the factory floor, particularly at the work-cell level. Here, advanced embedded microprocessors are found in a variety of machines and process controllers. These dedicated computers have plenty of power to control and respond to real-time manufacturing operations. Such systems are contributing significantly to improvements in cost, quality, and time in varied manufacturing processes.

Pen-based computing.   A major new advance in personal computing is the notebook computer with a pen-based user interface. Where keyboard-based notebook computers and handheld computers represent a continuation of personal computing on smaller scales, pen-based computing is a radically new model for end-user computing. Pen-based computing does not use keys or mice for the user interface. Instead—as the name implies—it relies entirely on pen strokes. Thus pen-based computers must recognize handwriting and pen gestures as opposed to keystrokes and mouse clicks.

Pen-based computing is expected to allow many people to use computers who previously could or would not. Since pen-based systems are highly portable and do not require both hands for use, they are popular for roving applications where the user may be standing and not have a lap available. Mobile factory floor personnel, warehouse personnel, salespeople, and service people are all candidates for pen-based computing. Ease of use, portability, and user interface will push computer support deeper into the organization—indeed, deeper into the whole value chain. Their low training requirements suggest that the pen-based systems can be effectively utilized by workers who currently lack computer support and may be computer illiterate.

LAN servers and superservers.   A significant advance in the PC's evolution was its deployment in traditional information systems roles, taking on responsibilities previously reserved for mainframe and midrange computers. PCs and workstations are used as servers or superservers—as low-cost distributed data base processors. Superservers are high-powered PCs with 10 to 100 times the processing power of normal PCs. Superservers (made by Compaq, NetFRAME, Parallan, Auspex, and Tricord) run the same PC or UNIX operating systems as the traditional PC servers, but they operate at speeds comparable to midrange computers and even low-end mainframes through the integration of multiple high-performance microprocessors into a single computer system.

Server PCs and superserver PCs make it possible to distribute data processing functions to small organizational units (e.g., sales offices, retail stores, warehouses, service centers, marketing offices). The cost and ease of use of PC-based computing makes it possible to cost-effectively provide computer support to many sites and users never before automated. Servers and superservers support the IS downsizing strategy. The goals of IS downsizing include decreasing overall costs (PC hardware and software is considerably less expensive than mainframe and midrange computers), increasing the ease of use of computer systems (PCs have more sophisticated user interfaces), and reducing the time needed to deploy new applications (PC tools are generally more efficient).

Supercomputers and parallel processors.   Supercomputers from Control Data Corporation, Convex, Cray Research, Fujitsu, Hitachi, and NEC represent the current mainstream of supercomputing. In manufacturing, supercomputers are used primarily in R&D and sometimes in high-end engineering applications, generally to provide the raw computing horsepower necessary for computation-intensive tasks such as finite element analysis, molecular modeling, fluid and aerodynamic modeling, linear programming, process simulation, economic simulation, and dynamical system modeling. They are extremely expensive machines and have historically been used for only the most demanding and critical applications. As the costs of supercomputers and parallel computers come down and as the value of reducing manufacturing process duration goes up, high-performance computers will find more and more applications in the manufacturing enterprise.

Parallel processing technologies from NCR, Thinking Machines, Bolt, Beranek and Newman, Kendall Square Research, Intel, and Motorola represent a way to get supercomputer power at midrange and mainframe prices. Parallel processing entails integrating many processing units into a single computer processing engine. Today, applications must be written specifically to take advantage of parallel processors; there are very few application development tools for parallel processing. As the technology matures, supercomputing through parallel processors will be made available to a wider user base in manufacturing. Business managers will use parallel computers to perform complex what-if business and market simulations; engineers will use parallel computers to conduct product testing on software models of the product rather than having to develop a real prototype; and quality systems will be able to visually inspect a product and use artificial intelligence to make quality judgments, much as humans would do.

Networking Technology

In addition to the more varied computer platform technology available today, computer networks in the manufacturing enterprise play a more and more critical role in tying the enterprise together. This is as true of the single-site manufacturer as of the globally dispersed manufacturer. Though a company with operations throughout the world needs a larger network than does a single-site operation, both need to be connected to their customers, their suppliers, and to other players in their value chains. Key manufacturing strategies are enhanced by network technology, all the way from the work cell up through the virtual enterprise with its highly globalized value chain. In the future, networks will play a greater role integrating the enterprise into the value chain and supporting its communication and information requirements. Fortunately, networking technology is rapidly evolving and able to meet the challenge.

Network technology is advancing at a rapid pace, and the breadth of technologies is expanding as well. Initially, data network technology consisted of only modems and communications circuits. Then network technology expanded to include terminal protocols, communication concentrators and multiplexers, and teleprocessing software on the mainframe. Through the 1980s, networking branched out to include networking protocol software and a much wider array of network media such as local area networks (LANs), fiber optics, wide area network switches, and communication carrier services. Network technology in the 1990s will expand into the computer operating system itself in the form of networkwide services and distributed application support. In fact, the 1990s will be the decade where the distinction between networking technology and computing technology disappears.

It is no coincidence that the movement toward multivendor international standards began with networking. The very essence of networking is the interconnection and interoperation of distinct systems. Networking thus leads many of the thrusts toward open systems, multivendor interoperability, distributed computing, and even application portability. In aggregate, these open system impulses are moving the industry toward network computing, where a network of far-flung computers acts as a single large virtual computer for each of its users. Network computing will allow greater flexibility in the locations where applications and data can reside, as well as in what type of computer can interoperate with the network. *In addition, networks are the conduits for new forms of interpersonal communications and coordination, supporting relationships among people that could not exist without technology's ability to overcome the constraints of geography, time, or the limited sensory nature of telephone interaction.*

Network technology is often referred to as the underlying technology "plumbing" necessary for modern information systems. Networking standards determine whether computers, terminals, applications, and data bases can interact with one another. Many people now consider the infrastructure to be more important than the computers and applications, which can be replaced much more easily than the "plumbing" itself.

The truly enabling network infrastructure should exhibit several key characteristics. It should

- Be seamless, hiding the complexities of the network plumbing from the users and application programmers.
- Be optimized for dynamically allocated bandwidth, so that applications can use as much bandwidth as is available, but only for the brief duration needed to transmit a message, screen, record, or file.
- Accommodate the very high bandwidths available on local area networks, as well as the moderate bandwidths available in the public wide area network.
- Allow any-to-any connectivity, so that future connectivity needs can be satisfied without having to redeploy network resources.
- Allow tens or hundreds of simultaneous logical connections from every computer to support the next generation of distributed and integrated applications.
- Have the same technical standards from very small networks to very large networks.

The technologies that fit these evolving needs are becoming available today, primarily in the form of LANs and the devices that interconnect LANs into wide area internetworks.

Mobile Networking
Enterprise data networking has been largely restricted to fixed enterprise locations. However, major new technologies and products could change this situation. In particular, cellular packet radio offers completely mobile data communications in both the local area environment and over wide area distances. Just as cellular phone systems allow telephones to be used on the run, packet radio systems allow laptop, notebook, or handheld computers to be in constant contact with the enterprise information systems. ARDIS, a company jointly owned by IBM and Motorola, provides a low-speed (4800 bps) radio data service that reaches over 8,000 cities and towns in the United States. New wide area radio services are now being developed that will provide higher data rates. Radio-based local area networks are also being developed by major vendors such as NCR, Motorola, and Apple. Radio LANs will free networking devices from having to be located at or near a LAN wall outlet.

Portable networking will have major impacts on the use of computers and information by anyone who must travel during business. Shop floor personnel, inspectors, sales personnel, and field service personnel can all gain access to or enter real-time information into the corporate information inventory. Application planners will be challenged to develop valuable and creative uses for this new capability. When combined with the expected growth in laptop, notebook, and handheld computers, radio technology will have a major impact in the 1990s.

Interoperability Protocols
Interoperability protocols are the languages by which computers (or printers or other networked devices) communicate. Interoperability protocols must be present in all networked computer systems to provide ready access to enterprise information and resources. However, interoperability protocols are problematic because there are so many incompatible standards. Manufacturing adds the complexity of robotics and computer controlled equipment with additional proprietary interoperability requirements.

To manage this explosion of incompatible protocols, the International Standards Organization (ISO) has developed over the past 10

years a rich set of protocols referred to as the Open System Interconnection (OSI) Suite. These standard protocols are vendor neutral (as are
the TCP/IP protocols of UNIX) and thus can be implemented on any
vendor's computer system. The manufacturing industry, led by General
Motors and Boeing, has spearheaded an effort to gain consensus on a
common set of interoperability protocols called the Manufacturing Automation Protocol/Technical Office Protocol (MAP/TOP) specification.
This protocol suite is based primarily on the OSI set of standards with
several extensions to accommodate the unique demands of manufacturing.

Network Computing

Open systems, distributed processing, and applications portability combine to create a fundamentally new capability termed network computing.
Broadly speaking, network computing is the reunification of distributed
processing. Network computing can be viewed as a set of networkwide
services provided by all cooperating processors on a network. The configuration and availability of services makes a network of computers look
like a single computer system to end-users and applications.

The primary benefits of network computing are scalability and
modularity. Network computing allows new applications to be developed on small machines serving a department or small manufacturing unit. This provides a low-entry mechanism for testing and tuning
new capabilities. If successful, the new application can be moved to
larger platforms (through portability) or can be replicated (through distributed processing) as many times as necessary. If a business unit is
dissolved or sold, that distributed portion of the information system
may be dissolved or sold with it. If a new business operation that ad-
heres to compatible network computing standards is acquired, it may
be brought into the information system through the addition of a new
distributed component.

Although there are some personnel and capacity considerations that
still favor centralized mainframe solutions, the characteristics of network
computing (including lower costs, greater flexibility, high levels of integration, and better performance) will be too attractive to resist.

Application Development Technology

Improved application development technology means that software developers are able to adapt and get software to market faster, with fewer

problems, and with more functions. This not only means that manufacturers have another tool for improving the cost, quality, and timeliness of their products and services, but also means that manufacturers must anticipate that their competition will take advantage of the same benefits. The primary application development technology is computer-aided software or systems engineering, or CASE. CASE is the primary medium for transforming software development from a craft to an engineering discipline.

Engineering disciplines use structured approaches to define problems and technical means to solve the problems. Whereas in most engineering situations the problems themselves are of a technical nature, problems in software development are business oriented and, thus, do not lend themselves to classical engineering approaches. This is one reason why it has taken so long for automation to be applied to the design and manufacture of software applications.

CASE can be divided into four distinct classes:

- Methods that define how to describe the business problem, the major steps, and approach for developing the system.
- Techniques that describe how to perform specific method steps.
- Tools that automate specific steps or procedures.
- Lifecycle management methodologies that describe the process, the work breakdown structure, and the project management approach.

Since CASE can apply to any tool, technique, or method that aids in the software development process, it includes a diverse array of products. Today, individual CASE tools might include graphical business modeling tools, data dictionary tools, screen painters, code generators, reengineering analyzers, repository data bases, style guides, data base definition tools, front-end code generators, fourth-generation languages (4GLs), documentation generators, training and demo development tools, prototype tools, and project management systems. It is possible to group these diverse CASE tools into five general categories:

- Front-end or Upper-CASE tools analyze the business requirements and develop applications or data models to satisfy those requirements.
- Back-end or Lower-CASE tools assist in constructing, testing, and documenting an application.
- The repository ties diverse CASE tools together through a central data base.

- Reengineering develops application models based on already existing code.
- Project support assists in tracking and controlling the software development project.

An early objective of CASE was to increase programmer efficiency so that code could be developed faster and systems could be implemented sooner. The emphasis of CASE is now on application effectiveness rather than on programmer efficiency. The goal of application development automation is manufacturability and maintainability, so that applications do not have to be repaired or replaced. This new emphasis is similar to that of the total quality movement in general manufacturing.

Specialized Application Environments

Electronic imaging, modeling and simulation, and expert systems are all specialized environments that will play an increasing role in manufacturing as time goes on.

Electronic Imaging

The first specialized application environment is electronic imaging. In the early 1980s, two separate IS trends started in U.S. industry—one driven by technology, the other organizationally driven. On the technology front, developments in mass storage technology resulted in a new data storage media called optical disks. These disks were capable of storing up to 1 gigabyte of digital data per 12-inch disk, an unprecedented density of data. Coincident with this major innovation, a new family of software applications based upon work flow software was developed. This work flow software managed the storage and retrieval of document images and the routing of these images over LANs to workstations throughout the organization. This software also included a programming environment that allowed the creation of applications for managing electronic images of paper documents in the same way as their paper counterparts have been for decades. The convergence of these two trends created the interest and demand for document image processing (DIP) systems.

Document image processing has often been used as a test bed for new concepts and products. For example, in the mid-1980s, DIP systems designers embraced an emerging systems architecture called client/server; in 1988, document image systems integrators began to deploy new high-speed networks called FDDI to help improve DIP system response time.

In the future we can expect this trend to continue with the integration of such developments as agent-oriented software, pen-based systems, and voice recognition into DIP systems.

By means of document images stored in "jukeboxes" of 10 to 280 high-density optical disks, document images are transmitted to and displayed on a variety of workstations and personal computers. Document images can be printed on laser printers or sent through fax gateways to standard fax machines. If on-line publishing systems or CAD systems are in use, information from these systems can be merged with DIP at the workstation or printer to create seamless documents.

Work management software, combined with the new graphical and window-oriented interface technologies, has made significant additions to DIP. These software products allow for the building of applications where documents (document images, CAD, electronic publishing, word processing) can be moved automatically through an office environment (or any network, for that matter) and sequenced through a set of work steps. Management reports, security, and interfaces to other software systems are also elements of these software products.

The current deployment of document image processing systems in manufacturing organizations is limited in impact but is growing rapidly. For the most part, DIP systems have been used to support CAD activities. In the future, however, it is likely that these systems will affect organizational design and management and will become an integral part of the next generation of manufacturing information technology.

The DIP approach to automated work management supports the shift of white-collar work activities from preparing to do the work (retrieve, gather, find) to doing the work (e.g., execute, train, and manage), as illustrated in Figure 6–7. In addition, DIP systems support the redefinition of work to off-load the nonexpert tasking (e.g., sort, compare, distribute, communicate) from the knowledge worker.

The impact of DIP on manufacturing will be felt throughout the organization. Imaging processing supports concurrent engineering by enabling engineers to share design and requirements information better with factory groups; by making the preparation, use, and support of technical documents easier; and by supporting electronic linkages to and from more traditional manufacturing computing environments such as administration, marketing, sales, finance, purchasing, human resources, contracts, product planning, and accounts payable. DIP is expected to play an important role in improving customer services and technical support.

FIGURE 6–7
Document Image Processing on the "White-Collar Factory"

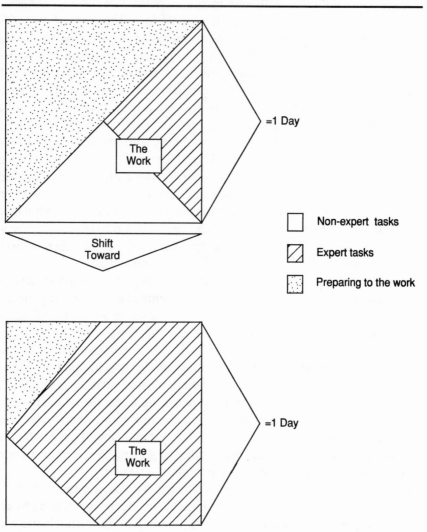

Advocates of document image processing believe it will address many of the important organizational challenges that manufacturing organizations will face in the 1990s (see Figure 6-8). These include issues such as

- Work force training.
- Job design.
- Flexible job/task assignment.
- Customer service.
- On-line training.
- Task rotation among staff.
- Answering customer questions in real-time.
- Support technology for manufacturing information systems.

In the final analysis, DIP is likely to be successful and pervasive because it is both an integrative and an additive element to the information technology evolution currently underway. The key elements of a document image processing system—work management software, client/server architecture, and a graphical user interface—are also the key elements of other significant developments and applications of IT.

Modeling and Simulation Technology

The second specialized application environment is modeling and simulation technology. Modeling is the process of using a simplified paradigm to analyze the important characteristics of some real-world system. Models are used to predict the outcome of a time-consuming, expensive, or complicated process without having to experience it in real-life form. For example, organizational modeling can predict the effectiveness of organizational structures; revenue/profit models can calculate the bottom-line impact of product price changes; marketing models can estimate the effect of marketing campaigns; resource models can assess the impact of product schedule changes; and economic models can estimate the direction of consumer spending. The benefits of predicting rather than experiencing the outcomes are obvious. They include lowering development costs, minimizing risk, getting results faster, and assessing quality sooner. Businesses that must compete on ever-shorter time frames embrace modeling as a standard tool of analysis. Recent developments allow modeling of more real-world phenomena than ever before. They even also allow us to analyze our world with unprecedented accuracy.

328

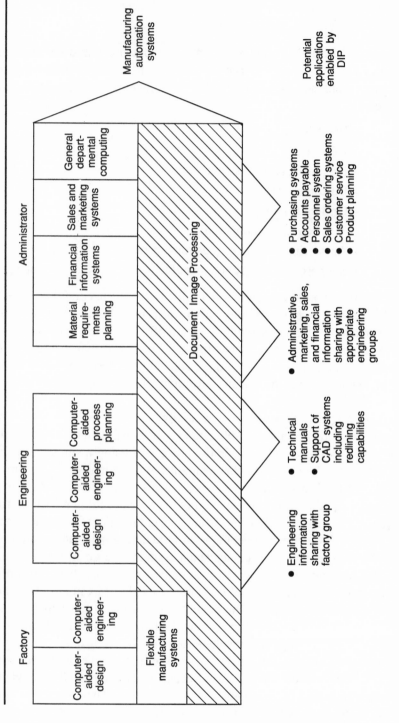

FIGURE 6-8
Document Image Processing in the Manufacturing Environment

Combined with calculus or linear algebra, models can be used to determine the optimum inputs (product mix, pricing, material, schedule, etc.) to achieve the most favorable output (profit, market share, durability, time, etc.). Optimization techniques operate on the mathematical models to determine the best option. Optimization routines included in some MRPII applications assist the manufacturer by determining the optimum mix of product, personnel, inventory, and material to maximize profit or minimize time-to-market at minimum cost. Modeling is not restricted to mathematics, however. Several common variations in modeling include narrative, physical, analog, symbolic, data, simulation, and procedural models.

Often the best solution to complex modeling problems is to use simulation techniques rather than analytic mathematics. Simulation is a means of reproducing an event or process in a controlled way, usually using a computer. Simulation does not attempt to calculate the answers given a set of inputs; instead it mimics the real system and the results are "observed" rather than calculated. Simulation entails dividing a process into activities, entities, and events that interact simultaneously but can be initiated and monitored by a computer, which advances the simulation clock many times faster than the passage of time outside the computer model. Simulation focuses on outcomes rather than the development of complex mathematical structures. Increased use of simulation led to the development of simulation languages for computers. Two major types of simulation are discrete events and continuous process systems. Examples of discrete events are the manufacture of automobiles or computers on an assembly line. Examples of continuous process systems are fluids flowing in the piping of a refinery or the air flow over and under an airplane wing section.

Analytic mathematical modeling has been used in industrial processes to develop equations of many macro- and microprocesses. The economic order quantity (EOQ) equation, used to calculate the best lot size, is a model that uses the costs of setting up a batch run and the costs of storing inventory to calculate the best batch size. There are many such examples in industry where equations are developed and manipulated to optimize policies and procedures. Often, these use linear programming and probability and statistics to solve a problem. In addition to these mathematical models, simulation and procedural models are used to develop a map of a process that can then be used to analyze the process for ways of improving it or reducing costs or understanding it better.

Expert Systems

Expert systems—a part of artificial intelligence—have emerged as a technology that can promote quality and productivity improvements in a range of industries, including manufacturing. An expert system is a computer program that emulates expertise in a specific domain or subject area. Companies are increasingly aware of the value of the knowledge and expertise that their employees possess. Because they reside in the knowledge workers, the intellectual assets of the firm may seem intangible, but that expertise can help any company differentiate itself in the marketplace, thus enhancing its competitiveness.

Expert systems are most useful in situations where specific, accurate information needs to be retrieved and applied to problem solving. The intelligent information retrieval functionality is exemplified by internal corporate expert programs and some sophisticated customer service operations. An example: a software users helpline, in which an employee provides technical assistance by using an expert system. Any occasion calling for consistent decision making, no matter what the industry area, can benefit from expert systems.[16] Some specific benefits from the use of expert systems are

- Access to knowledge, not just information.
- Better decision making, resulting in faster professional work.
- Improved quality and consistency, resulting in higher customer satisfaction.
- Structural process for collecting and documenting expertise, building corporate memory.
- Knowledge that is collected and organized, so that it can be offered as a product or service.
- Improved operations through detailed monitoring, and national procedures in place for crisis management.
- Closer relationships with customers when salespeople use expert systems to respond to inquiries.

Expert System Shells

Depending upon the complexity of the business problem, expert system development can be facilitated by the use of an expert system shell. Ex-

---

[16]For a discussion of expert systems used in different industries, see Edward Fiegenbaum, Pamela McCorduck and H. Penny Nii, *The Rise of The Expert Company* (New York: Vantage Books, 1989).

pert system shells embed the few existing ways to represent knowledge or to make inferences, but they do not include knowledge related to a specific domain. These generic outlines or templates allow for faster and less costly development of expert systems by simplifying the programming. The user/developer enters the domain knowledge, and the shell provides the reasoning structure in the form of "if . . . then" statements. Sometimes shells are built within a company, as described in the Du Pont case study later in this chapter. Today commercial shells are widely available in multipurpose forms and for specific business areas.

The manufacturing industry is particularly well-suited to exploit the benefits of expert systems technology, due to the relevant skills among employees and the nature of manufacturing processes. For example, engineers will generally adopt new technologies early; with their programming skills, they can then act as their own knowledge engineers and build expert systems. Manufacturing applications of expert systems include scheduling, planning, procurement, configuration, engineering, design, quality assurance, process control, and diagnostics. In addition, business applications are proliferating in the sales, service, and financial management areas.

Simulation and modeling, network computing, expert systems, and imaging are all major developments in information technology that will greatly affect manufacturing. *These do not simply represent an extension of current IT usage to higher speeds or volumes; rather, they are a fundamental change in the model for computing.* The cumulative technological trends that are fueling this change are increasing workstation power and networking speeds, network computing services, CASE tools, and multimedia information.

Taken individually, these technology advances do not suggest a specific future. Taken together and combined with the goal of making information systems flexible and powerful, however, these technologies lead to a vision of highly distributed processors networked together to support shared data and applications. This vision includes centralized repositories of data that are maintained by information systems professionals, with application development conducted by end-users using powerful and simple tools. In this vision, technology completely changes the relationships among people through communications, multimedia, and expert systems. Technology infrastructure is much more important than the applications themselves to developing competitive parity or advantage. While this vision is not really new to IT, it is becoming an attainable goal.

EXPERT SYSTEMS AT DU PONT

In this case study, we will see how a large, diversified company identified a critical new technology—expert systems—and established a vision
of how the technology could add value throughout the enterprise. Strong
leadership, support from senior management, and alignment with the
firm's business strategy and IT strategy set the stage for what has been
called one the most successful corporate implementations of expert systems. An understanding of the corporate culture and the proper way to
initiate change, along with a policy of valuing and empowering employees, characterized this transformation from the mid- to late 1980s.

What started out as a small think tank operation has evolved into a
companywide program called Project Leapfrog. The program is intended
to maintain the high level of interest in expert systems and to perpetuate
the spirit of innovation that has already provided competitive advantage.
Today, over 1000 expert systems are in use at Du Pont, with returns
averaging ten dollars annually for every dollar invested. The operating
impact is over $100 million per year.

About the Company

Du Pont has 1,700 products, some of which have up to 10,000 sub-
types. Its products include fibers (apparel), communication satellites,
agricultural and industrial chemicals, biomedical products, industrial and
consumer products, polymer products, imaging systems, coal, automotive products, electronics, and petroleum. This diversification of products, without any central product line, shapes the firm's organizational
structure—a very loose confederation of many business units of various sizes. The R&D program that supports basic research throughout the
entire company is also decentralized.

Strategic Alignment

For Du Pont, the manufacturing value-added resides in the following
corporate leveraged items:

- A unique response to customer needs.
- Finding the best practice.
- Economy of scale, or uniform practices.
- Integration of practices and systems.

Part of the justification for making the investment in expert systems was that they could contribute in each of these areas.

During the 1980s, the major growth technologies expected to have an impact on Du Pont were information management, advanced materials, and life sciences. Within information management, the specific technologies identified as critical were artificial intelligence (AI), simulation, and telecommunications. Thanks to the vision and advocacy of Ed Mahler, an engineer with years of experience at Du Pont, expert systems (a branch of AI) gained prominence as a strategically important technology. Today, Mahler is program manager for Du Pont's Decision Support and Artificial Intelligence Task Force. In Mahler's view, "Basically expert systems are an augmentation and substitution process . . . a systemic view of improving work practices" that will ultimately that have an impact throughout the value chain.

Introduction of Expert Systems

Before a company can make the decision to install expert systems, it must understand itself well—its structural organization, culture, work force, and human and nonhuman resources—in order to develop expert systems that properly and appropriately meet its needs. Once opportunity areas for improvement have been identified, it is important to understand how expert systems can leverage the resources of the company. Expert systems also offer many other benefits, ranging from quality improvement to increased customer responsiveness.

The Vision

With the cumulative knowledge of their peers, managers are breaking the boundaries of geography and time, making better, more timely decisions. Expert systems further enhance the ability of managers and all decision makers to make better decisions that are based on a more complete use of information. The vision of the artificial intelligence task force, as articulated by Mahler in an internal company publication, is "That all critical decisions will be made with the best knowledge and relevant information at the point of decision. We will achieve this through technology and empowered people."[17]

---

[17]Larry Chilcoat, "Victoria Plant Interviews Ed Mahler," *You & What's New* (Du Pont internal publication), February 1991, p. 3.

"What a marvelous world that is on us now, where we can delegate these dull, boring, routine decisions to a never-complaining computer partner. No longer is it just a tool, we can turn it into an apprentice. Expert systems are the glue that holds computer systems together, they perform the transformation that is required to finish the task. Although people are able to synthesize information based on incomplete data or imperfect data, in essence humans are experts at taking their best shots. A simple transaction system cannot do that." (Mahler interview)[18]

What distinguishes expert systems from conventional computer data processing is that they utilize "facts, rules of judgment, rules of expert decision making, and logic to discover lines of reasoning leading to the solution of problems."[19] Through expert systems, the computer is transformed into a reasoning tool. Expert systems combine a body of knowledge with a reasoning process based on human patterns of thought.

The key strategic issue here was to somehow develop a shell system that could serve as the basis for future tailoring and program modification to meet the needs of each user. The development of an expert system that could be easily used and modified by the user also fit well in the corporate philosophy of a decentralized system where each person could be productive independently and make significant decisions alone.

Development of the Expert System

Since there was no expert system, or tool, as Mahler would call it, that was simple enough for widespread adoption throughout the company, a new shell was designed for internal expert system development. It had to run on the existing hardware at Du Pont, which came from different vendors. The strategy was largely VAX-based, allowing users to develop their own expert systems on the desktop.

The Tool Kit, designed by Du Pont engineer Lester Shipman, requires no programming knowledge of the user and contains embedded statistics and graphics. Employees can attend a two-day course on how to use the shell. They also learn knowledge engineering principles and are introduced to commercially available shells.

This kit enabled Du Pont users to develop their own expert systems that gave them a personal sense of achievement and contribution. There

---

[18] Ed Mahler, interview with author, Wilmington, Del., June 25, 1991.
[19] Ibid.

also is a jump-start option where members of the Mahler's AI group come and provide consultation for a maximum of two days to get the system started. In addition, telephone support is available.

Dissemination Strategy

A key consideration, in addition to who will be using the expert system, is proper dissemination of the new technology. At Du Pont, working through the old-boy network was critical in getting the expert systems project initiated and in garnering support for its continued development. Networking was an important tool in spreading the word. Developing a task force made up of people from different backgrounds and departments not only leveraged various skills, but also gained the support of many departments. This was not an exclusive think tank made up of outside people, but people well known in the company and well aware of the issues at Du Pont. Mahler also gained the support of senior management, mainly from his boss, Raymond Cairns, the vice president for information systems.

From this core group, a second layer was added: site coordinators at the various plants and departmental locations. A third layer consisted of the hundreds of people trained in the two-day course. All these people are linked together by an electronic bulletin board system, so they can keep up with new uses of the expert system shell and gain access to frequently asked questions.

Thus, Mahler's AI program group offers the course, consulting, and telephone advice as various ways of enabling and empowering individuals to develop their own expert systems designed to meet their personal and varied needs. The AI group serves to help company members understand the powerful uses of expert systems, build their own system, and maintain the momentum. But to guard against making the company dependent on it, the AI group continually encourages users to be more independent and to take the risks necessary in learning about expert systems.

Mahler was careful to enlist the sponsorship of senior management when the potential of expert systems became apparent. To ensure managerial support at all levels for the new technology, the AI group offers an introductory four-hour presentation about expert systems and their applications for managers and engineers who will manage the system.

The assessment of whether a company is even capable of utilizing expert system technology and the issues of what type of expert system to develop must be based on the current computer capabilities of the company. At Du Pont, there was a certain level of computer familiarity. In addition to 3,000 programmers working with FORTRAN and COBOL, the firm also had 50,000 employees who could use software applications such as Lotus 123, but who could not write application programming. Ed Mahler was faced with the dilemma of developing an expert system that increased the productivity of each employee but that could be easily developed by nonprogrammers and could be tailored to meet the varied needs of each product group. Furthermore, Mahler wanted to use the existing PC-based hardware.

Ultimately, the expert systems were intended for end-users, not just for use by those who developed them. In Du Pont's case, expert systems were not going to be reserved just for the programmers, but rather were envisioned to help free the experts. It is these people and the customers whom the AI builders at Du Pont targeted when they chose to build a basic shell system.

Human Resources Considerations

Getting people to use expert systems at Du Pont depended on developing an expert system that could be used by employees with varying levels of computer skills. Building a complex or obscure system would only add to the anxiety of utilizing a new tool. Encouraging people to personally own (design, develop, implement, and use) expert systems allows expert systems to be utilized to their maximum potential. Employees feel not only that expert systems can help them, but also that they have a personal stake in its development. Before they can adopt expert systems and modify their attitudes toward artificial intelligence, they must see how their work can be enhanced. They should not feel threatened by the existence of expert systems. Effective managers will assure employees that their increased productivity does not mean that the company will start decreasing the work staff or cut jobs. Employees must see expert systems as a companion.

Applications Proliferate at Du Pont

Mahler believes that all problems at Du Pont boil down to three basic categories: diagnostics or troubleshooting, selection, and planning or scheduling. Du Pont has directed the application of expert systems to three critical areas in manufacturing: utility, the equipment used to make the product; process control, monitoring process variations (this

component can be equated to the diagnostics paradigm, including remote process control); and scheduling, which involves issues of priority
setting, JIT, and flexibility.

Diagnostics

Diagnostics can occur in all functions. In marketing, it tends to appear
in technical services. In manufacturing, process diagnostics is a common problem. Issues of low yields or equipment malfunction, or what
component of a computer is likely to be defective, are ones that can be
solved through the use of expert systems. Instead of expending hours
diagnosing the problem, pulling apart a computer, or replacing unnecessary parts, the expert system can pinpoint where the problem is and how
to fix it.

Selection

Selection is another basic problem. Selection of expert systems can provide the knowledge necessary for the consumer to make the right choice.
Through these types of expert systems, information contained in corporate rule books, performance guides, standards books, maintenance and
operations manuals is made easily accessible to the user. Given so many
consumer options, Du Pont realized it had to find a way to help the customer select the right product and distinguish the Du Pont product from
its other competitors. For example, each of the 600 kinds of neoprene
functions a little differently; an expert system helps the customer identify
the right type to use. Gone are the voluminous manuals or the lengthy
calls to the laboratory or technical services for proper advice. Once all
this information is inserted into the expert system, it can be accessed
innumerable times by countless users.

A type of selection service provided for customers in packaging
is the expert system called "Smart Choice." This particular expert system helps the consumer determine which of the 30 grades of Du Pont
"Bynel" coextrudable adhesive resin to select. Another expert system,
S.H.A.R.E. (Self-Help Automated Resource Evaluation), according to
company literature, helps electronics package designers in choosing
among Du Pont's line of ceramic thick film compositions. The Carpet
Advisor expert system helps designers and architects select the proper
carpet for customers. By inputting customer responses to various questions on carpeting requirements, such as cost, color, and stain resistance,
the Carpet Advisor can determine the best match between what Du Pont
has and what the customer needs.

Planning

Schedules can be thrown off easily if a machine malfunctions or if there is a discontinuous flow of materials. For example, scheduling the production of 200 kinds of polymers can be a tricky business when many are routed through common machinery.

Solving specific problems—Remote Access

One way expert systems leverage human resources is by providing consulting on recurring problems. "Principal consultant apprentice" expert systems free the expert by providing field engineers with answers to most basic issues. It was calculated that some 80 percent of all problems that field engineers have can be solved over the phone and do not require a local visit.

Another example of problem solving is a "sales tax advisor" expert system. Du Pont must pay sales taxes on materials that are used with plant equipment or in the office. This sales tax is not levied on materials that are made into product and shipped from the factory. Furthermore, these sales tax amounts vary from state to state. Distinguishing whether to apply the sales tax and how much to apply can be a difficult task, but an expert system can make these decisions consistently.

Developing a Corporate Memory.   Expert systems also help record the expertise gathered by the human expert over time. Instead of worrying about how to train personnel to become experts or losing valuable information as employees transfer or retire, the expert system serves as a reservoir of information and process documentation. This information becomes a corporate asset. In one case involving a complex process of distilling impurities in a chemical used for making solid-state electronics, the expertise of one engineer who could do this job was transferred into an expert system known as "Mike-in-the-Box." Thus, the knowledge of one expert became corporate know-how, allowing many other individuals not only to learn from this expert, but also to properly execute the diagnostic process. The expert system became a nonhuman advisor to many, available 24 hours a day. Just as importantly, the time of this one expert was freed to perform other more complex tasks.

Another example of developing a corporate memory involved a diagnostic problem in the fiber-dyeing process. Dying the fabric is quite difficult (considered by some to be an art form). A retired human expert was called in to help develop a system used in reducing the chances of an improper dye job. This expert developed a 300-rule system that was incorporated into an expert system to remind the operator of all the things that can affect the dye of a fabric, such as the temperature of the bath and the speed at which the fabric is run through the dye batch.

As a form of corporate memory, expert systems are an ego-neutral, permanent asset of the company. "Try finding 25 critical people in a particular field and none of them will be able to tell you how the whole process works. Through expert systems, the enterprise is reconstructing reality and providing knowledge that can empower the user."[20]

Economies of Scale.   Economies of scale is another benefit that can be realized through expert systems. The economies of scale can be enjoyed in the manufacturing of similar products, such as the nearly 200 types of polymer production, where knowledge in the production of one type of polymer can be applied to a large degree to the other types of polymer production.

Increased Customer Responsiveness.   Expert systems provide an efficient way of responding to customer needs. Quick turnaround in response time is a powerful value added factor that can improve a company's operations and customer satisfaction levels.

Lessons Learned

Planning and carrying out truly innovative changes requires a thorough understanding of the organization. According to Ed Mahler, successful applications depend 90 percent on organizational change and 10 percent on technology. Major lessons learned were

- Ownership of a system is the key to success.
- Integration with other systems is almost always necessary to achieve business results.
- Automating routine decision making reaps the highest monetary rewards.

Lessons were also learned about the development process. When using the dispersed expert systems approach, a company may go though

---

[20]Ibid.

three stages: maverick, experimentation, and culture change. In the first stage, a group of core individuals develop their own expert systems on a limited basis. In the second stage, the successes of the mavericks' experimentation lay the foundation for convincing the rest of the company of the benefits behind expert systems. Gradually these successes start to reach a critical level where the group can start to introduce expert systems on a widespread basis.

The critical success factors for expert systems development are adaptability, ease of use, accuracy, and low cost incurred for data distribution. "It is important to manage the expert systems development. If you don't manage it, it won't happen," says Mahler.[21] The expert system must match the firm's corporate environment; for example, the expert systems development at Du Pont was developed along the old-boy network, expertise, and respect based on experience.

Having explored new technologies, we will now explore the paradigm currently taking shape within manufacturing.

THE EMERGING INFORMATION TECHNOLOGY PARADIGM

The key to taking advantage of the changing IT paradigm is adopting a new vantage point from which to assess IT investment. Traditional IT investment follows a set analysis process that starts with business modeling, leads to data modeling, continues to application definition, and finally results in the selection of the technology that is most appropriate to support the applications and data. This seemingly pragmatic approach is one most information systems planning methodologies prescribe. Unfortunately, this approach can result in exactly the IT infrastructure problem described earlier—namely, a multiplicity of incompatible computers, incompatible networks, and incompatible workstations, each selected for suitability in an isolated application environment. Efforts to integrate subsequent applications are often thwarted by the combined stresses of potential incompatibilities.

The root of this problem is that optimizing separate pieces of an infrastructure for each new application is a short-sighted strategy. This approach fails to recognize properly that an infrastructure composed of

---

[21] Ibid.

computers, terminals, networks, and data bases has more lasting value than the applications that use it. Furthermore, a consistent IT infrastructure has the inherent ability to accept and integrate new technologies, applications, and connections. By analogy with the transportation system, the roadways and bridges have more lasting value than the current set of cars and trucks that use them. If the U.S. interstate highway system followed the same evolutionary path of most information systems, roads would be built only between cities that currently have proven interconnection needs. To achieve a high degree of enablement, however, an enterprise must be willing to invest in the flexibility represented by an multipurpose infrastructure rather than simply adding new and distinct information systems.

The 1980s showed that blockbuster applications have a decreasing ability to achieve competitive advantage and very little ability to sustain it. Peter Keen argues that grace period for IT-driven competitive advantage can vary from two to seven years. Two-year advantages result from new software applications; seven-year advantages are achieved when the networking and interconnection infrastructure is also involved in the new system.[22] Even American Airlines, which has been a primary exemplar of the use of large applications for competitive advantage, is moving away from this strategy. According to Max Hopper, Senior VP at American, "Developing an innovative new computer system will offer less decisive business advantage than before, and these advantages will be more fleeting and more expensive to maintain."[23]

Competitors can duplicate software applications to provide the same service, or even improve on the original concept with more features. Continuing improvements in application development automation [such as CASE tools and rapid application development (RAD) techniques] will further decrease the grace period of competitive advantage. To maintain IT-driven competitive advantage, an enterprise must continually improve its applications at least as quickly as the competition tries to catch up. Alternatively, the competitive leader can periodically change the differentiating applications to something radically new, again sending the competition back to the drawing board. What is needed for either of

---

[22]Peter G.W. Keen, *Shaping the Future*, Chapter 2, "Competitive Positioning Through Information Technology" (Boston, Mass: Harvard Business School Press, 1991), pp. 61–62.

[23]Max D. Hopper, "Rattling Sabre—New Ways to Compete on Information," *Harvard Business Review*, May/June 1990, p. 121.

these scenarios is an infrastructure (technical, human, organizational) that fosters rapid change and integration of diverse data stores, people, and applications. An IT infrastructure that has evolved based on least-cost support for isolated applications is least likely to enable new applications, particularly the types of applications that offer competitive advantage and thus represent radical uses of technology.

Information Technology Architectures Define an Enabling Infrastructure

The way out of the seemingly endless spiral of short-sighted technology planning is to develop an information technology architecture whose goal is global enablement rather than isolated optimization. The IT architecture must be defined according to criteria beyond simple support of existing applications and computers. Instead, an enabling IT architecture plan must take into account emerging computing and networking technologies, evolving communication patterns and connection needs, and changing application architectures and development tools. In essence, an IT architecture specification is based on presumed uses of emerging technology as well as on a prediction of future business scenarios that would drive the use of technology. Enabling IT architectures transcend the present status quo in an attempt to position the enterprise for the future.

Combined with data architectures, application architectures, and management architectures, IT architectures constitute a complete information systems architecture. IT architectures can be specified according to several levels of detail, from principles, to models, and to standards. The principles describe a company's fundamental beliefs and constraints regarding the use of technology.[24] Models describe the relationship among major IT components and the services that will be provided by the IT infrastructure. This service description is fundamental in assessing an architecture's degree of enablement by defining what the architecture is intrinsically capable of doing or not doing. Detailed architectural standards are necessary to ensure interoperation among diverse computers, networks, and applications.

---

[24]For a description of how principles can be used to define an IT architecture, see T. H. Davenport, M. Hammer, T. J. Mephisto, "How Executives Can Shape Their Company's Information Systems," *Harvard Business Review*, March/April 1989, pp. 11–27.

Manufacturing is at a turning point in information technology evolution. The advances in applications development, microprocessors, network technology, and operating system services now allow users to handpick IT architectures. Previously, IT architectures were completely defined and controlled by a few vendors with sufficient market clout to specify sets of compatible technologies. (IBM's SNA-3270-CICS is one very common example of a set of compatible technologies specified and controlled entirely by IBM.) The future of IT architectures revolves around the concept of open systems that unbundle technologies into component parts and allow some mixing and matching to suit given IT needs.

Open Systems Role in Information Technology Architectures

The new era of information technology is earmarked by the term *open systems*. To many people, open systems is synonymous with the UNIX operating system, but a broader definition is required. An open systems standard is any information technology standard that is published, and thus is supported, by multiple vendors. Open systems should also support some degree of mixing and matching among diverse standards so that customers have some ability to choose which standards should be assembled for their particular architectures.

The rise of open standards has fostered the growth of independent software developers, who are writing everything from communications protocols to electronic mail systems, often in high-level languages readily compiled for many computer system environments. Similarly, an entire industry of data communication vendors has emerged, selling everything from packet switches to LAN bridges and routers that simultaneously support a wide range of computer systems. Computer vendors no longer have a lock on the market for software or networking components compatible with their computers.

Well-implemented open system standards allow the user to focus on applications and their benefits rather than on technology infrastructure issues. *Technology compatibility across a broad range of equipment will make it possible to share information across the value chain and more effectively integrate organizations throughout the chain to optimize the performance of each.*

The two forces contributing to the move toward open systems are (1) the increasing influence of international standards bodies (stemming from customer demands for interoperation of equipment from multiple vendors), and (2) the prevailing trend toward disaggregating technologies from one another. This second force is most important, since it highlights an underlying move toward modular technology, and hence flexible technology.

In the past, there was little choice in how an information system was constructed. Once the operating system was specified, the computing hardware, the network, and the application architectures were also fixed. Once the terminal was chosen, the user interface was fixed. The combination of operating system and terminal, therefore, effectively determined the characteristics of the entire information system.

The present situation is less constrained. Computing hardware and operating systems have become somewhat disassociated, at least to the degree that any hardware platform can run a version of UNIX as well as its "native" proprietary operating system such as IBM's MVS or DECs VMS. This holds true even for PCs that are capable of running DOS, OS/2, or Mac O/S as well as streamlined versions of UNIX. Once the operating system is chosen, however, the system services available become fixed. The operating system services define whether an application written for one operating system may be transferred to another operating system—thus, they determine its portability.

Workstations and PCs have replaced terminals and offer graphical user interfaces. The rise of standard network protocols and network services has permitted the network to be unbundled from the computer hardware, operating systems, and workstation. Applications are now being written to run on many different computing platforms (which are combinations of hardware and operating system). However, many applications still incorporate intrinsic data management functions and constrain the choice of user interfaces. Furthermore, most applications are written so that the individual modules are not separable from one another, thus making it impractical to reuse modules in different applications or even to modify a single module (in response to a business process change) without affecting the other modules.

The emerging computing paradigm is one of substantially greater disassociation. System services are being extracted from the operating system so that application portability is greatly enhanced and workstations can support multiple graphical user interfaces. More importantly, the data management function is migrating from the application to stand-alone data base management systems (DBMS) so that common data can be accessed by any application on the network. Applications are being written in a much more modular form so that code may be reused or modified easily. The underlying technical advances that are making this increased disassociation possible are the new network computing standards and CASE tools and techniques.

The benefits of this trend affect many diverse aspects of how IT is managed. Information technology planners will be increasingly able to choose the standards and technologies that best fit their visions of their organization's future. Modularity will make it possible to incorporate or substitute new technologies without a wholesale change of infrastructure. Customers will enjoy lower costs as a result of increased competition and as technology based products become more standardized. Packaged software applications will be more prevalent as the pool of programmers for each computer platform increases due to applications portability.

The real power of this trend, however, is in how it affects the quality of the individual products that make up an information system. Disassociation allows each vendor to contribute according to its area of excellence, including processors, DBMS, workstations, networks, application modules, application development tools, and the like. The customer can take advantage of the continual improvements in each technology area. For manufacturing applications, this philosophy of disassociation could apply to the software modules that make up integrated MRPII applications. Some vendors will have better financial modules, while others will produce better process planning modules, while still others will be known for their inventory control modules. Manufacturing enterprises would be well served by a software industry that allowed the mixing and matching of application modules to form the best-fit application for each given manufacturer. The aim of an IT architecture definition is to position the enterprise to be able to take advantage of the best-of-breed in any technology or application area.

Migration to Flexible Architectures

Unfortunately, most enterprises have an installed base of computers, networks, and applications that cannot be suddenly turned off as a new infrastructure of enabling technology appears. *Migration from nonflexible systems to flexible and open systems will be the primary challenge for information technology planners in the 1990s.* Open systems (in the form of application portability standards, e.g., POSIX-X/Open), network computing standards, and CASE tools promise to increase the flexibility and integrateability of information systems radically. The price of this flexibility is increased responsibility on the enterprise to design its architecture proactively, rather than simply to buy a product or a vendor's prepackaged architecture. Once a custom IT infrastructure is designed, the IT architect is responsible for maintaining the architecture specification as state of the art. An organization can no longer afford the comfort of allowing a single vendor to define and upgrade the architecture.

Open systems by themselves will not guarantee competitive advantage or even ensure greater application functionality. Open systems are simply a powerful tool for enacting and enabling business strategies. The correct execution of an open system strategy will, however, facilitate application portability, avoid vendor lock-in, help speed application development, and can provide a rich basis for tight integration of applications. Off-the-shelf applications will also play a larger role in manufacturing information systems. The next major step in software integration will be in application package integration, or assembling off-the-shelf software to form customized integrated packages. This step will require some significant advances in application architectures as well as in CASE tool integrators. However, as application developers are able to easily port their products to many classes of machines (workstations, servers, midrange, and mainframes) and as applications can be replicated cooperatively across a network, the pressure to integrate diverse packages will increase dramatically.

Information Technology Enablers

Advances in information technology continually reshape views of how and when IT should be used. In the past, computer vendors marketed their products as clearly identified business solutions—for example, general ledger, warehouse management, or payroll. Information technology was almost always bought as a packaged solution. This situation has changed, in part because no vendor can prepackage the vast range of individualized uses of IT. Further, modern information systems are increasingly composed of parts from many vendors. Selecting IT components and evaluating the effectiveness of systems must be done from the perspective of the customer. IT planners have a greater responsibility than ever to keep abreast not only of customer needs, but also of evolving and emerging technologies, vendor product strategies, and standards developments.

In the normal evolution of technology usage, one technology will rise in prominence only to be phased out as a replacement technology emerges, as technology costs change, or as changes occur in some collateral technology. This evolutionary course implies that the most prominent technologies today (as determined by the installed base) are very likely not the best ones to satisfy current and emerging needs. In this sense, basing IT decisions on what is in widespread use today is akin to driving a car by looking through the rearview mirror. The driver will be well positioned to travel yesterday's roads using yesterday's technologies but will not see the turns in the road ahead.

The analysis of replacement technologies is the simplest to address because it does not require planners to develop new models for technology usage. Rather, replacement technology decisions are usually based on cost and performance criteria of a one-for-one replacement. For example, replacing one mainframe with a more powerful mainframe would require straightforward cost/performance analysis rather than an assessment of the role of the mainframe in corporate data processing.

Changes to the underlying cost structure also would seem to imply a straightforward analysis—indeed, cost decreases could allow a firm to simply continue doing what it is currently doing, but at a lower overall cost. In actuality, however, the analysis is more complicated because dramatic cost decreases can also allow technologies to be used in ways not previously feasible. One example is the rise in private enterprise backbone networks, prompted by the network price decreases following the AT&T divestiture in 1984. After the breakup, costs for high-capacity circuits plummeted, spurring corporations to set up private voice, data, and video networks. New locations never before feasible were connected to the corporate information highway. Video conferencing among business offices became much more practical. Therefore, changes to the underlying cost basis must be scrutinized carefully. This is particularly true for any technology that "touches" large numbers of end-users (e.g., PCs, PC software, network connections), because even small cost changes result in large savings as they are multiplied many times over.

One technology is a collateral technology of another when changes in one technology alter the desirability of the other. Changes to collateral technologies are often very difficult to identify, and their implications are often the hardest to assess. An example of this is the gradual decline in importance of IBM's SNA network technology. The ease of use and power of PC-based applications is credited with much of the early acceptance of PCs and, by association, local area networks (LANs). This has spurred a major trend toward the use of LAN-to-LAN wide-area-networking technologies instead of IBM's SNA, even though SNA is still the best technology for large-scale terminal-to-host connectivity and screen-oriented transaction processing.

It is significant that the trend toward interconnecting systems will only increase the impact of collateral technology changes. The price of disk drives and microprocessors affects PCs, PCs affect LANs, LANs affect application architectures, application architectures affect CASE tools, CASE tools affect code portability, code portability affects operating system functionality, and so on. It is no wonder that IT planning can be so challenging.

Finally, because a new generation of computer equipment has been developed every three to five years, it can be important for manufacturers to work closely with equipment vendors and software developers to help "pull" new technology into the market and define its functions and form. In addition, by deploying a new system early in its useful life, a manufacturer can get the most from the system before it becomes antiquated and perhaps gain an advantage in the market by using the system earlier and longer than competitors.

SUMMARY

In this chapter, we have examined the many roles that information technology plays in successful manufacturing strategies and the importance of information technology in enabling manufacturers to meet the challenges that lie ahead. The competitive renewal of U.S. manufacturing has been an issue of national importance since the late 1970s. Much has been written on the extent of the problem and what companies need to do to regain or maintain a competitive edge. The adoption of technology plays a prominent role; for some companies it is the dominant long-term solution. From the beginning of this period of heightened manufacturing awareness, businesses have been admonished to "automate, emigrate, or evaporate" by the most ardent proponents of technology. Billions of dollars have been invested in an effort to transform the vision of highly automated operations into reality. As a result, computer-integrateable tools exist for nearly every aspect of a company's operations, and what doesn't exist is under development. Technologically, barriers to computer-integrated manufacturing have all but been eliminated.

The major trends in information technology will greatly affect the ability to manufacture. These trends do not simply represent an extension of current IT usage to higher speeds or larger volumes. Rather, they represent a fundamental discontinuity with the current model for computing. The technological trends that, in aggregate, comprise this shift are workstation computing power and local area network speeds, network computing services, CASE tools, object-oriented techniques, and multimedia information. Taken individually, these technology advances do not point to a specific future path. Taken together, and combined with an overwhelming need to make information systems as flexible as they are powerful, these technologies illuminate a vision of highly distributed processors, networked together to support shared data and applications. This vision contains centralized repositories of data that are maintained by professional information systems professionals, with application development being conducted by the end-users themselves using powerful and simple tools. It incorporates an understanding that technology can completely change the relationships between people through communications, multimedia, and expert systems. And it includes an understanding that the technology infrastructure is more important than the applications themselves in achieving competitive parity, let alone advantage. Although this vision is not really new to the litany of IT propaganda, it is finally becoming a feasible target.

The deployment of manufacturing IT has become a high-stakes game with compulsory participation and companies in growing numbers are becoming involved. Whereas some companies have found technology to be an effective route to improved competitiveness, others have not. The challenge manufacturers now face is selecting the correct systems and implementing them with vision and determination. Now that we have examined the critical elements of the integrative manufacturing formula, in Chapter 7 we will discuss how the organization can be changed dramatically by a variety of improvement methodologies.

CHAPTER 7
TRANSFORMING THE ORGANIZATION: IMPROVEMENT METHODOLOGIES

INTRODUCTION

In the year 2000, manufacturers should be celebrating the integrity of the manufacturing enterprise, with empowered people and organizations servicing customers with as-needed expert knowledge and unprecedented, infinitely flexible production and support capabilities. This vision of the factory is considerably more than an abstract ideal. It is an achievable and necessary goal. Successfully transforming the manufacturing organization of the 1990s into the global enterprise of the 21st century is not a straightforward task. A combination of inspired, dedicated leadership and outstanding worker and enterprise performance is required for organizations to make the transition to manufacturing integrity and world-class performance.

This chapter includes a discussion of

- Benchmarking.
- Developing a performance improvement plan.
- Key techniques for methodology implementation.

BENCHMARKING AND BEST PRACTICES

In the year 2000, the *Fortune* 500 will most likely comprise a very different group of companies from that of today, with perhaps as many as half of those on today's list dropping out through merger, acquisition, or failure, to be replaced by other enterprises that today may be only a vision in an entrepreneur's mind.

Organizations determined to remain viable players in the next century will need to establish a vision of their own that will take them

---

This chapter was written with the assistance of Alex Nedzel.

forward. Realizing the vision will not be easy, particularly without inter-mediate programs that reflect the big picture and position the companies for their futures. "Key action programs are part of a holistic manufac-turing strategy. Taken together, they form a set of mutually reinforcing manufacturing choices that are being driven by the changing competitive environments."[1]

Organizations need to engage in an ongoing examination of what factors make some companies successful while others fail in a shifting business environment, and what lessons both the successes and failures provide. Organizations must also be willing to set aside all not-invented-here bias and take advantage of the best, no matter where it is found.

Overview

Beginning in the 1970s, historically successful manufacturers across the globe were challenged by new competitors introducing products and ser-vices that were both higher in quality and lower in price. Older organiza-tions implemented a process now called *benchmarking* to focus attention on understanding how these new competitors and others pioneered and mastered new processes and practices, particularly with respect to cus-tomer satisfaction, that enabled them to successfully penetrate markets and compete. Organizations use the results of benchmarking to identify, measure, design, and implement process and practice improvements that will enhance the enterprise's competitive position and add value to the products and services it delivers to its customers.

Xerox Corporation, a well-publicized advocate of benchmarking, defines benchmarking as the continuous process of measuring products and services against the toughest competitors or those companies recog-nized as industry leaders. This kind of *competitive* benchmarking is not as common as *noncompetitive* or *process* benchmarking, since it has been found that most competitive organizations do not like to share details of their organization and thus do not provide good models for emulation. In general, benchmarking is a continuous process in which an organiza-tion systematically and proactively measures the operations, processes, products, services, techniques, and methods of another organization(s) and compares the results with its own performance. Targets are estab-

---

[1]Ted Olson and Craig Giffi, *Competing in World Class Manufacturing* (Homewood, Ill.: Business One Irwin, 1990), p. 239.

lished for organizational improvement by identifying enterprises whose performance is outstanding, measuring their performance, characterizing how that performance was produced, and then extrapolating from those observations to create achievable but aggressive criteria for improving internal performance. Measurements derived from noncompeting industries or from otherwise dissimilar organizations are referred to as *best practices*.

Examining the processes and practices of leading companies enables other organizations to identify improvement opportunities and provides a prototype for the improvements or innovations required to become competitive or achieve competitive advantage. For example, why does it take Fujitsu only two years to introduce a new model car while it takes most competitors much longer? A look at the techniques Fujitsu uses to get its products to market shows that the company has applied the time-to-market lessons it learned in the engineering, manufacturing, and marketing of computers to this different product field. Any manufacturer should be able to apply these kinds of lessons.

Goals of Benchmarking

Benchmarks can provide information for a number of goals:

- To assess the strengths and weaknesses of internal operations.
- To improve current manufacturing processes and business practices.
- To capitalize on proven ideas and technology.
- To avoid the cost and time of developing new processes and practices from scratch.
- To establish more competitive performance targets and set realistic, long-term goals.
- To lay the foundation for continuous improvement programs throughout the organization.

Four Types of Benchmarking

Internal metrics measure period-to-period progress on typically departmental, tactical, or other divisional metrics. Many companies are multinational, multidimensional, and multimarket; therefore, they contain diverse sections that can offer valuable insight to each other.

Best-in-class metrics measure company performance against competitors in similar industries. Top performance is sometimes referred to as world-class.

Best practices compares similar practices (often cross-functional) against all industries worldwide.

Best possible, a metric in its infancy, identifies maximum attainable performance by applying best practice methods, organizational and cultural empowerment, and advanced, yet proven, technology. These metrics may also be visionary by using technology trends in conjunction with business process innovation methodologies discussed later in this chapter.

The Two Classes of Benchmarks

Quantitative Benchmarks (performance metrics). Metric benchmarking compares quantitative operating statistics from one company to those of another company or to industry standards. Quantitative benchmarks have inherent difficulties (e.g., incompatibility of metrics, poor comparability and availability of data, and inconsistency in reporting procedures and rules), but provide the advantage of measuring relative performance, thereby revealing the performance gap. That gap, however, is described in quantitative terms, and the benchmark does not outline practices targeted to reduce it.

Qualitative Analyses (practice benchmarks). Whereas metric benchmarking identifies and quantifies performance gaps, practice benchmarking helps close the gaps. It compares the operations, organizations, processes, and practices of one enterprise to those of another. Once the practices have been identified and understood, they are immediately transferable for integration by the enterprise.

The Value of Benchmarking and Best Practices

Perhaps benchmarking's most important benefit is that it requires an organization to develop and retain an outward perspective, canvassing and searching for ways to improve, innovate, and, thus, renew and change its formalized processes. Through benchmarking, an enterprise can gain a clear understanding of how its current processes satisfy customer requirements and how to improve satisfaction and enhance current processes by emulating practice leaders—critical information for any manufacturing organization.

Benchmarking also provides a way to differentiate an enterprise from its competition, as it identifies and focuses on practices that will position the enterprise beyond its competitors and leverages those practices that add incremental value to customers. Management can assess and evaluate its current practices and synthesize these with the enterprise's strategy in order to target the specific benchmarking processes.

Due to its cross-functional nature, another value of benchmarking is that it provides the opportunity for everyone in the company—from accountants to factory personnel—to contribute to the organization's improvement. No longer is innovation and process improvement the sole responsibility of a department such as product marketing, engineering, research and development, or manufacturing; the responsibility is extended across everyone everywhere in the enterprise.

There are a number of aspects of organizational performance that enterprises are well advised to benchmark. Of these, perhaps the most important are the organization performance measures, which should effectively measure manufacturing and business performance in a manner consistent with the overall goals of the enterprise.

Measures should be specific and consistent. For example, Federal Express, a recognized best-in-class company for logistics distribution, tracks service factors in order to produce its service quality indicator (SQI), which exemplifies the single-mindedness of its focus on customer satisfaction and provides an example of best practices in performance measures in the logistics, distribution, shipping, and inventory tracking process. Federal Express's SQI is a hierarchy of performance measures that break down service quality into 12 specific measures of customer dissatisfaction, which allow for a routine collection of detailed information that rolls up into an effective measure of customer satisfaction. No interpretation of data is necessary; no ambiguity is possible, because when the measure of performance shows improvement, customers are being better served. The 12 measures are

- Wrong day late.
- Right day late.
- Invoice adjustment required.
- Damaged packages (regardless of fault).
- Complaints reopened.
- Overgoods (identification lost, no label).
- Abandoned calls.

- Lost packages.
- Missed pick-ups.
- Telephone traces (incomplete information available in computer).
- Missing proofs of delivery on invoice (even if on-time and right place).
- International (same measures for international business).

The Benchmarking Process

There are nine steps to establishing a benchmarking program.

1. Understand the enterprise's current state. The enterprise must develop a clear understanding of what can and shall be improved internally and, therefore, what to benchmark. Benchmarking must first focus inward on the major processes, organizations, and operations that exist today, and secondly look outward toward the customer, the competition, and other industries. To accomplish this, a team must be formed representing a range of functions and skills and consisting of workers and management with differing functional backgrounds and a variety of analytical, organizational, and technical skills.

2. Determine candidate targets for benchmarking. Benchmarking can focus either on the enterprise's products and services by evaluating costs and quality or on key processes that can improve customer satisfaction or enhance internal performance. One important basis for choosing areas to benchmark is a clear understanding of what the enterprise and its customers require, both now and in the future; priority should be given to critical and frequently recurring processes that add or subtract the most value and that clearly serve or fail to serve the customer.

In order to characterize the gap between current and target performance and the potential benefits of targeted improvements, a variety of techniques can be employed, including metric comparisons, cycle-time measures, quality goals, and cost targets. Analyzing benchmark gaps will enable the organization to prioritize opportunities and begin to develop programs for closing the gaps. How will the improvements brought about by benchmarking be recognized and quantified? The answer lies in how performance of the organization is measured. Many organizations today lack adequate performance metrics and, thus, are not in a position to accurately assess the effects of benchmarking efforts.

3. Establish benchmark partners. An essential element of the benchmarking partnership is a willingness to enter into an open, two-way relationship that requires sharing information that is often considered proprietary or confidential. Those that have emerged as industry leaders by perfecting key processes or practices are frequently sought as benchmark partners. As already noted, although benchmark partners can be competitors, noncompetitive enterprises that have mastered important and transferable processes and that see merit in exploring continued improvements are often a better choice.

The optimal benchmark partner is addressing the same or a very similar set of customer requirements (customers can be external or internal to the organization) and is, of course, ready, willing, and able to collaborate. Candidates for benchmarking partnerships can be identified by employees, customers, or suppliers; located among customers and suppliers in an organization's own value chain; gleaned from trade journals, data bases, annual reports, market research, government data, or consultants; or gathered from professional association membership rosters. Qualifying partnerships can be as simple as telephoning the target organization, proposing a benchmarking partnership, and meeting the partner candidate to work out the details.

4. Conduct benchmarking. In benchmarking a process, the team begins by examining how the process flows, how much it costs, how long it takes to complete, and how efficient and defect free the process is today. Since this internal review involves multifunctional resources, it often prompts people to evaluate and rethink the process from their perspectives. Most organizations are unable to assemble fully trained benchmarking teams and must therefore provide training programs. Internal benchmarks should be calculated before visiting and benchmarking external partners, thereby providing early insights into improvement opportunities and making team members better focused and more likely to detect excellent practices in other organizations.

Next, the examination turns to the partner's process, an evaluation that focuses on the organizational structure, the work flow, performance measures used, and how technology supports the process. A questionnaire that includes every issue to be addressed during the site visit should be prepared (the partner should receive it well before the visit), and the benchmarking team should be thoroughly versed in the processes to be benchmarked. The site visits (most often reciprocal, but not necessarily targeting the same practice areas) should be conducted with every intention of establishing long-term relationships with the enterprises and employees involved. Immediately after the visits, the team should validate the results, determine and agree which findings present the greatest opportunities to each organization, and share insights and recommendations.

Throughout this work, it is important that the benchmark team establish and maintain good working relations with the partner's employees to enhance communications and ensure a complete understanding of the benchmarked area. If the benchmark target is a product or service, the team must translate the results of the evaluation into recommendations, processes, or practices for its own organization. For example, if the costs of a competitor's product are lower, the team must investigate the practices that have reduced its costs, such as fewer accounting people, just-in-time purchasing, or consolidation of supplier base. This investigation results in a complete list of prospective improvements.

After a site visit, the benchmarking team should set the organization's target level of performance for the benchmark and, by taking into account present performance, quantify the resulting gap. Specific improvements that could help close the benchmark gap should be applied.

5. Design and prototype improvements. To close the gap, the benchmarking team should first incorporate identified practice improvements in a limited or prototype fashion to control the impact of inexperience and enable the team to optimize the procedures before deploying them more broadly.

6. Implement changes and transform the organization. Refining these benchmarking prototype recommendations into the daily operation will complete management's commitment to process improvement. The benchmarking team will design programs for incorporating management's revisions into enterprisewide processes and a cost/benefit analysis must be provided. In addition, education and training are integral to the benchmarking process and need to be included in the program implementation plan. These programs are then scheduled, budgeted, and presented to senior management for authorization to proceed.

7. Monitor changes and refine operations. An effective system and methodology for monitoring performance of operations will enable an organization to continue its ongoing benchmarking efforts.

8. Planning for the future. When best practices are included, along with long-range performance targets taken from the enterprise's strategic and operating plans, the real value of benchmarking is realized. Long-range planning should compare the performance objectives of the enterprise with the best practices objectives of its benchmarking partners. Planning for change is always less painful than reacting to crisis and provides the necessary time for management training and buy-in.

9. Monitor and measure the new process. The final benchmarking step is performance measurement. Ensuring that the new procedures effect the changes anticipated requires persistent and effective measurements. If new metrics of performance are required, as is often the case, they must be carefully developed to ensure that they accurately measure the process and meet the needs of both the organization and the customers. Metrics can be expected to change over time (i.e.,"ship to commit" becoming "ship to request").

Figure 7–1 depicts a five-year program for process improvement. Benchmarking partner performance helps identify target processes and, in conjunction with current performance measurements, determines the benchmark gap. Strategic actions, based largely upon adapted partner practices, are selected and rolled into a business plan that will yield the desired improvements. These innovative actions drive radical, quan-

FIGURE 7–1
Five-Year Process Improvement Cycle

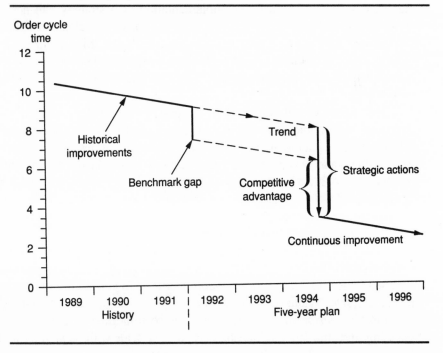

tum, one-time improvements, subsequently reconvening the continuous practice of improvement.

DEVELOPING A PERFORMANCE IMPROVEMENT PLAN

Although benchmarking and best practices may point an enterprise in the right direction for change, how does it actually get where it wants to be? Sustained performance improvement is more difficult, but it is essential if a company wishes to remain competitive. This section will serve as a working guide to developing a performance improvement plan, implementing it, and measuring its effect. It will discuss

- The methodologies or approaches that a company can use to increase performance.
- The implementation and skill building process.
- The significance of performance measurement metrics.

When a good strategy fails to meet its potential for success, the reason often lies in its implementation—not in some flaw inherent in the strategy itself. Because the implementation of a strategy can never be as exciting as the initial development, it is usually delegated below the management level and loses its executive clout. This, in turn, has often caused the implementation to be poorly measured and, if the results have not been measured accurately, then they are usually not rewarded properly.

That is the way it was done in the past, when results or objectives were not measurable. Today, through some of the methodologies that follow in this chapter, there are process steps and milestones that are measurable—and rewardable. Today, cultural and behavioral elements of change are incorporated into our methodologies. For example, in the past, world-class manufacturing measured turnover; now it measures each of the processes used to achieve the end result, including behavior, tools/techniques, and cross-organizational relationships.

Once the company has identified an improvement area, it should clearly articulate its specific objectives. Implicit in this crucial task is the need to develop concrete, measurable criteria to gauge current performance and later evaluate the results of a particular improvement strategy. The topic of *performance measurement* is so important in the strategic planning and implementation phases that it is dealt with separately and in great detail in the last section of this chapter.

Methodologies and Objectives

The appropriateness of a methodology depends largely on how well its attributes coincide with the company's goals. There are hundreds of methods to choose from, each with a set of performance objectives, an expected range or scope of influence, an anticipated time frame for implementation, and a group of manufacturing issues (i.e., problem sets) for which it is best suited. However, we have consolidated these options into three basic types of methodologies—cost reduction, business process improvement, and business process innovation. The planning team should match, as closely as possible, the company's needs with the methodology attributes on specific issues, such as performance objectives, focus, time frame, technology, and cultural change. Figure 7–2 illustrates the objectives, performance metrics, focus, and time frame of each methodology. The first phase in the process analysis approach—the overall strategic analysis of a company—was covered

FIGURE 7–2
Three Methodologies for Process Improvement

	Cost reduction	Business process improvement	Business process innovation
Objective	• Reduce cost of current process	• Continually improve the current process	• Dramatic improvement in cost, quality, time and/or environment through vision-driven process redesign
Performance metrics	• Cost	• Cost • Quality • Time	• Cost • Quality • Time • Culture
Methodology focus	• Tactical • Departmental/ function • Local • Interfaces • Market protection	• Strategic • Companywide • International • Coordination • Market share	• Visionary • Enterprise • Transnational • Integration • Market preeminence
Time frame	• Immediate	• 1–2 years	• 2–3 years

in Chapter 4. The next set of questions to consider is at the strategic planning level; the performance improvement team must match the objectives behind each methodology with the stated company vision and goals.

Cost Reduction

Cost Reduction (CR) methods are tactical measures taken quickly to address a current problem or trend. These application methods are in the most fundamental group of performance improvement measures, which target cost (i.e., labor, overhead, inventory) as the primary measurement metric. In some situations, the problems or trends are effectively resolved with cost reduction measures, but most often they also require more permanent, long-range treatment. From the standpoint of immediacy, however, cost reduction methods provide excellent tools to "stop the bleeding" and generate quick turnaround results. Although a reduction in costs is certainly one way of gauging a company's efficiency, there are other considerations, such as continuous improvement in time, responsiveness, and quality that the CR methodology does not address.

The cost reduction methodology, primarily directed at local or departmental levels of the company, focuses on the quick turnaround achievement of improvements in efficiency and the resulting reduction in costs for a particular process. Because CR efforts are departmental in nature, they tend to leave intact the current interfaces between departments or functions; they influence only intradepartmental or intrafunctional operations. (Cost reduction also tends to be procedure- rather than capital-intensive.)

The application of CR programs is most valuable in the pursuit of near-horizon goals, such as the short-term protection of markets where a narrow focus and immediate results are most critical. The installation of in-stock industrial equipment, standard computing, and off-the-shelf training programs are examples of relatively quick solutions that address the goals of task elimination, automation, and task improvement. These projects seldom require executive sign-off or guidance, as they are seen as independent endeavors. In situations where a more general effect is desired—one that affects different departments and functions and raises the overall business performance of a company—a special effort is required to coordinate cost reduction programs.

Cost reduction methodology can address both direct and indirect labor costs as well. Educational and training programs and other forms of efficiency improvements can also help reduce the costs associated with scrap, rework, and inspection. Inventory turn rates, schedule stability, and revenue throughput are other concerns that can be handled together because they deal with a common set of supply-side issues. The ability of CR programs to improve, even slightly, situations such as direct and indirect labor costs can have a significant impact in generating additional funds through increased savings and cash flow, which then become available to fund other programs.

Business Process Improvement

Business Process Improvement (BPI) addresses a more complex set of issues and focuses on the reorientation of company culture so that it embraces continuous improvement. BPI measures take place over a longer period of time and address the broader issues of a quality culture, time-reduction, and customer-responsiveness, as well as continuous improvement in cost.

Over the past two decades, many U.S. companies, as they search for systematic approaches to continuous improvement in cost, quality, delivery, and service, have become targets of serious international competitors. Over a very short period of time, several engaging new concepts and principles have been testing these companies' capacity not only to introduce technological change, but also to take enormous leaps in cultural transformation from a cost reduction perspective to a continuous improvement philosophy. This philosophy is reflected in the BPI methodology.

The goal of continuous process improvement methodology takes into account contributions from a variety of sources. The methods that Fredrick W. Taylor introduced in industrial engineering, which transformed factory processes, still provide the core approach to cost reduction and have given rise to a series of different approaches to continually improving manufacturing methods.[2] In addition to these various manufacturing methods, the principles of just-in-time, quick response, concurrent engineering, quality function deployment, computer-integrated manufacturing, and enterprise planning have gained popularity. Together

---

[2]Various manufacturing methods have been developed during the last 50 years. Some of the key contributors include Chandler, with organizational design principles; Ollie Wight, with integrated manufacturing system concepts; Michael Porter, with strategy redesign; Edward Deming, with total quality; and Robert Kaplan and Tom Vollman, with total cost and accounting redesign.

these methodologies and principles have expanded the options that manufacturing companies have to pursue the goal of attaining industry leadership or world-class performance status.

The idea of continuous process improvement embodied by BPI not only has been supported and advocated by stakeholders, including customers, investors, communities, and employees, who have all demanded serious improvement, but also has required their active *involvement*. Unlike cost reduction methodology, which targets departmental or independent functions for performance improvement, the problems and the solutions inherent in BPI are too complex and holistic for any single department, or even division, to handle, but they require the concerted efforts of all parties involved.

BPI cuts across departments and functions and requires the integration of technology training with culture reorientation and systems development. It differs from cost reduction measures in that it emphasizes sustained improvement; promotes integrative, collaborative behavior across company departments; and extends the focus from a cost reduction perspective to include quality improvement and time competitiveness.

Unlike CR programs, which rarely require executive guidance, BPI must be endorsed at the executive level and actively monitored by senior executives. These programs in aggregate require companywide efforts and should be included in the one- to two-year operating plans, serving as the key components in strategic planning. BPIs are appropriate for companies interested in increasing product quality, responsiveness to customers, market share, materials and inventory efficiency, productivity, and financial return. Successful use of the BPI methodology is highly dependent on a company's willingness to invest in its people (e.g., education, training, retention).

Business Process Innovation

Business Process Innovation (BPIN) prepares a company to respond to both today's customers and those of tomorrow, taking a more radical or revolutionary approach to improving the company's performance. Unlike cost reduction measures or continuous improvement, executives realize they must transform company practices and redefine the way it does business. BPIN relies on the interrelationship of all the processes that a company engages in to provide a product/service; the radical improvement of one or several will have a ripple effect on the other processes. This effect is achieved by using the compelling imagery of the companywide vision. Key enablers to both the vision and its implementation are information technology and best practices employed by best-performance companies regardless of industry and geographic boundaries.

The variety of objectives used for initiating a company's transformation include quantum improvement, 6 sigma quality, "5X" improvement, and sophisticated strategy formulation based on visioning. The time frame for BPIN is also considerably longer, roughly two to five years to inaugurate and implement. It will also be integrated with the back and/or front end of (continuous) business process improvement efforts. The benefits captured from this comprehensive reorientation have significant cost reduction, quality, and time implications. Furthermore, BPIN relies on the investigation and adoption of new or emerging information technologies, which are spawning new generations of information systems.

Until recently, cost reduction and continuous improvement methodologies provided innovative breakthroughs and, often, quantum improvements. Depending on the degree of investment and systematic management in these approaches, companies experience varying degrees of performance improvement. A company just now applying TQM or MRP will still experience dramatic internal improvement but perhaps achieve parity, at best, against its competitors. Today's companies must now measure their worth against the 1990s benchmark, which is increasingly more competitive.

In essence, BPIN is far more ambitious, leveraging the synergy generated from information technology advances and cultural enablement, and demonstrates a further commitment to best-in-class practices. Such new standards move toward the ideal market situation, where the company enjoys the benefits of the maximum security derived from the best possible preventive entry position. These companies, in their quest for maximum performance improvement are culturally ready to cast off the not-invented-here syndrome and adopt best practices regardless of geographic origin or industry. The compelling concept of BPIN can be appreciated in writings by such leaders as Thomas H. Davenport.[3]

Most businesses run on systems and processes rooted in 10-year-old technology, thereby not taking advantage of the past decade's *tenfold* increase in information technology. Companies now wish to use

---

[3]For further reading, see Thomas H. Davenport and James E. Short, "The New Industrial Engineering: Information Technology and Business Process Redesign," *Sloan Management Review* (Summer 1990) and Thomas H. Davenport, *Process Innovation: Redesigning Work Through Technology and People* (Boston, Mass.: Havard Business School, 1992), pp. 11–27.

contemporary and leading-edge information technology to reap unprecedented levels of performance improvement. In addition, the rise of consciousness in diversity, empowerment, and multinational leadership has provided companies with dramatically higher levels of usable "brain power" that would thrive with the integration of IT.

The BPIN methodology seeks quantum improvement in cost, quality, time, and/or environment, which it accomplishes through the vision-driven process redesign, examining a process as it cuts across an entire enterprise, and typically offering substantial improvement in cross-functional, cross-unit, and geographic integration. The methodology has the potential to introduce innovative processes that can transform an international company into a transnational corporation.

Corporations that undertake BPIN usually are seeking a position of market preeminence and recognize the need to maintain their competitiveness and guard against the erosion of their competitive edge. Continued innovation is the best protection against the position of having to take drastic, often compromising, measures just to survive. In addition to globalization, BPIN addresses such challenges as substantially improving the value of a product or service to customers; increasing customer responsiveness; drastically reducing the time necessary to design, sell, make, or deliver a product; eliminating inventory; and dramatically cutting overhead costs.

The methodology is new, powerful, and more difficult to carry out because of the challenges in developing and implementing a truly fresh and compelling vision. Even when such a visioning effort is successful, daunting challenges remain. BPIN requires a transformation across functional lines. Teams must therefore obtain wide support for the new processes and tolerance for the associated upheaval, and then be able to navigate the pitfalls encountered on the way to full implementation. Innovation of a major business process will require between two and five years to fully implement and become totally compatible with concurrent and subsequent continuous process improvement efforts.

Implementation

Implementation Steps

Planning the future, though difficult, can be easier than implementation. In this phase, other crucial questions develop: How does a company expect to implement and continue improving over time? What are the specific tools and techniques necessary for implementation? This section reviews the steps involved in implementing a particular methodology; this type of systematic review can also help the company select the type of methodology process it needs to implement. A company's vision and goals of where it wants to be can provide a much stronger degree of justification for change than can the fact that one methodology appears easier to implement. (The comparative review of implementation steps should, however, be viewed as a secondary consideration, since the implementation steps are similar whether for cost reduction or business process innovation. Looking at the process for implementation should not be used as a substitute for strategic planning.)

Techniques

Knowing the steps involved in implementing a particular methodology is enormously helpful, but identification of the skills or techniques required for the successful implementation of a particular methodology is also valuable. When management understands these techniques, it will be able to take better stock of the existing company resources and strengths, choose those techniques that might be of immediate use, and identify those in which the company should further develop and train its personnel. Figure 7–3 categorizes which techniques generally apply the expected levels of change, from internal data driving cost reduction, to external information driving improvement and to utopia states visioning techniques, which relate to radical expectations.

Performance Measurement

Measurement is important to all aspects of business performance improvement. Without it, a company cannot know where improvement efforts are needed or where they are paying off. In developing a strategy for improvement, the choice of methodology to select and the cost/benefit analysis that underlies each decision in improving performance ultimately draw support from measurement studies. Although the development of an effective measurement program associated with a particular strategic move is certainly difficult, it is essential in assessing the degree to which performance improvement efforts are successful. There are a number of ways to model these performance measurement efforts; however, some basic strategic considerations should be included when developing an effective measurement system that can be applied to all three types of methodologies.

FIGURE 7–3
Key Techniques for Process Improvement

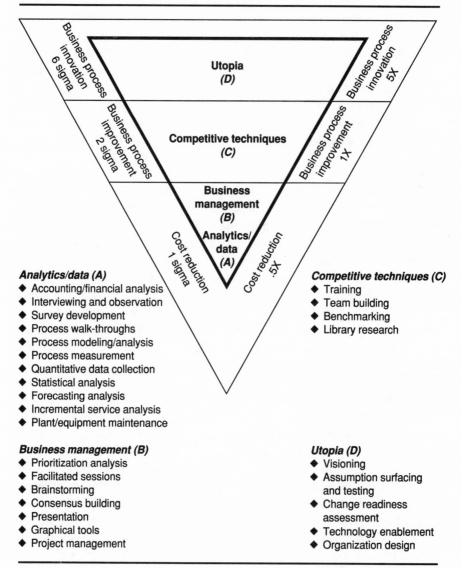

Identify Appropriate Performance Metrics.   Although a company can articulate overall improvement objectives quite easily in terms of the basic issues of cost, quality, time, and environment, specific metrics need to be developed for each process. The metrics must be easily measurable and should correlate to the overall objectives for improvement; by monitoring them over time, managers can keep apprised of progress against objectives.

In addition to identifying metrics to monitor overall process performance, measurement of performance in key activities within processes is also essential. Only in this way is there a basis for analyzing and streamlining the components of the process and their associated flows.

Obtain Baseline Measurements for the Purpose of Setting Improvement Objectives. Baseline measurements of the processes under analysis should be accomplished as quickly as possible, as they are the basis for setting improvement objectives and can serve as an opportunity to pilot the systems and methods needed to obtain each measurement.

Develop Efficient and Reliable Means for Administering the Measures at the End of the Project and on an Ongoing Basis. Based on their experience of having gathered the measurements for the baseline, the team will develop an ongoing process for collecting them, which can be as simple as calling for an existing report on a routine basis or as complex as acquiring new process monitoring sensors and developing an integrated information system for processing and reporting on the measurement data. As a result of this and the previous activity, the performance improvement team may conclude that a given metric is not conducive to ongoing, reliable, and cost-effective measurement for monitoring a particular activity. In such case a more practical metric should be chosen and tested.

Implement Effective Feedback Mechanisms. The final task in measurement is to ensure that once the measurement data is available, it is put to good use—in essence, the assurance that the measurements for an activity are reported to the process improvement team members associated with the activity in a timely fashion. There also needs to be a process in place within the team for factoring the measurement results into subsequent improvement plans.

Methodology Steps

We have already mentioned that the choice of methodology reflects the firm's priorities; for example, utilizing the cost reduction methodology implies that cost containment is a more important priority; using a business process innovation approach may suit a company interested in achieving a higher degree of globalization.

In the process analysis approach, understanding the mechanics of, or the process behind, a particular methodology can prove enormously valuable in increasing the success rate for establishing a methodology. When the performance improvement team understands the methodology from an implementation viewpoint, it can judge the capacity of the firm to implement the methodology, plan the implementation in a more systematic manner, and help the company utilize the information gained from past experiences.

Identifying the steps in the implementation process can give a great deal of meaning and direction to the efforts of the company, whether dealing with cost reduction, business process improvement, or business process innovation programs. The three methodologies may differ somewhat, but conceptually each follows the same phase development:

- Planning and managing.
- Process assessment and targeting.
- Performance measurement of target processes.
- Developing a plan.
- Designing changes and developing a prototype of change.
- Performance measurement of the prototype.
- Implementing the pilot program.
- Performance measurement of change.
- Final considerations.

The following sections describe this phase development for each methodology.

Cost Reduction (CR)

Planning and Managing
The most basic project management outlines a specific time frame for change, which is broken up into discrete parts, steps, or tasks involving not only the management of the project, but also the management of the organization, its people, and their expectations. This first stage is a continuing concern throughout the entire improvement process. Indeed, the project manager must be able to measure the progress that has been achieved in implementing (or developing a blueprint for) change and then

analyze the underlying causes of the change, or obstacles to change, and learn how to fine-tune the improvement process to achieve the desired result.

Process Assessment and Targeting

Process Analysis. At this stage, the performance improvement team should begin to analyze each process, identifying the objectives behind each one, with the goal of discovering which one requires improvement from a cost reduction or effectiveness point of view. Process managers can also analyze the different processes after they learn about each process structure and each subprocess's objectives. They begin by developing high-level models of major processes within the project scope. In these models, process flowcharts that graphically represent the sequence and relationships among activities in the target processes should be developed. Each flowchart should include the following:

- Inputs—the materials and information flowing into the process.
- Outputs—the materials and information flowing out of the process.
- Activity times—the time required to perform each activity in the process.
- Cycle times—the overall time required to complete the process once.
- Value-added/non-value-added classifications—an activity in the process is a value-added activity if it makes a direct, incremental contribution to the conversion of inputs to key outputs. If the contribution is indirect or nonexistent, the activity is non-value-added.
- Root causes—the events or reasons that underlie the need to conduct each activity in the process. If a root cause for a given activity cannot be readily identified, a good test is to determine what, if anything, would go wrong if the activity were removed from the process.

In addition to developing a flowchart, managers should identify the current service levels (which will be used in the phases involving performance measurement steps and benchmarking).

Process Analysis—Setting Priorities. Next, the performance improvement team should develop evaluation criteria for determining which steps should be taken first, identifying processes that need some type of cost reduction improvement and ranking which measures should receive top priority given various constraints (e.g., time, cost, etc.). In addition to identifying changes that promise the highest degree of cost reduction in relation to the initial implementation expense, other factors should be considered; organizational scope, implementation time, resources required, and the general likelihood of success are also important evaluation criteria. A related criterion is the nature of process ownership associated with each opportunity. Given such evaluation criteria, process managers and other players will be able to prioritize the high-level cost reduction opportunities and update the project plan to reflect the new measures.

Performance Measurement of Targeted Processes
The team should then conduct an incremental impact analysis of the selected processes to identify elements of work that may be eliminated to achieve the potential cost reductions identified earlier. As seems appropriate, the team should iterate back to previous steps to further refine the process targeting and cost reduction objective setting.

The entire discussion of performance measurement is central to assessing the impact of a particular change to a process. Once the specific process has been identified, it must be quantified in a meaningful way so that the current state of operation can be documented and measured against future performance. The performance improvement team can start by using the quantitative performance measures currently used by the organization to monitor the performance of the processes under analysis. Cost, for example, is a common metric used to gauge a company's performance. However, even though such measurements of performance often exist, frequently there are no meaningful measurements for many of the individual activities that make up the process.

In situations where there are holes in the current measurement approach, new appropriate measures need to be developed. These metrics should measure the efficiency of all activities within a process from a cost perspective. In addition to developing new forms of measurement, it is important to develop ones that can be administered by existing personnel or can be supported by the company in other ways. There is little use for developing elaborate measurement techniques if financial or human resources are inadequate to carry out such investigation.

Developing a Plan
The development of a performance measurement plan that utilizes the CR methodology must incorporate all the data acquired in the previous steps (e.g., assessing processes with company's objectives, analyzing

each process in detail to identify target areas, and developing baseline measurement of current processes). The development of a plan refines the initial prioritization of improvement opportunities discussed earlier.

Planners must also keep the details of design and implementation considerations in mind. The objective of developing a plan is to properly assess cost reduction opportunities by balancing factors such as implementation cost, payoff potential, risk, opportunity prerequisites/interrelationships, and time requirements. In developing a portfolio of short-, medium-, and long-term opportunities, the performance improvement team should not overextend or overburden the available implementation resources. It is usually a superior strategy to complete a few high-impact cost reductions before initiating a broader set of opportunities that overtax resources.

Designing Changes and Developing a Prototype of Change
Designers need to develop an analysis of the targeted process which will occur through the removal or reduction of as many non-value-added activities as possible. Planners should then develop a prototype representing the modified process, offering a way to simulate and test the operation of the cost reduction measure. A prototype can be considered the analog to a scientific experiment in a laboratory: a small-scale, quasi-operational version of the modified process that can be used to test various aspects of the design. It should not be confused with a pilot, wherein a process is implemented on a small scale and is in actual use.

Performance Measurement of the Prototype
After developing a prototype, the team should compare the anticipated results of the prototype with the current performance measurements obtained in the third step, measuring the targeted process. In this before-and-after analysis, the performance improvement team should consider the following: What do the potential cost savings look like? What needs to be done to achieve the contemplated change? Are the necessary resources in place? Who needs to be involved? Answers to these questions may prompt a revision of the cost reduction program.

After completing the analysis for the individual processes, the team will develop a consolidated analysis of the likely project benefits and corresponding implementation costs for the near, medium, and long terms. Once the team gains management approval, it can proceed with implementation.

Implementing the Pilot Program

The pilot program begins with the development of a plan for implementing the changes needed for each process, both organizational and technical, that is detailed enough to permit meaningful use of project management tools and embodies a heavy emphasis on the up-front training of employees affected by each intended process change. All parties involved must endorse the overall approach and reasoning behind the intended process changes; it is also necessary to review specific role changes. Finally, the performance improvement team needs to introduce the process improvement techniques so as to empower and equip employees with the necessary skills and training to implement the changes and even modify these changes as warranted.

In the implementation of the cost reduction measure, it is usually more appropriate to plan the intended process changes along a sequential pattern, rather than simultaneously. In this manner, the project can be managed as a series of successive cost reduction milestones that empower individuals, rather than one large, seemingly overwhelming task.

Performance Measurement of Change

Once the cost reduction measure has been implemented in the form of a pilot program, performance measurement is crucial to document the change, refine the anticipated expectations of its impact as outlined in the sixth step, performance measurement of the protype, and measure the actual results of the program. If the results of the pilot do not meet the team's expectations, then planners must reanalyze the new process to identify the areas where the anticipated impact was not achieved. Developing a measurement analysis of the pilot is crucial because comparing these results to past conditions gives the performance improvement team a gauge against which to measure the effect of the new changes. Planners should also correlate the pilot results with the prototype simulation.

In some cases, a modification of the process and the strategy might be in order to address the problems experienced in implementing the pilot. It is important to manage the expectations of senior management and keep them apprised of the latest results and analysis.

Business Process Improvement (BPI)

Planning and Managing

The planning and managing phase in BPI is similar to that in cost reduction, with the addition of a senior manager who takes specific responsibility for the particular process targeted for improvement. Whereas the CR approach tends to be limited to a particular department or function, thus not requiring the approval powers of a senior manager, BPI usually affects several departments or functions. The purpose of a designated senior process manager is not to remove others from responsibility for improvement design or implementation, but to champion with the resources and support necessary to authorize the efforts that may cross departments and functions. The BPI leader should be a senior manager who has control over a targeted process, demonstrates commitment to the BPI approach, and is available to lead the improvement effort.

To be successful on any scale, however, BPI efforts require broad cultural empowerment and participation, which are crucial to implementing the initial measures, and a guarantee of the company's commitment to continuous improvement in both word and deed. With the needed aid of senior management, the improvement team must show the company's commitment to continuous change. To this end, the improvement team must be sure to communicate the project objectives and the plan, and provide process improvement training for all employees involved with the process.

In addition, the process improvement team must have the requisite skills to address the targeted improvement opportunities or receive the appropriate skills training. It is likely that the team will be in place for at least a year to drive the initial implementation and support subsequent continuous improvement and measurement.

Process Assessment and Targeting
The basic steps outlined in the cost reduction methodology—analyzing the process (process flowcharts) and setting priorities (evaluation criteria)—also apply to BPI. In contrast to CR, which generally uses cost as the key measurement tool, the issues of quality, time, and responsiveness come into focus when the BPI methodology is utilized. Thus, a BPI analysis of potential areas for improvement must consider these additional concerns. Finally, the evaluation criteria for BPI are expanded to include items related to implementation cost, benefit, timing, and organizational and business risk.

Planners can begin to understand the business plan and formulate measures to improve different processes by continually looking at: (1) current and potential customer needs; and (2) the critical success factors of the enterprise, its customers, and suppliers. These two issues can help serve as a framework for assessing each process and determining both the specific processes that should be targeted and the type of improvement that might be in order.

As planners identify improvement opportunities, they should keep in mind that some may be justified from an activity optimization perspective, which may or may not bear directly on the organization's overall improvement goals. Others may be directly in line with the organizational improvement goals. All opportunities must be evaluated according to the level of impact on performance improvement and the advancement of company goals.

Once the team identifies specific processes for improvement, it should make sure that the staff is qualified to examine each process in detail. It is also necessary to provide those managers and employees directly involved in the process with the required skills and training, for they need to assume a role in the overall process improvement effort.

Performance Measurement of Targeted Processes
The same types of considerations used in the CR methodology are also appropriate for the BPI approach. These include measuring the current state of the particular process or processes, developing new measurements for significant activities that are not currently being measured, and establishing a baseline reading of present performance.

Developing a Plan
Building on the considerations appropriate for the CR methodology in completing the analysis for the individual processes, planners should develop a consolidated analysis of the likely improvement benefits and corresponding implementation costs and risks for the near-, medium-, and long-term elements of the portfolio. These cost/benefit reports should be presented to senior management for the appropriate approval and the authorization to proceed with the program.

Designing Changes and Developing a Prototype of Change
Designing changes for the BPI methodology is similar to the CR approach of streamlining the process and developing a prototype of the improvement measures.

Performance Measurement of the Prototype
A similar comparison of before-and-after situations needs to be developed from an individual process perspective and a consolidated picture. It is also essential to view these situations in the near-, medium-, and

long-term time frames, especially since BPI consists of continuous improvements. In addition to considering cost reductions, planners should also investigate the benefits of increasing responsiveness to customers, enhancing quality, and reducing cycle time.

Implementing the Pilot Program
The implementation of the BPI effort follows the same general procedures as outlined in the CR methodology, with the exception of the sequential project planning. The BPI program might be more effectively managed along a simultaneous planning frame (e.g., concurrent engineering) because the parallel use of resources permits substantial results to be achieved rapidly across the board. The plan for the sequencing of key milestones should therefore involve all available members of the process improvement team.

Performance Measurement of Change
The BPI effort requires the same type of performance measurement as is outlined in the CR methodology—comparing the results of the pilot with the measurements derived from current company performance and evaluating them against the anticipated impact envisioned with the prototype. Similar adjustments in process design, planning of implementation, and adjustment of expectations, may have to be made.

Business Process Innovation (BPIN)

Planning and Managing

A Business Plan.   Within the context of transforming the company, the task of planning and managing change requires a deeper understanding of where the company views its future and the level of commitment to these goals. Such a task is complicated by the fact that change is not always directed at a particular target, nor is transformation limited to the implementation of specific directed steps. Instead, what is required is an open, critical mind, able to assess the validity of every process and its contribution to overall company performance. In this context, innovation can range from a creative approach to improving a process, the omission of a particular process, or the reorganization of the flow of processes—and it requires the capacity to look at the purpose behind a particular process and envision a more effective way of accomplishing the results desired, which need be not confined to the current methods available, utilizing cutting-edge technology to develop that process.

Such innovation, however, can easily become misguided, or even inappropriate, because some individuals may forget the purpose behind the innovation and pursue innovation for innovation's sake. Innovation must start with a clear articulation of the company's mission and objectives, which should be generated from the strategic analysis of the company. Process innovation efforts must always be aligned with the business vision, which provides the overall strategic context for the innovation effort, functioning as a blueprint of sorts. The business or strategic vision represents the long-term, ideal state for the products, markets, organization, and culture of the enterprise. Senior management must take the initiative and responsibility to guide and develop this business vision and be aware of every innovative effort in terms of the business plan. Innovation efforts that lack executive championing are unlikely to receive the necessary funding and resource support and, therefore, are unlikely to achieve success.

Process Vision—Qualitative Objectives.   Once the company has developed a documented business plan and all the players understand that plan, it can begin to target processes. More than just rudimentary steps to analyze the process and identify its weaknesses and strengths, innovating a process requires an ability to see how the process fits in the whole plan and the capacity to envision the complete process independent of current practice or company policy. As planners develop the process vision, they should clarify the customer objectives of the targeted process, which can be considered the quantitative goals of innovation.

The performance objectives will identify the levels of improvement that the company seeks from the innovation and will differ substantially from company to company. Examples of quantitative goal setting include: "we will develop the ability to ship the product within one day of customer signoff"; or "we will reduce the unacceptable product variance rate to six standard deviations out on the normal distribution [6 sigma]". These objectives provide quantitative standards against which the success of the innovation effort can be measured.

Process Vision—Attributes.   Process attributes, the second component of the process vision, describe how the organization wants to structure its activities and organization over time and how various processes will then be implemented. Where multiple innovation efforts are underway, process attributes can serve as a guide to ensure that the innovations are consistent from a strategic perspective. One such attribute could be: All information about the status of an order in the process will be available to all users (including sales reps, manufacturing schedulers, customers, and so on) via computer inquiry. Given such an attribute, the team should develop all aspects of the process around that attribute—its structure, flows, inputs, and outputs, as well as its human and information technology requirements. The attributes begin to define the innovation scope and will guide the subsequent analysis and design activities.

Process Vision—Assessing Readiness for Change. Before dramatic change can be effective, the organization as a whole, and especially the people charged with implementing and designing the change, must understand and accept the need for such a change. Interviewing and conducting surveys are among the many valuable tools that can be used to assess the organization's general readiness to undergo change. Assessing the company's capacity or readiness for change should be an ongoing process because innovation is an ever-developing process. As the understanding that the company gains from these processes evolves, so too will the prescriptions for performance improvement.

An important element in the assessment of a company's capacity for change is the identification and subsequent strengthening of the company members' commitment to the innovation of the targeted process. The process of building commitment, which results from and accompanies the process of assessing a company's readiness for change, must begin with senior management. Company members will receive their cue from senior managers who both profess and exhibit active support of innovative efforts. Senior managers responsible for a particular process should also sponsor the innovation of that particular process, lending their resources and formal authority to the implementation of a specific innovation effort.

Process Assessment and Targeting

As seen in the CR and BPI approaches, targeting the process for improvement requires an understanding of the performance objectives of the different processes. When establishing guidelines for defining a particular process or function, planners should be aware that there may be considerable overlap from one process to another. This knowledge is critical to the success of the innovation effort, for it is not possible to make an informed selection for process innovation if this understanding of the organization's processes is lacking.

Processes should be identified at several levels of significance, starting with general processes or types of processes. (Typically, companies employ about 10 to 20 major processes.) The planning team should focus on capturing all *significant* candidate activities, rather than every single activity. The performance improvement team should also bear in mind that when it identifies all the major processes, the number should be manageable from a project perspective and the processes should be comprehensive enough to allow innovation.

Unlike CR and BPI, which depend on the team to select the processes targeted for improvement, the executive committee must select processes from the planning team's candidate list for innovation improvement. Furthermore, in the BPIN approach, an added dimension of innovation must be considered. The team should be careful to ensure that the scope of the innovation effort remains within the limits of the organization's capabilities and resources as stated in the company's overall mission and objectives. Even if all processes need to be redesigned, an organization cannot endure the magnitude of change that would be introduced if all processes were innovated simultaneously. An organization must recognize the level of change and upheaval it can successfully endure. In most situations, it is a good idea to stagger innovation processes so that key resources can gain experience and focus energy on delivering initial milestones successfully.

Finally, performance measurement teams should remember that innovation in one process will inevitably lead to the need to innovate, or at least modify, another process. (i.e., the order fulfillment process will connect to the manufacturing planning scheduling process). Thus, the selection of a process targeted for innovation tends to include consideration of several other closely related processes. In choosing processes for innovation, we recommend considering these criteria, listed in decreasing order of importance:

- Centrality of the process to the business vision.
- Receptivity of the people involved with the process to the major changes likely to be identified in the innovation effort.
- Manageability of the project scope.
- Level of urgency of the process.

Performance Measurement of Targeted Processes

As discussed before, an understanding of all the significant processes and their relationships with each other is essential before innovation of these processes can take place. This understanding lays the foundation for appropriate performance measurement of the current processes in three ways:

- It allows the people involved in the innovation effort to develop a common understanding of the current state.

- It provides the team with an understanding of the baseline from which it will proceed when implementing the innovation.

- It provides a basis for measuring the performance of the current process, which must be done to establish a baseline against which to gauge performance improvement.

Developing a Plan

As discussed, process innovation is much more comprehensive than straightforward streamlining and improvement. However, the information gained regarding the targeted process can also be used to develop a short-term improvement program that can be implemented while the innovation work within the future process vision continues.

In BPIN, the concept of change levers—looking at information technology and organizational structure (human resources) as the principle ways to enable or enhance a company's ability to transform itself—plays an important role in maximizing the company's capacity to develop and implement an innovation program. In the other two methodologies, CR and BPI, we regarded the company's capacity for change and improvement as being largely a function of current resources. (We consistently maintained that planners should be careful not to overburden the company's current resources or develop a plan that had little chance of being implemented.) Thus, in developing a plan, the performance improvement team should consider not only all the potential innovations that may be implemented, but also how the innovative use of information technology and human resources can actually enable the firm to realize more innovations.

The powerful role of information technology in allowing an organization to realize its strategic goals must be considered even before developing a new process design because traditionally, and as can be seen in the implementation of BPI, information technology is a basic tool for automating a process that has already been designed. In BPIN, however, information technology actually affects the process design and is recognized as one of the critical factors influencing the eventual nature and inspiration of the innovation.

In addition to considering the potential of leading-edge technology to enable a substantially improved business process, other considerations are state-of-the-art thinking and trends in organizational design and empowerment, with the goal of radically changing the way work is organized in the process being analyzed.

Although the consideration of these change levers occurs prior to the process design step, in reality the role of change levers is considered much earlier, when the performance improvement team starts developing a blueprint for action and a process vision (see the second step of BPIN, process vision).

Designing Changes and Developing a Prototype of Change

The approach of BPIN dramatically differs from that of CR and BPI in that of the process and related processes are transformed rather than merely modified. Thus BPIN design changes tend to be far more profound and follow a different design. In this phase, the performance improvement team starts to use all the data gathered (see previous steps) as a foundation for designing the process, but it views and analyzes such information from a more visionary perspective, where creativity becomes an essential tool in transforming the current process.

The use of brainstorming (see later section in Key Techniques) is valuable in allowing each individual and the group collectively to view the process from a fresh perspective and to develop equally unique solutions that outline possibilities for a creative, yet pragmatic, new structure for the process. The emphasis here is on the utilization of information technology and organizational design to increase the scope of what is pragmatic beyond current organizational resource.

Once the new process design is accomplished through creativity and change levers, a process prototype should be developed as was done in the CR and BPI methodologies. The prototype is crucial to simulating and testing the operation of the modified targeted process to reveal the probable results of the transformed process. It helps planners and senior management obtain a first glimpse of the new process and to establish baseline expectations. Naturally, from the point of view of innovation, prototyping should be seen as an iterative process intended to test and refine the fit among the new process structure, information technology, and the organization. Thus, the prototype needs to be tested in real-time in the form of a pilot (see the section on implementing the prototype). Since it is difficult to predict with complete accuracy the impact of information technology and organizational changes on the redesigned process, prototyping assists the team in coming to a better understanding of the magnitude of changes required.

Possible consequences of prototyping may include a reevaluation of earlier deliverables such as the performance objectives or detailed process design, and it may take several iterations to become satisfied with the quality and feasibility of the innovated process. Most examples of successful process innovation have taken from two to five years and were quite iterative; experience and knowledge gained at each step of the process applied to improve and refine the work already done.

Performance Measurement of the Protoype

Planners develop a before-and-after comparison, assess the impact of the new innovation, and measure its ability to realize the firm's long-term strategic objectives. In addition to cost, time, customer responsiveness, and quality considerations, the comparative picture should also factor in the business drivers of continued market competitiveness and globalization.

Implementing the Pilot Program

Because the implementation of the pilot program is considerably more complex in the BPIN model than in the CR and BPI models, the performance improvement team will find it useful to divide implementation into three phases:

- Detailed process, organization, and information systems design.
- Construction.
- Full-scale training and deployment.

Of course, implementation begins with the development of a thorough action plan for the detailed process and systems design. Design changes, however, will occur on both organizational and technical levels, and the work should be managed carefully, with a number of interim milestones. Management should be kept abreast of status, since each phase culminates in a work plan and budget for the next phase.

As in the CR methodology, planning the process implementation along a sequential timeline rather than in parallel can be more effective, particularly when more than one process is involved. (However, some substeps may occur in parallel). The sequence method allows the project to be managed as a series of successive quantum performance victories rather than as a large, single task without conclusive interim milestones. Once again, the same type of psychological empowerment can occur with the passing of each quantum victory.

Performance Measurement of Change
Performance measurement of the pilot innovation should be based on the same considerations as when measuring CR and BPI efforts.

Final Considerations

An important characteristic of the BPI and BPIN methodologies is that improvement is never considered complete. In the BPI approach, there is a cultural reorientation, based on value, toward regarding improvements not as singular events but as part of a continuum of evaluation and improvement, with the process improvement team evolving into an ongoing organization whose mission is to stay on top of improvement opportunities, oversee their implementation, and track the benefits actually obtained.

An organization must be committed to maintaining its competitive edge, not resting on past laurels, because innovation gives a company a competitive edge that may be far-reaching but not lasting; today's innovation will probably be tomorrow's standard. Keeping ahead of the industry requires a future-oriented perspective, always being at least one step ahead of other industry competitors. The role of the performance improvement team as the initiators, designers, and implementers of change is crucial to maintaining a company's commitment to continual improvement. The team should evolve into a permanent division of the company, with its responsibilities articulated along the following activities:

- Conduct ongoing process improvement training and empowerment in order to reach new and experienced employees as other targeted processes are added to the process improvement or innovation initiative.
- Reinforce, refresh, and update the training of the process improvement or innovation veterans so that the commitment to the process is kept alive.

- Assign process improvement team members to innovation initiatives in other areas (processes) of the enterprise.
- Ensure that the measurement systems in place provide accurate and sufficient reporting of performance for senior management's use. Measurement systems must be detailed enough to facilitate continuous improvement at the task level, as well at the strategic analysis level.
- Work regularly with senior management to ensure that process improvement and innovation initiatives remain a priority of the firm and that these initiatives properly reflect corporate priorities.

KEY TECHNIQUES FOR METHODOLOGY IMPLEMENTATION

The successful implementation of any particular methodology requires certain skills and attributes, called *techniques*. Understanding what they are and how they allow the organization to realize its performance improvement goals is important in assessing the company's capacity for improvement. Furthermore, the techniques that the company already successfully practices can be used to develop those that are either weak or nonexistent.

Because cost reduction, business process improvement, and business process innovation are a progression from the most simple to the most complex methodology, they have certain techniques in common. Techniques that are essential for CR are also useful for BPI and BPIN, and those needed in BPI are also needed in BPIN. As a company gains experience and knowledge in implementing performance improvement changes and in moving up from one methodology to another (CR to BPI to BPIN), it gains valuable new techniques and solidifies old ones.

Cost Reduction

As a technique, cost reduction is used to effect a one-time, short-term, relatively low impact change, such as automation of a labor-intensive process, which focuses on only one aspect of the business.

Acquiring Data and Quantitative Analysis Techniques
Most of the techniques used in the CR approach involve acquiring data for analysis and quantitative methods for computing current operations

(although not every one could be categorized as such), and, as a whole, form the foundation for decision making and setting priorities.

Accounting and Financial Analysis.   Accounting and financial analysis skills are important techniques in costing activities and in assessing the value of any investment. They are used to identify and properly allocate the direct and indirect costs attributable to a particular activity in a process. Basic accounting also enables the individual to understand financial reports, which are an important standard tool used in making more advanced cost accounting analysis.

Solid financial analysis skills are also important in weighing the benefits and likely payoffs of a cost reduction project against the investments that must be made and the risks that must be assumed. Central to these skills are discounted cash flow analysis, return on investment analysis, and probability-based decision analysis, wherein the costs and benefits of possible outcomes can be used in the context of the chances that the outcomes will occur.

Interviewing and Observation.   Developing the interview/observation model, which represents the primary source for gaining input and perspective on a cost reduction project, can be structured along the following considerations:

- *Determine the interview objectives*, such as the scope of coverage and types of information to be gathered. The scope generally involves identifying and focusing on the specific process or activities for which information is being sought.
- *Select an interview approach*, ranging from one-on-one, to small groups, to focus groups, and to foregoing interviews in favor of implementing a written survey.
- *Identify the people to be interviewed*, the focus being on those who are both able and willing to provide the information needed.
- *Sell and schedule the interviews*, because the interviewee must see one or more benefits to participating in order to generate a higher level of interest and participation on his or her part. Incentives can be structured along some form of quid pro quo sharing of data, or perhaps some anticipated benefits of the streamlined process.
- *Establish rapport*, to match interviewing style to the personal style of the interviewee.

- *Obtain complete and accurate responses*, by having a checklist of needed information as a tool in guiding the interview and by making sure that all the important data is obtained. It is much easier to obtain clarification real-time than it is after the fact.
- *Observe first-hand the process or activities discussed in the interview*, allowing the interviewer to test and reconfirm his or her understanding of the process.
- *Follow up with additional questions* when inconsistencies or a need for clarification are discovered.

Survey Development.   Surveys are most appropriate for gathering information when the number of sources from which to obtain data is substantial, when there is a need for ease of structuring information, or when there are anonymity requirements. At the process assessment and targeting stage of cost reduction projects, surveys may be of benefit in identifying which processes key managers and others are interested in and which processes have the greatest cost reduction potential. Surveys also represent a method for measuring the key aspects of performance for one or more processes or activities. There are several variables in survey design:

- Choice of survey participants.
- Anonymous versus attributed responses.
- Design and administration: in-house versus third party.
- Data gathering method: written versus telephone versus in-person.
- Types of questions: multiple-choice versus numeric versus open-ended narrative.
- Rewards or premiums for survey participants.

Whatever choices are made for these variables, in order to obtain a high response rate, the survey should be extremely well-organized, focused, and concise, and it should be presented in a structured way that poses the least amount of difficulty for the participants—the type of response being solicited should be clearly indicated so that the individual does not have to decide how to answer.

Process Modeling and Analysis.   Process modeling and analysis entails the following activities:

- Decompose a process into its constituent activities.

- Portray the activities and their interrelationships in graphical (flowchart) or tabular form.
- Examine inputs, flows, capacities, costs, times, and outputs as the activities are mapped.
- Determine the characteristics and constraints of the overall process based on the activity parameters.
- Use the model to explore the likely effects of change scenarios wherein changes are made either to the activities of the process, their characteristics, their interrelationships, or the process inputs.
- Apply simulation tools to various live process scenarios. In addition to reporting on simulated inputs, flows, and outputs, the team can utilize automated simulation tools capable of real-time graphic animation.

Depending on the situation, different dimensions of cost reduction or process improvement analysis can be emphasized:

- Value-added and non-value-added analysis.
- Costing/efficiency analysis.
- Throughput analysis.
- Cycle time analysis.

In a typical cost reduction project, at least two of these approaches are applied in combination.

Process Walk-Throughs.   A process walk-through is a series of interviews with relevant employees aimed at refining and adding the necessary detail to the project team's early understanding of the activities as they relate to the process flow, and at gaining any additional information necessary to properly document the process. The team can also enhance its understanding of the process by reviewing the following:

- Background and skills of the employees involved.
- Additional activities being conducted by employees.
- Identification of the process suppliers and customers and their key issues.
- Current problems and improvement ideas.
- Possible consequences of discontinuing an activity.

It will be easiest to structure a walk-through once modeling of the process has been developed, since identifying the potential for cost reduction or improvement will help justify the time and effort involved.

Process Measurement. Process measurement spans four areas:

- Identifying appropriate performance metrics for an activity within the context of the overall process objectives.
- Obtaining baseline measurements for the purpose of setting improvement objectives.
- Developing efficient and reliable means for administering the measures at the end of the project and on an ongoing basis.
- Implementing effective feedback mechanisms.

Quantitative Data Collection. Process modeling requires an understanding of the structure of a process. Such an understanding is typically gained by interviewing and observing and by assessing the quantitative aspects of the process, such as volumes, costs and times—in short, quantitative data collection. This type of data is usually obtained from accounting and measurement systems, which are often automated. Key dimensions of the quantitative data collection challenge include

- Ability to tap existing accounting and measurement systems for process data.
- Ability to specify, generate, and read ad hoc reports from computerized data bases.
- Surrogate analysis: the ability to gain insight into a hard-to-measure variable by identifying and measuring another, related variable that can be assessed either automatically or manually.
- Ability to design and conduct new measurements when neither the needed data nor an acceptable surrogate is currently available.

The activity of quantitative data collection is obviously related closely to the measurement discipline, since measurements are usually elements of quantitative data.

Statistical Analysis. Statistical analysis techniques are an important companion to quantitative data collection. In cost reduction work, it is important to understand the statistical significance of quantitative data gathered about a process before reliable conclusions regarding process performance can be drawn from the data. The statistical significance of a survey analysis is driven by issues of independence, sample size, and system complexity.

Correlation analysis, a branch of statistics, is also useful in process analysis work, where precise information about the correlation of various inputs with each other and with outputs can be of benefit. In addition, if a certain variable is to be used as a surrogate for another, more difficult-to-measure variable, correlation analysis is often the key to ascertaining and benefiting from the existence of the substitution or alternative measurement.

Lastly, statistics are the key to gauging and managing variability in activity performance measurements, which are often as (or more) important a performance metric as the absolute magnitude of the measurement. Referred to as statistical process control, the concept can enable improved optimization of maintenance costs, as well as of the direct and indirect costs of poor quality.

Forecasting Analysis.   Cost reduction and other types of process improvement are performed on processes with the expectation that the process will work better in some way after implementation—implying that the factors surrounding the process, such as demand, materials costs, and equipment efficiency can be forecast. The most common form of forecasting is time-series analysis, wherein future prices, volumes, and capabilities are predicted based upon a statistical examination of their historical behavior. The challenge is to recognize when one or more factors change so as to invalidate the assumptions of the past. Examples of such discontinuities might be

- The introduction of a substitute material with different price, performance, and volume characteristics.
- The addition of a major new customer or project with a quantum effect on demand levels.
- A shift in strategic corporate priorities.
- The impending introduction of a revolutionary new business process.

In these circumstances, the analyst must examine the changed context, determine its impact on the forecasting approach, and compensate accordingly.

Incremental Service Analysis.   Incremental service analysis is a technique for systematically examining the likely performance impact of process design changes. It breaks the contemplated change up into a series of small and manageable pieces, usually at the process activity level, and then tests the effects by successively (incrementally) evaluating the impact of each piece on the process. Depending on the objectives, the analyst may either accumulate the incremental results or analyze each change component on a stand-alone basis.

Plant/Equipment Maintenance.   The appropriate maintenance of plant and equipment has an obvious correlation to issues of cost and quality. Developing a maintenance strategy requires that two trade-offs be addressed:

- Maintenance investment versus level of service.
- Preventive maintenance versus failure correction.

On the surface, each trade-off appears to be one between incurring a cost or suffering a consequence that itself can be translated to cost. For example, the cost of a low level of equipment service may be poor quality, which relates directly to inspection, testing, scrap, and rework costs, not to mention the possible cost of customer dissatisfaction. Similarly, waiting for a piece of equipment to fail before servicing it results in downtime and process disruption costs, again with the possibility of customer dissatisfaction. Managing the trade-offs takes place on two fronts: understanding (and perhaps improving) the resiliency and flexibility of the business process, and managing the expected ongoing cost by balancing maintenance investments against the statistical likelihood and frequency of the negative outcomes.

Statistical process control (SPC), pioneered by Edward Deming, has made it possible to find a point of balance with fewer downside trade-offs. Its underlying principle is that process failures can be forecasted by monitoring the variations in the specifications of the product flowing out of various steps in the process. Once a pattern has been established, a certain level of product variation can be used to signal the need for almost routine maintenance on a piece of equipment before it actually fails.

Prioritization Analysis.   Prioritizing possible improvement opportunities is key to cost reduction and other methodologies, enabling the most attractive opportunities to be implemented first and remain above the line of available resource investment. There are a number of approaches to prioritization:

- *Ranking*, one of the most straightforward forms of prioritization, in which the analyst identifies a measure, such as return on investment, against which the options can be ranked and hence prioritized.
- *Pareto analysis*, which ranks opportunities according to how many occurrences of a negative event they would obviate, or, conversely, how many occurrences of a positive event they would cause. The traditional 80–20 rule (i.e., a majority of problems stem from a minority of possible causes), is actually an example of pareto analysis; it implies that if 80 percent of complaints can be eliminated by focusing on 20 percent of the root causes, then these causes should be the top priority.
- *Weighting*, which is necessary when multiple ranking criteria must be brought together in a prioritization analysis. Each criterion is assigned a particular weight, and each improvement opportunity is evaluated against each criterion. A composite rating for the opportunity is developed by adding together the criteria values with their weightings applied. The opportunities are then ranked based on their composite ratings.

Although the quantitative methods are an important aid in prioritization analysis, the improvement team must recognize that it is hard to turn all relevant evaluation criteria into numbers. Because of this, prioritization analysis entails subjective discussion and consensus building as well as quantitative methods.

Useful Management Techniques
The following techniques are not as easy to categorize under one heading, but they tend to follow the lines of managing a project and communications.

Facilitated Sessions.   Throughout the course of a performance improvement project, work needs to be accomplished by groups of people in meetings, often internal to the improvement team and sometimes involving people outside the core team. The role of the facilitator is very important in this area because he or she can ensure that

- There is a clear objective for the session.
- A sufficient number of participants will be attending to accomplish the objective.
- Each participant has adequately prepared to address the objective.
- Each participant makes the necessary contribution.
- The contributions are presented to and understood by all in a timely fashion.
- The contributions are evaluated or reconciled so as to achieve the objective.

These job requirements will draw on all of the management skills of the facilitator, and the meetings themselves will demand his or her undivided attention and focus.

Brainstorming.   A special type of facilitated session, brainstorming is a creative group process wherein participation is encouraged from all group members, regardless of their roles and relationships in the organization. The brainstorming session must have a nonjudgmental atmosphere, where the facilitator places an emphasis on unconstrained inventiveness, the acceptability of every idea, and the fact that thoughts can be shared without risk.

A typical session format is to elicit a single suggestion from each participant, going around as many times as there are suggestions. Although others are allowed to seek clarification, they may not modify, support, or refute any contribution. After all suggestions are on the chalkboard, the facilitator, with help from the group, organizes the contributions into manageable groups for subsequent discussion and evaluation.

Consensus Building.   The art of building consensus toward a recommended action, whether in a small-group workshop setting or in the later stages of an improvement project, is important to cost reduction and other improvement methodologies. In a work group, the participants sort through the options and reach consensus in a structured fashion.

Done correctly, management consensus building is simply the aggregation of numerous small-group encounters—some formal and structured, some not. If the improvement team is systematic in its interactions with executives on the management team, then a consensus within the management team will be achieved before the formal decision-making meeting, over which the improvement team has little direct control.

Presentation.   Strong presentation skills for team members—the leaders in particular—afford great advantage in working to build consensus around team recommendations. These skills should be fostered in the team.

Graphical Tools.   Graphical tools play two roles in process improvement projects: they allow team presentations to be as compelling and visual as possible, and they allow the modeling and understanding of processes to be as visual and straightforward as possible. Standard presentation graphics tools fill the former role, and a process modeling and/or simulation tool with a strong graphical interface, possibly animated, fills the latter.

Project Management.   Project management techniques, which must be applied throughout the course of a project, comprise six areas:

- *Structure the project*, which involves working with executive management to confirm the intended scope, deliverables, resources, and timing for the project; it should be completed before continuing with the subsequent steps of the project.
- *Plan the project*, which will result in a successively refined understanding of the project work plan, deliverables, resources, and timing.
- *Control the project*, which is important to the early detection and correction of insufficient work and/or cost overruns, and must be managed carefully in relation to the work plan.
- *Assess change* as the project evolves because, first, a greater or lesser number of improvement opportunities than expected may be identified; second, an individual improvement effort may prove less tractable than anticipated; third, more effort than anticipated may be necessary to gain acceptance of the recommended changes in the organization; and fourth, senior management may revise the project scope.
- *Report project status* to keep management expectations in line with the evolving prospects for the cost reduction project.
- *Conclude the project* by assessing and reporting final results and releasing team members to take on new assignments.

Business Process Improvement

Business process improvement concentrates on gradual improvement that builds bridges from the current state of performance to the desired state. BPI is a continuous improvement philosophy that introduces cultural change and is driven by knowledge, the current state of technology and systems, experience, and, typically, best-in-class (competitive) benchmarking. There are usually a half dozen changes occurring simultaneously, with the focus being on a performance improvement of 50 percent to 100 percent.

Each of the techniques for cost reduction methodology discussed in the previous section apply to business process improvement as well. In addition, the following four technique areas are relevant for business process improvement.

Training.   Business process improvement has two characteristics that underscore the need for an aggressive training program:

- The initiative requires broad participation within all affected areas of the enterprise.
- Employees must be positioned to apply continuous improvement techniques to their activities and processes on an ongoing basis, since improvement must be a continuum.

At the outset, the enterprise may need to bring in an outside party to design and implement appropriate programs and administer the training, but the transition to an in-house training and indoctrination capability is a necessity as initial implementation nears completion.

Team Building.   Team building is an important tool for enhancing the effectiveness of a group of people in their work, with process analysis and subsequent improvement implementation requiring one or more groups of people to work together effectively. Often delivered in the form of a one- to five-day off-site meeting for each working group, team building works toward the following objectives:

- Highlight the individual perspective and needs of each team member.
- Invest each member of the team with shared objectives and priorities relating to the overall improvement effort and the specific process to be improved.

- Provide the team members with dry-run experience, where they practice working together to solve problems and meet challenges.

Benchmarking.   Benchmarking, covered in depth earlier in this chapter, is extremely useful in assessing process design and performance. Its principal activities are to

- Identify the processes and characteristics to be benchmarked, and develop a survey outline.
- Apply the outline to gather data on in-house processes, with in-house data representing the first sample point in the benchmarking data base.
- Identify possible secondary sources for benchmarking data, such as industry associations, research firms, and literature.
- Identify and select companies that would be good benchmarking partners, which should have process problems and challenges analogous to those in-house but should usually not be direct or indirect competitors.
- Solicit and enlist the candidate benchmarking partners, gaining agreement on the data to be shared, roles, and deliverables.
- Agree on a research approach, calling for a mix of visits, telephone calls, personal interviews, and group meetings, with a flexible time frame.
- Report on results internally and to the partner firms.
- Map the benchmarking results to possible ideas for new process improvement initiatives.

Library Research.   To support both explicit and implicit benchmarking efforts in the course of process improvement, effective library research is important, either through an in-house organization or an outside on-line data base service or research firm. The resources available include

- Newspapers and magazines.
- Trade and industry journals.
- Association journals and proceedings.
- Books.
- Annual report and 10-K data.
- Proprietary research reports and newsletters.

Two types of research requests can be made: one-time and standing. The one-time request provides the researcher with a set of questions to research and indicates probable information sources for the researcher to investigate before responding. The standing request provides the researcher with a list of ongoing areas of interest for which sources are to be checked for new data on an agreed-upon schedule. With both types, there is an art to making the request broad enough to yield useful and complete information without being so broad as to deluge the team in paper.

Business Process Innovation

Business process innovation takes companies on a steep climb to a completely different plateau of performance. Unlike cost reduction and business process improvement, it is vision driven, with its eye on the future state of the organization, and is propelled by factors such as technology trends. It is multifocused, largely driven by time/quality/cost (in that order). It is multidepartmental, multidivisional, value chain dependent, and it often extends beyond the traditional. Business process innovation results in radical change.

Each of the techniques discussed in the sections for the cost reduction and business process improvement methodologies apply to business process innovation as well. The additional five technique areas are relevant for business process innovation.

Visioning.   Visioning is a key technique that distinguishes BPIN from other improvement methodologies. It provides organizations with a unique opportunity to create a future vision that will ultimately lead to quantum change. Visioning is the process of stepping back from current reality to design the future, with the innovation team working with senior management to describe the way the business should work in five or more years, first at the general business level and then at the process level.

It usually starts with an exercise to place people's implicit visions of the future on the table, using such techniques as assumption surfacing and testing, technology enablement, interviewing, brainstorming, and consensus building. The visions are made explicit and reconciled into a unified, internally consistent statement. Once the visions are openly articulated, their underlying assumptions can be identified, challenged, and modified, constrained only by the creativity of the management group and its facilitators. The innovation team has some discretion as to where in the process to use group brainstorming versus individual interviewing in its quest to generate ideas and build consensus.

Assumption Surfacing and Testing.   Assumption surfacing and testing bears conceptual similarity to the process of determining whether activities are value-added or non-value-added. It involves examining an aspect of a current process and asking the question, "Does this really need to be done this way?" Often, the initial answer is "Yes," to which the next question should be, "Why?" With some additional probing and thinking, assumptions underlying the "yes" answer will surface. On further thought, some of the assumptions may be found to be inaccurate, and others may be rendered obsolete by market developments or advancements in the enabling organization and technology. An example:

> The accounts receivable organization of a company is working to decrease billing and collection costs radically. They have chosen staffing and float as key performance metrics. The question arises: "Do we really need to send paper invoices?" The first answer is, "Of course."
> "Why?"
> "Because that's how you tell the customer what he or she owes. It's how you do business, remember?"
> "The customer may be as upset to have to process all our invoices as we are to generate them. What if we see if they'd be interested in working with us on a system to automatically debit their account by the order amount upon delivery and inspection?"
> "Huh...maybe..."

Once underlying assumptions are shattered, a potentially valuable process idea can gain a foothold.

Change Readiness Assessment.   Since radical change is central to the success of business process innovation efforts, an organization undertaking this kind of project must be capable of working with, accepting, and implementing radical new ideas. Change readiness assessment provides the organization with the opportunity to measure its receptivity to radical change prior to attempting it. The key variables are

- How strong and committed is the process sponsor?
- How resistant to change are the managers and employees who are involved in the process?
- How consistent or inconsistent is the change with the current process and culture?

- How skilled is the innovation team in orchestrating smooth implementation?

Once the assessment results are available, the innovation team may choose to put programs in place to address any change readiness gaps that are uncovered and press on, or it may conclude that the contemplated innovation is simply not practical in light of the gaps found.

Technology Enablement.   Technology enablement analysis, applied to process innovation at the process design stage, and somewhat at the visioning stage, is used to search the realm of recent information technology advancements and anticipate future developments relevant to the process under analysis. For example, laptop and pen-based computing technologies are enabling rapid change in the way companies sell and fulfill orders for complex products and services.

Technology enablement analysis can be conducted by identifying the generic ways in which information technology could be applied to a process for business benefit and assessing which of these generic applications may be relevant to the process under consideration. This analysis should be complemented by a simultaneous assessment of the expected technology during the ongoing innovation effort. Often, an application idea that would not make sense in terms of current technology can crystallize into a high-impact, feasible process innovation one or two years in the future. Sometimes, a company can work in collaboration with a technology provider to develop a leading-edge capability.

Organization Design.   Successful innovation usually depends as much on human factors as it does on technology and process. Organization design is the key to addressing the human factors because innovation must be implemented by employees. Some human factors to consider include

- Where in the process must cooperation and integration between departments be improved?
- Are there areas where the process itself obviates the need for solid-line reporting and peer relationships?
- Are there changes necessary to ensure that the entire process benefits from a single, authoritative, committed sponsor?
- What changes are necessary in individual management styles and priorities?

Organization design issues are also directly involved in innovation projects, which have a tendency to recommend process designs that span multiple existing business function boundaries, thereby raising issues of cross-functional integration. For example, the order fulfillment process could be viewed as starting with the marketing department and flowing to the customer, the salesperson, the sales support person, finished goods inventory management, manufacturing, distribution, and accounts payable. The need for attention to organization design, often at the broadest levels, serves as further illustration of the need for strong senior management sponsorship of the innovation effort.

DIGITAL'S END POINT MODEL: THE NEED FOR BUSINESS INNOVATION

The performance improvement efforts of the Distributed Systems Manufacturing (DSM) Group within Digital Equipment Corporation (DEC) will be used as a case study to better illustrate how methodologies can be analyzed and judged for their effectiveness. This case is an excellent example of how change expectations were met and surpassed through the integration of people, process, and technology.

Process innovation severely tests the abilities of any organization because of the complexity of implementing simultaneous changes in many systems and structures. Management must be realistic about the breadth and depth of planned changes, even in the face of uncertain or unanticipated results. Organizational changes provide the greatest challenge. These changes encompass educating and motivating employees, modifying attitudes and behavior, altering group and functional interactions, and sustaining the vision and effort for the duration. In the case of DEC, dramatic changes took place not only within a business unit, but also outside the enterprise, in its relationships with customers and suppliers.

Background

By 1985, DEC had spent three years developing its new manufacturing architecture and was eager to try it out. The DSM Group was selected as the test site for several reasons: DSM was a rapidly growing producer of network products within DEC's Computer Systems Manufacturing Group. In 1985, DSM had 1,100 employees distributed across its Boston-based headquarters, four engineering centers, and three plants located in Maine, Puerto Rico, and Ireland, which produced approximately 500 products that were traditionally shipped to other plants within the corporation; by the mid-1980s, demand for DSM's products from external customers, including OEMs, distributors, and direct customers, was increasing rapidly. Annual growth rates of 40 percent to 60 percent were anticipated for the period 1987 to 1989, and it was anticipated that DSM would generate almost $1.5 billion in revenue by 1990.

In 1985, DSM's $250 million networking business was not a core business for DEC, and because it was not willing to risk piloting the new architecture on a primary computer product area, DSM became a rational choice for the experiment. Furthermore, it was not as profitable in contrast to other business units—quite the contrary. The increased demand for network products was not foreseen, so no one really expected the growth to exceed $1 billion in the next three years. By the conclusion of the program implementation, DSM was introducing 2.5 times as many new products as it had before. This increased demand and new product introduction rate could never have been met without the changes in infrastructure that will be described in this section.

Everyone involved knew that making dramatic improvement in DSM would be a difficult assignment—and the proud history of achievements of the parent company would only increase the resistance to change. To make matters worse, networking, DSM's niche, was going through a period of product technology innovation, so there was no *immediate* impetus for DSM to change its manufacturing strategy.

The new Group Manufacturing Manager for DSM was asked to pilot the new companywide manufacturing architecture in this division.[4] The vision outlined how manufacturing, logistics, engineering, and various business activities would be integrated under a "one plan" concept. In addition to managing DSM's revenue growth, the new architecture was to ensure that headcount would remain flat. The program's financial objectives included doubling ROA with a 10 percent annual improvement in margins over the five-year period.

Conditions for Business Innovation

1) As the strategic plan evolved, a value chain view of the business, driven by "time-to-market," was an imperative that shaped all decisions.

---

[4]The author of this book, L. Scott Flaig, became Group Manufacturing Manager at DSM in 1985.

2) Therefore, involvement of customers and suppliers throughout the early planning process was the best way to nurture a value chain view and arrive at workable integrated innovations.

3) Determination of the cultural changes necessary to meet the preceding conditions and to carry out the plan was important because it raised awareness of culture change and enablement as key variables in business innovation.

4) Identification of the appropriate information technology enablers and incorporating them into the plan was especially critical and would provide distinct advantage, given the company's line of business.

These themes will recur throughout this case. None of these conditions by itself would have been sufficient to spawn business innovation; the excitement of the strategy grew from the synergy among these guiding principles.

The Plan

The Group Manufacturing Manager and his team put together a five-year strategic plan focused on making dramatic improvements in three key processes: supply/demand planning, manufacturing, and new product development. It called for a 60 percent reduction in manufacturing cycle time, a 50 percent reduction in time-to-market, and a tripling of the number of new product introductions per year. The plan was based on a vision of a virtually integrated enterprise called "The End Point Model."

The DSM team began the nine-month planning process with a competitive assessment (benchmarks) and an assessment of future customer requirements (customer needs analyses). Out of these efforts came a realization of the importance of reducing cycle time—the time from vendor shipment of parts to customer delivery of products—to meet increasing expectations for quick responsiveness to customers. Reducing manufacturing cycle time hinged on tighter linkages between the various groups within DSM, and between DSM and its customers and vendors, of whom there were thousands worldwide in 1985. Because of the geographical dispersion of DSM and its customers and suppliers, the only means of achieving the required integration was to create a virtually integrated enterprise supported by networked business processes.

The team developed an aggressive five-year plan consisting of programs and activities at the group and plant level, shown in Figure 7–4.

The cycle time reduction plan, for example, called for DSM to reduce its manufacturing cycle time from 40 weeks to 17 weeks over the five-year period. The plan was both IT and cultural change intensive, since its "Systems and Information Management Tools" component called for CAD, CIM, AI, Group Technology, and Advanced Manufacturing Systems to be implemented, and many of the programs had a strong impact on the way people in the organization worked.

The plan also had a section that dealt with plant level materials and information flows. Manufacturing Resource Planning (MRPII) Certification was a major track within the plan and a means of achieving organizational discipline and business integration. The measures associated with MRPII also served to monitor DSM's progress and achieve "build-to-order" (mass specialization) capabilities by 1990.

By 1988, the DSM organization had achieved the following results.

	Strategic		*Financial*
	Manufacturing		
Cycle time	52% decrease	Inventory	60% decrease
	Product		
Time-to-market	30% decrease	Revenue	Increase
Quality	95 to 99% error free	ROA	Increase 25 points
Delivery	85 to 95% on time	Margin	Increase 25 points
Product introductions	Increase 2.5×	Headcount	Flat

Catalyst for Change
If things are going well in a company, then there is no institutional catalyst for change. As Lou Gaviglia, then DEC's V.P. of Systems Manufacturing, put it, "There has to be a right time to make the kind of changes we were trying to make." In order for business process innovation to be initiated, at least one of two conditions must exist: there must be a serious business problem that has not responded to traditional

FIGURE 7–4
Digital Equipment Corporation
The Endpoint Plan

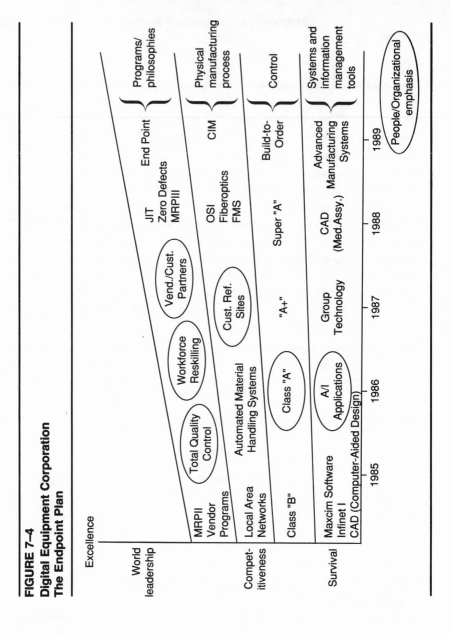

performance improvement tools, or there must be a compelling vision that will provide competitive advantage. As it turned out, the time was right for DSM because both conditions existed.

DSM had placed very poorly—close to last—in internal and external benchmarking studies of manufacturing performance. This information, coupled with information gathered in the assessment process, was used to create the impetus for change. The message to the organization was, "We have a big problem. We've got to get really serious about it. But if we stick together we can do it." If DSM's lackluster report card provided the pain, the End Point Model was held out by the team as a vision of manufacturing excellence to the rest of the organization.

Visions Cannot Be Mandated
Although the vision realized in the End Point Model should be credited to the project team, it certainly emanated from the prototype requested years earlier by a new Vice President for Materials, who served as a catalyst for change. In addition, following a costly systems failure in 1983, the firm sought planning and systems that were predictable and dependable in order to avoid repeated damage to reputation and customer satisfaction.

The prototype, which presented the notion of an integrated enterprise, was well received and became the subject of a number of high-level corporate committees, which developed models or architectures describing how Digital would do business differently. By 1985, it had evolved into a document called the Corporate Manufacturing/Materials Architecture. At this time, the Vice President of Systems Manufacturing, to whom DSM reported was also developing a Class A program for manufacturing excellence that included all computer manufacturing sites.[5] The program centered on MRPII Class A, providing the climate for DSM to activate a comprehensive manufacturing strategy.

Building a Team That Worked
In 1985, the Manufacturing Group Manager for DSM was given the unique opportunity to build upon the work on the prototype architecture by pulling together a team with as broad a knowledge base as possible. The team's task was to make the architecture a reality for DSM. "It's not just the vision. It's knowledge...vision is hollow if the

---

[5]Ibid.

company can't use its knowledge."[6] The mandate for the group was to be improved performance, rather than simply implementation of the architecture. That mandate provided a group sense of mission, as well as specific measurable goals.

The team was assembled with care; all functions and sites were represented. The core team was from staff, and the extended team included suppliers, customers, engineering, marketing, and five major vendors who were also DEC customers. These organizations were considered to be stakeholders, and their help in creating the enterprise plan was deemed critical to its success.

The team asked itself what cultural aspects would be necessary to achieve its objectives. The most crucial factor was determined to be that participants needed to value differences such as gender, race, nation, and function. (In fact, one of the team's hallmarks became its diversity.) Team members were selected carefully with an eye to their openness to change, and this criterion, along with others, was later used to select the vendors that were invited to be a part of the project.

The broader than usual cultural and gender diversity of the team was ultimately one of its great strengths and was essential in creating a plan to integrate a very diverse organization. The unique perspectives of the individuals and groups resulted in both a richer process and end result, because team members learned to listen to each other, challenged unspoken assumptions, and broadened each other's perspectives. Time was explicitly devoted to developing new values and to working out group processes and group dynamics. Meetings were held in all DSM sites so the team could experience the culture of each of the different locations. At the end of the nine months, they emerged with not only a plan, but with a strong group identity and cohesiveness, reshaped perspectives and values, new skills and behaviors, and a belief and commitment in their vision and their ability to work together to make a difference in DSM.

Thorough Planning Was Critical

The nine-month period that the team spent together was an essential ingredient in its ultimate success. During the first three to four months, there were intensive planning meetings, taking up almost 40 hours per week. These were needed to identify what was critical to the business, to determine what the competitive strategy was going to be, and to address technology enablers and human resource issues. The process fired up the

[6]Chuck Savage, interview with author, July 29, 1991.

team and set each individual and the group as a whole on intense personal and professional growth trajectories. By the end of the nine-month period, the team had already accomplished more than it ever imagined it could—and created the five-year End Point Model plan that would transform DSM into a world-class manufacturing organization. This transformation placed it first in subsequent internal and external benchmarking comparisons. The planning period, however, produced more than a plan.

Vendors and Customers as Partners

Developing the selection criteria for vendors and suppliers was a difficult process that took several months. The starting list of about 100 active suppliers and customers went through a lengthy process of elimination before it was reduced to about 20 candidates. To avoid seeming as though the program was being imposed on vendors, it was decided that End Point partners should be companies that were DEC customers as well as suppliers. This meant that, as customers, they stood to gain immeasurable benefits from the success of the project, giving them the incentive to participate. The solicitation process was quite thorough, exploring the companies' willingness to be a part of a new business process, and whether they met the stringent criteria that had been set. They had to be willing to take the risk, and be willing to make a major commitment. The team sought to identify companies that

- Were large key customers who could benefit significantly from their involvement in the program.
- Exhibited a corporate culture that valued difference.
- Were active worldwide, especially in areas where DSM had customers.
- Had a high-tech strategy—interested in new ideas and new products to help DSM meet its time-to-market objectives.
- Had reputations for excellence in manufacturing.

Many of the companies that were approached were skeptical at first. As vendors, they were interested because they knew that they had to respond to an initiative from a valued customer. However, as customers, they were less enthused until they perceived the potential benefit from the overall value chain. Customer/supplier internal constituencies also had to be managed: If company VPs couldn't be persuaded to talk to each other, then separate meetings had to be arranged for sales and vendors sides. Once they joined up, they became true business partners with a real vested interest in the success of the End Point Model. This was especially true for the five vendors who actually participated through the entire project.

Implementing the Plan

Spreading Commitment to the Whole Organization
The work in the planning phase was conducted largely within the team, with some participation from and training provided to the team's direct reports. As the mode shifted from planning to implementation, the energy of the whole organization needed to be mobilized. Members of the team, especially those from the plants where many of the implementation activities took place, as well as their direct reports, carried the message throughout the organization.

Redefining Measures of Success
By this time "excellence" had taken on some new and rather specific meanings. As part of the planning process, the team had rethought and redefined the way it measured success.

Old	*New*
Supply/demand	Demand/supply
Number of suppliers	Number of alliances
Partial orders	Complete orders
Delivery to commit	Delivery to request
Cost	Margin
Quality at dock	Quality at customer
Percent built to stock	Percent built to order

Measurement and Accountability
An important theme of the project was to establish a strong ethic and discipline around measurement and accountability within DSM. As noted earlier, MRPII Class A certification was one of the first milestones of the 1986 plan. It was also the basis for measuring DSM's progress. MRPII was a plant-level project, and accountability was established, starting with the plant manager, for 13 measures. Progress was tracked monthly,

and the results were posted prominently in each plant. Pictured in Figure 7–5 is a representation of the MRPII Report Card posted in the Augusta, Maine, plant. Several other advanced methodologies were essential to the success of the overall program, including JIT, QR, TQM, continuous flow manufacturing, and total cost management. All of these contributed to increased customer satisfaction and an improved bottom line.

Many of the Programs Had a Strong Organizational Impact
As previously noted, many of the programs had a strong impact on the skills and jobs within DSM. *Creating a motivated workforce, empowered through access to information and IT-based tools, was a conscious goal of the End Point Model plan.* Extensive investments were made in employee training and education to support the deployment of advanced systems and technology within the organization. As Lou Gaviglia has commented, part of empowering people means "giving back trust to small groups."

Another dimension of the organizational impact inherent in the plan was the shift required in longstanding paradigms about work and or-

---

FIGURE 7–5
Measurement and Accountability for Results are Critical to Success

---

Augusta, Maine: Quarterly MRPII Performance Report

	Q1	Q2	Q3	Q4	Q5	Q6	Q7
Top management planning							
business plan	0	0	100	100	100	96	92
sales plan	48	0	74	84	81	82	73
production plan	0	0	96	88	85	72	76
Operational planning							
master schedule	10	22	72	65	41	88	100
material requirements	0	91	72	69	96	91	97
capacity planning	0	0	100	80	75	95	100
Data base							
bills of material	96	97	86	100	96	100	100
inventory records	85	93	90	90	81	87	94
routing	0	0	0	97	100	100	100
Operational execution							
material acquisition	0	53	26	40	52	84	80
shop floor control	23	19	66	54	52	97	99
schedule performance	99	99	99	99	97	96	97
order administration	63	54	96	89	93	97	98
average	33.3	46	75	81	81	91	93
class	D	D	C	B	B	A	A

ganization. The very concept of an integrated *enterprise* conveyed an
expanded concept of organization, one that included DEC's customers
and vendors. Individuals and groups within DSM worked through the
implications and new behaviors necessitated by other, equally profound
changes in assumptions. Some of these are listed below.

Old	*New*
What's good for DEC	What's good for enterprise
Job/functional focus	Cross-functional/interorganizational process focus
Informal systems and lax controls	Formal systems and management discipline
Open-ended consensus building	Assigned accountability/rewards
White male dominance	Valuing difference

Organizational Resistance

Most organizations have an amazing ability to deny reality, regardless
of how seriously behind the competition they might be, and even when
documented by benchmarking studies. In fact, the denial syndrome really seems to be activated when there is a large delta in performance.
Responses often heard are: "we are different," "this issue is a temporary one," "it will go away," "we have programs in place already,"
or the ever-popular "let it be."[7] Many managers at DSM felt threatened by the changes underway because either they didn't feel capable or
they didn't understand the vision well enough, and therefore feared that
the journey would proceed without them. Others had serious doubts,
based on their knowledge and past success, which was more "management by art." Both forms of resistance had to be anticipated and
managed.

The sponsorship of senior corporate officials is essential in defusing
resistance to change. However, the senior manager of the group had the
responsibility of reinforcing the innovations on a day-to-day basis. The
team had anticipated the resistance and used a combination of hard and

[7]See Charles M. Savage, *5th Generation Management* (Maynard, Mass.: Digital Press, 1990).

soft interventions to manage it, providing education, information, and frequent opportunities for direct two-way communication with employees. The objective was to create a logic for change, so that employees could personalize it. An informal benchmarking process involved study group visits to U.S. and Japanese companies whose methods and technology the team admired. The commitment to education during the business innovation process was strong; during the first year, DSM allocated close to $2 million dollars for about 1,000 people, demonstrating to employees that management was equally serious about the changes and about enabling employees to use new tools and systems and helping them to change attitudes and behavior.

The DSM team institutionalized the *celebration* of both task-oriented and behavioral successes in order to encourage change. In line with DEC's employee values, and to encourage the adoption of the extensive use of IT that was part of the plan, every attempt was made to find new opportunities for employees whose jobs were eliminated by the use of technology. In fact, one of the many expert systems that was developed was an expert-based outplacement/career planning system.

The Short-Term Costs and Benefits of Fast-Paced Radical Change

Perhaps the most significant benefit was that DSM was able to make rapid, measurable progress toward its goals. As previously noted, this success was exploited by DSM's leaders to encourage and fuel further gains. Moreover, the organization was very charged-up during this period, and employees at all levels made tremendous professional and personal strides. Job satisfaction was greatly increased.

There was, however, a down side. Alongside the measurable progress, there was also a first-year, short-term dip in the inventory metric as inventory was consciously increased to buffer for change. The division endured some tough inventory reviews with senior management during this period as the team defended the plan and held out the promise of a turnaround—which did materialize. The VP of Systems Manufacturing, Lou Gaviglia, provided the executive buffer and the encouragement and trust to continue. He also acted as the sounding board to test ideas and, in particular, the necessary cultural changes.

The high degree of change, coupled with demands to keep up with normal production in a rapidly expanding business, created peak periods of stress that necessitated occasional deceleration.

Information Technology

Recognition of the importance of information technology in creating far superior capabilities in manufacturing, engineering, and logistics was a critical success factor. Probably the most significant technology enabler was the application of networking, both local and wide area. The experimentation with proprietary electronic connectivity with suppliers in the End Point Model only later came to be known as EDI. Networking enabled DSM to

- Execute worldwide forecasting at the product level.
- Link customers and suppliers directly to its planning process.
- Link worldwide logistics.
- Simultaneously source multiline items on a particular customer order, so it could do on-line scheduling, providing dependable ship dates from multiple locations.
- Perform remote engineering at multiple locations, improving time-to-market capability and project management.

The use of expert systems was another key technology enabler. The XCON (expert configuration) allowed DSM to configure systems on-line, and to simultaneously schedule line items on the order. Other applications of expert system technology were

- Forecasting and planning.
- Human resources management of skills and training programs.
- Shop floor process management.
- Sales assistant to aid customers in asking "what if" questions.
- Incorporating design for assembly needs in the engineering process.

Another major investment was made in CAD/CAM, allowing DSM to feed design information to manufacturing locations, and thereby driving the process equipment at the shop floor. This achievement was quite revolutionary at the time. Investments were also made in data base management, to provide worldwide data simultaneously to all locations. The team knew at the outset that technology would be an important component of its success. Many of the specific IT solutions evolved even during the implementation phase, largely as a result of teamwork as well as the newly created environment supportive of innovation and risk taking.

Lessons Learned

Inherent in the plan and in the name for DSM's vision itself—the End Point Model—was the concept of a future state that, once achieved, would represent the pinnacle of manufacturing excellence. Successful implementation of the plan created new insights within the organization about how things might actually work somewhat differently. Limiting the pilot to DSM, a business unit with distinct boundaries, probably helped to achieve the dramatic changes just described. The new vision that evolved was that of a learning organization that continuously adapts its behavior and its goals based on the anticipated and unanticipated results of the implementation of the existing plan. One of the first changes occasioned by this realization was the creation of strategic teams, made up this time not exclusively of senior management, but of middle management and supervisors who would review specific programs and recommend modifications.

The extended planning process was absolutely essential to success because it provided the opportunity to combine the vision with the knowledge DSM's people had of its business. By working as a team, by including all functions, and by respecting diversity, the DSM organization was able to develop a culture of change and build off of everyone's strengths. Both process technology and information technology had to be studied carefully in order to arrive at the model of virtual integration. Taking the time to establish guiding principles and to assess the magnitude of the undertaking proved to be justifiable once results started coming in.

The transition from planning to implementation was risky, as some changes could not be planned, but rather, had to evolve. Although the original purpose of the DSM project was to try out the new enterprise architecture, the End Point Model took on a life of its own and became a true example of business innovation. In spite of some ambiguity, sustaining the vision kept the process going. Plant managers had to broaden their knowledge base substantially, and departments, once independent of one another, learned that shared, networked information could benefit everyone. The team learned that radical change meant developing completely new measures of success and rewards and that giving individuals and groups regular monitoring and feedback helped to meet the improvement goals.

Given the team's knowledge of information technology enablers and the articulated architecture, the team could envision how DSM could be leveraged with customers and suppliers. Therefore they knew when they embarked on the journey that it was not merely an academic exercise, but a new way of doing business that would meet or exceed their collective expectations.

Subsequent decisions about how to shorten cycle time and work with customers as well as vendors were shaped by DSM's view of itself as part of a value chain. During the project, the team learned which criteria were important and how to develop the best possible relationships. The five customer/vendors who were partners in the End Point Model became even better customers and vendors. Before the program DSM had 750 suppliers; using the new criteria, fewer than 100 qualified to remain as true business partners.

Innovation, as demonstrated by DEC's DSM Group, was truly the integrative product of people, process, and technology. All were essential components for the eventual realization of a new model that was customer driven and sustainable, because the culture had come to expect continuous improvement.[8] Empowered people, enabled through information technology, could envision business and manufacturing processes that would virtually locate the entire DSM organization at the doorstep of every customer, worldwide.

The strategic and financial results shown at the very outset of this case speak for themselves. According to plan, in 1987 DSM plants became customer reference sites within DEC, no longer the sleepy manufacturing organization encountered in 1985. Shop floor employees gave tours for visitors who came to see what manufacturing excellence meant. Today, the eyes of the people involved in planning and implementing the End Point Model still light up when they think back and talk about this period that had such a profound effect not only on DSM but on the personal and professional lives of those involved.

SUMMARY

The three performance improvement approaches discussed in this chapter are powerfully equipped to attack the problems for which they were designed. Each represents a critical, systematic approach to targeting, analyzing, designing, and implementing solutions to the competitive is-

---

[8]In fact, the End Point Model's theme was later changed to "The Journey to Excellence."

sues that face manufacturing, although each demands a different level of skills and commitment. Cost reduction is the most limiting, resulting in a relatively low-impact change; business process improvement concentrates on gradual improvements (a "bridge builder"); and business process innovation takes a steep ascent to a drastically different level of performance (a "leap to greatness").

Because there is no single way to set and attain performance improvement objectives, the specific approach selected should be a function of the methodology experience of the organization and/or its consulting partner and the organizational unit driving the improvement initiative, as well as a function of the overall objectives and time frame.

Although we have sketched three approaches to performance improvement, they are not in themselves prescriptions for success. Once one has been chosen, the improvement team must tailor it to reflect the requirements and scope of the target processes. For example, when the information systems organization is responsible for developing the approach, the approach is often distinctly oriented toward developing an information system. In some cases, hybrid approaches will be warranted. For example:

- A cost reduction effort that is broadened to include some interdepartmental interface issues.
- A cost reduction effort that addresses the process improvement issues of quality and timeliness in addition to cost, but that remains focused on project-driven improvements.
- A continuous process improvement effort that begins with project-driven cost reduction.
- A business process innovation effort that is linked closely to pre- and post-implementation continuous improvement analysis and implementation.

The breadth and aggressiveness of the approach (e.g., the choice of methodology) must be commensurate with the amount of time and organizational energy that are available in the enterprise. Every manufacturer, whether it be Digital in its approach to performance improvement through innovation, Walgreens in its determination for quick responsive systems, or General Dynamics in an IT process redesign, must select effective change management test methods and techniques. The success of these companies was largely due both to their systematic and disciplined approach and to their commitment to measuring and rewarding progress.

As companies begin to further develop their model of choice, whether vertical or virtual, they will come to realize that each method will be exercised to a point of hypertrophy—that is, they will be in a constant iterative state of visioning, strategy formulation, program planning, and implementation. Visioning and innovation, enabled by a steady stream of new technologies, will become key executive initiatives. A steady stream of new market opportunities, new competitors and new vendors will further enrich the possibilities inherent in the virtual enterprise. The pressure to continually reduce cost in operations while reaching for zero defects in products and process will necessitate effective continuous improvement and cost reduction programs. All these methodologies will be pervasive for the competitive manufacturers of the 1990s.

CHAPTER 8
FACTORY 2000 AND BEYOND

Imagine a factory as precise as a fine watch, operating without queues or errors and situated to take advantage not just of lowest cost, but of access to highest-value markets. In this factory, production learning curves have been eliminated because design-for-manufacturability is inherent in every product; the unit cost of a manufacturing run of 1 is the same as for a run of 100,000. Manufacturers work extensively and directly with value chain members in product design efforts, which enhances the effectiveness and efficiency of both. Customers and suppliers communicate electronically with the factory. New products are developed on time—and introduced in astonishingly short cycles. Delivery is to the date and time requested by the customer. All orders are complete because customers will accept nothing less. Quality exceeds customer expectations because competition requires nothing less.

The challenge for manufacturers today, of course, is to successfully make the transition to this vision of manufacturing. By properly using people, process, and technology as the assets they are, each manufacturer can grow from its current state toward its "factory of the future." The pressure is on, and each manufacturer must articulate *today* its vision of what might be and must quickly follow up with strategy formulation, programs, and retraining if structural transformation of the enterprise is to be achieved in a competitive time frame.

Manufacturing in the Future

Many of today's key issues and concerns for manufacturers will persist through the next several years. Globalization and customer focus will intensify and become integrated on a broader scale, with renewed energy, resulting in the ability of customers anywhere in the world to expect and demand truly personalized service.

- Globalization is likely to mean greater uniformity of markets: The French and the Chinese will not become more different—they are as different as they are ever likely to be, and will only become more similar. Whether this presents more challenges or opportunities for manufacturers is uncertain.

- The focus on the customer will intensify. Customer service will take on more forms, such as product serviceability, usability, unpackability, storability, and assembled readiness—virtually anything that can ease a customer's use, purchase, storage, shipment, or maintenance of the product. Manufacturers will be much more responsive to customers and will have significantly enhanced capabilities to customize products and services and to treat customers in a manner that suggests each customer is the only customer.

- Today, most manufacturers sell much product and very little service. In the future, they will be more likely to sell much service and proportionately less product. Expectations are that added-value for the customer of the future will be 70 or 80 percent, driven by service. At IBM, arguably a successful global manufacturer, only 6 percent of employees—20,000 out of 400,000—are production employees.[1] The remainder provide some kind of support service.

- Looking internally, manufacturers will be required to develop transnational and global management skills, including the ability to communicate in many languages and with employees from a wide variety of cultures. Even simple communications will become complex.

- As global pollution increases, the environmental issues of manufacturing will begin to be addressed on a transnational basis, and international standards may emerge. As a result, sourcing based upon relaxed regulation or enforcement thereof is less likely to be a factor to manufacturers.

- Cost, quality, and delivery—like service—are performance criteria that will continue to play important roles for manufacturers and their customers. However, the emphasis on value will increase. Costs have finite limits; value does not. As enterprises become more efficient, opportunities to reduce waste—and thus cost—become scarcer. But there is always opportunity to add value, which enables a manufacturer to charge a higher price.

---

[1]Stanley Davis, *Future Perfect* (Reading, Mass.: Addison-Wesley, 1987), p. 9.

Framework for the Future: People, Process, and Technology

Leadership will be crucial, since change will abound. The future will see more multifunction employees and multifunctional management, and more workers will be intimately familiar with more of the enterprise through rotating assignments and broadly applied education and training programs. The ranks of middle management, traditionally responsible for tactical, day-to-day decisions, will be eroded by the need to speed up all business and manufacturing processes, as well as by refinements and improvements in the utility of more powerful decision support systems. The resulting organization will be much flatter and, correspondingly, more responsive to customer and industry opportunities.

A Vision of Change

How will the experience of workers on the factory floor change? One vision has highly skilled, computer-aided workers designing and managing manufacturing processes and relatively unskilled workers attending these processes. In another vision, highly intelligent process control systems that require little management guide low-skilled workers through manufacturing processes. A third vision involves well-engineered, highly automated, flexible work cells that require very skilled workers. A mix of these, perhaps even within a single plant, is possible.

The future will see a more integrated approach to quality and other cross-functional improvement methodologies. All levels of the enterprise, from senior management to the shop floor, will become involved in employing these disciplines and methodologies and in leveraging the benefits they produce.

New processes and methodologies will be a critical part of the factories and businesses of the future. In many instances, these methods will be derived from visions of a possible future and the opportunities that future holds. Organizations must search out the themes, trends, and developments that hold promise for substantial opportunities 3, 5, or 10 years into the future. Enterprises that have invested sufficiently in infrastructure will find they are able to roll out new methodologies, processes, and procedures in timely support of these opportunities.

Although many manufacturers will continue to employ benchmarking to improve products and processes, the very finest manufacturers will look beyond best practices to best-possible practices and use projected or extrapolated performance rather than measured performance to drive innovation and improvement. Best-possible performance goals will enable organizations that outperform all others to improve even more.

Products will become more modular, making room for the customer in the final configuration, assembly, and integration roles, and they will also become more intelligent, with on-board "smart" devices alerting customers, servicers, and manufacturers to potential problems before they occur. Maintenance and replacement will precede, not follow, breakdown, maximizing uptime and equipment utilization.

"Evolution, it seems, is now moving fast enough to be visible," wrote Charles Garfield in his book *Peak Performers*.[2] This must surely be true for many of the technologies that support manufacturing. Technological advances in material sciences, manufacturing processes, and production will enable many manufacturers to make products smaller, more energy efficient, and nearly maintenance free.

Communications and information technologies will support substantial growth in the amount of product support and other services manufacturers provide their customers. Furthermore, a continuum of not-yet-invented support services will arise within and among value chains, based upon a ubiquitous electronic connectivity beyond the most advanced implementations available today.

Manufacturers in the year 2000 will have substantially fewer suppliers than they do today. However, the total population of suppliers will probably not decrease dramatically because value and supply chains will lengthen as a result of increased specialization. The future is not likely to find a predominance of either highly centralized factories or of small factories with large distribution centers. Almost all products will be distributed faster and with less expense through the removal of air, water, and other non-value adding or nonfunctional components.

For many manufacturers, the challenge of the 1990s has been to speed up the flow of information and materials across the value chain. As the enterprise, through alliances and partnerships, comes to incorporate more of the total value chain, the challenge will no longer be to to expe-

---

[2]Charles Garfield, *Peak Performers* (New York: Avon, 1986), p. 16.

dite activities throughout the value chain, but to integrate planning tightly across the value chain. In the future, as in the past, enterprise strategies will derive from industry developments and organizational strengths and weaknesses. But in the future, the tactics that support these strategies will derive more and more from value chain considerations that lie outside the enterprise, rather than from factors internal to the organization.

In the past, inward-looking organizations approached cost reduction, continuous improvement, and innovation as independent and individual methodologies for improving manufacturing performance. In the future, these methodologies will interact and intertwine both within the organization and across the value chain, making organizational improvement considerably more complex and challenging. And, of course, government regulation and policy will continue to be wildcards as long as politics, rather than economics, persists as a predominant influence.

A Brilliant Future

Each organization will have its own "Factory 2000" as a goal. Since reaching it will be more a matter of methods than of milestones, however, manufacturers must continually do and be their best, and consequently will need the best people. The enterprise's work force will need to be organized in support of unprecedented achievement, with the best people drawn to an enterprise that has a compelling vision and an organizational culture that values and empowers talented workers. "Intelligent people prefer to agree [rather] than to obey," noted Charles Handy.[3] If the enterprise is to compete in the year 2000, its most intelligent and talented people must be motivated by clear vision and be rewarded for achievement.

In the future, an organization's ability to learn and to manage change will become even more important than it is today. Improved performance often comes from well-managed change and from innovation. Since the primary impediment to innovation is resistance to change, organizations that learn how to better prepare their workers to embrace change will adapt better and are likely to innovate better. World-class manufacturing companies of the future will place a premium on these strengths and will make it very difficult for others to compete without such skills.

---

[3]Charles Handy, *The Age of Unreason* (Boston, Mass.: Harvard Business School Press, 1989), p. 162

Leading manufacturers will join world-class value chains consisting of partners whose near-perfect integrity of operations is a strategic imperative. Partners in these chains will be selected from among the best manufacturing enterprises across the globe and, like precious jewels, will be chosen for their brightness, their brilliance, and their unmatched appeal. Any performance weakness in the chain will cause the weak link to be discarded, like a flaw disqualifying an otherwise beautiful gem. The manufacturing framework, properly applied, allows an organization to polish its strengths until they gleam, and to align, integrate, and focus its resources to optimize performance along the integrated value chain—an effort that is sure to appeal.

Manufacturers face many hazards and challenges as they plot their courses toward the opportunities of the future, but the integrative manufacturing framework described in this book offers a practical, powerful tool that every manufacturer can use to navigate those waters, structure high-level policy discourse, and formulate and align strategies. Its universal applicability makes it ideal for planning and managing across the value chain, thus providing a common perspective for building strategic partnerships and for optimizing the value chain's capacity to deliver value to its customers. Properly applied, this framework provides a highly serviceable planning architecture for the manufacturer aspiring to world-class performance.

INDEX

Other titles of interest to you from the Business One Irwin/APICS Library of Integrated Resource Management . . .

MANAGING HUMAN RESOURCES
Integrating People and Business Strategy
Lloyd S. Baird

By teaming examples of successful human resources experiments with his own practical tips on human resource objectives, employee recruitment, and appraisal, Baird examines and reveals the success potential for integrating people and business strategy. (268 pages)
ISBN: 1-55623-543-7

MANAGING FOR QUALITY
Integrating Quality and Business Strategy
V. Daniel Hunt

Maintaining a standard of quality doesn't have to cost a lot, but neglecting this standard can cost your company plenty. Hunt, author of the best-selling *Quality in America,* provides another excellent guide for achieving your quality goals—and effectively managing quality costs. (360 pages)
1-55623-544-5

EFFECTIVE PRODUCT DESIGN AND DEVELOPMENT
How to Cut Lead Time and Increase Customer Satisfaction
Stephen R. Rosenthal

Effective Product Design and Development will help you steer clear of long development delays by pointing out ways to detect design flaws early, and by showing how to empower the entire work team to recognize time-absorbing mistakes. You will discover how to shorten the cycle of new product design and development and turn time into a strategic competitive advantage. (341 pages)
ISBN: 1-55623-603-4

INTEGRATED PROCESS DESIGN AND DEVELOPMENT
Dan L. Shunk

Shunk's book is a no-nonsense, reader-friendly guide that not only defines the information requirements for integrated process design, but also outlines the procedures you must take to achieve it. You will discover ways your company can benefit from new and future technological trends, value-adding through design, value-added tracking, and more. (260 pages)
ISBN: 1-55623-556-9

INTEGRATED PRODUCTION AND INVENTORY MANAGEMENT
Revitalizing the Manufacturing Enterprise
Thomas E. Vollmann, William L. Berry, and D. Clay Whybark

Slash production and distribution costs by effectively monitoring inventory! This strategic guide explains the inventory control processes that strengthen the customer service function and improve purchasing forecasts and production schedules. (385 pages)
ISBN: 1-55623-604-2

Available in fine bookstores and libraries everywhere.

The Educational Society for Resource Management

Please send more information about...

If you enjoyed this book, continue your learning through other APICS-sponsored educational opportunities.

❏ APICS Publications—More than 400 textbook and courseware items. *(#01041)*

❏ The APICS Certified in Integrated Resource Management (CIRM) process—A full curriculum and self-assessment system focusing on the functions and interrelationships of 13 areas of the business enterprise. *(#09016)*

❏ The APICS Certified in Production and Inventory Management (CPIM) process—A self-assessment system providing in-depth knowledge in the core areas of production and inventory management. *(#09002)*

❏ APICS Membership and Educational Programs—A wealth of opportunities, from 2 1/2-day workshops and courses to APICS' six-day all-encompassing international conference and exhibition. *(#82021)*

Name:_____

Title: _____

Company:_____

Address:_____

City: _____

State: _____

ZIP:_____

Phone (w): _____

BUSINESS REPLY MAIL
FIRST-CLASS MAIL PERMIT NO 2858 FALLS CHURCH, VA

POSTAGE WILL BE PAID BY ADDRESSEE

ATTN: MARKETING DEPARTMENT
AMERICAN PRODUCTION AND INVENTORY
CONTROL SOCIETY INC
500 W ANNANDALE RD
FALLS CHURCH VA 22046-9701